NEW MATERIALISMS ANCIENT URBANISMS

The future of humanity is urban, and knowledge of urbanism's deep past is critical for us all to navigate that future. The time has come for archaeologists to rethink this global phenomenon by asking what urbanism is and, more to the point, was. Can we truly understand ancient urbanism by only asking after the human element, or are the properties and qualities of landscapes, materials, and atmospheres equally causal?

The nine authors of *New Materialisms Ancient Urbanisms* seek less anthropocentric answers to questions about the historical relationships between urbanism and humanity in Africa, Asia, and the Americas. They analyze the movements and flows of materials, things, phenomena, and beings—human and otherwise—as these were assembled to produce the kinds of complex, dense, and stratified relationships that we today label urban. In so doing, the book emerges as a work of both theory and historical anthropology. It breaks new ground in the archaeology of urbanism, building on the latest 'New Materialist', 'relational-ontological', and 'realist' trends in social theory.

This book challenges a new generation of students to think outside the box, and provides scholars of urbanism, archaeology, and anthropology with a fresh perspective on the development of urban society.

Susan M. Alt is Associate Professor of Anthropology at Indiana University and Faculty Curator at the Glenn Black Laboratory of Archaeology. Her research interests include the relationships of migration, violence, and gender to the built environment, especially involving the origins of Mississippianism. She is author or editor of *Cahokia's Complexities* (2017), *Medieval Mississippians* (2015), and *Ancient Complexities* (2010).

Timothy R. Pauketat is Professor of Anthropology and Medieval Studies, and Director of the Illinois State Archaeological Survey at the University of Illinois. The author or editor of 15 books, Pauketat seeks to understand through large-scale archaeology the big historical relationships between politics, religion, climate, and urbanism.

NEW MATERIALISMS ANCIENT URBANISMS

Edited by Susan M. Alt and Timothy R. Pauketat

LONDON AND NEW YORK

First published 2020
by Routledge
2 Park Square, Milton Park, Abingdon, Oxon OX14 4RN

and by Routledge
52 Vanderbilt Avenue, New York, NY 10017

Routledge is an imprint of the Taylor & Francis Group, an informa business

© 2020 selection and editorial matter, Susan M. Alt and Timothy R. Pauketat; individual chapters, the contributors

The right of Susan M. Alt and Timothy R. Pauketat to be identified as the authors of the editorial material, and of the authors for their individual chapters, has been asserted in accordance with sections 77 and 78 of the Copyright, Designs and Patents Act 1988.

All rights reserved. No part of this book may be reprinted or reproduced or utilised in any form or by any electronic, mechanical, or other means, now known or hereafter invented, including photocopying and recording, or in any information storage or retrieval system, without permission in writing from the publishers.

Trademark notice: Product or corporate names may be trademarks or registered trademarks, and are used only for identification and explanation without intent to infringe.

British Library Cataloguing-in-Publication Data
A catalogue record for this book is available from the British Library

Library of Congress Cataloging-in-Publication Data
Names: Pauketat, Timothy R., editor. | Alt, Susan M., 1959– editor.
Title: New materialisms ancient urbanisms / edited by
Timothy R. Pauketat and Susan M. Alt.
Description: Abingdon, Oxon ; New York, NY : Routledge, 2019. |
Includes bibliographical references and index.
Identifiers: LCCN 2019008451 (print) | LCCN 2019012675 (ebook) |
ISBN 9781351008488 (eBook) | ISBN 9781351008471 (Adobe Reader) |
ISBN 9781351008457 (Mobipocket Unencrypted) |
ISBN 9781351008464 (ePub3) | ISBN 9781138542464 (hardback : alk. paper) |
ISBN 9781138542501 (pbk. : alk. paper)
Subjects: LCSH: Cities and towns, Ancient. | Material culture–History–To 1500. |
Urban ecology (Sociology)–History–To 1500. | Urban landscape architecture–
History–To 1500. | Urban archaeology. | Social archaeology.
Classification: LCC HT114 (ebook) |
LCC HT114 .N48 2019 (print) | DDC 307.76093–dc23
LC record available at https://lccn.loc.gov/2019008451

ISBN: 978-1-138-54246-4 (hbk)
ISBN: 978-1-138-54250-1 (pbk)
ISBN: 978-1-351-00848-8 (ebk)

Typeset in Bembo
by Newgen Publishing UK

 Printed in the United Kingdom by Henry Ling Limited

CONTENTS

List of figures	*vii*
List of contributors	*x*
Acknowledgments	*xiii*

1 Introducing New Materialisms, rethinking ancient urbanisms   1
   Timothy R. Pauketat

2 From weeping hills to lost caves: A search for vibrant matter
  in greater Cahokia   19
   Susan M. Alt

3 Chaco gathers: Experience and assemblage in the ancient
  Southwest   40
   Ruth M. Van Dyke

4 Assembling the city: Monte Albán as a mountain of creation
  and sustenance   65
   Arthur A. Joyce

5 Assembling Tiwanaku: Water and stone, humans and monoliths   94
   John Wayne Janusek

6 Immanence and the spirit of ancient urbanism at Paquimé
  and Liangzhu   130
   Timothy R. Pauketat

vi Contents

7 The gathering of Swahili religious practice: Mosques-as-assemblages at 1000 CE Swahili towns   158
   Jeffrey Fleisher

8 Urbanism and the temporality of materiality on the medieval Deccan: Beyond the cosmograms of social and political space   184
   Andrew M. Bauer

9 Cities, the Underworld, and the infrastructure: The ecology of water in the Hittite world   218
   Ömür Harmanşah

10 Commentary: *The City and The City*   245
    Oliver J. T. Harris

Index   *260*

FIGURES

2.1	Map of greater Cahokia showing major civic–ceremonial precincts	20
2.2	LiDAR image of the greater Cahokia region	23
2.3	LiDAR view of the Emerald Acropolis' core area	24
2.4	A thunderstorm cell passing over the Emerald Acropolis in 2015	25
2.5	3D reconstruction of select Emerald Acropolis buildings in EB1	26
2.6	LiDAR view of the Cahokia precinct	29
2.7	Plan map of the St. Louis precinct	30
2.8	Karst features south of greater Cahokia	32
2.9	Exchange Avenue figurine made from carved flint clay	34
3.1	Locations of Chacoan outlier great houses and road segments between ca. 1020–1100 CE	43
3.2	Fajada Butte, an isolated sandstone remnant of Chacra Mesa, is the topographic focal point of Chaco Canyon and the home of the Sun Dagger petroglyph	45
3.3	Sandstone masonry great-house walls rise into the New Mexico sky	46
3.4	Stars revolve around true North, as seen above the symmetrical foot drums of Great Kiva A in the center of the plaza of Pueblo Bonito	47
3.5	The four-storey Chacoan great house, Pueblo Bonito	47
3.6	Active mineral extraction equipment operating just outside the Pierre's Chaco outlier community along the Great North Road	58
4.1	Map of the Valley of Oaxaca	66
4.2	Mound 1 at San José Mogote	71
4.3	Idealized reconstruction of Rosario phase buildings and Monument 3 on Mound 1 at San José Mogote	74
4.4	View of Mound 1 at San José Mogote with Monte Albán in the background	76
4.5	Aerial view of Monte Albán with the Main Plaza circled	77

viii List of figures

4.6	Panorama of the Main Plaza of Monte Albán	78
4.7	Hypothetical reconstruction of Building L-sub at Monte Albán	79
4.8	Photograph of in-situ orthostats from Building L-sub	80
4.9	Carved slabs reset in Building J: (a) Example of a slab depicting a revered ancestor; (b) Monument J-41	81
5.1	Oblique view of Tiwanaku in relation to local sites, landforms, and the southern portion of Lake Titicaca	95
5.2	Top image: Composite 1930s aerial photo of Tiwanaku. Bottom image: Detail of the north portion of the network	100
5.3	The reconstructed Kalasasaya complex, facing northwest	104
5.4	Map showing movement of sandstone to Khonkho Wankane and Tiwanaku on either side of the Corocoro range, and movement of volcanic stone to Tiwanaku from Ccapia and Copacabana	105
5.5	Choquepacha Fountain, Tiwanaku's water temple	109
5.6	View east from atop Pumapunku, highlighting the view of Mount Illimani and view west from the balcony platform of Kalasasaya, highlighting a view of Mount Ccapia	110
5.7	Hydraulic features in the Akapana platform	114
5.8	The Kochamama Monolith Triad, located just east of the intersection of the Mollo Kontu and Perimeter Canal	115
5.9	The Andesite Corridor that frames Mount Kimsachata in the distance (facing south)	116
5.10	Three of Tiwanaku's five known presentation monoliths, shown to relative scale: Fraile (A), Bennett (B), and Ponce (C)	118
6.1	Physiographic map of the Casas Grandes region	136
6.2	Ramos Polychrome pottery jar, 20 cm tall, showing polychrome serpent and associated imagery	137
6.3	Paquimé residential room block, view to north with unexcavated mound to right, 2009	138
6.4	Paquimé infrastructural features	139
6.5	Physiographic map of the Liangzhu locality	141
6.6	Schematic plan map of Liangzhu city's major earthen and watery features	143
6.7	Engraved images of a mask or essence of a Liangzhu water spirit	144
6.8	Non-urban and urban assemblages, simplified	150
7.1	Eastern African coast and sites mentioned in the text	161
7.2	Development of mosques at Shanga, Kenya	164
7.3	Excavated mosques at Shanga, showing earlier wattle-and-daub mosques and later *Porites* mosque above	165
7.4	Pemba Island, Tanzania	167
7.5	Plan of early *Porites* mosque at Chwaka	169
7.6	Plan of later Friday mosque with early mosque inset, Chwaka, Pemba Island	176
7.7	Friday mosque at Chwaka excavated	177

List of figures **ix**

7.8	Deposit in the mihrab of the Chwaka Friday mosque: (a) general view; (b) close-up	179
8.1	Location of sites and capital centers noted in text	185
8.2	City plan of Warangal (A–B) and patterns of movement (C) into and out of the city	189
8.3	The Maski Durgada Gudda inselberg	195
8.4	MARP study region	197
8.5	Distribution of prehistoric and Medieval Period settlement terraces overlain on high-resolution satellite imagery of the Durgada Gudda	200
8.6	Topographic map showing the distribution of several recorded settlement terraces and associated retention walls amongst the uppermost rock slopes of the Durgada Gudda	201
8.7	Colluvium from upper settlement terrace of MARP-82	203
8.8	Examples of room blocks (A,B), spatial divisions (C), and defensive walls (D) on the Durgada Gudda	205
8.9	Example of Vijayanagara gateway (A) and associated cross-valley wall (B)	208
9.1	Map of the Anatolian peninsula during the Hittite Empire	227
9.2	Hattuša (modern Boğazköy), ceremonial capital of the Hittite Empire	229
9.3	Hattuša (Boğazköy), Chamber 2 at Südburg Sacred Pool Complex with hieroglyphic Luwian inscription	230
9.4	Hattuša (modern Boğazköy), Südburg Sacred Pool Complex	231
9.5	Hattuša (Boğazköy) Southern ponds, computer reconstruction	234
9.6	Arm-shaped terracotta libation vessels from Hattusha's Southern Ponds	234
9.7	Sarissa, modern Kuşaklı	236
9.8	Yalburt Yaylası Mountain Spring monument: The Hieroglyphic Luwian inscription of Tudhaliya IV (1237–1209 BCE)	237

CONTRIBUTORS

Susan M. Alt is Associate Professor of Anthropology at Indiana University, Bloomington, with research interests in the ontological relationships of water, earth, gender, ritual, and human society. Her archaeology focuses on the lower Ohio and central Mississippi valleys, particularly the American Indian city of Cahokia and its upland shrines and settlement complexes. She is the author of numerous articles and editor or author of three books, including *Cahokia's Complexities* (Alabama, 2018).

Andrew M. Bauer is Assistant Professor in the Department of Anthropology at Stanford University, where his research and teaching interests broadly intersect archaeological method and theory and environmental anthropology, with particular emphasis on the politics of environmental production in pre-colonial South India. He has published several books, including *Climate Without Nature: A Critical Anthropology of the Anthropocene* (Cambridge, 2018, with Mona Bhan), *Before Vijayanagara: Prehistoric Landscapes and Politics in the Tungabhadra Basin* (American Institute of Indian Studies, 2015), and *The Archaeology of Politics: The Materiality of Political Practice and Action in the Past* (Cambridge Scholars, 2011, co-edited with Peter Johansen), as well as numerous articles and essays.

Jeffrey Fleisher is Associate Professor of Anthropology at Rice University. His regional specialty is on the ancient Swahili coast of eastern Africa, focusing on rural and non-elite residents in and around first- and second-millennium urban centres. His current research focuses on the use of open and public space at the UNESCO World Heritage Site of Songo Mnara in southern Tanzania, and on issues of mobility in Iron Age Zambia. He is the editor/author of three books, most recently *Speaking with Substance: Methods of Language and Materials in African History* (Springer, 2019, co-authored with Kathryn de Luna).

Ömür Harmanşah is Associate Professor of Art History at the University of Illinois at Chicago. His current research focuses on the history of landscapes in the Middle East and the politics of ecology, place, and heritage in the age of the Anthropocene. He is the author of *Cities and the Shaping of Memory in the Ancient Near East* (Cambridge University Press, 2013) and *Place, Memory, and Healing: An Archaeology of Anatolian Rock Monuments* (Routledge, 2015). Since 2010, he has directed Yalburt Yaylası Archaeological Landscape Research Project, a diachronic regional survey in west–central Turkey. He is also the lead principal investigator for a three-year multi-institutional, collaborative project titled 'Political Ecology as Practice: A Regional Approach to the Anthropocene', supported by the Humanities Without Walls Consortium, funded by a grant from the Andrew W. Mellon Foundation.

Oliver J. T. Harris is Associate Professor of Archaeology at the University of Leicester. He is the author (with John Robb and others) of the *Body in History* (Cambridge, 2013) and (with Craig Cipolla) of *Archaeological Theory in the New Millennium* (Routledge, 2017). His research focuses on archaeological theory, especially New Materialism, assemblage theory, and affect, as well as the Neolithic and Bronze Age of Britain and Europe. He is co-director of the Ardnamurchan Transitions Project, which investigates long-term landscape histories in Western Scotland, and in 2016 was awarded a Philip Leverhulme Prize for Archaeology.

John Wayne Janusek is Associate Professor of Anthropology at Vanderbilt University and has worked in the highland South American Andes for over thirty years. He is an archaeological anthropologist interested in multiple dimensions of past urbanism, including political ecology, landscape, materiality, other-than-human animacy, ritual practice, and environmental archaeology. His books include *Identity and Power: Tiwanaku Cities through Time* (Routledge, 2004), *Ancient Tiwanaku* (Cambridge, 2008), and *Khonkho Wankane: Archaeological Investigations in Jesus de Machaca, Bolivia* (editor, Berkeley, 2018).

Arthur A. Joyce is Professor of Anthropology at the University of Colorado Boulder. He has conducted interdisciplinary research in Oaxaca on issues of power, politics, religion, landscape, and ecology. He is author or editor of five books including *Mixtecs, Zapotecs, and Chatinos: Ancient Peoples of Southern Mexico* (Wiley–Blackwell, 2010), *Polity and Ecology in Formative Period Coastal Oaxaca* (Colorado, 2013), and *Religion and Politics in the Ancient Americas* (Routledge, 2018, with Sarah Barber). He has held research fellowships from the American Museum of Natural History, Dumbarton Oaks, and the American Council of Learned Societies.

Timothy R. Pauketat is Director of the Illinois State Archaeological Survey and Professor of Anthropology and Medieval Studies at the University of Illinois, Urbana-Champaign, having previously taught at the Universities of Oklahoma and SUNY-Buffalo. He is the author or editor of 15 books, including *An Archaeology of the Cosmos* (Routledge, 2013) and *Archaeology of Ancient North America*, with Kenneth

xii List of contributors

Sassaman (Cambridge, 2019). He is interested in the relationships of urbanism, climate change, affect, agency, and history in North America and beyond.

Ruth M. Van Dyke is Professor of Anthropology at Binghamton University–SUNY. Her archaeological research employs phenomenological and spatial methods to investigate the intersections of memory, materiality, and ideology. She has published over 50 articles and book chapters, and she is author or editor of 6 books, including *The Chaco Experience* (SAR, 2008) and *Archaeologies of Memory* (Wiley–Blackwell, 2003, with Sue Alcock). Her primary work is focused on the rise and decline of the Chaco phenomenon in the Southwest United States. She also directs a historical archaeology project investigating identity and memory in nineteenth-century Texas, and she is currently at work on an interdisciplinary study of the materiality of pilgrimage.

ACKNOWLEDGMENTS

This volume is the culmination of an archaeological research project funded by the John Templeton Foundation (grant 51485)—The Foundations of Ancient American Indian Religion and Civilization at Cahokia's Emerald Acropolis—that ran from 2014 to 2017 (T. Pauketat and S. Alt, co-PIs). That project investigated the rise of an American Indian city, Cahokia, based on extensive fieldwork at an unusual Cahokian shrine complex (see Chapter 2). It also evaluated the relationship of urbanism and religion more generally with reference to other early cities around the world. To achieve the latter, we invited a remarkable set of scholars to participate in two scholarly seminars. The first was funded by the John Templeton Foundation and held in April 2017 at the School for Advanced Research (SAR) in Santa Fe, New Mexico. We are grateful to President Michael Brown and our friends at the SAR, especially Leslie Shipman, for generously supporting that event. And we apologize to Alamo Car Rental for the alignment problem, but the road into Chaco driven by participants Oliver Harris, Jeff Fleisher, and Tim Pauketat, along with visiting archaeologist Jeff Kruchten, that final cold, wet, muddy, snowy April morning was primarily at fault.

The energy of the first meeting in Santa Fe was matched only by the vitality of a second one in Dragoon, Arizona, making the discussions leading up to this volume among the best intellectual exercises of our lives. The second seminar was held in February 2018 at the Amerind Museum and Research Center in Dragoon, with the financial support of the Amerind Foundation. We are most grateful to Amerind Executive Director Christine Szuter, who witnessed our gregarious and productive group of seminarians, and we certainly appreciate all the hard work that the group put into those gatherings and this book. Thank you, Ruth, Art, John, Jeff, Andrew, Ömür, and Ollie! Back at the University of Illinois, a special thanks goes to Janice Pankey and Cathy Cunningham at the Illinois State Archaeological Survey, who managed the financial accounting of the project and thought their way around all

xiv Acknowledgments

bureaucratic obstacles in our way. A big thank you to the former director of the Illinois State Archaeological Survey, Thomas Emerson, for letting them do it.

Finally, a special note of gratitude goes to Matthew Gibbons and Routledge Press for taking on this project. Molly Marler, Elizabeth Risch, and Katie Wakelin helped to usher it into existence. The cover photo, an interior wall of a sunken courtyard at Tiwanaku, was inspired by an original taken by John Janusek.

1

INTRODUCING NEW MATERIALISMS, RETHINKING ANCIENT URBANISMS

Timothy R. Pauketat

Urbanism is shaping the entire planet—its people, its non-human organisms, its landscapes, and its climate. It is an inescapable dimension of humanity and history. In countless direct and indirect ways or in one or another guise, it impacts everyone alive today, even those not living in densely settled landscapes. That is, not only are well over half of the world's human beings living under ostensibly urban conditions, but many of the rest inhabit suburban, exurban, and so-called rural landscapes that would not exist but for urbanism.[1]

It is unfortunate, then, that archaeologists of urbanism tend to define their subject narrowly and qualitatively—as distinct kinds of places, infrastructures, and human population densities in opposition to other kinds of human entities and phenomena (Adams 1966; Childe 1950; Marcus and Sabloff 2008). Early urbanism, they say, was a specific sort of cultural construction designed to meet human needs (cf. Soja 2000). Unfortunately, such studies of cities, infrastructures, and institutions are anthropocentric to a fault, assuming rather than demonstrating that people mediated all urban developments in the past (see Barad 2007; Morton 2017).

The upshot of this book is that we need to approach urbanism at the outset by recognizing its other-than-human causal and consequential complexities and contingencies. The contributors to this book seek to build such an approach by examining the other-than-human ingredients in urbanism. They do this by elevating the ontological—the ways of being and relating in the world. In so elevating the ontological, the authors brush up against archaeologies of religion, among other things (see Fowles 2013; Insoll 2011; Pauketat 2013). Indeed, the seminars upon which this book is based explicitly sought to understand the religious dimensions of early urbanism. This makes sense, of course, because religion and spirituality, at least as lived, cannot be separated from ways and theories of being (i.e., ontology). And because urbanism is ultimately a way of living (Wirth 1938), we must consider

2 Timothy R. Pauketat

the religious aspects of that living when broadening the discussion of the development of early urbanism.

Such is the purpose of this book, and authors assume phenomenological, relational, and 'New Materialist' approaches to the past in order to achieve that purpose, merging historical information about the ontologies of past people with analyses of the affective powers of substances, materials, phenomena, things or peoples (Bennett 2010; DeLanda 2006; Ingold 2012). The emphasis in this New-Materialist statement of purpose should be placed on the word 'new', since no one in this volume seeks a return to the older (modernist) forms of materialist theory, where aggregate material conditions were used as explanations of whole societies and historical epochs. New Materialisms (there are a number of varieties) allow for animate and agentic forces other than people to cause history. Of course, New Materialisms have been criticized for dehumanizing humanity and for sanitizing human history—purging it of its power, politics, and inequalities (cf. Cole 2013; Rekret 2016; Tompkins 2016). Such criticisms are legitimate, if slightly misplaced.

Certainly, authors in this volume do not seek to excuse the moral, political, and ethical responsibilities of being human, in the past or present. People do deserve the credit or the blame for much in the past and present. Climate change, for instance, needs to be blamed on people—specifically, corporations and politicians. Water crises in the Atacama Desert and the city of Detroit, as other examples, are similarly to be blamed on politicians and their corporate allies. Then again, the cultural and physical violence done to victims, on the one hand, and the privileges and power of antagonists, on the other, have deeper, longer-term, and more insidious roots and involve material and biological agents that continue to shape the world and all of the things and bodies therein long after human antagonists wash their hands of their offenses. These need to be evaluated (Bauer and Ellis 2018).

In the end, if the job of an archaeologist is to evaluate historical cause and effect, then it is increasingly clear that purely anthropocentric explanations, even of the political dimensions of urban phenomena, give short shrift to critical material, substantial, and phenomenal relationships that will help us to evaluate the politics, morality, and ethics of people. We ignore them to our detriment and, hence, New Materialisms and related realist approaches are having a profound influence on archaeology today (Alberti 2016; Harrison-Buck 2018; Jones and Alberti 2013; Thomas 2015). That which unites such approaches is their philosophical decentering of people in the production of human history, although there is a fair amount of variability in the degree to which other-than-human materials, substances, or phenomena are afforded primacy in ostensibly human history (e.g., Ingold 2007c). Moreover, many of the approaches were ultimately derived in some fashion from the phenomenology of Martin Heidegger (1996), as exemplified by Tim Ingold (2000). In addition, most owe a debt to Indigenous-American theories of persons, places, and things that decenter the modern notion of the human individual (Deloria 2006; V. Watts 2013). This is certainly the case for a number of the chapters in this volume, and is the basis of a host of 'relational' approaches today (Alberti and Marshall 2009; Baltus and Baires 2018; C. Watts 2013).

Beyond these relational archaeological approaches, there are also other symmetrical, actor-network, and object-oriented approaches that theorize things as co-mediators of social life (Olsen et al. 2012; Webmoor 2007; Witmore 2007). These are inspired by the ontological realism of Bruno Latour and Graham Harman (Harman 2010; Latour 2005; Latour et al. 2011), and they dovetail with the so-called 'archaeology of the contemporary world' (Dawdy 2017; Graves-Brown et al. 2013). The latter focus on critical analyses of objects and architecture in human constructions of alternative futures and are inspired by Walter Benjamin's (1999) and Henri Bergson's (2007) decidedly more humanistic theorizing of images, objects, and architecture.

The realist philosophies from which this book's authors find inspiration stem less from the humanist-tinged thinking of Latour, Harman, Benjamin, or Bergson and more from the 'transcendental empiricism' of Gilles Deleuze (1994), the affect-rich geography of Nigel Thrift (2008), the materialism of Jane Bennett (2010), the quantum physics of Karen Barad (2007), and the assemblage theory of Manuel DeLanda (2006, 2016). Accordingly, the authors of this volume direct their archaeological inquiries toward understanding substantial, material, spatial, atmospheric, phenomenal, and infrastructural genealogies that have entangled people and other-than-human causal forces in specific contexts in the past and, from there, have defined humanity and delimited history in urban ways.

Indeed, more than some of the varieties of recent archaeological thinking noted above, a central distinguishing aspect of our New Materialism is that history yet matters in it, not simply as 'one damn (human) thing after another', to adapt a well-worn phrase, but as the analyses of continuous flows and movements of matter, substance, and energy, as measured through time and across space. These flows and movements are entangled, bundled, or assembled in ways as to define and redefine all entities, including seemingly tightly integrated and clearly demarcated organic and inorganic things and bodies. Things and bodies themselves are, in other words, always emergent; no things pre-exist such flows and movements (Barad 2007). Rather, they come into being as flows and movements mediate larger webs of relations. The biographies, genealogies, and histories of such flows and movements, from chemical reactions and weather events to urbanization, need to be understood as co-constructive (Ingold 2007a, 2007b, 2013).

The matter, media, and atmospheres through which substances take shape, beings come into being, and social relationships happen are not merely resources used by people to construct societies, to make things, or to oppress. Even urban infrastructures are not simply about human invention and economic investment. Rather, they are comprised of fluid, permeable, and metamorphological relationships vital to the constitution and history of peoples, places, and things themselves. Histories are always being assembled, disassembled, and reassembled relationally (e.g., Ingold 2011). To some extent, the crystalline properties of rocks, the fluid qualities of life-giving water, or the sensory-rich engagements of beings moving through affective atmospheres or permeable fields of vibrant matter in some times and places help to explain that which we ordinarily box up as urbanism.

4 Timothy R. Pauketat

In what follows, I introduce how assemblages, affects, stratifications, territorializations, rhizomes, haecceities, conversions, and more might allow us to rethink the problems of early urbanism. The chapters that follow then do the work of tracing the flows of matter, the locomotions of atmospheric or cosmic phenomena, and the genealogies of moving beings and bodies in and out, on or under, and through or against urban or would-be urban assemblages. The result is anything but your typical book on ancient cities.

Theoretical packaging

Not surprisingly, many early anthropological, sociological, and archaeological theories were attempts to come to grips with the origins and existence of urbanism (Childe 1950; Frazer 1945; Marx and Engels 1970; Tylor 1873). Writing in 1864, the French historian Fustel de Coulanges (1980) sensed the ontological underpinnings of it all when he proclaimed that the earliest cities of the Mediterranean were founded on religious principles, if not actually established by the gods through human interlocutors. Some archaeologists today would affirm the same, recognizing for example that native African, Asian, and American cities were, by design, emplacements of cosmic order on earth (e.g., Fash and López Luján 2009; Kus 2012; Malville and Gujral 2000; Wheatley 1971). Of course, such a broad conclusion begs questions about the nature of urbanism that have proven difficult to answer—in large part because urbanism comes with considerable conceptual baggage that needs to be unpacked and repacked.

Typical materialist approaches treat urbanism as a one-off human development, hiding the reality that past urban, proto-urban, and non-urban places, as well as uncentralized but populated landscapes, assumed a diverse array of sizes, densities, configurations, and materialities (cf. Childe 1950). In the past, there were low-density urban landscapes in Southeast Asia, the Yucatan, and the Amazon; high-density cityscapes in Mesopotamia, China, and central Mexico; and pulsating pilgrimage complexes everywhere in between (Fletcher 2009; Heckenberger et al. 2003; Marcus and Sabloff 2008; M. E. Smith 2007). There were cities of fixed concrete and stone structures, with their 'phantasmagorical' qualities (see Harmanşah, Chapter 9), and there were tent cities (ranging from great encampments of Roman legions to gatherings of peripatetic Paleolithic foragers at places such as Gobekli Tepe). In the present volume, this range falls between the extremes of the mountaintop materiality of Monte Albán, on the one hand, and the temporary bent-pole buildings at Cahokia's Emerald Acropolis, on the other (see Alt and Joyce, Chapters 2 and 4). The enigmatic Chacoan phenomenon was arguably something in between (see Van Dyke, Chapter 3), its socio-historical web covering an area so vast as to suggest that the 'city', in this case, might need to be conceptualized as a regional phenomenon (consider Benson 2017).

Urbanism was and is in no way limited to cities, however those might be defined, and Meredith Chesson (2015, 2019) has also suggested the existence of an alternate 'slow' kind of urbanism seen in the burgeoning villages of the Neolithic Levant.

Kenneth Ames et al. (2016) likewise see in the crowding of plank-house settlement around Prince Rupert Harbour in northwestern North America an instance of emergent urbanism. Indeed, one might imagine instances where Mesopotamian- or Mesoamerican-style urbanism never developed, as in Amazonia and parts of Asia and North America, even though many urban qualities might still be apparent in these instances. Consequently, it seems apparent that urbanism need not be synonymous with compact, bounded, and permanent places distinguished by dense human populations. Likewise, cities need not be the products of states, or states the results of cities (Sinopoli and Suvrathan 2016; Yoffee and Terrenato 2015). Instead, any number of relationships might possess an urban dimension, which is to say an urbanity. Any dense architectonic or infrastructural field might be called urban, especially those where the moving bodies, materials, substances, and phenomena were stratified (see below).

To delimit what I mean by such a general definition, I want to lay out some substantial and material fundamentals. Of these, the most basic if not also familiar is the assemblage. A review of the assemblage, along with a series of related concepts, enables us in subsequent chapters, to reopen interrogations into things that many wrongly assume are already settled—city, infrastructure, politics, and event among them.

Assemblage

All things-that-mediate are, in essence, assemblages of qualities and properties that are always subject to rearrangement and dissolution (Harris 2017). To mediate is, in some sense, to assemble or relate, although how that mediation or assemblage happens would vary as widely as there are things in the world, with some assemblages—say, cities—being comparable to each other (DeLanda 2006; Kostof 1992). The reasons for such comparability will be due to the scale and density (or 'intensity') of the assemblage, its permeability (boundedness or 'territorialization'), and its motions or transformational proclivities (durability, directionality).

Some assemblages might be so loose or ephemeral as to be hardly noticeable or historically meaningful. For example, urbanism itself might be difficult to identify—especially the continuous low-density varieties known in the tropics (Fletcher 2009) or the 'slow urbanism' of the Levant (Chesson 2019). Such loose or slow assemblages, of course, might undergo more rapid, or 'fast' transformations, or 'assemblage conversions', from the inside-out or outside-in such that they disproportionately mediate some landscape or other relational field (Bennett 2010:42; Deleuze and Guattari 1987:325). These instances of rapid or fast urbanism would presumably then be recognizable to sentient beings as cities. Thus, various early cities discussed in this book—Monte Albán, Cahokia, Tiwanaku, Liangzhu—were designed and built during great construction events such that their builders must have understood that radical social changes were underway (see Alt, Joyce, Janusek, and Pauketat, Chapters 2, 4–6). Other cities or urbanities discussed herein—Maski and Chaco, for instance—were more organic, rhizomatic, or slow in character (Van Dyke, Chapter 3, and Bauer, Chapter 8).

6 Timothy R. Pauketat

The importance of distinguishing the two cannot be overstated. They exemplify how things (read, cities)—as entities that mediate (a.k.a. agencies)—emerge from less-thingly substantial or material fields in Deleuzian thought (see Joyce, Chapter 4). Deleuze and Guattari (1987:261–262) distinguished the looser, more open or spatially distributed mode—sometimes called a haecceity—from the more rigidly delineated or individuated mode.

> There is a mode of individuation very different from that of a person, subject, thing, or substance. We reserve the name *haecceity* for it. A season, a winter, a summer, an hour, a date have a perfect individuality lacking nothing, even though this individuality is different from that of a thing or a subject. They are haecceities in the sense that they consist entirely of relations of movement and rest between molecules or particles, capacities to affect and be affected.
>
> (Deleuze and Guattari 1987:262)

Such delimiting processes or events create form from formlessness, a process that happens from the inside-out and the outside-in at all scales—from the molecule up to the city.

> [T]he bigger something is ... or the more microscopic it is, the more its thinghood recedes. ... Water, soup, and butter, being divisible, remain the substances that they are, even if their quantity is altered. ... Things persist, and remain. ... This is why it is odd to say that food or any kind of consumable is a thing. If things had a very fleeting existence they would lose their capacity to belong to the world, a capacity which presupposes a certain duration and persistence. They would be more like events or occurrences.
>
> (Finlayson 2013:99–100)

Cities, as things, might emerge on their own to affect the world around them, or they may be ascribed objective reality, more or less, by their surroundings and by other beings, especially people. All entities are comprised of both modes of individuation to variable degree: 'At most, we may distinguish assemblage haecceities ... and interassemblage haecceities, which also mark the potentialities of becoming within each assemblage' (Deleuze and Guattari 1987:262). Urbanism is an interassemblage haecceity. And yet just as clouds materialize or disappear at certain altitudes under variable atmospheric conditions or as rain is absorbed to become groundwater (only to reappear as—and to therefore territorialize—places such as seeps and springs), so the urbanism that initially appears as discrete cities on the landscape might later become unrecognizable when rural interstices fill up with urban development.

The point is this: we would also not easily recognize those qualities of urban assemblages that give them their dynamism were we to focus solely on the entities that we call cities. This is because cities and other less-bounded forms of urbanisms are more than just grouping of things. They are arrangements of *immaterial or affective* elements, qualities, and movements as well, as Yannis Hamilakis (2017:171) has discussed with regard to other sorts of assemblages. (Some of these immaterial or affective arrangements are also 'immanent' linkages to a wider relational field or 'stratum' [see below]).

A great deal of that which we label urbanism does not involve things at all, but consists of formless substantial and material 'attachments' (Latour 2005). Take the soil in which grows the food that feeds a city; it has little actual fixed form apart from the fields in which it is found (see Latour 1999). Similarly, the charred remains of food that archaeologists routinely recover are probably best understood as the leftovers of non-things—substances that were consumed, digested and converted into human energy and flesh—rather than discrete things. This is not to say that such pure matter or inchoate substance did not assume form from time to time. It is just to recognize that a good part of the movements of the sediments and consumables of human urban experience are as formless matter, not objects or things with any lasting stability. And such forms must have affected other forms, and ultimately people and urbanism, in historically important ways.

Immanence

Significantly, such formless matter has vital tendencies and 'intra-active' properties (Barad 2007), among them being the ability—under the right circumstances or states—to become bounded or 'territorialized' and, conversely, unbounded and 'deterritorialized' (Deleuze and Guattari 1987). These are the movements between substantial and phenomenal realms, on the one hand, and thingly realms, on the other, also called 'mattering' by Karen Barad (2007). Certain physical and chemical properties of substances or compounds, for example, are attracted to others under certain conditions, depending on the atmosphere of which they are a part. Thus, hydrogen molecules might join with oxygen to produce water under certain atmospheric regimes. Similarly, water vapor comprises part of the earth's atmosphere, invisible under certain temperature and pressure conditions, but mattering nevertheless. Most definitely, water vapor defined the atmospheres of some ancient cities, such as Cahokia (see Alt, Chapter 2), in ways that attracted or repelled people. In similar ways, the affects of modern cities attract or repel people from places nicknamed after their qualities: grey city, sun city, sin city, the big apple, and the big easy.

That is, there are many less-thingly or more-substantial and phenomenal existential states or atmospheres involved in urban contexts than meets the eye. Years ago Robert Hall (1989, 1997) argued that engagements of people with earth, water, steam, sweat, sunlight, and lightning, among other substances and phenomena, were paramount to understanding social life in precolonial North America. All afforded reactions in other physical, chemical, elemental, or biological relationships and, hence, became entangled in complicated webs of historical relations. In this book, Jeffrey Fleisher's coral construction materials (Chapter 7), Susan Alt's and Ömür

Harmanşah's subterranean water (Chapters 2 and 9), John Janusek's and Arthur Joyce's mountains (Chapters 4 and 5), Andrew Bauer's boulders (Chapter 8), and Ruth Van Dyke's sandstone cliffs (Chapter 3) are excellent examples. These afford places agency owing to their vital tendencies and intra-active qualities.

The strands of these sorts of relational webs are 'immanent', which is to say rhizomatic, pervasive, and omnipresent in ways that undergird the fundamental qualities of entities. The steamy or watery qualities of some urbanities are prime examples (see Pauketat, Chapter 6). Water in one state or another comprises organisms, landscapes, and atmospheres. It is immanent and, for that reason, immanently powerful. People perceive this power, sometimes in spiritual terms.

Such immanence, in fact, produces a kind of palpable vibrancy or spiritual 'affectivity' (see below) to the things manifest in such relational realms that are then engaged by people as spirits or lifeforces. Dissecting such complicated immanent entanglements might be the only way of coming to grips with immaterial, substantial, or non-thingly but affective qualities of the interrelated phenomena of urbanism.

Affectivity and stratification

Students of modern cityscape palimpsests and ruins have recognized as key to urban dynamics the affective *properties* or *qualities* exuded by materials, substances, elements, molecules, chemicals, phenomena, and so forth, and felt by sentient beings. That is, some cities have haunting, spiritual qualities owing to the variable material and temporal qualities of the architecture from different eras or architectural ruins; both can exude 'auras' (Benjamin 1999; Dawdy 2010; Olivier 2001). Shannon Dawdy (2017:33) explains how the climate, insects, and indexical styles of New Orleans buildings contributed to their charm and 'antique' aura mere decades after their construction. Aura, as a kind of affect, sits between the human senses and the things themselves and informs the ways one moves around and experiences landscapes.

For all intents and purposes, aura and other affects are that which mediate relations. They are the 'attachments' of Bruno Latour's networks and the strands of Tim Ingold's (2000) 'meshworks' and Deleuze and Guattari's (1987) 'rhizomes'. They are, in essence, that which gives any *thing* its thinghood and any object or being its agency. Restating an earlier point, no *thing* exists except as an assemblage, multiplicity, haecceity, or bundle of affects. Even cities are not simply assemblages of buildings, people, and institutions, as mentioned earlier. Rather, they possess considerably more 'intensity' than that (to borrow from Deleuze and Guattari 1987). Urbanisms consist of bundles of bundles—'roiling maelstroms'—of affect and layer upon folder layer of experiential qualities (Thrift 2004; 2008:171).

Of course, such affects—bundled/assembled/folded or not—are highly influential when it comes to the senses of beings and are thus central to the experiences and memory work of people and places. One constructs memories in social contexts through materials and spaces (Halbwachs 1992). In cities, the sights, sounds, and smells of cooking foods, residential districts, and domestic animals alternatively leave clear impressions that can be recalled and that train the body to move or feel in routinized ways. The climate of a region, the colors of public spaces, the spicy flavors of a district's cuisine, or the lingering aftertaste of locally crafted earthen pots enhance such memories and body-knowledge. Immigrants probably move to cities not because of an abstract analysis of economic potential but because of how they feel.

Once there, cities shape the memories, identities, and imaginations of people (Harmanşah 2013; Pauketat et al. 2015; A. T. Smith 2003; Soja 2000). To live in a Neolithic village was to become Neolithic, so to speak (Hodder and Cessford 2004). To make a tool, craft a pot, or build a pyramid was to generate society (Dobres 2000; Joyce 2004; Pauketat 2000; Pauketat and Emerson 1991). To walk through Chaco Canyon or to view the world from the upper city of Kalhu was, and is, to gather history unto oneself and carry it forward (Harmanşah 2013; Van Dyke 2007). To live in an urban landscape is to become urban. In this sense, cities truly are what cities do (Yoffee and Terrenato 2015).

Contrariwise, the attractions of some city might have been that which altered the perceptual movements of human bodies, perhaps bringing about a hitherto unknown degree of self-awareness and, in the process, altering humanity. Perhaps the configuration of tillable soils, flowing water, and clear skies of that location articulated with the movements of the heavens, leading to the building of a monument or the founding of a city, much as Fustel de Coulanges suggested. Or perhaps something just felt right, and people stayed (Thrift 2004, 2008).

There are long-term historical effects. Stone would be sensed in ways very unlike wood, earth, or water. And such diverse sensorial qualities engage human beings in very different ways owing to the material's relative hardness, impermeability, fluidity, and durability, among other affects, all producing a different historicity for stone cities compared to those of, say, wood or thatch, even ignoring for the time being the complicated genealogies of place that develop after the affective fact. The greyness of Aberdeen, the bustle of Mumbai, the waterscape of Venice, and the sunny, sage-scented skies of Santa Fe affect people in different ways with divergent long-term outcomes.

Might such qualities attract or repel beings to a location, even before urbanism appears? If so, how might they articulate those beings, along with other things, through relationships such that they birth urbanism? How relevant to any urbanity were atmospherics, weather, water, and terrain? To what extent do we need to evaluate not just the qualities of some substantial domain, but the particularities of its flows and transmogrifications (Edgeworth 2011; Strang 2014)? And what is it that distinguishes (or does not distinguish) urbanism—as something that people may or may not perceive in certain historical moments—from everything else?

Such questions lead to a consideration of one more dimension of a process described up to this point only as assemblage, territorialization, and immanence. This is the 'stratification' of relational zones, where the processes of assemblage and territorialization are segregated or layered into subfields (Deleuze and Guattari

1987:40ff., 502–503). Soil accumulates at an interface between strata. Water precipitates, flows, and percolates through and along strata. Wooden buildings degrade into dust or burn to become smoke and ash at the interface of earth and sky. Celestial bodies range through relational fields of the sky. Whether it be actual geological strata along which percolating groundwater is captured—the surface of the earth on which soils form and farmers plant their crops—or the dome of the sky across which celestial objects move irrespective of the happenings down below, strata are quasi-independent realms of intra-acting and interacting substances, materials, phenomena, and things. Infrastructures are strata produced through the engagements of people with other forces that then take on a durability and related causal power all their own.

Existing as a wholly or partially independent plane is the important point, because the key to urbanism, several authors in this volume argue, is the folding together of such otherwise autonomous realms and the creation of dense relational fields. For instance, there is good reason to recognize that celestial bodies were in some ways related to the formation of both urbanism and organized religion (Pauketat, Chapter 6; see also Krupp 1997). There may be equally good reason to point to the partitioning of relationships into multiple superimposed strata or sub-strata, via the creation of infrastructures or the founding configuration of places, as that which generates the dynamics that we typically associate with urbanism (Harmanşah, Chapter 9).

That is, urbanism is not merely a dense, territorialized assemblage of people. It is a thickly folded, layered, or zoned multiplicity that, in such a state, generates complex intra-assemblage and inter-assemblage spheres of activity, organizations, and institutions at scales and degrees of intensity—and with assemblage-conversion potentialities—that change the course of history. With regard to the latter assemblage conversion, it is worth mention that such foldings or articulations of strata might have had a rhizomatic genesis that nevertheless produced nodes or moments (i.e., events) of 'rupture … brought about by the coexistence and articulation of heterogeneous elements' (Hamilaikis 2017:171). Alt (2006) has previously made a similar point about 'hybridity' and the rise of Cahokia (see Chapter 2).

New Materialism's methodology

Evaluating such causal relationships in New Materialist terms is a two-step process. The first step is similar to the ways that archaeologists have previously unpacked object biographies, genealogies of practices, and landscape histories (Harmanşah 2014; Joyce 2000; Meskell 2004; Pauketat and Alt 2005; Van Dyke 2007; Weismantel and Meskell 2014). This step entails that we trace the material relations and untie, unfold, and disassemble the knots, folds, bundles and assemblages of our cases.

This step often begins with contextual or ethnographic information—the associations, attachments, or entanglements that seem to have been manifest in, or to have resulted from, some urban history. Cities and centers are themselves such knots, of course, as are the ontologies, if you will, of descendants and neighbors. All chapters in this volume make some use of such information. The point, of course, is not to reassert a constructivist position that people mediated all things in culturally unique ways, but rather to affirm that other-than-human materials and phenomena did and still do assemble human and other-than-human entities.

The second step involves a re-evaluation of causality and a re-theorizing of that which we call urbanism. In the present cases, this step leads to a re-thinking of the ways in which large-scale, even geopolitical, relationships happen simultaneous with and immanently linked to the fundamental, phenomenal, affective, substantial, and material flows that comprise those big historical relationships (Harris 2017). Things emerging and submerging in and out of history thoroughly infuses and constitutes the substrate of early urbanism. The key seems to be in properly characterizing how—at what scale and in what dimensions—this happens by focusing on those affective qualities of substance, material, and phenomena that influence others. None of these are irrelevant to considerations of something so seemingly complex, and yet so elementally and ontologically simple, as urbanism. These atmospheric relations, flows of water, terrestrial movements and features are the 'primary ontological units' that undergird urbanism (Barad 2007).

The argument can be no better made than via the American Indian city of Cahokia, which Susan Alt argues in Chapter 2 emerged from the immanent realms of earth and water. The relations, and their causal priority, are laid bare at Cahokia's outlying Emerald shrine complex, where water both pours down from above and seeps up from below. By way of engaging the powerful interface, people marked the locations with monumental constructions that, in turn, superimposed people and powers in urban and religious ways, thus constituting Cahokia.

As at Cahokia, Ruth Van Dyke argues in Chapter 3 that substance-thick and large-scale agricultural haecceities became territorialized at higher orders and in trans-dimensional ways. Van Dyke focuses her examination of Chacoan assemblages on the terroritializing and deterritorializing properties of the assemblage, in her case the fundamentals of places—earth, sky, water, rock, and maize—and human sensory experience. Those fundamentals were, in some ways, tenuous, and remain so today. In the past, time and movement through the Chacoan world was, according to Van Dyke, a dialectical territorialization and deterritorialization that produced and belied Chacoan urbanism.

In Chapter 4, Arthur Joyce sees in the Mesoamerican city of Monte Albán a novel articulation of animacies, particularly those of mountains, with people. Mountains impelled people and, in some sense, assembled them and their different pasts into a multi-temporal field actualized by materials of different durabilities. Similar to Chaco, territorializing relationships lead Joyce, following Barad (2007), to infer the realization of Monte Albán as an 'agential cut'—a tightly bundled assemblage that emerges to disproportionately influence history thereafter.

The city as articulation reaches a cosmic denouement in John Janusek's examination of Tiwanaku in Chapter 5. Janusek identifies the landscape as an 'ecoregime', by which he means 'a field of articulations that assembled mountains, celestial movements, water flows, humans, and nonhuman lithic persons as a coherent, if shifting, master cartography'. Tiwanaku was a place of intersecting moving bodies, human and celestial forms meeting in the shadows of mountains. Of particular note are the affects of the monoliths, which—being pieces of mountains—assembled people as much as people did them, all in a relational dance that, to some considerable extent, was Tiwanaku urbanism.

Affects are very much at issue in my own comparison of Paquimé, a multi-story adobe complex in Northwest Mexico, with Liangzhu, a sprawling city of earth and wood in Neolithic China. My point, in Chapter 6, is that the conversion of regional fields of articulation, assembled around grain agriculture and water, into stratified urbanities was the result of novel human 'anticipations' (to borrow Andrew Bauer's term, see Chapter 8) of immanent and affective non-human forces through infrastructure. Paquimé and Liangzhu were works in progress where non-human agencies were harnessed through infrastructures, the effects being both urban and religious.

Jeffrey Fleisher seeks in Chapter 7 to understand the ontological underpinnings of 'founded' Swahili towns through the examination of mosque construction. He understands Swahili towns to have been locales of 'great fluidity and movement' subject to continual deterritorializing forces centered on mosques that themselves were not simply religious structures but material flows. Mosques as assemblages territorialized materials 'connected to the ecology of the fore/nearshore' and associated people with powerful lifeforces, even as they enabled a syncretization of native and non-native spiritual practices. Through them, religion and cities came into being.

Such a syncretization is precisely what Andrew Bauer recognizes in the medieval-period Deccan Plain of South India. In Chapter 8, Bauer draws the contrasts between various cosmic centers and Maski. All are urban, but religious principles are not apparent at Maski, as compared to other medieval centers, suggesting the need for

> an approach to Medieval urbanization that looks beyond the city plans of imperial capitals or monumental centers to track the ways that the production of spatial forms and their corresponding sociality was assembled by a range of materials, things, and people.

We need a different approach to urbanism to understand why religious practices, similar to those seen in earlier chapters of this book, 'were not significant to the constitution of urban space or related forms of social alterity'.

Such a different approach is developed by Ömür Harmanşah in Chapter 9. Here, Harmanşah argues that the affects of Hittite cities in Assyria were 'creative, improvisational, and irreducibly material' aspects of urbanities. Cities were vibrant because of their affects, continuously transformed and reconfigured in ways that both 'are always deeply entangled with collective interventions of human communities to the environment' and that help to explain 'how, when, and why cities emerge in a particular landscape'. Echoing points made in the first half of the book, Harmanşah describes cities as 'ungoverned and eclectic assemblages of living and nonliving entities' that can be designed before they were ever lived in. Geological and architectonic structures, 'mortal and immortal actors', and politico-religious ceremonies 'were seamlessly continuous' in Hittite urban assemblages.

In his Chapter 10 commentary, Oliver Harris gives us four New Materialist conclusions based on the preceding chapters. First, following Deleuze, he distinguishes the virtual (city) from the actual (city), helping to explain how urbanism develops from ostensibly non-urban relations. Second, he makes the all-important point that New Materialist approaches to urbanism in no way abandon the study of humanity and historical process—quite the opposite. Third, New Materialist approaches to urbanism are consonant with, yet go well beyond, anthropological concerns with ontologies, politics, and power. Indeed, his fourth point is that there really is something about the city, as a Deleuzian sort of articulation (of form and content or affect and matter) that students of history and humanity need to consider much more deeply.

Conclusion

Harris would agree that, as a group, the contributors to this book redirect the discussions about the causes and consequences of urbanism, a very human phenomenon, by expanding the field of explanation to other-than-human realms. This is a materialist move to be sure, but a 'new' one that insists on historical understandings of all of the moving parts of our more-than-human world. Generally speaking, authors of various chapters

1. reject overly essentialized categorizations of cities, infrastructures, or events;
2. identify the affective powers and rhizomatic qualities of other-than-human things, non-things, and landscapes that existed even before, as Harmanşah puts it, people arrived on the scene, thus explaining how, when, and why urbanism took root in particular landscapes;
3. delineate certain powers and qualities as, in effect, religious, making religion in some ways causal to urban developments; and
4. interrogate ontological, infrastructural, architectonic, and geological processes as that which stratified human and other-than-human relationships to produce urbanism.

In so doing, the contributors to this book expand the field wherein we might understand how humanity, specifically urban humanity, was constructed to recognize that people

5. do not simply make themselves, and
6. were not always human in the same way.

14 Timothy R. Pauketat

That recognition would not come as a surprise to any of the descendants of the cities and urbanities analyzed in this book. If we were to transport ourselves back in time to any one of these urbanizing landscapes and ask the people who they were, how they felt about their home, and why they did what they did, some would doubtless profess their ontological sensibilities that certain substances, materials, and phenomena were powerful, energized by spirits, or conducive to communications with other-than-human beings. Many would agree that larger-than-life mediators were, to some significant extent, responsible for the urbanity in question. Some would proclaim, as many do today, that they dwell in their city because they cannot imagine life otherwise.

But whether or not people knew it in any discursive way, the upshot is that there were, and are, actual other-than-human causal forces that affected human history and that humanized/urbanized beings, and that will yet affect human futures and humanities-to-come. Such powers exist today even in nominally secular cities— cosmopolitan Paris, international Mexico City, commercial Singapore—where the affective powers of skyscrapers, public spaces, and central business districts assemble life around orderly infrastructures. These are all, in some sense, ontological—even religious—mediations similar to those of Cahokia, Chaco, Monte Albán, Tiwanaku, Paquimé, Liangzhu, Maski, the Swahili coast, and the Hittite cities. These all conveyed other-than-human order to disordered human lives and inchoate flows of matter and movements of things by assembling affects across very different scales, dimensions, or periodicities. And they all point to the promise of realizing profound lessons about our own urban futures by looking back at ancient urbanisms from newer vantage points.

Note

1 Not incidentally, well over half of human beings alive today affiliate themselves with one of the world's major religions, and many of the rest would consider themselves unaffiliated but spiritual beings as well.

References

Adams, Robert McC. 1966 *The Evolution of Urban Society*. Aldine, Chicago.
Alberti, Benjamin 2016 Archaeologies of Ontology. *Annual Review of Anthropology* 45: 163–179.
Alberti, Benjamin, and Yvonne Marshall 2009 Animating Archaeology: Local Theories and Conceptually Open-ended Methodologies. *Cambridge Archaeological Journal* 19(3):344–356.
Alt, Susan M. 2006 The Power of Diversity: The Roles of Migration and Hybridity in Culture Change. In *Leadership and Polity in Mississippian Society*, edited by B. M. Butler and P. D. Welch, pp. 289–308. Center for Archaeological Investigations, Occasional Paper No. 33. Southern Illinois University, Carbondale.
Ames, Kenneth M., Kisha Supernant, Andrew Martindale, Susan Marsden, Bryn Letham and Robert Gustus 2016 *A Hunter-Gatherer-Fisher Urban Landscape in Prince Rupert Harbor, British Columbia?* Paper presented at the 81st Annual Meeting of the Society for American Archaeology, Orlando, Florida.

Baltus, Melissa R., and Sarah E. Baires (editors) 2018 *Relational Engagements of the Indigenous Americas: Alterity, Ontology, and Shifting Paradigms.* Lexington Books, Lanham, MD.

Barad, Karen 2007 *Meeting the Universe Halfway: Quantum Physics and the Entanglement of Matter and Meaning.* Duke University Press, Durham, NC.

Bauer, Andrew M., and Erle C. Ellis 2018 The Anthropocene Divide: Obscuring Understanding of Social-Environmental Change. *Current Anthropology* 59(2):209–227.

Benjamin, Walter 1999 *The Arcades Project.* Translated by H. Eiland and K. McLaughlin. Harvard University Press, Cambridge, MA.

Bennett, Jane 2010 *Vibrant Matter: A Political Ecology of Things.* Duke University Press, Durham, NC.

Benson, Larry V. 2017 The Chuska Slope as an Agricultural Alternative to Chaco Canyon: A Rebuttal of Tankersley et al. (2016). *Journal of Archaeological Science: Reports* 16:456–471.

Bergson, Henri 2007 *The Creative Mind: An Introduction to Metaphysics.* Translated by M. L. Andison. Dover Publications, Mineola, NY.

Chesson, Meredith S. 2015 Reconceptualizing the Early Bronze Age Southern Levant without Cities: Local Histories and Walled Communities of EB II-III Society. *Journal of Mediterranean Archaeology* 28(1):51–79.

——— 2019 The Southern Levant during the Early Bronze Age I-III. In *The Social Archaeology of the Levant: From the Past to the Present*, edited by A. Yasur-Landau, E. Cline and Y. M. Rowan, pp. 163-182. Cambridge University Press, Cambridge.

Childe, V. Gordon 1950 The Urban Revolution. *Town Planning Review* 21:3–17.

Cole, Andrew 2013 The Call of Things: A Critique of Object-Oriented Ontologies. *Minnesota Review* 80:106–118.

Dawdy, Shannon Lee 2010 Clockpunk Anthropology and the Ruins of Modernity. *American Anthropologist* 51(6):761–793.

——— 2017 *Patina: A Profane Archaeology.* University of Chicago Press, Chicago.

DeLanda, Manuel 2006 *A New Philosophy of Society: Assemblage Theory and Social Complexity.* Bloomsbury, London.

——— 2016 *Assemblage Theory.* Edinburgh University Press, Edinburgh.

Deleuze, Gilles 1994 *Difference and Repetition.* Columbia University Press, New York.

Deleuze, Gilles, and Felix Guattari 1987 *A Thousand Plateaus: Capitalism and Schizophrenia.* Translated by B. Massumi. University of Minnesota Press, Minneapolis.

Deloria, Viine, Jr. 2006 *The World We Used to Live In: Remembering the Powers of the Medicine Men.* Fulcrum Publishing, Golden, CO.

Dobres, Marcia-Anne 2000 *Technology and Social Agency.* Blackwell, Oxford.

Edgeworth, Matt 2011 *Fluid Pasts: Archaeology of Flow.* Bristol Classical Press, London.

Fash, William L., and Leonardo López Luján (editors) 2009 *The Art of Urbanism: How Mesoamerican Kingdoms Represented Themselves in Architecture and Imagery.* Dumbarton Oaks, Washington, DC.

Finlayson, James G. 2013 To the Things Themselves Again: Observations on What Things Are and Why They Matter. In *The Oxford Handbook of the Archaeology of the Contemporary World*, edited by P. Graves-Brown, R. Harrison and A. Piccini, pp. 94–104. Oxford University Press, Oxford.

Fletcher, Roland 2009 Low-Density, Agrarian-Based Urbanism: A Comparative View. *Insights (Institute of Advanced Study, Durham)* 2(4):2–19.

Fowles, Severin M. 2013 *An Archaeology of Doings: Secularism and the Study of Pueblo Religion.* School for Advanced Research Press, Santa Fe, NM.

Frazer, James George 1945 *The Golden Bough: A Study in Magic and Religion* (originally published 1922). Macmillan, New York.

Fustel de Coulanges, Numa Denis 1980 *The Ancient City*. Johns Hopkins University Press, Baltimore.

Graves-Brown, Paul, Rodney Harrison and Angela Piccini 2013 Introduction. In *The Oxford Handbook of the Archaeology of the Contemporary World*, edited by P. Graves-Brown, R. Harrison and A. Piccini, pp. 1–23. Oxford University Press, Oxford.

Halbwachs, Maurice 1992 *On Collective Memory*. Translated by L. Coser. University of Chicago Press, Chicago.

Hall, Robert L. 1989 The Cultural Background of Mississippian Symbolism. In *The Southeastern Ceremonial Complex*, edited by P. Galloway, pp. 239–278. University of Nebraska Press, Lincoln.

————— 1997 *An Archaeology of the Soul: Native American Indian Belief and Ritual*. University of Illinois Press, Urbana.

Hamilakis, Yannis 2017 Sensorial Assemblages: Affect, Memory and Temporality in Assemblage Thinking. *Cambridge Archaeological Journal* 27(1):169–182.

Harman, Graham 2010 *Towards Speculative Realism: Essays and Lectures*. Zero Books, Winchester, UK.

Harmanşah, Ömür 2013 *Cities and the Shaping of Memory in the Ancient Near East*. Cambridge University Press, Cambridge.

————— 2014 Event, Place, Performance: Rock Reliefs and Spring Monuments in Anatolia. In *Of Rocks and Water: Towards an Archaeology of Place*, edited by Ö. Harmanşah, pp. 140–168. Oxbow Books, Oxford.

Harris, Oliver J. T. 2017 Assemblages and Scale in Archaeology. *Cambridge Archaeological Journal* 27(1):127–139.

Harrison-Buck, Eleanor 2018 Relational Matters of Being: Personhood and Agency in Archaeology. In *Relational Identities and Other-Than-Human Agency in Archaeology*, edited by E. Harrison-Buck and J. A. Hendon, pp. 263–284. University of Colorado Press, Boulder.

Heckenberger, Michael J., Afukaka Kuikuro, Urissapá Tabata Kuikuro, J. Christian Russell, Morgan Schmidt, Carlos Fausto and Bruna Franchetto 2003 Amazonia 1492: Pristine Forest or Cultural Parkland? *Science* 301:1710–1714.

Heidegger, Martin 1996 *Being and Time*. Translated by J. Stambaugh. State University of New York Press, Albany.

Hodder, Ian, and Craig Cessford 2004 Daily Practice and Social Memory at Çatalhöyük. *American Antiquity* 69(1):17–40.

Ingold, Tim 2000 *The Perception of the Environment: Essays in Livelihood, Dwelling and Skill*. Routledge, London.

————— 2007a Earth, Sky, Wind, and Weather. *Journal of the Royal Anthropological Institute* 13(s1):S19–S38.

————— 2007b *Lines: A Brief History*. Routledge, London.

————— 2007c Materials against Materiality. *Archaeological Dialogues* 14(1):1–16.

————— 2011 *Being Alive: Essays on Movement, Knowledge and Description*. Routledge, London.

————— 2012 Toward an Ecology of Materials. *Annual Review of Anthropology* 41:427–442.

————— 2013 *Making: Anthropology, Archaeology, Art and Architecture*. Routledge, London.

Insoll, Timothy (editor) 2011 *The Oxford Handbook of the Archaeology of Ritual and Religion*. Oxford University Press, Oxford.

Jones, Andrew Meirion, and Benjamin Alberti 2013 Archaeology after Interpretation. In *Archaeology after Interpretation: Returning Materials to Archaeological Theory*, edited by B. Alberti, A. M. Jones and J. Pollard, pp. 15–35. Left Coast Press, Walnut Creek, CA.

Joyce, Rosemary A. 2000 Heirlooms and Houses: Materiality and Social Memory. In *Beyond Kinship: Social and Material Reproduction in House Societies*, edited by R. A. Joyce and S. Gillespie, pp. 189–212. University of Pennsylvania Press, Philadelphia.

———— 2004 Unintended Consequences? Monumentality as a Novel Experience in Formative Mesoamerica. *Journal of Archaeological Method and Theory* 11(1):5–29.

Kostof, Spiro 1992 *The City Assembled: The Elements of Urban Form through History*. Thames and Hudson, London.

Krupp, Edmund C. 1997 *Skywatchers, Shamans and Kings: Astronomy and the Archaeology of Power*. Wiley, New York.

Kus, Susan 2012 Matters of Belief: Middle-Range Theory, Religion, and the "State". In *Beyond Belief: The Archaeology of Religion and Ritual*, edited by Y. M. Rowan, pp. 11–22, vol. 21. Archeological Papers of the American Anthropological Association. Washington, DC.

Latour, Bruno 1999 *Pandora's Hope: Essays on the Reality of Science Studies*. Harvard University Press, Cambridge, MA.

———— 2005 *Reassembling the Social: An Introduction to Actor-Network Theory*. Oxford University Press, Oxford.

Latour, Bruno, Graham Harman and Peter Erdélyi 2011 *The Prince and the Wolf*. Zero Books, Winchester, UK.

Malville, John McKim, and Lalit M. Gujral (editors) 2000 *Ancient Cities, Sacred Skies: Cosmic Geometries and City Planning in Ancient India*. Indira Gandhi National Centre for the Arts, and Aryan Books International, New Delhi.

Marcus, Joyce, and Jeremy A. Sabloff (editors) 2008 *The Ancient City: New Perspectives on Urbanism in the Old and New World*. School for Advanced Research Press, Santa Fe, NM.

Marx, Karl, and Frederick Engels 1970 *The German Ideology*. International Publishers, New York.

Meskell, Lynn M. 2004 *Object Worlds in Ancient Egypt: Material Biographies Past and Present*. Berg, London.

Morton, Timothy 2017 *Humankind: Solidarity with Nonhuman People*. Verso, London.

Olivier, Laurent 2001 Duration, Memory and the Nature of the Archaeological Record. In *It's About Time: The Concept of Time in Archaeology*, edited by H. Karlsson, pp. 61–70. Bricoleur Press, Gothenberg.

Olsen, Bjørnar, Michael Shanks, Timothy Webmoor and Christopher Witmore 2012 *Archaeology: The Discipline of Things*. University of California Press, Berkeley.

Pauketat, Timothy R. 2000 The Tragedy of the Commoners. In *Agency in Archaeology*, edited by M.-A. Dobres and J. Robb, pp. 113–129. Routledge, London.

———— 2013 *An Archaeology of the Cosmos: Rethinking Agency and Religion in Ancient America*. Routledge, London.

Pauketat, Timothy R., and Susan M. Alt 2005 Agency in a Postmold? Physicality and the Archaeology of Culture-Making. *Journal of Archaeological Method and Theory* 12:213–236.

Pauketat, Timothy R., Susan M. Alt and Jeffery D. Kruchten 2015 City of Earth and Wood: Cahokia and Its Material-Historical Implications. In *Early Cities in Comparative Perspective, 4000 BCE-1200 CE*, edited by N. Yoffee, pp. 437–454. Cambridge University Press, Cambridge.

Pauketat, Timothy R., and Thomas E. Emerson 1991 The Ideology of Authority and the Power of the Pot. *American Anthropologist* 93(4):919–941.

Rekret, Paul 2016 A Critique of New Materialism: Ethics and Ontology. *Subjectivity* 9(3):225–245.

Sinopoli, Carla M., and Uthara Suvrathan 2016 The City in the State. In *Social Theory in Archaeology and Ancient History: The Present and Future of Counternarratives*, edited by G. Emberling, pp. 109–128. Cambridge University Press, Cambridge.

Smith, Adam T. 2003 *The Political Landscape: Constellations of Authority in Early Complex Polities*. University of California Press, Berkeley.

Smith, Michael E. 2007 Form and Meaning in the Earliest Cities: A New Approach to Ancient Urban Planning. *Journal of Planning History* 6(1):3–47.

Soja, Edward W. 2000 *Postmetropolis: Critical Studies of Cities and Regions*. Blackwell, Oxford.

Strang, Veronica 2014 Fluid Consistencies: Material Relationality in Human Engagements with Water. *Archaeological Dialogues* 21(2):123–150.

Thomas, Julian 2015 The Future of Archaeological Theory. *Antiquity* 89(348):1287–1296.

Thrift, Nigel 2004 Intensities of Feeling: Towards a Spatial Politics of Affect. *Geografiska Annaler* 86B(1):57–78.

———— 2008 *Non-Representational Theory: Space | Politics | Affect*. Routledge, London.

Tompkins, Kyla Wazana 2016 On the Limits and Promise of New Materialist Philosophy. *Lateral* 5(1). https://doi.org/10.25158/L5.1.8 (accessed 25 Nov. 2018).

Tylor, Edward B. 1873 *Religion in Primitive Culture*. Harper, New York.

Van Dyke, Ruth M. 2007 *The Chaco Experience: Landscape and Ideology at the Center Place*. School for Advanced Research Press, Santa Fe, NM.

Watts, Christopher (editor) 2013 *Relational Archaeologies: Humans/Animals/Things*. Routledge Press, London.

Watts, Vanessa 2013 Indigenous Place-Thought and Agency Amongst Humans and Non-Humans (Woman and Sky Woman go on a European World Tour!). *Decolonization: Indigeneity, Education and Society* 2(1):20–34.

Webmoor, Timothy 2007 What about 'One More Turn after the Social' in Archaeological Reasoning? Taking Things Seriously. *World Archaeology* 39(4):563–578.

Weismantel, Mary, and Lynn Meskell 2014 Substances: 'Following the Material' through Two Prehistoric Cases. *Journal of Material Culture* 19(3):233–251.

Wheatley, Paul 1971 *Pivot of the Four Quarters: A Preliminary Enquiry into the Origins and Character of the Ancient Chinese City*. Edinburgh University Press, Edinburgh.

Wirth, Louis 1938 Urbanism as a Way of Life. *American Journal of Sociology* 44:1–24.

Witmore, Christopher L. 2007 Symmetrical Archaeology: Excerpts of a Manifesto. *World Archaeology* 39(4):546–562.

Yoffee, Norman, and Nicola Terrenato 2015 A History of the Study of Early Cities. In *Early Cities in Comparative Perspective, 4000 BCE-1200 CE*, edited by N. Yoffee, pp. 1–24. Cambridge University Press, Cambridge.

2

FROM WEEPING HILLS TO LOST CAVES

A search for vibrant matter in greater Cahokia

Susan M. Alt

At one time, not long ago, city and urbanism were two words thought not to apply to pre-Columbian Native America north of the Rio Grande. Anthropological and Indigenous theories emphasized, and still emphasize, the animistic practices and communal qualities of American Indian social relations in ways that might seem to inhibit the formation of urbanism (e.g., Deloria 2003; Hallowell 1960; Waters 2004). However, archaeological thinking and new discoveries from a series of major excavations at and around 'greater Cahokia'—a concentration of civic–ceremonial 'precincts' that comprise a novel kind of city (Figure 2.1)—are substantially changing our views of the causes and consequences of American Indian urbanism and North American history (Alt 2010; Emerson et al. 2018; Pauketat and Alt 2015a; Pauketat et al. 2015).

In this chapter, I consider greater Cahokia, the city, and its various outlying pieces as an assemblage that includes not just humans, but also other-than-human persons, places, things, and materials (sensu Deleuze and Guattari 1987). That is, Cahokian urbanization was not just a matter of mounds, plazas, buildings, and people but also nonhuman and other than human forces and qualities. Particularly important were the 'vibrant' aspects of places and materials that 'territorialized' and were territorialized by Cahokians (see Deleuze and Guattari 1987; also Pauketat, Van Dyke, Chapters 1 and 3). I explore those vibrancies as they were assembled through locations seldom previously considered as part of Cahokian urbanism.

My consideration of Cahokia's urban landscape begins with recent excavations at a religious shrine complex—the Emerald Acropolis—and continues into the caves and sinkholes of the greater Cahokia region. By doing this, I hope to engender a far different—and broader—sense of greater Cahokia than can be derived from a more traditional model built around a regional hierarchy of sites differentiated by population, architecture, artifacts and purpose (Fowler 1974; Milner 1998). Through religious sites, caves, and sinkholes, I rethink greater Cahokia's entire relational

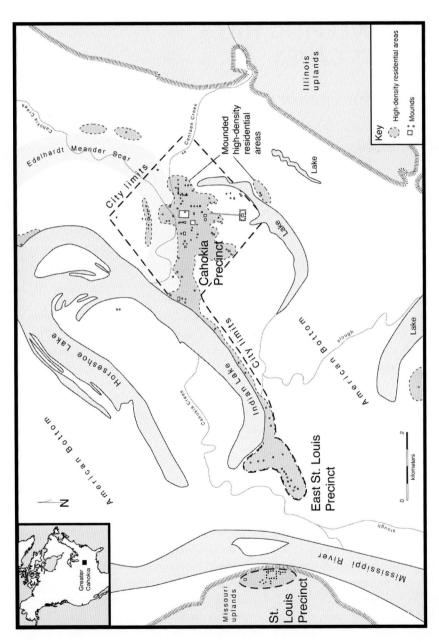

FIGURE 2.1 Map of greater Cahokia showing major civic–ceremonial precincts (map by T. Pauketat)

landscape and, by extension, refine our understanding of its urbanization, which happened in the mid-eleventh century CE. The underworld cave and sinkhole sites, in particular, lead me to the imagery of Cahokian carved stone figurines and rock art and, from there, to a new understanding of greater Cahokia's landscape-based urban ontology.

To convey my new understanding in the space available, I will also draw upon Indigenous ontologies, in part via ethnohistoric sources and in part based on the writings of Native American scholars (Blackhawk 2006; Bruchac 2004; Deloria Jr. 1995; Echo-Hawk 2000; Simpson 2014; Todd 2016; Waters 2004). Following current academic and Indigenous understandings, I look to the oral histories of Siouan speakers as likely derived in some way from Cahokia, although other modern peoples, including Caddo-language speakers, likely had ancestors at Cahokia as well (Diaz-Granados et al. 2015; Hunter 2013; Kehoe 2007; Kelly and Brown 2012). Siouan speakers include the Assiniboine, Iowa, Oto, Dakota, Omaha, Missouri, Mandan, Hidatsa, Crow, Quapaw, Kansa, Lakota, Ponca, Winnebago and Osage people. Their oral histories, recorded by native and non-native anthropologists and missionaries after European contact in the sixteenth century CE, can offer potential insights into that which may have mattered to Cahokians.

Assemblage thinking

Along with others in this volume, I make generous use of the concept of the assemblage (see especially Chapter 10). Following Deleuze and Guattari (1987), assemblages are diametrically opposed to the hierarchical mode of thought typical of urban analyses (e.g., DeLanda 2006). Assemblages cannot be essentialized; they are not monolithic or immutable entities but instead are alive with potential and promise. They are always emerging. More importantly for my present purpose, assemblages involve more than people. Many assemblages were not dependent on humans at all (Barad 2007). Nonhuman assemblages may also be alive, agentive and engaging, based as they are on materials with properties of motion or flow that animate them, along with the many other-than-human persons who lived alongside past human beings (Bennett 2010). Together, all of these things defined assemblages that at various times and in various ways affected human history.

Assemblages in this sense are understood in ways more nuanced and complex than the sorts of artifact or architectural assemblages traditionally employed by archaeologists. Archaeologists typically break their analytical assemblages into their constituent bits to better analyze specific categories of things such as lithics, pottery, or architecture. Doing so may help us understand those things in some ways, but the process also impoverishes our understanding by severing materials from their associations and connections as part of a lived world. By contrast, a New Materialist sort of assemblage thinking encourages us to analyze wholes as something more than the sum of their constituent parts. That is, a pot is never just a pot, but is part of all of the other pots ever made and the potential pots in an assemblage yet to come. One pot bundles together clay and temper, the ideas in a potter's head, or even all

22 Susan M. Alt

of the pots those ideas might have become. The pot's form may be a reminder of the shape of a gourd, the color of a stone, or the water in a nearby stream. It might entangle plants in the fields or the rabbits from the woods, later dropped into the cook pot, with the person who scooped out the cooked contents or burned a finger, with the wood smoldering under it, and with the cooking smells wafting over the community.

As my description above hints, assemblages, even assemblages of pots, did their assembling affectively by creating atmospheres that pulled people into relationships with other-than-human beings and by defining the terrain wherein human–human relationships took place. Assemblage would have resulted *from* vibrant materials that were themselves territorializing the wider landscape. We should think of these as 'vibrant' landscapes, following Jane Bennett (2010).

With regard to urban developments, the questions become more complicated. Viewing Cahokia or any city as an assemblage means that there must be an accounting of all the persons, places, and things that were part of it (see Chapter 1). It requires consideration of the affective qualities that people encountered as well as those they created, not just an instrumental accounting of resources to be utilized or conditions to be exploited or overcome. And it requires that we consider its process of becoming as parts of it were altered, added, or removed (DeLanda 2006, 2016). How were these landscapes 'territorializing' each other, rhizomatically connected and connected to the doings of human persons (see definitions in Chapter 1)? Here I broach the question, how does tracing the wider world of vibrant places, if not also the human perceptions of such things, change how we see enigmatic religious– urban phenomena such as Cahokia in late pre-Columbian North America?

The Cahokian urban assemblage

Greater Cahokia was located on the American Bottom floodplain of southwestern Illinois, across the river from modern St. Louis (Figure 2.2). A large village before 1050 CE, the human population of the greater Cahokia region swelled by over a third following an influx of immigrants in the decades before and after that turning point (Alt 2006, 2008; Slater et al. 2014). At that time, Cahokians land-leveled old village areas and then constructed monumental platforms of earth, large plazas, and neighborhoods over those areas. The result was an interconnected grouping of three monumental precincts that together covered some 20 square kilometers. The principal precinct, Cahokia proper, covers most of that area, or about 12 to 14 square kilometers (see Figure 2.1). There are also outlying small precincts of varying size within the region that replicate the types and densities of architectural features common to the central precincts (Alt 2018b). These were nested within rural landscapes and, sometimes, situated adjacent to other types of sites, such as 'shrine centers' (Alt and Pauketat 2018).

That is, although often incorrectly and simplistically conceived as a central city surrounded by secondary and tertiary settlements, the urban phenomenon of greater Cahokia was actually a multiplicity of places—outlier precincts, shrine complexes,

A search for vibrant matter in greater Cahokia 23

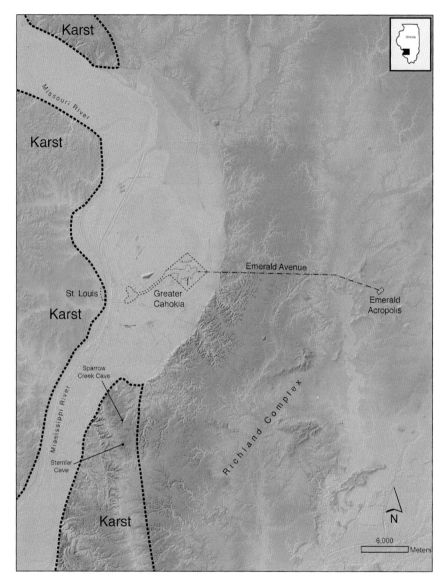

FIGURE 2.2 LiDAR image of the greater Cahokia region, highlighting karst zones and the Cahokia–Emerald relationship (image by S. Alt)

farmsteads and farming villages, and other ceremonial, mortuary and ritual 'nodes' surrounding a dense core of people, domestic housing, public architecture, plazas and monumental constructions (Alt 2018b; Emerson 1997a; Pauketat et al. 2017) Greater Cahokia stretched from a western precinct in modern-day St. Louis eastward across the Mississippi River to the precincts of East St. Louis and Cahokia proper. From there, it continued eastward, following for a 24-kilometer-long

24 Susan M. Alt

'roadway' into the Illinois uplands to the Emerald Acropolis, a shrine center (Alt 2018b; Emerson et al. 2018; Pauketat et al. 2015, 2017).

Emerald Acropolis

Located on a glacial drift ridge in the uplands 24 kilometers east of downtown Cahokia, the 'Emerald Acropolis' (Pauketat et al. 2017) consisted of 12 earthen mounds on top of a ridge, the largest being 7 meters tall with 2 terraces and a small summit mound (Figure 2.3). Beneath these mounds, the ridge had been terraformed, presumably by Cahokians around 1050 CE, to more closely align with a lunar standstill—specifically a 'maximum northern moonrise' that happens every 18.6 years (Pauketat et al. 2017). Cahokians did this by shaping the ridge's sides and summit, placing several mounds in rows aligned with the lunar standstill and establishing other shrines atop more distant hills.

Of great importance to my present purpose are the geomorphological characteristics of the Emerald ridge as they facilitated interactions with water. First and foremost, the ridge contains a perched water table, a condition deriving from

FIGURE 2.3 LiDAR view of the Emerald Acropolis' core area showing Excavation Blocks (EBs) and modern agricultural terraces on the lower southern and western slopes (courtesy of the Emerald Acropolis Project and S. Alt)

an impermeable layer under the ridge that caused water to be hung up in the hill instead of immediately draining through the hill's soils and buried glacial gravels (Grimley and Phillips 2015). This condition, as described by modern residents who lived near Emerald, causes water to ooze from the sides of the ridge throughout much of the year, especially following rainstorms (this highly problematic condition was mitigated by modern farmers who placed drainage pipes through the hillside). If anthropomorphized, one might interpret the hill, in some ways, as weeping. Also, modern landscape modifications and continued farming have clogged the principal outlet for this perched water table: a spring that sat downslope and to the north of the primary mound at the site (Snyder 1962).

These modern alterations to the landscape highlight differences in the values and needs of modern and ancient peoples. While seen as obstacles by modern farmers, these water features were probably what drew people to the Emerald location in the early 1000s and, possibly, provoked the original emplacement of the shrine center atop that specific glacial ridge. Emerald then and now provides a uniquely theatrical vantage point to experience the fierce thunderstorms that happen throughout the Midwest's springs and summers. This vantage point is due not only to its elevation, but because the Acropolis is located in an open expanse of prairie (Oliver 2002). Storm cells can be seen forming far off to the west, in the direction of Cahokia, and are then heard and felt as they approach. Standing on Emerald in the midst of a storm is to truly be enveloped by it, as the very ground shakes with each burst of thunder and its accompanying lightning (Figure 2.4).

As it turns out, it is entirely likely that, for the ancient Cahokians, thunder, lightning, and water from the sky would have been perceived very differently than groundwater, especially that which seeped out of a hillside. To Siouan speakers (especially the Dakota and Omaha), thunder, lightning, and rain belonged to the 'thunderers', masculine sky-rain spirits who in some legends confronted underground beings in epic battles. Groundwater, on the other hand, would have more likely been associated with underground beings, spirits, and feminine forces. The water hills from which groundwater seeps are often mentioned by the historical heirs and descendants of Cahokians: the Omaha, Dakota, and Osage visit such

FIGURE 2.4 A thunderstorm cell passing over the Emerald Acropolis in 2015 (EB6 to the right, photo by T. Pauketat)

places to pray and appeal to the spirits at such springs (Bailey 1995; Dorsey 1894; Fletcher and La Flesche 1992; La Flesche 1921, 1930).

Archaeologically, there can be little doubt that Emerald's waters attracted people from distant places, perhaps owing to the convergence of both types of water—from the sky and from the ground—in lunar alignment. There is archaeological evidence of the intermittent occupation of, and travel to and from, the Acropolis. For instance, the buildings and artifacts at Emerald, as identified in seven excavation blocks and a magnetometry survey, suggest that Emerald was not a year-round settlement (Alt 2018a; Alt and Pauketat 2018; Pauketat and Alt 2015b; Pauketat et al. 2017). That is, while evidence exists that hundreds of thatched-roof buildings sat atop the ridge at any one time, there were few to no food-storage pits or likely storage buildings during these occupations. In addition, debris of year-round domestic life is lacking at Emerald, with most of the material culture recovered associated with ceremonial events connected in some ways to a series of shrine buildings (see below). Some of the pottery found in these same deposits suggests that people from modern-day Indiana, 200 km to the east-southeast, were among those visiting Emerald (and other Cahokian places) between 1000 and 1100 CE. A roadway led from Cahokia to Emerald, and another roadway may have led from Emerald toward southern Indiana (Pauketat 2013; Skousen 2016).

Perhaps also owing to convergent properties, Emerald featured an unusually large number of circular structures, most of which were sweat lodges or steam baths (see Emerson 1997a). Sweat lodges here, and at Cahokia proper, likely brought people into intimate contact with water in several ways (Figure 2.5). Water was poured over heated rocks to produce steam or a vapor. Heat and moisture from this process

FIGURE 2.5 3D reconstruction of select Emerald Acropolis buildings in EB1; small sweat lodge in the center, shrine house to the left, and other support buildings (as modeled by Alex David Jerez Roman, Emerald Acropolis Project)

then provokes water in the form of sweat elicited from human bodies. Producing sweat was necessary to expunge impurities or disease such that a person who has gone through this process is then purified or cured. Lakota priest and Heyoka (water spirit contrarian) Black Elk described emerging from the sweat lodge or steam bath as an act of rebirth from Mother Earth (Brown 1953; Bucko 1998).

Water also had a great deal to do with another type of Emerald Acropolis shrine building. These were small, rectangular semi-subterranean buildings, with floor areas little more than 15 square meters and reminiscent of traditional pre-Cahokian domestic houses in the region (Alt 2016). This traditional form, however, was engaged by people visiting Emerald in nontraditional ways, probably related to the religious practices new to eleventh-century greater Cahokia. These included applying a distinctive yellow plaster—made from silty clay and water—to shrine building floors (Alt 2016). The shrines were terminated by rain or poured water, as indicated by omnipresent, water-laid, laminated silts over the decommissioned yellow floors.

Some shrines were renewed with multiple yellow plaster floors, each separated by thin layers of water-washed silt. In several instances, Cahokians re-excavated into the fill over the yellow floor, seemingly to reanimate or make offerings to the location or the yellow floor—incinerated baskets, charred seeds and corn, woven bags and larger textiles (prayer blankets?), heat-exploded chipped-stone hoe blades, and fragmented pottery jars, bowls and other vessels have been found. One fired-clay figurine fragment had been modeled to look like a female human body, with a clearly depicted vulva.

The identification of ancient footprints in the laminated soils of three different buildings suggests the presence of people during the watery ceremonies, as if people were intervening in the process whereby the open basin was being in-filled with water-laid sediment. The most telling such intervention with water at Emerald was associated with a large, square public building, sometimes interpreted as a place of council. Within this possible 'council house' (or temple), a young woman's flexed skeletal remains were found interred in the middle of central post pit, after the roof support post had been removed. Similar to instances known in greater Cahokia's precincts, she had been immersed in water and surrounded by water-washed silts. It is unclear how long she lay in that state before being completely buried with earth by living people involved in the burial (Alt 2015).

So it seems that most everything of importance at Emerald began and ended in water. The glacial drift ridge—earth filled with water—itself was possibly the most significant relational configuration. The ridge might have been perceived to attract thunderstorms. Shrine house floors were smeared with a mixture of earth and water. And offerings were made to, or into, water.

The Cahokia precinct

The evidence of watery relations at Cahokia is no less clear than at Emerald, though in a different relational configuration (Dalan et al. 2003). The primary precinct and its 30-meter-tall 'Monks Mound' and the massive grand plaza (surrounded by 120 other mounds, smaller plazas, and neighborhoods) sit in the Mississippi floodplain in the midst of standing and flowing lakes and streams, respectively (Figure 2.6). Water and water management were necessarily part of urban life.

The main plaza was constructed on a slight north-to-south grade using thick mantles of sandy sediment that directed the flow of surface water, from rains or snows, downward and toward the southern end of the plaza in the direction of a special set of ridge-top burial mounds (Alt et al. 2010; Dalan et al. 2003). In that direction, and around the edges of the precinct, were large pools of water that began as borrow pits—places where sediments were excavated by Cahokians to terraform the city and create the mounds at its foundation (Fowler 1997). While these deep and wide borrow pits were often in-filled shortly after their original excavation, others were left open, perhaps to be used as sumps for draining water into from other areas of the site (Baires 2017; Dalan et al. 2003). The use of such borrows for theatrical or ceremonial purposes is, however, also evident by the siting of mounds on the edges overlooking borrow-pit water (see Figure 2.6). In one case, a rectangular platform and a strip of unborrowed land was left protruding into the middle of a large, watery borrow pit surrounded by earthen platforms, creating what would have made for a dramatic stage, encircled by water to enhance any activities occurring there (Dalan et al. 2003). It is tempting to wonder whether these water bodies were experienced similarly to ponds that formed in natural sinkholes in the uplands beyond the city (see below).

Of more immediate concern, however, are the associations of water with the dead, a common feature of religious beliefs among Cahokia's descendants and others across the Mississippi valley and into the Plains. Beyond the southern end of the Grand Plaza is what Sarah Baires (2017) calls a watery realm of the dead. As opposed to the higher, drier land in the central portion of the Cahokia precinct, a realm of the living, the southern end of the complex was built in the swampiest, wettest part of the city, seemingly enhancing a liminality in that part of the site where groundwater, especially in the springtime, often sits at the surface. That swampy portion of the precinct is bisected by a kilometer-long earthen causeway built about 1050 CE at the very foundations of the city (Baires 2014, 2017). The causeway, in turn, leads to one of the more prominent ridge-top burial mounds at Cahokia, assembling through human movement (in a Deleuzian sense) a linkage to a watery realm of the dead.

Indeed, water, and swamps were common around all of the precincts of, and in, the city of greater Cahokia. Such a swampy environment would have infused the city with specific sensibilities. The denizens of the wateriest places at Cahokia—frogs, turtles, wading birds, waterfowl, and mosquitos—would have created the affective basis for such sensibilities. Perhaps even the very air of the city would have been infused with water, seen today as mists and fogs in the mornings and events due to the region's notoriously high summertime humidity.

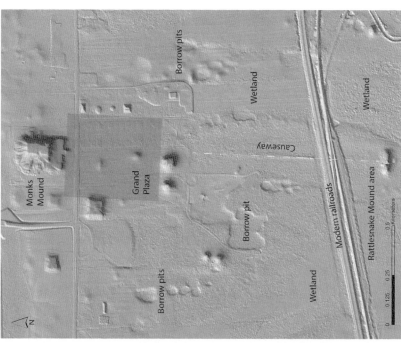

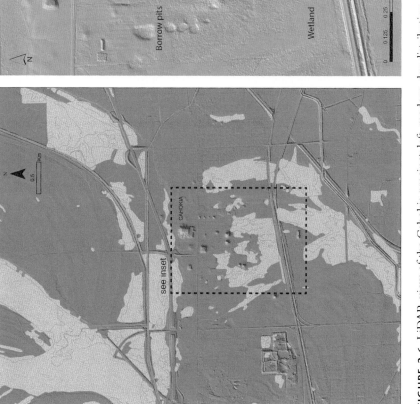

FIGURE 2.6 LiDAR view of the Cahokia precinct: left, modern-day distribution of surface water and wetlands; right, close-up of central mounds, plaza, and causeway (public domain data; images by S. Alt)

30 Susan M. Alt

Lost caves

The watery world centered on Cahokia extended beyond the city and floodplain in three directions besides east, or toward the Emerald Acropolis (see Figure 2.2). To the north, south, and west were other watery features—sinkholes, springs, and caves—that virtually framed the greater Cahokian assemblage in the center. The most important portion of that framing was to the west under modern-day St. Louis. In that location, just 8 kilometers west of Monks Mound, sat one of the three central precincts of greater Cahokia. Though this precinct was destroyed by the expansion of St Louis in the nineteenth century, maps from the time show that it was made up of 27 mounds, rectangular and circular platforms arranged around a rectangular plaza, with a great ridge-top mortuary mound to the north (Peale 1862).

As it turns out, the St. Louis precinct sat directly atop a karst field, which is to say a natural underground drainage system characterized by caverns and subterranean streams that open onto the surface via sinkholes and springs (Figure 2.7). The St. Louis karst field derives from its underlying soluble limestone bedrock that afforded the formation of fissures, which over time became sinkholes that over tens of thousands of years funneled water from the surface down through the limestone underground, resulting in a Swiss-cheese like structure to the subsurface bedrock. The results are many miles of caves with openings in various parts of the modern-day city of St. Louis and along the rocky river banks of the Mississippi River. The opening to one of these, via a sinkhole, was immediately adjacent to one of the central platforms in the precinct's main cluster. The opening to another was situated

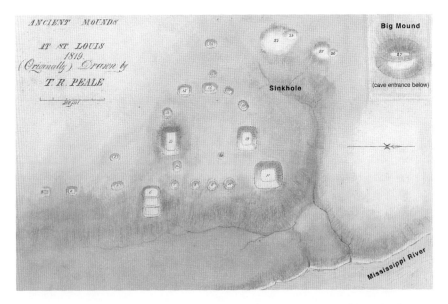

FIGURE 2.7 Plan map of the St. Louis precinct, showing Big Mound inset in the upper right (*Beck's Gazetteer 1822*, page 23b, public domain)

near the base of the precinct's great mortuary mound (Rother and Rother 1996). The latter subterranean opening was sealed sometime after 1859, before which 'adventurous boys of North St. Louis crawled into the sides of the "Indian Mound" that stood on Broadway, near Brooklyn Street' (Rother and Rother 1996:123). The caves under this imposing tumulus, also known as the 'Big Mound',

> were entered by a short, narrow tunnel, and were of various sizes. The largest room was about twenty feet square and seven feet high. On stormy and wintery days, the boys would explore and amuse themselves by the light of tallow candles. Whenever the boys were reported missing from the Mound or Webster schools, the police would search the caves.
>
> (Rother and Rother 1996:123)

Unfortunately, the Big Mound was removed in 1869, and St. Louis's known caves and entrances were all severely impacted by modern activity. Many were simply filled in and sealed up, and others were used for a variety of purposes including, since the eighteenth century, the brewing and cold storage of beer. Yet the fact of their existence makes clear that the St. Louis precinct was quite possibly constructed atop a subterranean landscape in order to assemble whatever was in those caves. Indeed, it is possible that, similar to the Emerald Acropolis, the St Louis precinct could have been an access point for people on the surface into the underworld, which was likely a place of the dead. It is even possible, though speculative, that the St. Louis precinct might have been an intermittently occupied shrine complex, similar to Emerald, inhabited by few living people year round.

Other karst plains

There are other karst plains immediately behind the dramatic rocky bluffs that demarcate the edge of the Mississippi River flood plain north and south of greater Cahokia (see Figure 2.2). Neither area has seen much archaeological investigation, although there are several Cahokia-related sites near karst features south of Cahokia that hint of ancient interests below ground. These include a possible Cahokian shrine house adjacent to one sinkhole overlooking the Mississippi floodplain (McElrath 1986). They also include a larger Cahokian settlement, at what is now known as Dugan Airfield, on a high hill overlooking a karstic landscape (Skousen 2018). This site produced Cahokian architecture and artifacts along with one feature containing 'a large number of fossils' (Skousen 2018:175), as did the nearby, unexcavated 'Sink' site. The Sink site is reported to have produced Cahokian pottery and chert that was likely quarried from an adjacent sinkhole (Woods and Mitchell 1978). Indeed, much of the so-called Ste. Genevieve, Salem, and St. Louis formation cherts associated with Cahokia and other early Cahokian settlements in the Mississippi floodplain in the tenth and eleventh centuries CE may have been obtained from some of the 10,000 sinkholes within a day or two's walk of greater Cahokia (Kelly 1980; Koldehoff 2006).

It is important to highlight the fact that these karst landscapes are themselves unusual in many ways. On the ground surface, some of the sinkholes appear as dry, round depressions, while others act as ponds collecting rain water, and some lead directly into the earth and, later, exit by way of springs and almost-magically reappearing streams (Figure 2.8, left). The topographic band of karst south of Cahokia is several kilometers wide and underlain by an extensive network of narrow underground stream passages, some passable by human beings (Panno and Luman 2012; Panno et al. 1999, 2009). Above ground, individual sinkholes form microenvironments that facilitate habitats for unusual plants, amphibians, reptiles, birds, bats, and/or insects that cannot or do not live elsewhere in the greater Cahokia region. For some species these places are temporary homes, or they may spend part of their life cycle in karst features.

For people in the past, movement across a field of sinkholes would have been memorable, and entering into an underground cavern remarkable if not transformative. Footprint petroglyphs mark the entrance of some such sites (Bushnell 1913). One would have been fully aware of entering an entirely alien world unlike the above-ground world. The first sensation would have been that of going from bright daylight into the darkness of the earth (Figure 2.8, right). The next sensations would have been of temperature and odors. The air in a sinkhole is warmer on cool days, and cooler on hot days, and it carries the smells of the earth. Farther underground, the colors and shapes of the flowstones, mineral deposits and even bacteria colonies are visible with torchlight. The sounds of running, dripping, falling water are audible. The affects are vibrant, and might easily have been envisioned as alive, making the overall karst landscape, if not the greater Cahokian realm in general, a unique assemblage of immense beauty and power that linked the land of the living with a dark, watery realm below ground.[1]

FIGURE 2.8 Karst features south of greater Cahokia: left, Sparrow Creek Cave stream exits the earth; right, entrance to Stemler Cave (St. Clair County, Illinois; photos by S. Alt)

Water spirits

The extent to which Cahokians passed through the karst features and into the underworld beneath the St. Louis precinct or north and south of Cahokia, is not certain. However, to the west of St. Louis is another karst cave system known to have been entered by Cahokians.[2] There, in 'Painted Cave', are multiple and at times overlapping polychrome pictographic images of Cahokian culture heroes, mythic beings, and other-than-human spirits (Diaz-Granados et al. 2015). Among these are what Carol Diaz-Granados and colleagues interpret to be the Siouan character 'First Woman', her vulva (which is a portal to the spirit realms), 'First Man', 'Thunderers', earth monsters, and more. First Woman, linked by modern-day Osage elders to the moon, is said to consort with serpents and is associated with the underworld, rebirth, and renewal in Siouan narratives (Diaz-Granados and Duncan 2000; Diaz-Granados et al. 2015; Wagner et al. 2004). First Man is more associated with the sun, the sky, and the Thunderers. One image from 'Picture Cave', interpreted as first woman's vulva, was painted near the cave entrance such that the sun would shine on it once a day, perhaps recapitulating the intimate relationships between First Man and First Woman. Another image of an apparent masculine 'culture hero' with a headdress, mace, and bow (Diaz-Granados and Duncan 2000), is also a likely Cahokian Heyoka, not unlike Black Elk of the Lakota (Hall 1997).

The rock art in Picture Cave in some ways confirms the Cahokian sense of the power and historical significance of the watery underworld suggested by the placement of the St. Louis precinct. Additional confirmation takes the form of a suite of supernatural beings that were carved by Cahokians from a soft red stone, or 'flint clay' derived from sinkholes west of the St. Louis precinct (Emerson and Hughes 2000; Emerson et al. 2002, 2003). These Cahokian carvings take various forms, such as that of frog-shamans, warriors, and anthropomorphic gods or goddesses. These carved stone beings, some of whom were buried in or near shrine houses, convey Cahokians' entanglement of these beings with the underworld and water.

Masculine figures were sometimes drilled to be used as smoking pipes, but feminine forms were not (Alt and Pauketat 2007; Emerson 2015). And several of these feminine goddess objects have been found in association with the twelfth-century version of the Cahokian rectangular shrine house or temple (Emerson 1997b). Of these, one features a goddess birthing plants from her hands while she emerges from a funeral basket (considered an underworld portal); another manipulates a similar basket; a third hoes the back of a monstrous serpentine earth spirit; yet another pours water out of large marine shell (Figure 2.9).

Clearly, water and water spirits were integral to greater Cahokian life. Among Siouan-speaking descendants or neighbors of descendants, water is one of the four major powers—water, wind, earth, and fire (Bailey 1995; Dorsey 1894; Fletcher and La Flesche 1992; La Flesche 1921, 1930). The world began as water and the first creatures were water creatures (Berezkin 2007; Hall 1997; Martin 1995; Radin and Reagan 1928). These are just a few of the numerous Siouan associations of life and people with water.

34 Susan M. Alt

FIGURE 2.9 Exchange Avenue figurine made from carved flint clay, showing feminine character pouring liquid from what's likely to be a marine shell cup (courtesy, Illinois State Archaeological Survey)

Discussion and conclusion

Did the people of Cahokia think of it as a city comprised of three precincts surrounded by a host of other towns, shrine complexes, and farming settlements? Did they distinguish the special portals into the underworld as part and parcel of their urban lifestyle? Or did they think of Cahokia as a vast assemblage of many portals, points of articulation where they might relate to the seen and unseen powers of their world?

There is every reason, from a New Materialist point of view, to view Cahokia as a 'multiplicity' of water—not just one thing 'defined by the outside'—and existing through the many sites where people might tap into a complex field of engagement fraught with possibilities of supernatural encounters (Deleuze and Guattari 1987:9). The Emerald Acropolis provides us with a window into Cahokian interactions with water, from intimate experiences in sweat lodges and shrine houses to the alignments with the moon. The Cahokia precinct's watery landscape placed people in a 'maelstrom' of watery relations that pulled in the living and the dead (see Chapter 1, citing Thrift 2004). Caves with pictographs and petroglyphs and flint clay carvings of goddesses and spirits show us the Cahokians' own access to underworld portals. Thus, the experience of urban Cahokia could have never been divorced from the powers emanating from the thousands of sinkholes, caves, springs and underground passages and streams.

Of course, of the various landscapes in and around greater Cahokia, the latter were among the most vibrant, even if commonly ignored in archaeological descriptions of the region and its origins. The affects of the sinkholes, caves, springs, and underground passages require a better archaeological accounting if we hope to understand broader historical relationships. Envisioning those as the rhizomatic parts of a greater Cahokian assemblage instead of as a hierarchy of sites and things used in human social and political transactions will ultimately help us trace the entanglements of people, places, and things that we label urbanism.

Taken all together, evidence from the weeping hill of Emerald, the watery worlds of the Mississippi floodplain, the lost caves of the region, and the images of people who experienced these vibrant landscapes constituted Cahokian urbanism. The precise historical reasons why urbanization occurred at, or as, Cahokia around 1050 CE will remain debated no doubt because the analytical perspectives brought to bear on the questions of Cahokia do not consider the vibrant characteristics of place that mattered most to the Cahokians and their immediate descendants.

The facts of the region's watery portals require that we ask: Was Cahokia emplaced where it was because of entanglements and interactions with otherworldly spirits and forces? Of course. But only if we understand that which motivated people to include the materials and landscapes wherein resided powerful other-than-human forces of change.

Notes

1 For example, inside Stemler Cave, there is a section of black-colored ceiling where a bacteria colony grows and, due to micro-water droplets within the bacteria, the ceiling sparkles as if with stars in a night sky. In other passages of the same cave are white, smooth, and shiny flowstones that look like bones growing out of the walls. While the Illinois caves, much as the St. Louis caves have experienced over 200 years of Euro–American alterations, the experience of them yet remains unique and compelling.
2 There are similar suggestive rock art in caves in and beyond the greater Cahokia region. One rock shelter located in the Shawnee Forest of Southern Illinois discovered and investigated by Len Stelle, possessed the unusual property of a stream that runs next to the cave 'turns to blood' during the winter solstice. This occurs because the water contains a high iron content and iron-eating bacteria that produce 'a red orange slurry'. This 'bloody water' was used to create images on the rocks inside the grotto. The images themselves are argued by Len Stelle to be women's medicine, with one image in particular, based on ethnographic analogy, appearing to be that of a medicine woman. He also identified a particular kind of fern growing in excess around the rock shelter that is well known in ethnobotanical literature for its use for women's reproductive disorders. Interestingly, Dorsey

reported that Omaha women who had trouble conceiving would go to a cave entrance in order to pray to conceive. Yet another small cave closely intertwines rock art with water. The Bushnell Ceremonial Cave is near the late Cahokian settlement of Common Field in Missouri and combines watery interactions with cave imagery. This small cavern contains petroglyphs with thunderer imagery pecked into the stone along the cave floor, across which flowed water. It is only possible to enter the cave in the dry season. This cave floods every spring, hiding the images and even at times the cave entrance itself under deep water.

References

Alt, Susan M. 2006 The Power of Diversity: The Roles of Migration and Hybridity in Culture Change. In *Leadership and Polity in Mississippian Society*, edited by B. M. Butler and P. D. Welch, pp. 289–308. Center for Archaeological Investigations, Occasional Paper No. 33. Southern Illinois University, Carbondale.

——— 2008 Unwilling Immigrants: Culture, Change and the 'Other' in Mississippian Societies. In *Invisible Citizens: Captives and Their Consequences*, edited by C. M. Cameron, pp. 202-222. University of Utah Press, Salt Lake City.

——— 2010 Complexity in Action(s): Retelling the Cahokia Story. In *Ancient Complexities: New Perspectives in Pre-Columbian North America*, edited by S. M. Alt, pp. 119–137. University of Utah Press, Salt Lake City.

——— 2015 Death, Sacrifice and Religion at Cahokia. In *Medieval Mississippians: The Cahokian World*, edited by T. R. Pauketat and S. M. Alt. School of American Research Press, Santa Fe, NM.

——— 2016 Building Cahokia: Transformation through Tradition. In *Vernacular Architecture in the Pre-Columbian Americas*, edited by C. T. Halperin and L. Schwartz, pp. 141–157. Routledge, London.

——— 2018a Putting Religion Ahead of Politics: Cahokian Origins as Viewed through Emerald's Shrines. In *Big Data and Ancient Religion in the North American Midcontinent*, edited by B. Koldehoff and T. R. Pauketat, pp. 208–233. University of Alabama Press, Tuscaloosa.

——— 2018b *Cahokia's Complexities: Ceremonies and Politics of the First Mississippian Farmers*. University of Alabama Press, Tuscaloosa.

Alt, Susan M., Jeffery D. Kruchten and Timothy R. Pauketat 2010 The Construction and Use of Cahokia's Grand Plaza *Journal of Field Archaeology* 35:131–146.

Alt, Susan M., and Timothy R. Pauketat 2007 Sex and the Southern Cult. In *The Southeastern Ceremonial Complex*, edited by A. King, pp. 232–250. University of Alabama Press, Tuscaloosa.

——— 2018 The Elements of Cahokian Shrine Complexes and the Basis of Mississippian Religion. In *Religion and Politics in the Ancient Americas*, edited by S. Barber and A. Joyce, pp. 51–74. Routledge, London.

Bailey, Garrick A. 1995 *The Osage and the Invisible World from the Works of Francis La Flesche*. University of Oklahoma Press, Norman.

Baires, Sarah E. 2014 Cahokia's Rattlesnake Causeway. *Midcontinental Journal of Archaeology* 39(1):1–19.

——— 2017 *Land of Water, City of the Dead: Religion and Cahokia's Emergence*. University of Alabama Press, Tuscaloosa.

Barad, Karen 2007 *Meeting the Universe Halfway: Quantum Physics and the Entanglement of Matter and Meaning*. Duke University Press, Durham, NC.

Bennett, Jane 2010 *Vibrant Matter: A Political Ecology of Things*. Duke University Press, Durham, NC.

Berezkin, Yu. E. 2007 'Earth-Diver' and 'Emergence from Under the Earth': Cosmogonic Tales as Evidence in Favor of the Heterogenic Origins of the American Indians. *Archaeology, Ethnology and Anthropology of Eurasia* 32(1):110–123.

Blackhawk, Ned 2006 *Violence over the Land: Indians and Empires in the Early American West*. Harvard University Press, Cambridge, MA.

Brown, Joseph Epes 1953 *The Sacred Pipe: Black Elk's Account of the Seven Rites of the Oglala Sioux*. University of Oklahoma Press, Norman.

Bruchac, Margaret M. 2004 Earthshapers and Placemakers. In *Indigenous Archaeologies: Decolonising Theory and Practice*, edited by C. Smith and M. H. Wobst, pp. 52–74. Routledge, London.

Bucko, Raymond 1998 *The Lakota Ritual of the Sweat Lodge*. University of Nebraska Press, Lincoln.

Bushnell, David I., Jr. 1913 Petroglyphs Representing the Imprint of the Human Foot. *American Anthropologist* 15(1):8–15.

Dalan, Rinita A., George R. Holley, William I. Woods, Harold W. Watters, Jr. and John A. Koepke 2003 *Envisioning Cahokia: A Landscape Perspective*. Northern Illinois University Press, DeKalb.

DeLanda, Manuel 2006 *A New Philosophy of Society: Assemblage Theory and Social Complexity*. Bloomsbury, London.

——— 2016 *Assemblage Theory*. Edinburgh University Press, Edinburgh.

Deleuze, Gilles, and Felix Guattari 1987 *A Thousand Plateaus: Capitalism and Schizophrenia*. Translated by B. Massumi. University of Minnesota Press, Minneapolis.

Deloria, Vine, Jr. 1995 *Red Earth, White Lies: Native Americans and the Myth of Scientific Fact*. Scribner, New York.

——— 2003 *God is Red: A Native View of Religion*. Fulcrum Publishing, Golden, CO.

Diaz-Granados, Carol M., and James R. Duncan 2000 *The Petroglyphs and Pictographs of Missouri*. University of Alabama Press, Tuscaloosa.

Diaz-Granados, Carol M., James R. Duncan and F. Kent Reilly III (editors) 2015 *Picture Cave: Unraveling the Mysteries of the Mississippian Cosmos*. University of Texas Press, Austin.

Dorsey, James Owen 1894 A Study of Siouan Cults. In *Eleventh Annual Report of the Bureau of Ethnology*, pp. 351–554. Government Printing Office, Washington, DC.

Echo-Hawk, Roger C. 2000 Ancient History in the New World: Integrating Oral Traditions and the Archaeological Record in Deep Time. *American Antiquity* 65(2):267–290.

Emerson, Thomas E. 1997a *Cahokia and the Archaeology of Power*. University of Alabama Press, Tuscaloosa.

——— 1997b Cahokian Elite Ideology and the Mississippian Cosmos. In *Cahokia: Domination and Ideology in the Mississippian World*, edited by T. R. Pauketat and T. E. Emerson, pp. 190–228. University of Nebraska Press, Lincoln.

——— 2015 The Earth Goddess Cult at Cahokia. In *Medieval Mississippians: The Cahokian World*, edited by T. R. Pauketat and S. M. Alt, pp. 55–60. School for Advanced Research Press, Santa Fe, NM.

Emerson, Thomas E., and Randall E. Hughes 2000 Figurines, Flint Clay Sourcing, the Ozark Highlands, and Cahokian Acquisition. *American Antiquity* 65:79–101.

Emerson, Thomas E., Randall E. Hughes, Mary R. Hynes and Sarah U. Wisseman 2002 Implications of Sourcing Cahokia-Style Flint Clay Figures in the American Bottom and the Upper Mississippi River Valley. *Midcontinental Journal of Archaeology* 27:309–338.

——— 2003 The Sourcing and Interpretation of Cahokia-Style Figurines in the Trans-Mississippi South and Southeast. *American Antiquity* 68:287–313.

Emerson, Thomas E., Brad H. Koldehoff and Tamira K. Brennan (editors) 2018 *Revealing Cahokia's Urbanism: Rediscovery and Large-Scale Excavations of the East St. Louis Precinct*. Illinois State Archaeological Survey, University of Illinois, Urbana.

Fletcher, Alice C., and Francis La Flesche 1992 *The Omaha Tribe* (vols. 1 and 2, originally published 1911). University of Nebraska Press, Lincoln.

Fowler, Melvin L. 1974 *Cahokia: Ancient Capital of the Midwest.* Addison-Wesley Module in Anthropology, No. 48. Reading, MA.

——— 1997 *The Cahokia Atlas: A Historical Atlas of Cahokia Archaeology.* Illinois Transportation Archaeological Research Program, Studies in Archaeology, No. 2. University of Illinois, Urbana.

Grimley, David A., and Andrew C. Phillips (editors) 2015 *Ridges, Mounds, and Valleys: Glacial-Interglacial History of the Kaskaskia Basin, Southwestern Illinois.* Guidebook 41, Illinois State Geological Survey. University of Illinois at Urbana-Champaign, Champaign.

Hall, Robert L. 1997 *An Archaeology of the Soul: Native American Indian Belief and Ritual.* University of Illinois Press, Urbana.

Hallowell, Alfred I. 1960 Ojibwa Ontology, Behavior, and World View. In *Culture in History: Essays in Honor of Paul Radin,* edited by S. Diamond, pp. 19–52. Columbia University Press, New York.

Hunter, Andrea A. 2013 *Ancestral Osage Geography in Osage Nation NAGPRA Claim for Human Remains Removed from the Clarksville Mound Group (23PI6), Pike County, Missouri.* Osage Nation Historic Preservation Office, Pawhuska, OK.

Kehoe, Alice B. 2007 Osage Texts and Cahokia Data. In *Ancient Objects and Sacred Realms: Interpretations of Mississippian Iconography,* edited by F. K. Reilly III and J. F. Garber, pp. 246–261. University of Texas Press, Austin.

Kelly, John E. 1980 Formative Developments at Cahokia and the Adjacent American Bottom: A Merrell Tract Perspective. Unpublished PhD dissertation, Department of Anthropology, University of Wisconsin, Madison, WI.

Kelly, John E., and James A. Brown 2012 Search of Cosmic Power: Contextualizing Spiritual Journeys between Cahokia and the St. Francois Mountains. In *Archaeology of Spiritualities,* edited by K. Rountree, C. Morris and A. A. D. Peatfield, pp. 107–129. Springer, New York.

Koldehoff, Brad 2006 Chipped-Stone Resources of Monroe County. In *Late Woodland Frontier: Patrick Phase Settlement along the Kaskaskia Trail, Monroe County, Illinois,* edited by B. Koldehoff and J. M. Galloy, pp. 367–376. Transportation Archaeological Research Reports No. 23. Illinois Transportation Archaeological Research Program, University of Illinois at Urbana-Champaign, Champaign.

La Flesche, Francis 1921 The Osage Tribe: Rite of the Chiefs; Sayings of the Ancient Men. In Thirty-Sixth Annual Report of the Bureau of American Ethnology, pp. 35–597.

——— 1930 The Osage Tribe: Rite of the Wa-Xo'-Be. In Forty-Fifth Annual Report of the Bureau of American Ethnology, pp. 529–833.

Martin, Lawrence T. 1995 Animal Forms of Manidog in the Anishinabe Earth-diver Story. *Papers of the Twenty-Sixth Algonquian Conference* 26:240–250.

McElrath, Dale L. 1986 *The McLean Site.* American Bottom Archaeology, FAI-270 Site Reports, vol. 14. University of Illinois, Urbana.

Milner, George R. 1998 *The Cahokia Chiefdom: The Archaeology of a Mississippian Society.* Smithsonian Institution Press, Washington, DC.

Oliver, William 2002 *Eight Months in Illinois, with Information to Immigrants.* Southern Illinois University Press, Carbondale.

Panno, Samuel V., and Donald E. Luman 2012 *Sinkhole Distribution and Associated Karst Features of Monroe County, Illinois.* Illinois State Geological Survey, Champaign.

Panno, Samuel V., Donald E. Luman and Julie C. Angel 2009 *Sinkhole Density and Distribution of Cahokia Quadrangle, St. Clair County, Illinois.* Illinois State Geological Survey, Champaign.

Panno, Samuel V., C. Pius Weibel, Carol M. Wicks and James E. Vandike 1999 *Geology, Hydrology, and Water Quality of the Karst Regions of Southwestern Illinois and Southeastern Missouri*. Guidebook 27. Illinois State Geological Survey, Champaign.

Pauketat, Timothy R. 2013 *An Archaeology of the Cosmos: Rethinking Agency and Religion in Ancient America*. Routledge, London.

Pauketat, Timothy R., and Susan M. Alt (editors) 2015a *Medieval Mississippians: The Cahokian World*. School for Advanced Research Press, Santa Fe, NM.

Pauketat, Timothy R., and Susan M. Alt 2015b Religious Innovation at the Emerald Acropolis: Something New Under the Moon. In *Religion and Innovation: Antagonists or Partners?*, edited by D. Yerxa, pp. 43–55. Bloomsbury, London.

Pauketat, Timothy R., Susan M. Alt and Jeffery D. Kruchten 2015 City of Earth and Wood: Cahokia and Its Material-Historical Implications. In *Early Cities in Comparative Perspective, 4000 BCE-1200 CE*, edited by N. Yoffee, pp. 437–454. Cambridge University Press, Cambridge.

——— 2017 The Emerald Acropolis: Elevating the Moon and Water in the Rise of Cahokia. *Antiquity* 91:207–222.

Peale, T. Ramsey 1862 Ancient Mounds at St Louis Missouri in 1819. In *Annual Report of the Board of Regents of the Smithsonian Institution, Washington 1862*, pp. 386–391.

Radin, Paul, and A. B. Reagan 1928 Ojibwa Myths and Tales. *Journal of American Folklore* 41:61–146.

Rother, Hubert, and Charlotte Rother 1996 *Lost Caves of St. Louis*. Virginia Publishing, St. Louis.

Simpson, Audr 2014 *Mohawk Interruptus: Political Life across the Borders of Settler States*. Duke University Press, Durham, NC.

Skousen, B. Jacob 2016 Pilgrimage and the Construction of Cahokia: A View from the Emerald Site. Unpublished PhD dissertation, Department of Anthropology, University of Illinois, Urbana.

——— 2018 *Early Mississippian Settlement along the Kaskaskia Trail: The Dugan Airfield and Booster Station Sites*. Illinois State Archaeological Survey, Technical Report No. 96. University of Illinois, Urbana.

Slater, Philip A., Kristin M. Hedman and T. E. Emerson 2014 Immigrants at the Mississippian Polity of Cahokia: Strontium Isotope Evidence for Population Movement. *Journal of Archaeological Science* 44:117–127.

Snyder, John Francis 1962 Certain Indian Mounds Technically Considered. In *John Francis Snyder: Selected Writings*, edited by C. C. Walton, pp. 230–273. Illinois Historical Society, Springfield.

Thrift, Nigel 2004 Intensities of Feeling: Towards a Spatial Politics of Affect. *Geografiska Annaler* 86B(1):57–78.

Todd, Zoe 2016 An Indigenous Feminist's Take on the Ontological Turn: 'Ontology' Is Just Another Word for Colonialism. *Journal of Historical Sociology* 29(1):4–22.

Wagner, Mark J., Mary R. McCorvie and Charles A. Swedlund 2004 Mississippian Cosmology and Rock-Art at the Millstone Bluff Site, Illinois. In *The Rock-Art of Eastern North America*, edited by C. Diaz-Granados and J. R. Duncan, pp. 42–64. University of Alabama Press, Tuscaloosa.

Waters, Anne 2004 *American Indian Thought*. Blackwell, Oxford.

Woods, William I., and Robert D. Mitchell 1978 *A Survey of Aboriginal Chert Sources in the Waterloo, Illinois, Area*. Report submitted to the Illinois Department of Transportation by the Office of Contract Archaeology. Southern Illinois University, Edwardsville.

3

CHACO GATHERS

Experience and assemblage in the ancient Southwest

Ruth M. Van Dyke

Prologue

Chaco Canyon is a place that gathers. There assembled we find clouds and stars, rabbits and ravens, stones and shadows. There enfolded we find corn and pollen, water and earth, turquoise and cacao. Woven into Chaco's fabric we find ancestors and descendants, scholars and tourists, park rangers and stakeholders.

Cities are gatherings, places where buildings, people, materials, activities, experiences, and memories overlap and intertwine with a density that defies disentanglement. Religious experiences are gatherings, with meaning emergent in the midst of shared liturgies, rare practices, and extraordinary affects. Religious experiences and cities (or at least dense gatherings of people) are both part of the gathering that is Chaco.

"The events of one's life take place, *take place*" (Momaday 1976:142, emphasis mine). In *The Chaco Experience*, I argued for the importance of affect and place – sandstone cliffs and canyon walls – in understanding Chaco (Van Dyke 2007). Chacoan elite leaders, I contended, manipulated monumental architecture, ancestral relationships, and the natural landscape to create a bodily experience for pilgrims and visitors; this experience legitimated Chaco Canyon (and its elite leaders) as central to the ancient Pueblo world. I was essentially arguing for the primacy of *religious* knowledge and practices at Chaco, as opposed to the economic or political dimensions favored by some other schools of thought. But what I did not yet understand was that these categorical separations are Western constructs. As beautifully demonstrated by Severin Fowles's (2013) *An Archaeology of Doings*, for indigenous peoples in the Southwest United States, religious "doings" are inseparable from all other dimensions of life.

Fowles took inspiration from Latour's (1993) critique of modernist attempts at "purification," often cited as a seminal work in a "new materialist" turn across the humanities and social sciences, or a speculative realist turn in continental philosophy (e.g., Harman 2010, 2011, 2016; Bryant et al. 2010). While I remain critical of attempts to erase all distinctions between people and things (see Van Dyke 2015b), I will allow that new materialist ideas derived from thinkers such as Bennett (2010), Barad (2007), and Ingold (2000, 2007, 2011, 2013) potentially provide useful ways to move past the categorical blinders imposed by Western thought and engage with non-Western ontologies. Archaeologists are creatively examining bundles, entanglements, and meshwork of disparate things, people, feelings, and ideas linked by noncategorical relationships and associations (e.g., Boivin 2008; Harris 2014; Hodder 2012; Olsen 2010; Pauketat 2013). Some scholars have advanced the term "assemblages" for these groupings, following Deleuze and Guattari (2007; see also DeLanda 2006).

In this chapter, taking the building blocks of my earlier work as my starting point, I want to explore the potential for the DeLeuzean idea of *assemblage* to help us think about the distributed (or deterritorialized) yet holistic (or territorialized) nature of Chaco across space and time. Chaco is a place that gathers people and topography, sensory experiences and ancestral connections. I follow Pauketat's (this volume) dictum to "trace the material relations and untie, unfold, and disassemble their knots, folds, bundles and assemblages."

An overview of Chaco

Chaco Canyon is a compelling archaeological locale well known as the center of one of the most complex sociopolitical phenomena in the ancient North American Southwest. The northern Southwest is home to Indigenous peoples whose ancestors have farmed this landscape for millennia, raising corn, beans, squash, and turkeys. Since about 700 CE, Pueblo ancestors lived in apartment-style roomblocks (or pueblos) that conform to rigid tenets of construction and spatial organization. Between 850 and 1150 CE, something unusual happened – ancient Pueblo people erected massive great houses at the heart of Chaco Canyon – a place of brown sandstone cliffs, wheeling ravens, and blue skies. Great houses such as Pueblo Bonito and Chetro Ketl remain as some of the best-preserved prehispanic ruins in the Southwest, with standing walls in excess of eight meters in height. These colossal structures represent a substantial investment of ancient labor and design, and they stand alongside other kinds of Chacoan monumental construction, including great kivas, earthworks, and road segments stretching for up to 50 kilometers across the high desert terrain. The monumental ensembles, sometimes glossed as Bonito style architecture, coexist with hundreds of small habitation sites in the canyon. The buildings, roads, and earthworks comprise a formal, highly structured landscape – a density of settlement that might be called urban. It is difficult for archaeologists to come up with firm figures for the density of people, however – population estimates range from lows of about 1,250 (Bernardini 1999), to highs approaching 6,000 canyon residents (Hayes 1981). Caches of unusual paraphernalia, including carved and painted birds and flowers, oddly shaped staffs, cylinder jars that held cacao, decorated baskets, jewelry of turquoise and shell – point to a rich body of religious practices and beliefs. Astronomical alignments and rock art tell us that Chacoans were concerned with solstices, equinoxes, and lunar standstills. Indigenous colleagues tell us Chaco Canyon was and is a significant place in tribal histories.

Chaco Canyon proper is only a small part of the story, however. Ancient Chaco Canyon was not a single locality but a phenomenon that spanned a region of at least 60,000 square miles (Figure 3.1). Over a hundred outlying Chacoan settlements lie beyond the canyon, across the surrounding San Juan Basin and adjacent areas. These outliers minimally consist of one or more Bonito style great houses, great kivas, earthworks, and road segments, and they are usually associated with a surrounding community of small habitation sites. Interactions among these communities varied across three centuries of Chacoan dominance in the northern Southwest. Following changes in architecture and material culture, scholars divide these centuries into the Early Bonito (850–1020 CE), Classic Bonito (1020–1100 CE), and Late Bonito (1100–1150 CE) phases.

In over 130 years of Chacoan scholarship, archaeologists have developed a wide range of models to explain the "Chaco Phenomenon." I will not attempt to recount them all here, but I will make an observation pertinent to our discussion: scholarly points of contention revolve around different perspectives on Chaco as a gathering. For some archaeologists, Chaco was the dense, urban center of a large polity. For others, it was the relatively empty ceremonial center of a loosely tied confederation. For a third camp, Chaco was merely a rather large farming community. Colleagues also have divergent views on what kinds of ties would have held Chaco together, as they construct models around social, economic, political, and/or religious arguments (see for example authors in Heitman and Plog 2015; authors in Lekson 2006; Lekson 2015; Ware 2015). In part, these divergent views exist because some scholars have focused tightly on excavated materials and architecture in Chaco Canyon, while others have focused broadly on survey data, outliers and the wider landscape. And of course, scholars have particular theoretical or contemporary political perspectives that inform their views.

I suspect all Chaco scholars could agree that religion is critical to understanding Pueblo societies past and present. But beyond that, there continues to be a wild and thorny thicket of arguments, models, and emphases. Some colleagues are interested in Chaco Canyon primarily as home to a large community of very successful farmers, whereas others see Chaco as a potentially unique or extraordinarily complex experiment in sociopolitical hierarchy. Some build on Pueblo ethnography to argue for specific forms of sociopolitical organization: house societies; matrilineages; sodalities. Others focus on tracing the movements and connections of materials into and out of the canyon. Looking through a regional lens, some Chaco scholars see the canyon as a center place from which power, people, and ideas emanated, or to which pilgrims flocked for ceremonial events presided over by elites. Chaco as an archaeological assemblage is huge, diverse, and constantly shifting. No single archaeologist or group of archaeologists possesses mastery of all our current knowledge about Chaco. Can a new materialist perspective contribute something new to these ongoing debates and conversations?

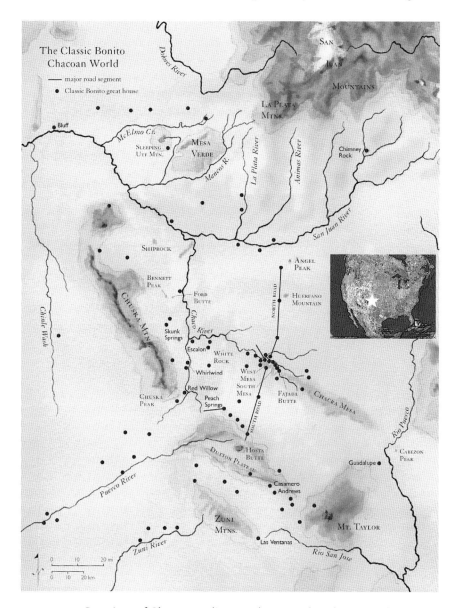

FIGURE 3.1 Locations of Chacoan outlier great houses and road segments between ca. 1020–1100 CE (drafted by Molly O'Halloran, with modifications by R. Van Dyke)

Chacoan assemblages

In this chapter, I explore using the idea of *assemblage* from Giles DeLeuze, by way of Miguel DeLanda, thinking about the distributed and flexible nature of the Chaco phenomenon (DeLanda 2006, 2016; DeLeuze and Guattari 2007 [1980]). In *A Thousand Plateaus*, Deleuze and Guattari developed the concept of the assemblage as an anti-essentialist, realist ontology in which wholes cannot be reduced to parts, because wholes are not aggregates of parts, but of contingent, continually shifting relations. But (and this is important), assemblages do not only contain materials – the familiar stuff of architecture and artifacts – nor can we think of them as the sum total of materials plus people plus ideas. Rather, relational and emergent assemblages are constantly and simultaneously being reconfigured along different kinds of dimensions, existing simultaneously at multiple spatial and temporal scales.

Territorializing processes gather – they bring people, places and things together, and they help to hold the assemblage together. Territorializing processes might involve topographically attractive places (*axis mundi*), enchanting experiences, abundant food and resources, clear boundaries, shared identities, political stability, feelings of communitas and solidarity, and shared beliefs and practices. By contrast, deterritorializing processes pull assemblages apart. Deterritorializing processes might involve failed crops or famine, fires and earthquakes, conflicts and violence, inequalities, exclusion and segregation. These are not exhaustive lists. Assemblages are anti-essentialist. Deterritorialization and reterritorialization are always relative, always connected, always in motion. There are some similarities here with the Marxist concept of dialectical tension, but without the implied limitations of two opposing poles. Assemblages are simultaneously, constantly, multi-dimensionally pulling (and being pulled), pushing (and being pushed), gathering (and being gathered), resisting (and being resisted).

Chaco must have been a multiscalar, distributed phenomenon encompassing elements that archaeologists have variously labeled social, economic, political, religious, architectural, and so forth. The concept of assemblage may give us better insights into these dimensions, because assemblages involve a wide assortment of entities: humans, objects, places, animals, plants, houses, monuments, ideas, social bonds – and because these entities can be described as territorializing and deterritorializing at different spatial and temporal scales. In the discussion that follows, I describe territorializing and deterritorializing processes at Chaco, organizing my thoughts around assembling places, experiences, and histories. Yet, there are no categorical boundaries among the materials, ideas, and relationships described in these sections of the chapter. DeLeuze and Guattari used tropes of rhizomes and plateaus to try to transcend our modernist need to create categories and hierarchies. In true rhizomatic fashion, we must realize that every idea, material, and relationship at Chaco is an emergent part of another.

The place: Earth, sky, water, stone, corn

Chaco Canyon, in northwest New Mexico, is an aesthetically powerful place, in part because of the sky-filled topography of the Colorado Plateau. The canyon – in the center of vast dish of the San Juan Basin – contains hidden spaces, but the mesas that bound it are high places. Wind and water erosion created the landforms of the Colorado Plateau over the past million years, slicing through sandstone strata and leaving isolated, oddly shaped remnants such as Fajada Butte, stranded in "Fajada Gap" between Chacra and South Mesa (Figure 3.2). Fajada Butte, Chacra Mesa,

FIGURE 3.2 Fajada Butte, an isolated sandstone remnant of Chacra Mesa, is the topographic focal point of Chaco Canyon and the home of the Sun Dagger petroglyph (photo by R. Van Dyke)

and West Mesa can be seen for miles to the north, west, and south of the canyon. From Chaco, these sandstone mesas offer spectacular views in nearly every direction toward distant peaks such as Huerfano Mountain, Shiprock, the Chuskas, Hosta Butte, and Mount Taylor. Intervisibility of prominent, distant peaks and oddly shaped landforms is important in the Pueblo world (Bernardini 2013; Bernardini and Peeples 2015). A Hopi man once told me that he finds it amusing that Anglo archaeologists have spilled so much ink trying to figure out why Chaco arose where it did, when the answer – Fajada Butte – is staring us in the face. He declined to elaborate, but this distinctive and highly visible knob clearly evokes meaningful relationships with deities, stories and/or ancestors for Indigenous peoples today. At the same time, as implied by the word "canyon," these highly visible, stone landforms exist in dualistic complementarity with the closed, hidden, protected, invisible spaces inside Chaco's sandstone walls. This visible/invisible drama is one characteristic of the kind of place Mircea Eliade called an *axis mundi* – a center place, balancing point of the world. People gathered in Chaco Canyon, in part, because of its topography, its light and shadow, sandstone and sky (Figure 3.3).

The canyon itself embodies a kind of topographic balanced dualism, and balanced dualism (or complementarity) is a well-known organizing principle for Indigenous peoples on the Plateau (e.g., Fox 1972; Ortiz 1969; White 1942). When Chacoans cut and shaped stone from the canyon walls to build their massive great houses, they crafted their buildings according to principles of balanced dualism on

FIGURE 3.3 Sandstone masonry great-house walls rise into the New Mexico sky (photo courtesy of Cloudy Ridge Productions)

multiple planes, juxtaposing the visible and the hidden, the sky and the earth, the movements of the sun and moon (Figure 3.4). The Chacoan assemblage involves the spatial distribution of buildings, earthworks, and monuments at multiple scales and according to recognizable rules of planning and orientation (Lekson 1986). Chacoan great houses and great kivas echo the canyon's dualistic character within the symmetrical layout of the structures themselves, and in the paired opposition between great houses and great kivas (Figure 3.5). Great houses are skyward, highly visible, rectilinear, relatively accessible spaces, while their great kiva counterparts are subterranean, hidden, circular, more restrictive spaces. The bright sunlight and open spaces of a great-house plaza would have contrasted sharply against the darkness found in great kivas and inner great-house rooms (Van Dyke 2017). Classic Bonito builders favored solar or lunar orientations (Sofaer 2007), and archaeologists have long recognized a north–south organizing principle at Chaco (Fritz 1978; Lekson 2015; Marshall 1997). Bonito style architecture is territorializing, demonstrating the presence of shared ideas about the cosmos and shared ideas about how to situate oneself on the landscape. These ideas radiate through multiple scales, from the canyon itself, to the structures erected around and within it, through outlier communities, across the greater San Juan Basin and perhaps beyond. The major road segments extending from Chaco – the Great North Road and the South Road – balance one another in terms of direction, and they also balance one another in terms of the hidden (Kutz Canyon to the north) and the visible (Hosta Butte to the south) (Marshall 1997), gathering the greater Chacoan landscape together. Over

FIGURE 3.4 Stars revolve around true North, as seen above the symmetrical foot drums of Great Kiva A in the center of the plaza of Pueblo Bonito (photo courtesy of Cloudy Ridge Productions)

FIGURE 3.5 The four-storey Chacoan great house, Pueblo Bonito, with its multiple great kivas, from the canyon rim above the structure, looking south (photo by R. Van Dyke)

48 Ruth M. Van Dyke

three centuries, a reflexive relationship developed between the architecture, landscape, and people. To experience the stone, the sky, the monumental construction in Chaco was to feel oneself to be at the center place, at the heart of the axis upon which life balanced (Van Dyke 2007).

Yet ancient farmers never would have set foot in Chaco without arable land and water. On the high desert of the Colorado Plateau, hot, clear, dry, sunny days are the norm. Today, as in the past, Chaco Canyon receives less than nine inches of precipitation per year, most of it in the form of late-summer thunderstorms or mid-winter rain and snow (Dean 1988:122–126). For Indigenous residents of the Colorado Plateau, water is life (Tuwaletstiwa and Tuwaletstiwa 2015). Springs, seeps, and lakes are portals to the world below, homes of deities, ancestors, or supernatural beings. Animals such as toads and serpents that can move between water and land are considered powerful messengers between these realms. It is not surprising, then, that many animistic artifacts found at Chaco bear the forms of animals associated with water – particularly ducks and toads or frogs (Brody 1984; Pepper 1920:91, 186;Vivian et al. 1978). When it rains in Chaco, the canyon is temporarily transformed into a space of misty mornings, croaking spadefoot toads, flying ants, and brilliant sunsets. Ironically, the baking hot, tan and brown sedimentary rocks of Chaco Canyon are the remains of muddy strata that once lay beneath an inland sea. Interspersed with black humic coal deposits and fossil casts of mud worms and sharks' teeth, the cliffs of Chaco juxtapose today's arid desert with its watery, marine past.

Nevertheless, the high desert of the Colorado Plateau is an unforgiving and difficult place to farm. Ancient peoples clustered along sandy drainages and devised the means to catch all the water available, inventing ways to coax corn, beans, and squash from the earth. Another of Chaco's territorializing dimensions was that this wide, shallow, ephemeral river with many major confluences contained excellent areas for the cultivation of corn (Geib and Heitman 2015). Some scholars believe that Chaco arose where it did due to its suitability for farming and water control. A sand dune across the confluence of the Chaco and the Escavada Washes may have trapped moisture or even created a shallow lake (Force et al. 2002;Vivian et al. 2006, in press). Vivian (Vivian and Watson 2015;Vivian et al. in press) describes extensive irrigation works, particularly on the north side of the canyon. In this view, hierarchical leaders emerged to organize the labor needed for these territorializing, labor-intensive irrigation practices. Wills (2017; Wills and Dorshow 2012; Wills et al. 2016) agrees that agriculture was central to Chaco, but disagrees with respect to the extent of irrigation features in the canyon. Rather, Wills contends that familiar Pueblo methods of agricultural production were employed among dispersed fields held by social groups both within and beyond Chaco Canyon – in effect, another way to see farming as a territorializing force drawing together communities within Doyel et al.'s (1984) Chaco Halo.

Assemblages of water, arable soil, sunlight, human labor and ingenuity contributed to create corn, and the corn then in turn participated in assemblages involving grinding, cooking, consumption, and ceremonies. The tremendous quantity of corn pollen and grinding stones in great houses suggests the critical importance of corn, and of women (who were almost certainly responsible for grinding) at Chaco (Geib and Heitman 2015; Heitman 2016). Chaco as a place of stones, light, water and soil, then, lead us to think about Chaco territorialized by the gatherings of buildings and labor, through cosmographic symbolism and bodily experience, agricultural practices and the nurturing of life.

The experience: Senses, bodies, movement

The term *place* emphasizes the lived experiences and meanings bound up in a particular space. Place-making – the construction of a meaningful landscape – is a sensual experience involving sight, sound, smell, memory, emotion, and movement (sensu Basso 1996). Lived spatial experiences help to affirm and challenge ideas about the world and our place in it.

For many societies, including Indigenous peoples of the Colorado Plateau, sight is the most important of senses. On an open, horizontal landscape with clear skies and prominent topographic features, Chacoan residents and visitors would have been acutely aware of what they could see, and what could be seen (Van Dyke et al. 2016). From the high places of Chaco Canyon, the viewer seems encircled by distant peaks and oddly shaped landforms (Vivian 1990:35; Hayes and Windes 1975; Lekson 2002). Shrines, road segments, and other strategically placed sites all suggest that distinctive volcanic plugs, buttes, and mountain peaks held special significance across the Chacoan world. By the Early Bonito phase, Chacoans systematically situated great houses and great kivas within sight of iconic landforms, particularly Huerfano Mountain and Hosta Butte.

Great houses not only embodied dualistic ideas – these structures were meant to be viewed. Chacoan great houses exhibit the solid mass, verticality, contrasting backgrounds, and clear forms characteristic of architecture built to be seen (sensu Moore 1996). Chacoan great-house builders both within and beyond Chaco Canyon enhanced visibility by means of massive construction, vertical locations, and associations with dramatic landforms. Builders positioned most outlier great houses with lines of sight to Chaco Canyon or to iconic Chacoan high places, and shrines facilitated these links. Shrines created an intervisible and communicative part of the territorializing assemblage. Recently, colleagues and I used ArcGIS viewshed analyses to demonstrate how Chacoan shrines on high places created long-distance connections of intervisibility across the Chacoan world that may have involved shared senses of place, signaling and communication (Hayes and Windes 1975; Van Dyke et al. 2016). And just as people at shrines or elevated great houses could see over vast distances, the sites could be seen from afar by outlier dwellers and by Chacoan visitors.

Although vision is an important sense, it is not the only sense: Recently, archaeologists have begun thinking seriously about the study of ancient sound (Scarre and Lawson 2006; Schofield 2014; Villanueva-Rivera et al. 2011). Ethnographic as well as archaeological sources reveal a wide variety of musical

50 Ruth M. Van Dyke

instruments that may have been used at Chaco: drums, copper bells, kiva bells, tinklers, rasps, bullroarers, conch shell trumpets, flutes, and whistles (Brown 2005; Weiner 2015). Rhythmic chants, stomps, and claps may have been part of Chaco's acoustic experience. Topography and monuments affect how sound travels, from magnified sounds inside confined spaces to the booming echoes between canyon cliffs. A reconstructed great kiva at the Chacoan outlier of Aztec West is the best extant approximation we have of an enclosed Chacoan great kiva space, complete with floor vaults that could have been used as foot drums. Through experiments in this space, we know that great kivas enhance low-frequency resonances – the same resonances associated with trance and mental imagery (Devereux 2006; Loose 2010).

Acoustic researchers at Chaco have been particularly interested in conch shell trumpets – an instrument likely employed in the context of ritual events at Chaco (Brown 2005:299–300; Loose 2012; Mills and Ferguson 2008:347, Table 1). Richard Loose (2012) recreated a shell trumpet using a *Strombus galeatus* shell, and he used digital software to measure the pitch and loudness when blown. His shell produced a sound with a decibel level similar to that produced by a motorcycle or a handheld drill. Primeau and Witt (2018) modeled the reach of a conch shell trumpet blast at dawn from Pueblo Bonito; following suit, we have attempted the same at two out-lier communities (Van Dyke et al. in press) Like the sonorous toll of a church bell in a medieval village, the blast of a conch shell trumpet could have been an effective way to call people together or to reach everyone within an outlier community – an acoustic territorializing force.

The sandstone cliff face between the great houses of Pueblo Bonito and Chetro Ketl in Chaco Canyon has long been noted for its unusual acoustic properties. In Navajo oral traditions, this cliff face is where deities taught Navajo hero twins how to produce the vocal tones used in ritual chants, accompanied by shell trumpet, eagle bone whistle, and reed flute. John Stein, Loose, and others experimented with amplified music, sine waves, flutes, and conch shell trumpets in this area, dubbed the "amphitheater." Reverberations lasted for 2 seconds (comparable to a concert hall), with a secondary, 3.5-second delayed echo from across the canyon to the south. The torus curve of the cliff causes unusual effects, including virtual sound image, in which sounds seemed to be emanating from within the cliff, and acousma, in which sounds produced nearby were heard as garbled or spooky, unintelligible noises. Stein et al. (2007) think the acoustic properties of this space must have been known to and used by Chacoans, perhaps in the context of ritual performances.

Summer rains in Chaco bring the sounds of thunder and running water, as well as another loud, unusual sound – the braying mating call of the spadefoot toad. For Pueblo people, toads and frogs are associated with water, rain, fertility, and corn. The rain comes, the toads come, the corn grows and is harvested. Women grind corn on stone manos and metates, and at Hopi, certain ritual dancers (Hopi katsin' mana) perform the grinding of corn, using rasps to imitate the sound of the manos and metates – rasps that are decorated with frogs and toads (Van Dyke 2015a). Given the unusual, short-lived, but deafening nature of spadefoot calls at Chaco, and given the importance of toads/frogs, rain, and corn at Chaco, it seems very likely that these sounds and the associated bundles of ideas figured prominently in Chacoan ritual as well.

Another unusual sensory experience at Chaco would have been taste – in particular, the taste of bitter cacao. Patty Crown (Crown and Hurst 2009; Crown et al. 2015) has demonstrated that the cylinder vessels – the same ones cached in ancestral burial rooms and repeatedly redecorated – once held cacao. The nearest source for cacao beans is in Veracruz, Mexico, 1700 miles to the south. The frothy, bitter cacao drink was a staple of Mesoamerican elite consumption, imbibed as part of religious ceremonies and as part of the sealing of trade agreements and alliances. We now know that these exotic beans were exported to Chaco, where special vessels were made (after the Mesoamerican model) for their consumption. Given the small quantity of known vessels (< 100) and the rare nature of these beans in Chaco, cacao consumption clearly was an experience accessible only to a few.

Other exotic goods to excite or delight the senses would have included turquoise, conch shells, lignite, brightly colored cherts and obsidians, stone beads, and macaw feathers. We know that these materials were moving around the Chacoan world (e.g., Cameron 2001; Hull et al. 2014; Thibodeau et al. 2012; Watson et al. 2015). Barbara Mills and Matthew Peeples are currently involved in a massive undertaking, collating all the artifact data from across the Chacoan world to be used in social network analysis, adding another perspective to our understandings of Chacoan regional relationships (Mills et al. 2019). Materials such as pink chert, glassy obsidian, or rare and bitter cacao must have been valued for reasons that transcended functionality.

Sights, sounds, smells, tastes, textures – all experiences take place through the medium of the human body, and the human body is always in motion. While archaeologists are fond of our top-down maps, Chaco was experienced from the vantage point of human bodies who were situated in particular times and spaces. In my vision of Chaco, during its heyday, Chaco was a ritual center visited by outlier dwellers who would have arrived on foot after walking for hours or days across the high desert terrain along prepared road surfaces, trails and drainages. We need to think about a Chacoan assemblage as involving an interplay of bodies with topography and trails, buttes and canyons. And travelers would have visited others' communities and joined other pilgrims all along the way, so we need to think about experiences of communitas, and the myriad social relationships that would have been forged, reinforced, and perhaps challenged on a daily basis during these journeys.

Roads undoubtedly had cosmographic and symbolic purposes, but they also directed movement into and away from Chaco. It is easier to walk on road segments than on adjacent, unmodified terrain. In the canyon, and at outliers, road segments were likely used for processions. As they led travelers to sites such as Pueblo Alto (in a high place, with excellent visibility) and Pueblo del Arroyo (in a low place, with more restricted visibility), road segments prescribed movement, creating spatial experiences that emphasized the visible and the hidden. Travelers moving across the dunes experienced an interesting "now you see it, now you don't" phenomenon when following prescribed approaches to Chaco along the roads. Procession routes created specific kinds of visual experiences that culminated in the dramatic spectacle of particular great houses. Pueblo Alto and Pueblo del Arroyo were situated to maximize viewer impact upon approach to the canyon from the north and south, respectively. Once in Chaco, staircases, mounds, and restricted access further directed visitors' and residents' bodies, creating and limiting different kinds of sensory experiences.

Despite recent arguments to the contrary, there is compelling material evidence for Chaco as a pilgrimage center: monuments that could not have been built by resident labor, massive deposits of unusual objects, and clear evidence for archaeoastronomical observances. Some of my colleagues (Plog and Watson 2012) have recently disputed this characterization of Chaco, arguing that there are not enough broken pots and deer bones in the mound at Pueblo Alto to constitute evidence for periodic feasting. I might here point out that feasting and pilgrimage are not synonymous, any more than monumental architecture and pilgrimage are synonymous. And, once in Chaco, visitors or pilgrims entered a landscape that was carefully choreographed to astound the senses and to convey the indisputable idea that Chaco Canyon (and by extension its elite leaders) were the right and proper center of the Pueblo world.

Historical relationships: Time, memory, ancestors

Time, memory, and ancestors also were territorializing forces gathering in Chaco Canyon. Pueblo peoples speak of cyclical returns to landscapes occupied by ancestors, building new sites atop old, and constructing shrines on the places where ancestors dwelled. Chaco has been one such place throughout its history.

Chaco Canyon was the home of two of the largest Basketmaker III (4th–6th centuries) villages on the Colorado Plateau. Chacoan builders clearly cared about these ancestral communities, establishing a J-shaped shrine atop one of them (Site 29SJ423). They carefully enshrined ancestors (founders?) in Early Bonito phase Pueblo Bonito. Rooms in the oldest part of this early great house became crypts for a group of people whose remains we have now radiocarbon dated to the ninth century (Plog and Heitman 2010) and who we now know represented a matrilineage (Kennett et al. 2017). Over time, more people were added to these burial rooms, together with astronomical amounts of shell, turquoise, macaws, cylinder jars, and other exotica. Heitman (2015) presents a compelling argument for house societies at Chaco, anchored by the tangible remains of ancestors.

Over three centuries, Chacoans engaged in processes that Crown and Wills (2003) termed "cyclical renewal," making frequent, repetitive (and structurally unnecessary) additions and remodelings to great houses and great kivas. Some Chacoan kivas have up to 31 layers of plaster (Kluckhohn 1939:8). Representational media such as rock art panels, kiva murals, masks, and pottery show signs of superposition, or repeated obliteration and redecoration (Hibben 1975:34; Smith 1952:19–21, 1990; Young 1988:192). Cylinder vessels were repeatedly redecorated, either by washing or scraping away the black-on-white designs, or by reslipping, repainting,

Chaco gathers: Experience and assemblage **53**

and refiring (Crown and Wills 2003). The repeated, cyclical celebration of rituals at Chaco would have created a sense of continuity with the past and the future. Architecture itself invoked linkages with the past in a process that I have argued was a material dimension of the construction of social memory (Van Dyke 2003, 2007). Mounds and berms in front of great houses stand in for large trash middens that would have signified long-term occupation. When Chacoans incorporated great kivas into the Bonito style repertoire during the eleventh century, they referenced Basketmaker III subterranean gathering places. Some Chacoan road segments seem to have been "time bridges" linking new buildings to those constructed by ancestors (Fowler and Stein 1992).

Perhaps Chacoans believed that time itself revolved around the canyon, as evidenced by the cyclical, repetitive, circular movements of the sun and the moon. Solar and lunar observations marked by architecture and rock art lent weight to the concept of Chaco Canyon as the center of the world. Like farmers everywhere, Pueblo peoples are acutely aware of the sun's daily and seasonal peregrinations across the sky (Harrington 1916:45–48; McCluskey 1977; Parsons 1939:212; Stevenson 1894:29; Tedlock 1983). Anna Sofaer and her colleagues (e.g., Sinclair et al. 1987) have demonstrated that Chacoans were concerned with solstices and equinoxes. More recently (Sofaer 1997) has argued Chacoans marked lunar standstills as well. This latter interpretation is more controversial, yet seems borne out by rock art, by some great-house alignments, and perhaps most compelling, by the position of the Chimney Rock outlier great house (Malville 2004). If ancient Puebloans were keeping track of the movements of the sun and moon on the horizon, then solstices, equinoxes, and standstills might have signaled occasions for people all over the Basin to gather in the canyon.

And, when the center of Pueblo power moved from Chaco to the outlier of Aztec, 50 kilometers to the north, many of these ideas moved as well. In fact, the builders of Aztec created a landscape that cited downtown Chaco in its layout and design, with three new great houses (Aztec North, West, and East) standing in for Pueblo Alto, Pueblo Bonito, and Chetro Ketl at Chaco (Van Dyke 2008, 2009), and the Animas River at Aztec standing in for the Chaco Wash. Repeated references to ancestors and practices of the past were an important territorializing force at Chaco, and these ideas and practices are manifest in architecture, in objects, and movement among and around places, and in the very movement of planetary bodies in the skies.

Chaco territorialized and deterritorialized

A Chacoan assemblage is a flexible entity encompassing not only collections of materials and spaces but gatherings of people, relationships, topography and ideas. We cannot merely look at maps of site distributions or settlement patterns – we must think about the ways in which these various gatherings and groupings were constantly territorialized and deterritorialized in time, space, and mind. Shared architectural ideas and shared ritual practices could have been powerful territorializing

54 Ruth M. Van Dyke

forces, but language, topography, distance, and social relations may have been among the deterritorializing forces at work here.

The canyon gathers

The concept of center place would have been a powerful, ideological territorializing force. Ancestors, intervisibility, dramatic topography, architecture emphasizing balanced dualism and directions – all of these elements coalesced to represent Chaco Canyon as a center place. Center place figures prominently in most contemporary Pueblo migration stories, with Tewa, Keres, Hopi, and Zuni peoples each contending, for example, that they have now arrived in the center place where each was ordained to live, and this concept has deep roots for the Pueblo world (Dongoske et al. 1997; Ferguson and Hart 1985; Parsons 1939). Although, from a contemporary perspective, Puebloans do not consider Chaco Canyon to be the proper center place, a millennium ago their ancestors might well have seen it that way.

Chaco cannot be understood if one's focus remains tightly on the canyon center. Rather, the greater Chaco landscape, and the canyon–outlier relationships are key (Van Dyke and Heitman in press). Elsewhere I have posited that residents of canyon and outlier settlements, such as those along the Chuskan slopes, gathered periodically to share resources, marriage partners, and ritual knowledge. They would have been mitigating the deterritorializing aspects of spatial distance against reterritorializing processes that included shared ideas about how the world works. From a Marxist perspective (Van Dyke 2008), I posited that when contradictions within this dialectical relationship reached a tipping point, a group of small-scale, dispersed farmers transformed into a centralized, hierarchical rituality whereby secret ceremonial knowledge legitimated elite political authority. From a DeLeuzean perspective, that tipping point must have involved the (temporary) triumph of territorializing forces.

Early Bonito ceremonial gatherings blossomed in Chaco in part because of the ways the natural topographic properties of the canyon fit with elements of a Pueblo worldview. For ancient Puebloans looking outwards from Chacoan high places, the canyon seemed an *axis mundi* connecting the visible and hidden, sky and earth, north and south. Builders increasingly formalized these relationships on the surrounding landscape. Road segments balanced and connected opposing directions, high and low great houses, and visible and hidden natural spaces. The canyon was a fulcrum, a point of fixity halfway between these geographic opposites.

By the Classic Bonito phase, Chaco Canyon was the central focal point of a set of highly formalized hierophantic practices. People traveled from the slopes of the Chuska Mountains and from other areas of the San Juan Basin to gather in the canyon for ritual events and festivities probably coordinated with astronomical events such as solstices and lunar standstills (e.g., Sofaer 1997, 2007). Canyon builders organized labor on a large scale, erecting settings for ritual activities and directing the experiences of visitors. Those who orchestrated and presided over these events – whether corporate groups, individuals, or matrilineages – derived status and prestige from their positions. But they did not hold Chaco together by virtue of charisma or coercion. Rather, the Chacoan assemblage at its most cohesive would have been territorialized by shared beliefs in the importance of repetitive (cyclical), elaborate ritual practices. At its height, Chaco Canyon was a place of density, gathering stone, water, sky, corn, cosmography, architecture, people, ancestors, ideas. Experiences, beliefs, and ideas that we might term "religious" would have permeated most (all?) facets of the Chacoan assemblage (sensu Fowles 2013).

Chaco pulled apart and reassembled

Although it is easy to think about Chaco as an urban place, a gathering place pulling the ancient Pueblo world together, the concept of a constantly emergent, rhyzomatic suite of assemblages reminds us to think about the constant negotiations and tensions that must have been present, not only at Chaco's rise, but during its heyday in the eleventh and twelfth centuries, and afterwards. Intervisibility may be one archaeologically accessible way to apprehend some of these tensions. Although some outlier great houses have line-of-sight connections with Chaco (either directly, or facilitated by shrines), others (like Casamero) are isolated. And, although many outlier great houses visually dominate their local communities, some (such as Whirlwind) are only visible from afar, suggesting visitors or neighbors were the intended audience, rather than local residents. If we assume that being able to see one another is territorializing and not being able to see one another is deterritorializing, then nuanced examinations of intervisible relationships within and among Chaco outliers are likely to help us tease out these forces across the eleventh and twelfth centuries.

The most formal outlier great houses date from the Classic and Late Bonito phases, as Chaco pushed outwards through emulation and colonization. The outlier of Aztec provides an excellent illustration of the tensions that accompanied these processes – meant to be territorializing, but ultimately deterritorializing. During the 1080s, some combination of Chacoans and local people began work on Aztec – a new Chaco Canyon 50 kilometers to the north. They recreated a Chacoan landscape on the banks of the Animas River, with architectural and topographic relationships mirroring those in the central canyon. These builders seem to have been re-territorializing the Chacoan idea in a new location – attempting to shift attendant religious, social, and political assemblages away from the canyon and coalesce them in a new center place. Perhaps, initially, Aztec did not attract much of a following, as evidenced by the hasty adobe construction of the first great house in the group (Aztec North) (Turner 2019). But, as social and environmental pressures may have helped deterritorialize Chaco Canyon, the verdant banks of the Animas River probably began to look more attractive. But Chaco Canyon was far from over. In the early 1100s, the ritual leaders of Aztec found themselves in direct competition for followers with the leaders of Chaco, as Chacoan builders responded with a new monumental building program of their own (Van Dyke 2004). But, by

1150, although people continued to live in Chaco Canyon, it was no longer central to the Pueblo world.

Ultimately, Aztec leaders' attempt to create a new Chaco was unsuccessful. Changes in architectural styles, material technology, subsistence remains, and burial practices indicate that areas of Aztec West were used for small-scale domestic habitation during the 1200s (Morris 1919, 1928). This shift away from Chaco-derived great house ceremonialism took place against a backdrop of increasing social and environmental instability across the Four Corners region. As deterritorializing forces (temporarily) again prevailed, the idea of Chaco became an element in newly emergent Indigenous assemblages across the northern San Juan. But that is a story for another day.

Contemporary assemblages

Today, the landscape, archaeology, memory, and idea of Chaco continues to territorialize assemblages that involve a wide range of contemporary human stakeholders – Pueblo and Navajo descendants and residents, scholars, universities, National Park Service employees, tourists, energy and mining corporations, cultural resource management firms, and the U.S. Department of the Interior. It is not possible to discuss Chaco without being cognizant of the many ways in which these stakeholders are currently involved in struggles over the relative importance, past treatment, and future disposition of the Chacoan assemblage.

The Colorado Plateau is home to 20 indigenous Pueblo groups, including the Hopi (who speak Uto-Aztecan), the Zuni (who speak Penutian), the Acoma and Laguna (who speak Keresan), and 16 eastern pueblos (who speak Keresan and Kiowa-Tanoan) situated along the Rio Grande River and its tributaries. The plateau is also occupied by the Numic-speaking Ute, Pai, and Paiute, and the Athabaskan-speaking Navajo and Jicarilla Apache. Nearly all these groups have oral traditions that involve Chaco Canyon, and Pueblo peoples are indisputably Chacoan descendants. Pueblo peoples each have an origin story that involves emergence from a world below, followed by migrations to a center place where the people are destined to live (Dongoske et al. 1997:603; Parsons 1939:215, 230). Archaeological sites mark the peoples' paths of migration, and Chaco frequently figures as one of the places they stopped at along the way (Colwell-Chanthaphonh and Ferguson 2006; Ferguson and Hart 1985:20–23; Kuwanwisiwma 2004). Pueblo people describe nonlinear concepts of time. For them, Chaco Canyon is a place that is continuously touched in memory and has continued to be visited in person by Pueblo elders and others in the course of Pueblo "doings" (sensu Fowles 2013).

Today, however, the legal terrain of Chaco Canyon is surrounded by the sovereign tribal lands of the Navajo Nation. The canyon figures prominently in Navajo oral traditions as home of the Great Gambler who enslaved all the Navajo people (Begay 2004). Surrounding prominent landforms such as Hosta Butte and Huerfano Mountain are storied places for Navajo histories (Kelley and Francis 1994). Navajo residents were forcibly evicted from Chaco Canyon during the mid-twentieth century after the establishment of the area as a National Monument. Yet the Navajo position as Chacoan stakeholders has been repeatedly questioned by scholarly and some Pueblo groups for a range of contemporary political reasons, contributing to tensions (Schillaci and Bustard 2010).

Most Chaco scholars have some proprietary feelings about the canyon, and this has created friction among our ranks ever since Richard Wetherill and George Pepper first sank their spades into Pueblo Bonito in 1896 (McNitt 1957:150–151). Edgar Lee Hewett's distress at the Hyde Expedition's Pueblo Bonito excavations contributed to the passage of the 1906 Antiquities Act (Snead 2001:31–64). Hewett and Neil Judd infamously avoided one another throughout the 1920s as they staged parallel (but never contemporaneous!) excavations in neighboring great houses (Lister and Lister 1984:65–117). Even in contemporary times, with academic prestige seen as a limited good, it seems we cannot resist the urge to dismiss and denigrate one another's work (see, e.g., Wills 2012; Plog and Watson 2012; Plog 2015; Ware 2017).

If this were not enough, the Chacoan landscape today is threatened with yet another deterritorializing transformation, as oil and gas development expands to surround Chaco Culture National Historic Park (Reed in press). The legal situation is complex but, in short, subsurface and surface rights in the United States are partible, and the U.S. Bureau of Land Management (BLM) owns most of the mineral rights beneath the San Juan Basin surrounding the national monument. Under pressure from developers and the current U.S. administration, the BLM has leased most of these mineral rights for development (Figure 3.6). Although Section 106 of the U.S. Antiquities Act prevents the wanton destruction of discrete archaeological sites beyond the park, it does little to protect the viewscapes, soundscapes, clear skies, long roads and other less-tangible categorically definable dimensions of Chaco. As an archaeologist and activist, I am working with colleagues to convince land managers and government officials that Chaco did not and does not stop at the park's boundaries (Van Dyke and Heitman in prep). But despite our best efforts to preserve the archaeology, the Chacoan assemblage is shifting, as the oil trapped in the Mancos Shale beneath the land is territorialized as part of a neoliberal, global, corporate industrial assemblage.

In 2017, I was part of an effort to organize a meeting involving scholars, Indigenous descendants, park personnel and government representatives, to look for a productive path forward.

"Why," I asked an Indigenous colleague at that meeting, "do you think all of us who care about Chaco also seem to feel the need to claim it exclusively for our own needs and purposes, even though in the process we tear one another, and Chaco, apart?"

"I believe," he replied, "it is something in the canyon itself that causes us to behave this way."

Acknowledgements. My thanks to Tim Pauketat, Susan Alt, and our fellow seminarians for stimulating discussions about urbanism, religion, and "new materialism." This work could not have taken place without the generous support of

FIGURE 3.6 Active mineral extraction equipment operating just outside the Pierre's Chaco outlier community along the Great North Road, approximately 15 kilometers north of Chaco Canyon, New Mexico (photo by R. Van Dyke)

the Templeton Foundation, the School of Advanced Research, and the Amerind Foundation. I alone am responsible for any errors or misconceptions presented herein.

References

Barad, Karen 2007 *Meeting the Universe Halfway: Quantum Physics and the Entanglement of Matter and Meaning.* Duke University Press, Durham, NC.

Basso, Keith H. 1996 Wisdom Sits in Places: Notes on a Western Apache Landscape. In *Senses of Place*, edited by S. Feld and K. H. Basso, pp. 53–90. School of American Research Press, Santa Fe, NM.

Begay, Richard M. 2004 Tsé Bíyah 'Anii'áhí: Chaco Canyon and Its Place in Navajo History. In *In Search of Chaco: New Approaches to an Archaeological Enigma*, edited by D. N. Grant, pp. 54–60. School of American Research Press, Santa Fe, NM.

Bennett, Jane 2010 *Vibrant Matter: A Political Ecology of Things.* Duke University Press, Durham, NC.

Bernardini, Wesley 1999 Reassessing the Scale of Social Action at Pueblo Bonito, Chaco Canyon, New Mexico. *Kiva* 64(4):447–470.

Bernardini, Wesley, Alicia Barnash, Mark Kumler and Martin Wong 2013 Quantifying Visual Prominence in Social Landscapes. *Journal of Archaeological Science* 40(2013):3946–3954.

Bernardini, Wesley, and Matthew A. Peeples 2015 Sight Communities: The Social Significance of Shared Visual Landmarks. *American Antiquity* 80(2):215–235.

Boivin, Nicole 2008 *Material Cultures, Material Minds: The Impact of Things on Human Thoughts, Society, and Evolution.* Cambridge University Press, Cambridge.

Brody, J. J. 1984 Chaco Art and the Chaco Phenomenon. In *New Light on Chaco Canyon*, edited by D. G. Noble, pp. 13–18. School of American Research Press, Santa Fe, NM.

Brown, Emily J. 2005 Instruments of Power: Musical Performance in Rituals of the Ancestral Puebloans of the American Southwest. PhD dissertation, ProQuest Dissertations, Columbia University, Ann Arbor.

Bryant, Levi, Nick Smicek and Graham Harman (editors) 2010 *The Speculative Turn: Continental Materialism and Realism.* RE Press, Melbourne.

Cameron, Catherine M. 2001 Pink Chert, Projectile Points, and the Chacoan Regional System. *American Antiquity* 66(1):79–101.

Colwell-Chanthaphonh, Chip, and T. J. Ferguson 2006 Memory Pieces and Footprints: Multivocality and the Meanings of Ancient Times and Ancestral Places among the Zuni and Hopi. *American Anthropologist* 108(1):148–162.

Crown, Patricia L., and W. Jeffrey Hurst 2009 Evidence of Cacao Use in the American Southwest. *Proceedings of the National Academy of Sciences* 106(7):2110–2113.

Crown, Patricia L., Jiyan Gu, W. Jeffrey Hurst, Timothy J. Ward, Ardith D. Bravenec, Syed Ali, Laura Kebert, Marlaina Berch, Eric Redman, Patrick D. Lyons, Jamie Merewether, David A. Phillips, Lori S. Reed and Kyle Woodson 2015 Ritual Drinks in the Pre-Hispanic US Southwest and North Mexican Northwest. *Proceedings of the National Academy of Sciences* 112(37):11136–11442.

Crown, Patricia L., and W. H. Wills 2003 Modifying Pottery and Kivas at Chaco: Pentimento, Restoration, or Renewal? *American Antiquity* 68(3):511–532.

Dean, Jeffrey S. 1988 Dendrochronology and Paleoenvironmental Reconstruction on the Colorado Plateaus. In *The Anasazi in a Changing Environment*, edited by G. J. Gumerman, pp. 119–167. Cambridge University Press, Cambridge.

DeLanda, Manue 2006 *A New Philosophy of Society: Assemblage Theory and Social Complexity.* Continuum, London and New York.

——— 2016 *Assemblage Theory.* Edinburgh University Press, Edinburgh.

Deleuze, Gilles, and Félix Guattari 2007 (1980) *A Thousand Plateaus: Capitalism and Schizophrenia.* Continuum, London and New York.

Devereux, Pau 2006 Ears and Years: Aspects of Acoustics and Intentionality in Antiquity. In *Archaeoacoustics*, edited by C. Scarre and G. Lawson, pp. 23–30. McDonald Institute Monographs, Cambridge University Press, Cambridge.

Dongoske, Kurt E., Michael Yeatts, Roger Anyon and T. J. Ferguson 1997 Archaeological Cultures and Cultural Affiliation: Hopi and Zuni Perspectives in the American Southwest. *American Antiquity* 62(4):600–608.

Doyel, David E., Cory D. Breternitz and Michael P. Marshall 1984 Chacoan Community Structure: Bis sa'ani and the Chaco Halo. In *Recent Research on Chaco Prehistory*, edited by W. J. Judge and J. D. Schelberg, pp. 37–54. Reports of the Chaco Center 8. Division of Cultural Research, National Park Service, Albuquerque.

Ferguson, T. J., and E. Richard Hart 1985 *A Zuni Atlas.* University of Oklahoma Press, Norman.

Force, Eric R., R. Gwinn Vivian, Thomas C. Windes and Jeffrey S. Dean 2002 *Relation of "Bonito" Paleo-channels and Base-level Variations to Anasazi Occupation, Chaco Canyon, New Mexico.* Arizona State Museum Archaeological Series 194. University of Arizona Press, Tucson.

60 Ruth M. Van Dyke

Fowler, Andrew P., and John R. Stei 1992 The Anasazi Great House in Space, Time, and Paradigm. In *Anasazi Regional Organization and the Chaco System*, edited by D. E. Doyel, pp. 101–122. Maxwell Museum of Anthropology Anthropological Papers 5. Maxwell Museum of Anthropology, Albuquerque.

Fowles, Severin M. 2013 *An Archaeology of Doings: Secularism and the Study of Pueblo Religion*. School for Advanced Research Press, Santa Fe, NM.

Fox, Robin 1972 Some Unsolved Problems of Pueblo Social Organization. In *New Perspectives on the Pueblos*, edited by A. Ortiz, pp. 71–85. School of American Research Advanced Seminar Series. University of New Mexico Press, Albuquerque.

Fritz, John M. 1978 Paleopsychology Today: Ideational Systems and Human Adaptation in Prehistory. In *Social Archaeology: Beyond Subsistence and Dating*, edited by C. L. Redman, M. J. Berman, E. V. Curtin, W. T. Langhorne Jr., N. M. Versaggi and J. C. Wanser, pp. 37–59. Academic Press, New York.

Geib, Phil R., and Carrie C. Heitman 2015 The Relevance of Maize Pollen for Assessing the Extent of Maize Production in Chaco Canyon. In *Chaco Revisited: New Research on the Prehistory of Chaco Canyon, New Mexico*, edited by C. C. Heitman and S. Plog, University of Arizona Press, Tucson.

Harman, Graham 2010 *Towards Speculative Realism: Essays and Lectures*. Zero Books, Winchester, UK.

——— 2011 *The Quadruple Object*. Zer0 Books, Alresford, UK.

——— 2016 *Immaterialism*. Polity Press, Cambridge.

Harrington, John 1916 The Ethnography of the Tewa Indians. In *29th Annual Report of the Bureau of American Ethnology for the Years 1907–1908*, pp. 29–636. Government Printing Office, Washington, DC.

Harris, Oliver J. T. 2014 (Re)assembling Communities. *Journal of Archaeological Method and Theory* 21:76–97.

Hayes, Alden C. 1981 A Survey of Chaco Canyon Archaeology. In *Archaeological Surveys of Chaco Canyon, New Mexico*, edited by D. M. Brugge, A. C. Hayes and W. J. Judge, pp. 1–68. National Park Service Archaeological Series No. 17A. Chaco Canyon Studies, Washington, DC.

Hayes, Alden C., and Thomas C. Windes 1975 An Anasazi Shrine in Chaco Canyon. In *Papers in Honor of Florence Hawley Ellis*, edited by T. R. Frisbie, pp. 143–156. Papers of the Archaeological Society of New Mexico 2. Archaeological Society of New Mexico, Santa Fe, NM.

Heitman, Carrie C. 2015 The House of Our Ancestors: New Research on the Prehistory of Chaco Canyon, New Mexico. In *Chaco Revisited: New Research on the Prehistory of Chaco Canyon, New Mexico*, edited by C. C. Heitman and S. Plog, pp. 215–248. University of Arizona Press, Tucson.

——— 2016 "A Mother for All the People": Feminist Science and Chacoan Archaeology. *American Antiquity* 81(3):471–489.

Heitman, Carrie C., and Stephen Plog (editors) 2015 *Chaco Revisited: New Research on the Prehistory of Chaco Canyon, New Mexico*. University of Arizona Press, Tucson.

Hibben, Frank C. 1975 *Kiva Art of the Anasazi at Pottery Mound*. KC Publications, Las Vegas.

Hodder, Ian 2012 *Entangled*. Wiley-Blackwell, Oxford.

Hull, Sharon, Mostafa Fayek, Frances Joan Mathien and Heidi Roberts 2014 Turquoise Trade of the Ancestral Puebloan: Chaco and Beyond. *Journal of Archaeological Science* 45:187–195.

Ingold, Tim 2000 *The Perception of the Environment: Essays on Livelihood, Dwelling, and Skill*. Routledge, New York and London.

——— 2007 Materials Against Materiality. *Archaeological Dialogues* 14(1):1–38.

———— 2011 *Being Alive: Essays on Movement, Knowledge, and Description*. Routledge, London.

———— 2013 *Making: Anthropology, Archaeology, Art and Architecture*. Routledge, London.

Kelley, Klara B., and Harris Francis 1994 *Navajo Sacred Places*. Indiana University Press, Bloomington.

Kennett, Douglas J., Stephen Plog, Richard J. George, Brendan J. Culleton, Adam S. Watson, Pontus Skoglund, Nadin Rohland, Swapan Mallick, Kristin Stewardson, Logan Kistler, Steven A. LeBlanc, Peter M. Whiteley, David Reich and George H. Perry 2017 Archaeogenomic Evidence Reveals Prehistoric Matrilineal Dynasty. *Nature Communications* 8: 14115.

Kluckhohn, Clyde 1939 Discussion. In *Preliminary Report on the 1937 Excavations: Bc50–51, Chaco Canyon, New Mexico*, edited by C. Kluckhohn and P. Reiter, pp. 151–162. University of New Mexico Bulletin 345, Anthropological Series 3(2). University of New Mexico, Albuquerque.

Kuwanwisiwma, Leigh J. 2004 Yupköyvi: The Hopi Story of Chaco Canyon. In *In Search of Chaco Canyon*, edited by D. G. Noble, pp. 41–47. School of American Research Press, Santa Fe, NM.

Latour, Bruno 1993 *We Have Never Been Modern*. Translated by C. Porter. Harvard University Press, Cambridge, MA.

Lekson, Stephen H. 1986 *Great Pueblo Architecture of Chaco Canyon, New Mexico*. University of New Mexico Press, Albuquerque.

———— 2002 *Sky Determines*. Paper presented at the 101st Annual Meeting of the American Anthropological Association, New Orleans.

———— 2015 *The Chaco Meridian: One Thousand Years of Political and Religious Power in the Ancient Southwest* (second edition). Rowman and Littlefield, New York.

———— (editor) 2006 *The Archaeology of Chaco Canyon: An Eleventh-Century Pueblo Regional Center*. School of American Research Press, Santa Fe, NM.

Lister, Robert W., and Florence C. Lister 1984 *Chaco Canyon: Archaeology and Archaeologists*. University of New Mexico Press, Albuquerque.

Loose, Richard W. 2010 Archaeoacoustics: Adding a Soundtrack to Site Descriptions. In *Threads, Tints, and Edification, Papers in Honor of Glenna Dean*, edited by E. J. Brown, K. Armstrong, D. M. Brugge and C. J. Condie, pp. 127–136. Papers of the Archaeological Society of New Mexico 36. Archaeological Society of New Mexico, Albuquerque.

———— 2012 That Old Music: Reproduction of a Shell Trumpet from Pueblo Bonito. In *Glen Canyon, Legislative Struggles, and Contract Archaeology: Papers in Honor of Carol J. Condie*, edited by E. J. Brown, C. J. Condie and H. K. Crotty, pp. 127–133. Papers of the Archaeological Society of New Mexico 38. Archaeological Society of New Mexico, Albuquerque.

Malville, J. McKim (editor) 2004 *Chimney Rock: The Ultimate Outlier*. Lexington Books, Lanham, MD.

Marshall, Michael P. 1997 The Chacoan Roads: A Cosmological Interpretation. In *Anasazi Architecture and American Design*, edited by B. H. Morrow and V. B. Price, pp. 62–74. University of New Mexico Press, Albuquerque.

McCluskey, Stephen C. 1977 The Astronomy of the Hopi Indians. *Journal for the History of Astronomy* 8:174–195.

McNitt, Frank 1957 *Richard Wetherill: Anasazi*. University of New Mexico Press, Albuquerque.

Mills, Barbara J., Matthew A. Peeples, Leslie D. Aragon, Benjamin A. Bellorado, Jeffery J. Clark, Evan Giomi, and Thomas C. Windes 2018 Evaluating Chacoan Migration Scenarios Using Dynamic Social Network Analysis. *Antiquity* 364:922–939.

62 Ruth M. Van Dyke

Mills, Barbara J., and T. J. Ferguson 2008 Animate Objects: Shell Trumpets and Ritual Networks in the Greater Southwest. *Journal of Archaeological Method and Theory* 15(4):338–361.

Momaday, N. Scott 1976 *The Names*. Harper and Row, New York.

Moore, Jerry D. 1996 *Architecture and Power in the Ancient Andes*. Cambridge University Press, Cambridge.

Morris, Earl H. 1919 *The Aztec Ruin*. Anthropological Papers of the American Museum of Natural History 26, Part 1. American Museum of Natural History, New York.

——— 1928 *Notes on Excavations in the Aztec Ruin*. Anthropological Papers of the American Museum of Natural History 26(5). American Museum of Natural History, New York.

Olsen, Bjørnar 2010 *In Defense of Things: Archaeology and the Ontology of Objects*. Altamira Press, Lanham, MD.

Ortiz, Alfonso 1969 *The Tewa World: Space, Time, Being and Becoming in a Pueblo Society*. University of Chicago Press, Chicago.

Parsons, Elsie Clewes 1939 *Pueblo Indian Religion*. University of Chicago Press, Chicago.

Pauketat, Timothy R. 2013 Bundles of/in/as Time. In *Big Histories, Human Lives: Tackling Problems of Scale in Archaeology*, edited by J. Robb and T. R. Pauketat, pp. 35–56. School of Advanced Research Press, Santa Fe, NM.

Pepper, George 1920 *Pueblo Bonito*. Anthropological Papers of the American Museum of Natural History, vol. 27. American Museum of Natural History, New York.

Plog, Stephen 2015 Understanding Chaco: Past, Present, and Future. In *Chaco Revisited: New Research on the Prehistory of Chaco Canyon, New Mexico*, edited by C. C. Heitman and S. Plog, pp. 3–29. Amerind Studies in Anthropology. University of Arizona Press, Tucson.

Plog, Stephen, and Carrie C. Heitman 2010 Hierarchy and Social Inequality in the American Southwest, A.D. 800–1200. *Proceedings of the National Academy of Sciences* 107(46):19619–19626.

Plog, Stephen, and Adam S. Watson 2012 The Chaco Pilgrimage Model: Assessing the Evidence from Pueblo Alto. *American Antiquity* 77(3):449–477.

Primeau, Kristy E., and David E. Witt 2018 Soundscapes in the Past: Investigating Sound at the Landscape Level. *Journal of Archaeological Science: Reports* 19:875–885. www.sciencedirect.com/science/article/pii/S2352409X17300949

Reed, Paul in press Protecting the Greater Chaco Landscape: Preservation and Advocacy. In *New Perspectives on the Greater Chaco Landscape*, edited by R. M. Van Dyke and C. C. Heitman. University Press of Colorado, Boulder.

Scarre, Chris, and Graeme Lawson (editors) 2006 *Archaeoacoustics*. McDonald Institute for Archaeological Research, University of Cambridge, Cambridge.

Schillaci, Michael A., and Wendy J. Bustard 2010 Controversy and Conflict: NAGPRA and the Role of Biological Anthropology in Determining Cultural Affiliation. *PoLAR: Political and Legal Anthropology Review* 33(2):352–373.

Schofield, John 2014 The Archaeology of Sound and Music. *World Archaeology* 46(3):289–291.

Sinclair, Rolf M., Anna Sofaer and John J. McCann, Jr. 1987 Marking of Lunar Major Standstill at the Three-slab Site on Fajada Butte. *Bulletin of the American Astronomical Society* 19:1043.

Smith, Watson 1952 Kiva Mural Decoration at Awatovi and Kawaika-a. Papers of the Peabody Museum of Archaeology and Ethnology 37. Harvard University Press, Cambridge, MA.

——— 1990 *When Is a Kiva?* University of Arizona Press, Tucson.

Snead, James E. 2001 *Ruins and Rivals: The Making of Southwest Archaeology*. University of Arizona Press, Tucson.

Sofaer, Anna 1997 The Primary Architecture of the Chacoan Culture: A Cosmological Expression. In *Anasazi Architecture and American Design*, edited by B. H. Morrow and V. B. Price, pp. 88–132. University of New Mexico Press, Albuquerque.

———— 2007 *Chaco Astronomy: An Ancient American Cosmology*. Ocean Tree Books, Santa Fe, NM.

Stein, John R., Richard A. Friedman, Taft Blackhorse and Richard W. Loose 2007 Revisiting Downtown Chaco. In *The Architecture of Chaco Canyon, New Mexico*, edited by S. H. Lekson, pp. 199–224. University of Utah Press, Salt Lake City.

Stevenson, Matilda Coxe 1894 The Sia. In *Bureau of American Ethnology 11th Annual Report*, pp. 3–157. Smithsonian Institution, Washington, DC.

Tedlock, Barbara 1983 Zuni Sacred Theater. *American Indian Quarterly* 7(3):93–110.

Thibodeau, Alison, John T. Chesley, J. Ruiz, David J. Killick and Arthur Vokes 2012 An Alternative Approach to the Prehispanic Turquoise Trade. In *Turquoise in Mexico and North America: Science, Conservation, Culture, and Collection*, edited by J. C. H. King, C. R. Cartwright, R. Stacey, C. McEwan and M. Carocci, pp. 66–74. Archetype, London.

Turner, Michelle I. 2019 Becoming Chacoan: The Archaeology of the Aztec North Great House. PhD dissertation, Department of Anthropology, Binghamton University–SUNY.

Tuwaletstiwa, Phillip, and Judy Tuwaletstiwa 2015 Landscape: The Reservoir of the Unconscious. In *Subjects and Narratives in Archaeology*, edited by R. M. Van Dyke and R. Bernbeck, pp. 113–120. University Press of Colorado, Boulder.

Van Dyke, Ruth M. 2003 Memory and the Construction of Chacoan Society. In *Archaeologies of Memory*, edited by R. M. Van Dyke and S. E. Alcock, pp. 180–200. Blackwell, Oxford and Malden, MA.

———— 2004 Memory, Meaning, and Masonry: The Late Bonito Chacoan Landscape. *American Antiquity* 69(3):413–431.

———— 2007 *The Chaco Experience: Landscape and Ideology at the Center Place*. School of Advanced Research Press, Santa Fe, NM.

———— 2008 Temporal Scale and Qualitative Social Transformation at Chaco Canyon, New Mexico. *Cambridge Archaeological Journal* 18(1):70–78.

———— 2009 Chaco Reloaded: Discursive Social Memory on the Post-Chacoan Landscape. *Journal of Social Archaeology* 9(2):220–248.

———— 2015a The Chacoan Past: Creative Representations and Sensory Engagements. In *Subjects and Narratives in Archaeology*, edited by R. M. Van Dyke and R. Bernbeck, pp. 83–99. University Press of Colorado, Boulder. doi: 10.5876/9781607323815.c004

———— 2015b Materiality in Practice: An Introduction. In *Practicing Materiality*, edited by R. M. Van Dyke, pp. 3–32. University of Arizona Press, Tucson.

———— 2017 The Chacoan World: Light and Shadow, Stone and Sky. In *The Oxford Handbook of Light in Archaeology*, edited by C. Papadopoulos. Oxford University Press, Oxford. doi: 10.1093/oxfordhb/9780198788218.013.9

Van Dyke, Ruth M., R. Kyle Bocinsky, Thomas C. Windes and Tucker J. Robinson 2016 Great Houses, Shrines, and High Places: A GIS Viewshed Analysis of the Chacoan World. *American Antiquity* 81(2):205–230.

Van Dyke, Ruth M., Timothy De Smet and R. Kyle Bocinsky in press Viewscapes and Soundscapes. In *New Perspectives on the Greater Chaco Landscape*, edited by R. M. Van Dyke and C. C. Heitman. University Press of Colorado, Boulder.

Van Dyke, Ruth M., and Carrie C. Heitman (editors) in press *New Perspectives on the Greater Chaco Landscape*. University Press of Colorado, Boulder.

Villanueva-Rivera, Luis J., Bryan C. Pijanowski, Jarrod Doucette and Burak Pekin 2011 A Primer of Acoustic Analysis for Landscape Ecologists. *Landscape Ecology* 26:1233.

Vivian, R. Gwinn 1990 *The Chacoan Prehistory of the San Juan Basin*. Academic Press, New York.

Vivian, R. Gwinn, Dulce N. Dodgen and Gayle Harrison Hartmann 1978 *Wooden Ritual Artifacts from Chaco Canyon, New Mexico: The Chetro Ketl Collection*. Anthropological Papers of the University of Arizona 32. University of Arizona Press, Tucson.

Vivian, R. Gwinn, Carla R. Van West, Jeffrey S. Dean, Nancy Akins, Mollie S. Toll and Thomas C. Windes 2006 Chaco Ecology and Economy. In *The Archaeology of Chaco Canyon: An Eleventh Century Regional Center*, edited by S. H. Lekson, pp. 45–66. School of American Research Press, Santa Fe, NM.

Vivian, R. Gwinn, and Adam S. Watson 2015 Reevaluating and Modeling Agricultural Potential in the Chaco Core. In *Chaco Revisited: New Research on the Prehistory of Chaco Canyon, New Mexico*, edited by C. C. Heitman and S. Plog, pp. 30–65. Amerind Studies in Anthropology. University of Arizona Press, Tucson.

Vivian, R. Gwinn, Adam S. Watson and Samantha Fladd in prep *Chaco Water*. University of Utah Press, Salt Lake City.

Ware, John 2015 *A Pueblo Social History: Kinship, Sodality, and Community in the Northern Southwest*. School for Advanced Research, Santa Fe, NM.

——— 2017 A Feminist Critique of Chacoan Archaeology: Comment on Heitman's (2016) Feminist Science and Chacoan Archaeology. *American Antiquity* 82(3):609–610.

Watson, Adam S., Stephen Plog, Brendan J. Culleton, Patricia A. Gilman, Steven A. LeBlanc, Peter M. Whiteley, Santiago Claramunt and Douglas J. Kennett 2015 Early Procurement of Scarlet Macaws and the Emergence of Social Complexity in Chaco Canyon, New Mexico. *Proceedings of the National Academy of Sciences* 112(27):8238–8243.

Weiner, Robert S. 2015 A Sensory Approach to Exotica, Ritual Practice, and Cosmology at Chaco Canyon. *Kiva* 81(3–4):220–246.

White, Leslie A. 1942 *The Pueblo of Santa Ana, New Mexico*. Memoirs of the American Anthropological Association 60. American Anthropological Association, Menasha, WI.

Wills, Wirt H. 2012 On the Trail of the Lonesome Pine: Archaeological Paradigms and the Chaco "Tree of Life." *American Antiquity* 77:478–497.

——— 2017 Water Management and the Political Economy of Chaco Canyon During the Bonito Phase (ca. AD 850 to 1200). *Kiva* 83(4):369–413.

Wills, Wirt H., and Wetherbee B. Dorshow 2012 Agriculture and Community in Chaco Canyon: Revisiting Pueblo Alto. *Journal of Anthropological Archaeology* 31(2):138–155.

Wills, Wirt H., David E. Love, Susan J. Smith, Karen R. Adams, Manuel R. Palacios-Fest, Wetherbee B. Dorshow, Beau G. Murphy, Hannah V. Mattson and Patricia L. Crown 2016 Water Management at Pueblo Bonito: Evidence from the National Geographic Society Trenches. *American Antiquity* 81(3):4449–4470.

Young, M. Jane 1988 *Signs from the Ancestors: Zuni Cultural Symbolism and Perceptions of Rock Art*. University of New Mexico Press, Albuquerque.

4

ASSEMBLING THE CITY

Monte Albán as a mountain of creation and sustenance

Arthur A. Joyce

One of the earliest urban centers in the Mexican Highlands was the mountaintop city of Monte Albán inhabited by Zapotec-speaking peoples in the Valley of Oaxaca (Figure 4.1). The urban center was founded at about 500 BCE through a unique convergence of mountains, rain, maize, earth, and people. As one of Mesoamerica's earliest cities, Monte Albán has been a focus of research and debate concerning the origins and nature of Native American urbanism (Blanton et al. 1999; Joyce 2010; Marcus and Flannery 1996). In this chapter, I argue that the relations between people, maize, rain, and earth and related phenomena involved the emergence of new kinds of beings, including deities and animate buildings as well as changes in acts such as rainfall and sacrifice through which vital forces were transferred among such beings. Boundaries among humans and between humans and other beings were reconfigured in ways that constituted new forms of ontology, identity, authority, materiality, and community.

I argue that such changes were actualized through Monte Albán, a mountain of creation and sustenance, an *axis mundi* where earth, sky, and underworld came together, and a rain place that brought fertility and well-being to the earth. I trace the genealogy of relationships and reconfigurations through which Monte Albán came to be constituted as an urban assemblage, beginning with the nearby site of San José Mogote two centuries prior to the founding of Monte Albán. Although the reconfiguring of relations among animate beings was crucial to the founding and growth of Monte Albán, they also created contradictions and tensions that were played out over the next several centuries. I emphasize the inseparability of mountains, people, rain, earth, and maize in the development of urbanism at Monte Albán and throughout Mesoamerica. I employ generalizations concerning Native American ontology and religion based largely on ethnohistoric and ethnographic research that, following Harris and Robb (2012), undoubtedly simplify a great deal of historical, cultural, and situational variability (Harrison-Buck 2012; Joyce 2019;

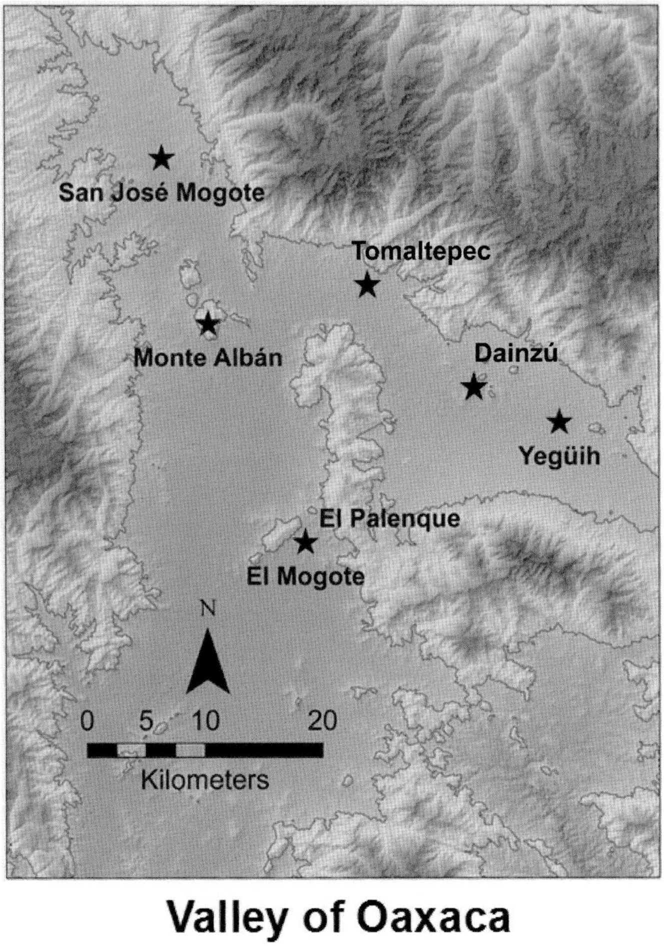

66 Arthur A. Joyce

Valley of Oaxaca

FIGURE 4.1 Map of the Valley of Oaxaca showing sites mentioned in the text (drawn by Sarah Barber, used with permission)

Joyce and Barber 2015). Doing so helps me to make a larger New Materialist argument that urbanism was a process that involved considerably more than human beings.

Agential cuts and Mesoamerican vitality

From a New Materialist perspective, social life involves the unfolding of complex assemblages defined as "temporary co-presences, deliberate arrangements, and articulations of things, beings, enunciations, memories and affects" (Hamilakis 2017:176). Entities within assemblages are assemblages themselves and can be detached and incorporated into other assemblages and so retain a relative autonomy and heterogeneity, but there are also properties and capacities that emerge from relations within assemblages (see Barad 2007; Bennett 2010; Delanda 2016; Deleuze and Guattari 1987; Harris 2017; Pauketat this volume). Karen Barad (2007) uses the term intra-actions to acknowledge the ontological inseparability of relational entities within an assemblage. The characteristics and dynamism of assemblages are a result both of the properties of and relationships among their constituent elements, which are simultaneously material and expressive, along with capacities to affect and be affected (DeLanda 2016; Deleuze and Guattari 1987).

Assemblage processes—the relationalities among constituent entities, including territorialization, deterritorialization, and stratification—constitute agencies within assemblages (see Pauketat, Chapter 1; Van Dyke, Chapter 3). Assemblage processes are topological in that they enact what Barad (2007) terms an "agential cut" through which the material and semantic properties and boundaries of entities are constituted. Agency therefore is a relational property of assemblages. Boundaries may be diffuse or can lead to qualities of differentiation and thus individuation, what Deleuze and Guattari (1987:260–263) refer to as a "haecceity." The agential cut therefore constitutes a temporary resolution of both the ontic and semantic properties of the assemblage, enacting what matters and what is excluded from mattering in both a material and meaningful sense. Because they are simultaneously material and meaningful, Barad (2007) refers to the intra-actions within assemblages as material-discursive practices. Humans are not outside of assemblages, but are entities within assemblages themselves, ontologically equivalent to other entities. Assemblages therefore enact agential cuts through which different kinds of humans as well as other-than-humans are constituted, along with exclusions that leave openings for contestation. From this perspective; knowing, sensing, and experiencing emotions are not confined to humans, but are distributed acts embedded within broader material-discursive configurations.

Thus, rather than reifying configurations such as city, community, polity, identity, authority, and institution, this perspective focuses attention on the dynamic relationships through which these phenomena are constituted, negotiated, contested, and transformed. From this perspective, urbanism, like religion and sacrality, becomes a relational property—an urbanity—that, as discussed throughout this volume, refers to a dense, layered convergence of assemblages and affects, of human entanglements and infrastructure (see Pauketat, Chapter 1 for a discussion of urbanism from a New Materialist perspective).

For many ancient and modern Native Americans a wide variety of living entities animated by vital, life-giving forces were central to the assemblages through which much of life was constituted (Barber and Olvera Sánchez 2010; Furst 1995; Pauketat 2013; Zedeño 2009). This existential unity blurs the boundaries between the natural, cultural and divine worlds and means that religious experience was enmeshed with daily life. As argued by Monaghan (1995, 2000), distinctions between the natural and supernatural therefore do not apply very well to Mesoamerica. Rain, clouds, earth, and other phenomena important to the daily lives of people were also manifestations of deities and the divine. Such a relational ontology means that in

68 Arthur A. Joyce

ancient Mesoamerica life was constituted not simply through the interactions of people, but was produced through ongoing relations among a diversity of animate beings that included earth, rain, maize, ancestors, deities, mountains, buildings, time, and numerous other entities.

The life forces that animate all living things therefore defined what it was to be sacred in ancient Mesoamerica and the acts through which these forces were transferred, transformed, and concentrated among beings were the focus of religious experience. Life therefore was constituted through the interactions of a far greater diversity of animate entities than recognized in most modern, Western ontologies. The ontological contrast is between an agential cut within assemblages of people and other-than-human animate and inanimate entities where much of the vibrancy of matter (sensu Bennett 2010) emanates from the same vitality that animates humans, as opposed to an agential cut that attempts to stratify existence between the living and a vast expanse of inert matter.

Yet this does not mean that all beings and practices were equivalent. Different beings manifest different kinds and degrees of these forces (López Austin 1988, 1989; Monaghan 1995:197–198). For example, certain beings, especially deities and rulers, assembled vital forces beyond those of others, which gave them greater power to affect the world. Since all living beings shared the same animating forces, distinctions among them were more fluid such that they had the capacity to transform from one state to another as in practices of *nahualism* and *tonalism* (Foster 1944; Sahagún [c. 1540–1585] 1950–1982). Likewise, the transferal of vitality from earth and rain to maize meant that the plants became the "children" of the gods of rain and earth (Monaghan 1990, 1995). Like humans, as social persona many other-than-human beings went through a life cycle marked by ritualized acts, including birth rites, usually conceptualized as acts of animation, and death rites termed practices of closure or termination through which vital forces were dispersed (Stross 1998). Likewise, other-than-human beings also required sustenance to maintain their animacy, just as humans must eat to live.

The properties and capacities of animate beings to transfer, transform, link, and concentrate vital forces were not necessarily inherent to individual beings or actions, but rather were created through assemblage processes that enchained diverse entities, including the complex ways in which humans engaged with the various animate aspects of their world. Therefore, much of human existence from disposing of refuse, making pottery, and working agricultural fields involved engagements with the sacred in the sense of these animating forces (Hutson and Stanton 2007). Yet certain acts, assemblages, entities, and phenomena had in their relationality more potent abilities than others to affect and manipulate vital forces. The activation of these capacities often involved ritualized practices (sensu Bell 1992) that included special materials, staging, and knowledge. For example, sacred bundles that assembled items including those with the ability to transfer vitality to other beings—what Zedeño (2009) terms index objects—activated and connected people to vital forces, including those of divinities and ancestors (Pauketat 2013). Thus, we might think of all aspects of human social life in prehispanic Mesoamerica as involving a continuum of degrees of sacrality and religious salience and will refer to the most powerful of these practices and beings somewhat arbitrarily as sacred and religious.

Given the importance of maize to human life in Mesoamerica, it is not surprising that flows of vitality in the growth of maize were of particular concern to people (e.g., Monaghan 1995; Vogt 1976). The origins of maize and the transferal of vitality involving people, rain, earth, clouds, wind, and other related phenomena was a fundamental component of creation narratives. In Mesoamerican creation stories, the current world was the result of a sacred covenant whereby people petitioned deities for agricultural fertility and prosperity in return for sacrificial offerings (Monaghan 1990, 1995; Tedlock 1996). Since humans literally consumed the gods as maize, earth, and rain, both sides of the exchange can be seen as forms of sacrifice through which vital forces were transferred. The sacred covenant therefore establishes sacrifice as cosmogenic and a fundamental condition of human existence involving relations of debt and merit between humans and the gods.

Generally speaking, in prehispanic Mesoamerica many things could be offered in sacrifice including the blood of humans and animals, human hearts, copal, maize dough, and incense although they varied in the degree to which vital forces were transferred (Freidel et al. 1993:204; López Luján 2005:35–37). As argued by Monaghan (1990), death itself was a sacrificial act through which people fed the gods (also see Becker 1993). By the Classic period (200–800 CE), if not before, the life force was especially potent in the blood of rulers, making their sacrifice perhaps the most effective means through which the gods could be petitioned (Schele and Miller 1986). Given that rulers could at times take on the essence of deities, it is not surprising that sacrifices were also made to them, including possibly payments of taxes and tribute (Monaghan 2009). Sacrificial offerings therefore recapitulated and activated a sacred covenant between humans and deities that was established as a fundamental aspect of the cosmic creation.

Although scholars have tended to project contact-period ontologies and religious practices into the deep past, several lines of evidence indicate that most aspects of these emerged during the Formative period (1900 BCE–200 CE). Archaeologists have noted a correspondence between people's increasing dependency on maize-based agriculture during the Formative and an increasing focus on effecting flows of vitality involving maize, rain, and earth through ritualized practices (Guernsey 2010; Taube 1996, 2000). Following Hutson and Stanton (2007), innovations in both farming and religion can be viewed as kinds of work designed to influence the circulation of vitality through maize, rain, earth, and people. For example, modern Mixtec farmers "speak of sacrifice as a stimulus to growth and generative of life, the way we might speak of fertilizer" (Monaghan 1995:213). As is visible in the growth of maize, it was possible for the plant to assemble and concentrate the vitality of rain and earth independent of the actions of humans. People therefore sought in various ways to insert themselves into these assemblages so as to affect flows of vitality to facilitate maize growth. Given the importance of maize to human life, those people who were able to most effectively petition the gods for fertility and prosperity gained political influence. Maize, rain, and earth, however—simultaneously as natural phenomena and as divinities—could be capricious and unpredictable in ways that confounded the work of people (Monaghan 2000).

In the next section, I consider archaeological evidence from the Middle Formative period Valley of Oaxaca that show how people's increasing dependence on and obligations to maize, rain, and earth came to transform life in ways that would eventually constitute Monte Albán as a city. While changes in farming practices were undoubtedly significant in Formative period social change, I suggest that the most transformative aspects of people's work involved the acts and animate entities that most powerfully affected flows of vitality in assemblages involving maize, earth, rain and, increasingly, people.

Assembling earth, rain, and maize at San José Mogote

Throughout Mesoamerica the reordering of relationships within assemblages involving people, earth, rain, maize, and related phenomena began in the latter half of the Early Formative period, particularly among the Gulf Coast Olmec, and became more prevalent by the Middle Formative (Taube 1996, 2000), although with a considerable degree of interregional variation. By the Middle Formative, manifestations of maize and rain deities were found in many regions (Taube 1996, 2000) as were quatrefoil motifs signifying the centering of the world through the merging of cosmic planes of sky, earth, and underworld—perhaps associated with caves, water, and the earth's interior (Gillespie 1993; Guernsey 2010). Human sacrifice became an important means for petitioning the gods of earth and rain for fertility (Grove 1999). The earliest examples of the mountain of creation and sustenance are found at this time as well (Grove 1999), which in Mesoamerican creation narratives was the place where the gods retrieved maize for the first humans. These sacred mountains, therefore, were liminal places of creation where sky, earth, underworld, and ancestors merged as well as sources of rain and fertility where sacrifices were performed (Freidel et al. 1993; Grove 1999; Markens 2013, 2014).

As in other parts of Mesoamerica, I argue that these changes can be seen in the archaeological record of the Oaxaca Valley. The reordering of assemblages involving maize, rain, earth, and people are especially evident on the summit of a natural hill that rises 15 meters above the site of San José Mogote located 12 kilometers north of Monte Albán. During the Middle Formative Rosario phase (700–500 BCE) people capped the hill with architecture, which Flannery and Marcus (2015) designate Mound 1 (Figure 4.2). Mound 1 was the focus of the reconfiguring of assemblages that would be instrumental in the founding of Monte Albán (Marcus and Flannery 1996).

Although Mound 1 was unoccupied at the beginning of the Rosario phase, the increasing influence on human lives of maize, rain, and earth might have drawn people to the prominent hilltop. Rather than a place renowned for connections to powerful humans, as it would be later in its history, Mound 1 may have been attractive because of its liminal placement where sky, rain, clouds, and earth converge.

FIGURE 4.2 Mound 1 at San José Mogote (photo by Arthur Joyce)

Source: From Joyce and Barber 2015: Figure 6 © The Wenner-Gren Foundation for Anthropological Research.

The hill rises into the sky, and rain and earth flow down its slopes during storms. That the community was drawn to Mound 1 by this confluence of materials is also indicated by the innovative acts carried out there during its initial reoccupation.

Shortly before the construction of the initial version of the platform on Mound 1 (Structure 19B), at least five pits were dug into the surface of the hill (Flannery and Marcus 2015:89–104). Each pit was filled with river sand and contained incomplete skeletal remains of one or two people covered with red pigment along with other items including ceramic vessels, a figurine, marine shell, jadeite beads, and a fish otolith. It is possible that these interments were sacred bundles relocated by the community to Mound 1. These features begin a pattern seen through the remainder of the Formative period, whereby offerings were emplaced prior to or at the onset of the construction of public buildings. The pits contained items that have been identified as index objects with animating properties identified in archaeological, ethnohistoric and ethnographic cases, including red pigment, marine shell, greenstone, and human bodies (Freidel et al. 1993; Mock 1998; Zedeño 2009). Many of these objects were exotic, non-local items with the capacity to index water (shells, fish). Greenstone had iconic associations with rain, maize, and fertility (Taube 2000); while red pigments may have been iconically associated with blood (Freidel et al. 1993:244). The vessels may have held food, blood or other items that fed the building, as recorded ethnographically in rites of animation in Mesoamerica (Stross 1998).

Following the construction of Structure 19B, a temple (Structure 28) was built on top of the platform (Flannery and Marcus 2015:141–155). Four large ceramic vessels were emplaced beneath each corner of the recessed floor of the temple,

72 Arthur A. Joyce

which invoked a quatrefoil with the floor of the temple as the center place and *axis mundi*. Sacrificial acts were likely carried out in the temple as indicated by the discovery of a broken obsidian bloodletter, a human clavicle with cut marks, and a quail bone found on the floor.

Offerings emplaced during the initial construction or remodeling of public buildings likely transferred vitality to earth deities, which for the first time animated the buildings, perhaps merging them with the hilltop, and making the hybrid entity a living, divine being and a new form of community member (Becker 1993; Mock 1998). The bundling of powerful objects with the remains of revered ancestors within a building constructed through communal labor doubtless drew together and territorialized the collective actions and histories of the families of San José Mogote. Sacrificial blood and perhaps earth offerings invoked the sacred covenant and petitioned the deities of earth and rain for fertility. Mound 1 therefore represents a reconfiguration of assemblages and affective fields whereby people and ancestors were brought into preexisting assemblages involving rain and earth. The agential cut enacted by this reconfiguration inserted people into the flows of vitality that converged on Mound 1, transforming human agency so as to allow people to more effectively meet their obligations to the divine and facilitate the growth of maize.

The prominence of the hill on which Mound 1 was constructed would have made the mound continuously visible to the entire community. The vertical separation of the plaza below and the public buildings above likely had the sensorial capacity to create distinctions between those given and those denied access to the restricted ceremonial spaces on the summit. The small number of objects in the offerings in Structures 19 and 28 further suggests that animating practices may have involved only a few participants. The emplacement into the earth of exotic items imported from distant places, which held animating power and invoked rain and maize, would have been moving experiences. Regardless of the original intentions of the builders of Mound 1, the organization of space enacted an agential cut that created the capacity, as yet virtual and unrealized, to enhance social distinctions involving status, political power, religious knowledge, and access to the divine.

In approximately 600 BCE, the Structure 28 temple on Mound 1 was burned to the ground (Marcus and Flannery 1996:129). The sudden destruction of Structure 28 could have triggered a crisis for the entire community by radically deterritorializing assemblages that were part of the community's relations with the earth, rain, and maize. Following the destruction of the temple, major changes are evident in the use of Mound 1. Rather than rebuilding the temple, an architecturally elaborate residence was constructed over the ruins (Flannery and Marcus 2005, 2015). Another large platform (Structure 14) was built north of the residence on which a new temple was constructed (Structure 37). The orientation of these buildings was changed from 8 degrees west of north to 3–6 degrees east of north, which would become the dominant one for public buildings at Monte Albán following its founding in ca. 500 BCE (Peeler and Winter 1992).

The residence consisted of a patio surrounded by at least three buildings with adobe and stone foundations (Flannery and Marcus 2015:417–443). Artifacts recovered from the residence comprised typical domestic tools and refuse along with items used in ceremonies, including figurines, a ceramic whistle, three fragments of obsidian bloodletters, and a ceramic anthropomorphic effigy vessel (Marcus and Flannery 1996:131–133). The effigy vessel is one of the earliest examples of a type of brazier used throughout the remainder of the prehispanic era to burn incense as an offering to divinities. A young woman buried beneath a wall at the time of the construction of the building has been interpreted by Flannery and Marcus as a possible offering (2005:426).

The residence contained the region's first formal stone masonry tombs (Marcus and Flannery 1996:133), demonstrating that certain people were now buried in special locations that differentiated them from non-tomb interments. The most elaborate, located beneath the patio, was Tomb 10, a two-chambered tomb whose walls and floor had been coated with plaster. If a version of the sacred covenant was part of Middle Formative religion, which seems likely (Joyce 2000; Taube 1996), then people interred in tombs would not have sacrificed their bodies at death in the same way as people buried in simple graves. Ancestors buried in tombs could be directly consulted by their living descendants through tomb reopening ceremonies (Urcid 2005:34–40), thus preventing their deterritorialization from the assemblage centered on Mound 1. Both the initial interment of the dead and later tomb ceremonies involving the remains of ancestors would have been intensely affective and sensorial experiences likely involving limited numbers of participants in the cramped, humid setting of the tomb in the presence of human remains in different states of decay. Tombs contained and stabilized the bones of the ancestors, making them more durable and creating memory and history through discursive memories of ancestors, whether real or fictive, and through the activation of habit memories in the performance of tomb rituals.

Another important discovery from Mound 1 was Monument 3 (Figure 4.3), located in a corridor between Structures 14 and 19 (Marcus and Flannery 1996:129–130). Monument 3 depicts a naked man with eyes closed and with the trilobe heart glyph on his chest with blood emanating from the heart. The individual's calendrical name or the name of his captor is also shown. The age of the monument has been highly contested (e.g., Cahn and Winter 1993), although Flannery and Marcus (2015:177–192) provide detailed stratigraphic and radiocarbon evidence that would seem to demonstrate the Rosario phase age of the monument. Monument 3 therefore represents the earliest evidence for human sacrifice, writing, and calendrics in Oaxaca. Human sacrifice was a new and more dramatic means of invoking the sacred covenant and transferring vital forces to petition the earth and rain for fertility and prosperity (Joyce 2000; Monaghan 1990; Tedlock 1996; Urcid 2011a). It was undoubtedly an emotional experience for participants: the sensorial impact of death, the hemorrhaging of blood, the summoning of deities. Human sacrifice thus actualized multiple temporalities, including the cosmic creation as well as previous acts of sacrifice and associated experiences that were recalled mnemonically by participants.

The evidence from Mound 1 at San José Mogote indicates a convergence and a fundamental reconfiguring of relationships in assemblages involving people, rain,

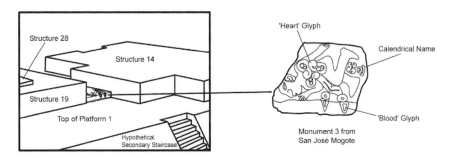

FIGURE 4.3 Idealized reconstruction of Rosario phase buildings and Monument 3 on Mound 1 at San José Mogote

Source: After Urcid 2005: Figure 1.3; redrawn with permission from Javier Urcid.

earth, maize, and animate beings. Animate entities assembled on Mound 1, including its buildings, the resident family, ancestors, and perhaps objects like bloodletters and effigy vessels, were now repositioned as central to relations between people and divinities. The change in building orientation is significant in that in prehispanic Mesoamerica there was a close association between site orientations and layouts, the movement of celestial bodies/deities, and conceptions of time. The earliest evidence for the use of the 260-day ritual calendar suggests that time and relations with divinities were now cyclical and that the animate beings assembled on Mound 1 likely were pivotal players in calendrical ceremonies through which multitemporal fields were assembled. Human sacrifice, autosacrifice, animating offerings, and the burning of incense made Mound 1 a place of sacrifice where cosmic planes were merged and obligations to divinities were met (Freidel et al. 1993; Joyce 2019; López Austin 1988, 1989; Monaghan 2009). Mound 1, therefore, was a liminality that folded together its human and other-than human residents with the sky, clouds, and rain above and the earth, ancestors, and offerings interred within its core, making it an *axis mundi* where the cosmic planes of earth, sky, and underworld converged. Designs on a ceramic vessel recovered as an offering in a Rosario phase adobe tomb in Mound 1 references this convergence, including depictions of a quatrefoil and possibly vegetation, perhaps maize (Javier Urcid, personal communication 2018). Sacrificial practices invoked the sacred covenant and the cosmic creation, making Mound 1 a place of creation. This inference is strongly supported by an offering beneath the floor of a later, Nisa phase (100 BCE–200 CE) temple on Mound 1, which consisted of a tableau of anthropomorphic effigy vessels depicting the story of the Rain God, assisted by lesser attendants from the four quarters of the world, freeing maize from the mountain of creation and sustenance to feed humanity (Urcid 2009). Through the coming together and intra-actions of rain, earth, maize, humans, animate buildings, ancestors, and so forth, Mound 1 was transformed into a mountain of creation and sustenance. The agential cut of these new assemblages enabled people to more effectively do the work needed to meet their obligations to powerful divinities—earth and rain—so as to insure the growth of maize and the broader well-being of humanity.

These assemblages also affected relations among people. For the first time in Oaxaca an agential cut was enacted that differentiated the occupants of Mound 1 from the rest of the community, particularly in terms of their enhanced ability to engage with powerful divinities. The offerings suggest that the public buildings were now living, divine beings and community members, with the human residents of Mound 1 likely positioned as caretakers of these buildings and with primary access to them. Human sacrifice, interment in tombs, and the close association of residences and powerful animate buildings, evident for the first time on Mound 1, all became means through which a separate noble identity was instantiated for the remainder of the prehispanic era (Joyce 2010). Social distinction was thus created not only episodically during public ceremonies, as it had been in earlier eras, but instead continuously through the quotidian practices of dwelling. This *new centrality* in assemblages through which vitality was transferred to meet divine obligations and to petition deities for fertility and prosperity would have been a source of political as well as spiritual power for the family living on Mound 1, which probably included the Oaxaca Valley's first hereditary rulers. These are the first indications that through the affordances of special religious implements, buildings, spaces, landscapes, and climatic phenomena, rulers and their families were becoming mediators between people and the powerful divinities that largely controlled maize growth. This partitioning of relationships with the divine therefore began to stratify and stabilize social distinctions (Pauketat Chapter 1). Evidence from succeeding centuries suggests, however, that earlier forms of communal authority and access to the divine persisted in creating lines of flight that would eventually be actualized centuries later at Monte Albán (Joyce and Barber 2015).

Mound 1 can therefore be considered a kind of infrastructure through which both social differences and cosmic planes were stratified and mediated (sensu Deleuze and Guattari 1987:502–505). Evidence for a similar stratification can be seen at contemporaneous sites elsewhere in Mesoamerica, including La Venta and Chalcatzingo (Grove 1999). In the Valley of Oaxaca, prominent public buildings continued to act as sacred mountains through the remainder of the prehispanic era (Markens 2013, 2014) as they were in other parts of Mesoamerica (López Austin and López Luján 2009).

The transubstantiation of a prominent hill into an animate being that assembled other powerful animate entities, which together enacted cosmogenic ceremonies through which deities were petitioned for fertility and well-being, created the region's first mountain of creation and sustenance. Yet towering above Mound 1, only 12 kilometers to the south, and easily visible in the distance, loomed an even more impressive mountaintop with assemblage-conversion capacities that would soon supplant Mound 1 as the focal point for transformations in relations between people and the divine. This mountain is known today as Monte Albán (Figure 4.4).

FIGURE 4.4 View of Mound 1 at San José Mogote with Monte Albán in the background (photo by Arthur Joyce)

Source: From Joyce and Barber 2015: Figure A14.

Monte Albán as a mountain of creation and sustenance

Monte Albán was founded in ca. 500 BCE by people from San José Mogote and nearby communities (Marcus and Flannery 1996). The site is located on several hills in the center of the Oaxaca Valley that rise as much as 375 meters above the valley floor (Figure 4.5). During the first several centuries, people from nearby areas were drawn to Monte Albán, and the site grew into the region's largest community, reaching 442 hectares, with an estimated population of 10–20,000 by the Late Formative Pe phase (300–100 BCE), with most people residing on hillslope terraces. The archaeological evidence shows that the founding and initial development of Monte Albán involved strong continuities in the assemblages involving people, earth, rain, and maize that came together during the Rosario phase at San José Mogote. The assemblages that coalesced on Mound 1 at San José Mogote simultaneously bundled together many of these forces and affects at Monte Albán as a haecceity and composition of desire (sensu Deleuze and Guattari 1987:399–400), soon beckoning people and other animate beings to converge on the cloud-swept mountaintop through its newly emergent virtual capacities. As a series of mountains towering over the center of the Oaxaca Valley, Monte Albán included many key elements of these assemblages even before the arrival of people, elements such

FIGURE 4.5 Aerial view of Monte Albán with the Main Plaza circled (photo by Arthur Joyce)

as the confluence of earth, sky, clouds, wind and rain as well as Monte Albán's centrality within the valley and between the celestial realm, earth and underworld. Water not only fell from the sky as rain, but emerged from the underworld as springs (Tricarico 2015). Monte Albán may already have been a more prominent and powerful mountain of creation and sustenance, *axis mundi*, and proto-urban conglomerate of powerful sacred substances and affects, including deities and divine forces, which drew people to it. Although Mound 1 at San José Mogote acted as a potent assemblage converter for Monte Albán, in the process the former was simultaneously deterritorialized and the site largely abandoned for a time (Flannery and Marcus 2005, 2015).

The evidence also suggests that relations among animate entities continued to be negotiated and transformed at Monte Albán following the arrival of people. A major aspect of these negotiations involved the working out of incongruities among assemblages centered on differently positioned human actors regarding access to the divine and the political influence such access conferred (Joyce 2010). These tensions likely began at San José Mogote with the emergence of hereditary rulers residing on Mound 1, and culminated in conflict at the end of the Formative period at Monte Albán.

As at San José Mogote, the demands of the earth and rain required people to find ways to petition deities so as to transfer vitality to maize, and this involved the construction and animation of buildings and spaces that facilitated people's intra-actions with the divine through various kinds of ritualized acts. One of the earliest activities at Monte Albán was construction of a ceremonial precinct focused on a

FIGURE 4.6 Panorama of the Main Plaza of Monte Albán (photo by Sarah Barber)
Source: From Joyce and Barber 2015: Figure A13, used with permission.

large, public plaza and surrounded by animate buildings (Figure 4.6). The initial version of the Main Plaza, dating to the Danibaan (500–300 BCE) and Pe phases, consisted of the plaza along with the western row of buildings and much of the eastern half of the enormous North Platform (Winter 2001:284–286). The construction of the Main Plaza precinct was a massive project that far exceeded anything at San José Mogote and included earth offerings to animate the buildings (Joyce 2019). Most offerings were modest in scale, suggesting restricted ceremonies similar to those at San José Mogote. Several human interments within early public buildings may also have been offerings analogous to the secondary burials beneath Structure 19B at San José Mogote.

Evidence from the Main Plaza suggests the increasing territorialization of assemblages involving people, rain, earth, ancestors, and associated deities including the merging of the essence of certain humans and gods. Beginning with the Danibaan phase, images of deities changed from stylized gods represented on ceramic designs (Blomster 2010; Taube 1996) to beings that were more clearly related to important deities documented for later periods (Urcid 2001). The later Formative period at Monte Albán saw the first occurrence of effigy vessels depicting the Rain Deity as well as the God of Ancestors, often referred to as the Old God, along with the Wide-Billed Bird, which symbolized the Zapotec deity *Pitáo Cozáana*, the Creator God or Sun God (Urcid 2005:54). Taube (2004:177) suggests that this deity may be derived from the Olmec, as was the Zapotec Rain Deity, known as *Cociyo*. Evidence from imagery and the recovery of stone masks indicates that by this time the wearing of Rain Deity masks in ritualized settings could actualize the abilities of certain humans to merge with the essence of the god as occurred in later periods. Similarly, the first few centuries of Monte Albán also saw the earliest evidence for a form of *nahualism* known as *xicani* (Urcid 2001:297), which involves the temporary merging of a human with the essence of an animal or celestial phenomenon (Hermann Lejarazu 2009). X*icani* had the ability to communicate with ancestors and perform human sacrifice and were thus rainmakers as well (Hermann Lejarazu 2009). Ritual specialists who organized and led ceremonies on the plaza were likely equated with important actors in creation narratives, especially the Rain Deity (Sellen 2002).

Much of our understanding of the practices through which people, gods, and ancestors intra-acted within assembles at Monte Albán comes from two remarkable programs of architectural sculpture found in the southern end of the plaza. The first was located in Building L-sub, which contained more than 300 carved orthostats often referred to as the *danzantes*. Most of the orthostats were removed from Building L-sub when it was partially dismantled around 250 CE (Urcid 2011a). Although traditionally interpreted as victims of human sacrifice, Urcid (2011a) has reinterpreted the program as an age-graded organization, perhaps a warrior sodality, carrying out autosacrifical rituals to invoke ancestors as oracular conduits, possibly in preparation for battle. Urcid's approach is based on meticulous research on the variability in the imagery, the life histories of the buildings in which they were set, comparative studies of image and text programs elsewhere in Mesoamerica, and largely hypothetical reconstructions of how the carved stones were originally arranged based on their form (e.g., corner stones) and on projections from in situ examples. Through identification of different types of figures depicted on vertical orthostats, he suggests that the stones were arranged so as to display a four-tiered ranking system based on age and achieved status (Figure 4.7). Urcid hypothesizes

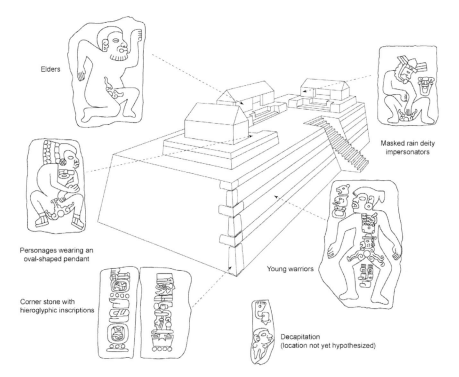

FIGURE 4.7 Hypothetical reconstruction of Building L-sub at Monte Albán representing an age-graded organization shown performing autosacrifice (drawing by Elbis Domínguez Covarrubias)

Source: After Urcid and Joyce 2014: Figure 9.2, used with permission.

FIGURE 4.8 Photograph of in-situ orthostats from Building L-sub with horizontal figures depicting ancestors and vertical ones depicting young adults performing autosacrifice (photo by Arthur Joyce)

Source: From Joyce and Barber 2015: Figure A3.

that higher-status individuals, including elders and people manifesting the Rain God, were displayed on the walls of the superstructures, with lower status ones on the facade of the platform below. All of the vertical figures are shown bleeding from their groins. Smaller, horizontal orthostats placed above the vertical slabs are interpreted as ancestors based on pan-Mesoamerican conventions (Figure 4.8). The cornerstones of the program contained short hieroglyphic texts that refer to at least two rulers, their enthronements, and the defeat and decapitation of an enemy. Human sacrifice is also represented by four depictions of decapitated heads.

The second iconographic program consists of approximately fifty finely incised slabs (Figure 4.9a) whose original location is not precisely known, although most were later reset in Building J (Urcid and Joyce 2014). Although long interpreted as depictions of places conquered by Monte Albán, recent analyses show that the slabs depict only a single place, likely a sector of Monte Albán itself (Carter 2017; Urcid and Joyce 2014). Rather than referring to the names of particular places, Urcid and Joyce (2014) argue that the sign inscribed above the toponym refers to the personal name of the individual represented by the inverted head below the toponym. We agree that the inverted heads depict deceased individuals, but since they are identified with only a single place, probably Monte Albán, we interpret them as revered ancestors, rather than sacrificed enemies. The projection of

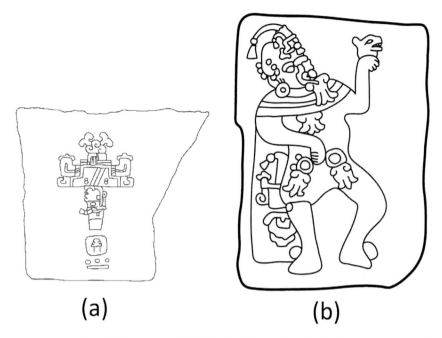

FIGURE 4.9 Carved slabs reset in Building J: (a) Example of a slab depicting a revered ancestor (drawing by Elbis Domínguez Covarrubias; after Urcid and Joyce 2014: Figure 9.7, used with permission); (b) Monument J-41 (after Joyce 2010: Figure 5.6d; redrawn with permission from Javier Urcid)

the heads beneath the toponym could reference the descent of the dead into the underworld and might be a further reference to sacrifice, if all forms of death were considered forms of sacrifice (Monaghan 1990, 2009). A possible cornerstone from the program (Monument J-41) depicts the only portrait of a ruler known for this period (Figure 4.9b). He is shown performing autosacrifice and human sacrifice through decapitation, while manifesting the Rain Deity.

In contrast to the southern end of the plaza, a frieze on the North Platform included graphic references to aquatic themes, including shells, bands of flowing water, and rain (Urcid 1994:64–65). Although the upper section of the frieze was destroyed in antiquity, the remaining portion includes what Acosta (1965:816) described as serpentine imagery, which may represent *Cociyo*. The frieze covered the sides of what may have been a sunken court, which in ancient Mesoamerica was equated with caves that merged cosmic planes, allowing for communication with divinities (Freidel et al. 1993:350–355). The juxtaposition of mountains, caves, and water are defining features of the mountain of creation and sustenance, viewed as the source of rain and fertility for many Native Americans today as it was in the prehispanic era (Barabas 2006; López Austin y López Luján 2009; Markens 2014).

The Main Plaza and its animate buildings and spaces can be seen as forms of infrastructure enacting agential cuts that extended and further stratified the kinds of assemblages and agencies first configured at Rosario-phase San José Mogote and elsewhere in Mesoamerica. As a mountain of creation and sustenance the Main Plaza was an *axis mundi* that stratified and mediated the cosmic planes of earth, sky, and underworld. The spatial arrangement of architecture, iconography, and text on the Main Plaza may have resembled and perhaps reassembled ceremonial centers at other Mesoamerican cities (Grove 1999), whereby the cosmos was rotated onto the surface of the site such that north represented the celestial realm and south the place of the dead in the underworld (Joyce 2000). Regardless of the meaning of its spatial layout, the Main Plaza bundled animate entities associated with the earth (living humans, plants, animals, and animate buildings), the underworld (ancestors, earth offerings, sacrificial victims, and the God of Ancestors), and the celestial realm (rain, clouds, sky, mist, and the Rain Deity). Practices on the plaza created sensorial experiences with all three of these cosmic strata. Digging beneath the earth in the construction of buildings and the emplacement of offerings invoked the underworld. The mountaintop on which the Main Plaza was built rose into the sky, making both celestial bodies and the valley below more visible. During the rainy season Monte Albán is often enveloped in clouds, making it literally a rain place. Some buildings may have been aligned with celestial bodies, tracking the cycles of their movements and therefore sacred time (Sprajc 2018).

Cosmic strata were mediated through acts afforded by the Main Plaza. Clouds, rain, fog, and earth came together on the mountaintop, transferring vitality to maize. In return, cosmogenic ceremonies including human and autosacrifice assembled animate entities, including people, buildings, and bloodletters that transferred vitality back to the earth and rain to fulfill human obligations as established in the sacred covenant and to petition deities once again. The resulting sustenance brought to earth was experienced in the house gardens grown on residential terraces in the city, in the agricultural fields visible in the valley below, and in the food consumed on a daily basis and during ritual feasts, perhaps accompanied by sacrifices that returned vitality to the gods. Likewise, autosacrifice invoked powerful ancestors from the underworld who assisted people in worldly matters. The Main Plaza also gathered cyclical notions of time and history actualized in the invocation of the sacred covenant and the cosmic creation as well as in notions of cyclical death and rebirth instantiated in sacrifice, rainfall, the growth of maize, animating practices, ancestor veneration, and in observations of the movement of celestial bodies.

The scaling up of assemblages centered on the Main Plaza also enacted an agential cut that stratified people and things in the Valley of Oaxaca according to whether or not they were incorporated within the agencies and affective fields extending from Monte Albán. The plaza was an arena where earth, rain, maize, deities, ancestors, and thousands of people could have participated in public ceremonies. Settlement pattern data indicate that by the Pe phase people were drawn not only to Monte Albán, but also to nearby settlements (Kowalewski et al. 1989:123). Archaeological research at San José Mogote and Tomaltepec has identified similarities to Monte Albán in deities, architecture, and the layout of public buildings and elaborate residences (Flannery and Marcus 2015; Whalen 1988).

These data suggest that assemblages centered on Monte Albán extended to and created affective relationships with communities in this part of the valley. Nearby communities were also involved in trade and exchange with Monte Albán (Minc et al. 2016) and may have provided agricultural surpluses to the city as a form of taxation, and perhaps sacrifice (Kowalewski et al. 1989:123–126). Presumably, in return, people from those communities gained access to the mountain of creation and sustenance and the fertility it conferred. At a greater distance at the sites of El Mogote, El Palenque, and Dainzú, however, archaeologists have found evidence of differences in public architecture and conflict with Monte Albán (Redmond and Spencer 2008; Urcid 2014). Affective fields were therefore extended beyond Monte Albán in ways that constituted a community of people, places, and other animate and inanimate entities incorporated within the assemblages centered on the Main Plaza.

The Main Plaza as a liminal place where sky, earth, and underworld converged increasingly stratified and spatialized people according to access to the divine, to wealth, and to political power. Although the Main Plaza proper was an inclusive arena, ceremonies carried out in restricted spaces, such as on platform temples, enacted agential cuts that stratified people according to whether or not they had access to these spaces, the rituals carried out within them, and the divinities contacted through them. Such a stratification of people through space and cere- mony can be seen in Urcid's (2011a) reconstruction of the imagery on Building L-sub. Likewise, during the Danibaan and Pe phases, the most elaborate residences at Monte Albán tended to cluster around the North Platform (Joyce 2000:84), suggesting an association of wealthier and more powerful people with the celestial realm and the Rain God. Similarly, effigy vessels and urns depicting the Rain God, and a variety of zoomorphic vessels representing animals associated with water (e.g., ducks, conchs, frogs, and toads) are commonly found in tombs and burials with elaborate offerings (Caso et al. 1967).

Although status differentiation increased, the boundaries between nobles and prominent commoners appear to have been somewhat blurred, especially in terms of relationships with divinities as well as the political influence that these relationships conferred (Joyce 2019; Urcid and Joyce 2014). Only rulers were clearly associated with human sacrifice, but prominent commoners were also shown performing autosacrifice and invoking ancestors (Urcid 2011a). If the people wearing Rain God masks on the imagery from Building L-sub were non-nobles, as argued by Urcid (2011a), then influential commoners, nobles, and rulers were able to embody the deity. Likewise, while the most elaborate stone masonry tombs were restricted to the nobility, adobe tombs have been excavated in the residences of commoners (Martínez López et al. 2014), indicating that prominent commoners and not just nobles, were interred in ways that facilitated communication with the dead. The hieroglyphic inscriptions and imagery referring to the relationships of rulers with divinities are focused on named personages, while the image and text program of Building L-sub indicates a more communal involvement with the divine. The data therefore suggest a degree of incongruity, tension and perhaps competition between the overlapping assemblages of divinities involving rulers and those involving communal organizations of non-nobles, thereby creating deterritorializing forces. The settings in which hereditary rulers and communal organizations negotiated and potentially contested relations with the divine and the political authority they conferred probably included public rituals, such as communication with ancestors, autosacrifice, and perhaps ritual preparations for battle as well as more restricted rituals within tombs along with access to special ceremonial roles like rainmakers and diviners. I suspect that these contrasting, but overlapping, human-focused assemblages first emerged at Rosario phase San José Mogote via the remarkable coming together of earth, rain, maize, and bodies.

Appropriating the divine, reconfiguring the political

Until the Terminal Formative Nisa phase, the data suggest that the programs of imagery and text on the Main Plaza helped to keep at bay tensions between assemblages involving divinities and rulers and those involving divinities and communal organizations of non-nobles by downplaying the actions of rulers, while foregrounding communal involvement with divinities (Joyce 2010; Joyce and Barber 2015). By the Nisa phase, however, the evidence suggests that nobles were becoming more prominent relative to communal organizations in the assemblages through which obligations to divinities were met in return for human sustenance; this would have been a source of great political power, but may have exacerbated social tensions and deterritorializing forces (Joyce 2010). The first high-status houses built directly on the plaza and on the North Platform date to this time and would have strengthened elite oversight of the ceremonial center. Evidence indicates that nobles were increasingly monopolizing animating practices involving the transferal of vitality to divinities (Joyce 2019). Although modest offerings of a few ceramic vessels have been found in public buildings at this time, most offerings included materials that were probably beyond the reach of commoners. During the Nisa phase, animating offerings became more elaborate and included exotic and highly valued objects made from jade, marine shell, and turquoise, and pottery along with mosaic masks, effigy vessels, and human skeletons that may be the remains of sacrificial victims. One remarkable offering included two whale ribs that had been notched to make them into musical instruments (Caso et al. 1967:103–105). Most of the offerings found in public buildings were in highly restricted locations that limited the number of participants, although others may have been able to observe from a distance. Such a spatial separation probably further stratified social distinctions related to status and access to the divine. No mere consequence of anthropocentric politics, this new power emerged precisely through the intersection of humans with the material capacities of the mountain, its animate buildings, and the increasingly exotic offerings through which vitality was transferred to the divine.

The most elaborate offering was Burial XIV-10 found on a stone pavement associated with a cistern on the eastern side of the Main Plaza (Acosta 1949). It contained the remains of two adult males, two adult females and a sub-adult, who were likely sacrificial victims. The skeletons were accompanied by ceramic vessels and ornaments of jade, marine shell, and pearl. The males were interred wearing stone mosaic pectorals, including an elaborate jade bat mask with eyes and teeth of marine shell. Near the burials were five ceramic boxes incised with the glyph for "water" and images of maize sprouts (Urcid 2011b). The offering was emplaced at the time of the closure of the cistern, suggesting it may have been associated with the termination of the building and the release of vitality. Near the cistern was evidence for ritual feasting, including ovens that contained hundreds of small bowls and extensive evidence of burning. The cistern offering was unusual in that it was located in a place that would have allowed for large audiences to participate. The evidence suggests that this offering was dramatic and impressive in scale, involving the interment of prominent people and prestige goods, feasting, and perhaps human sacrifice. Given its scale and elaboration, the ceremony was likely sponsored by the rulers of Monte Albán.

Materials within Nisa-phase offerings referenced a relatively restricted set of themes (Joyce 2019), including humans merging with deities (deity masks), sacrifice/ancestors (human and animal remains, red pigment), water/rain (shell, greenstone, whale bone), maize and fertility (greenstone, flower ornaments), and perhaps food and drink (ceramic vessels and possibly their contents). Taken together, these materials invoke the sacred covenant whereby humans offer sacrifices to deities in return for rain, maize, and ultimately sustenance. In many cases, the offerings assembled objects that referenced sacrifice with others that referenced fertility, such as greenstone and shell accompanying human bodies or ceramic vessels covered with red pigment. As material manifestations of the sacred covenant, the objects bundled within the offerings likely activated a capacity to transfer vitality to animate buildings, deities, or both.

Of course, the rulers of Monte Albán mobilized human and material resources to their advantage in ways that extended the affective fields centered on the Main Plaza. The conquest of El Palenque suggests that Monte Albán's rulers used coercion to gain influence over some communities (Redmond and Spencer 2006), although Dainzú and other sites probably remained independent (Sherman 2005; Urcid 2014). Captives taken in warfare afforded rulers with a powerful means through which to petition deities through the transference of vitality via human sacrifice. Monte Albán's nobility also had the wealth and connections to increasingly control social valuables such as jade and elaborate pottery through which debts and obligations could be extended to other communities. Many of these social valuables were likely also animate beings that required special treatment in their production, and which afforded their users with enhanced abilities to connect with the divine.

The transformations in the assemblages centered on the Main Plaza during the Nisa phase further territorialized those assemblages involving hereditary rulers and divinities, while creating deterritorializing forces involving communal organizations (Joyce 2010). By the end of the Terminal Formative, tensions between communal and noble relations with the divine and the broader influence that they provided may have

86 Arthur A. Joyce

erupted in ways that reconfigured these assemblages enacting another sort of agential cut—a political upheaval at Monte Albán. At this time, both of the major iconographic programs on the Main Plaza were dismantled, and some monuments were defaced and buried under new buildings. Since these iconographic programs defined corporate groups, their dismantling and destruction may indicate the suppression of communal religious practices and authority. A temple on the North Platform was also burned (Winter 1994:15) and a wall for defense and/or monitoring of access was built around parts of the site (Blanton 1978). That violence was aimed at the buildings and images which constrained elite authority shows that power was not simply a human–human relationship, but instead emerged from a complex assemblage that included many other-than-human entities as well as people. Violence may also have been directed toward people as suggested by a structure on the northwest corner of the Main Plaza that could have served as a control point limiting access. The recovery of 27 projectile points in this building suggests that coercive force may have been involved (Martínez López and Markens 2004). By the Early Classic period most powerful forms of engagement with divinities were focused on the nobility such that social differentiation became even more rigidly stratified (Joyce 2010).

Conclusions

In this chapter, I have argued that the founding and early history of Monte Albán involved the coalescence of assemblages constituted through a complex set of ontological entanglements. Although these assemblages were first evident in the dramatic changes that occurred on Mound 1 at San José Mogote, they were more fully actualized following the founding of Monte Albán. Even before its founding, Monte Albán may have already been a sacred mountain, *axis mundi*, and proto-urban conglomerate of powerful animate beings and affects awaiting only human intervention to fully crystalize urbanity into a city fundamentally differentiated from other communities in the valley. After the arrival of humans, Monte Albán's focal position in the assemblages through which obligations to the earth and rain were repaid through sacrifice, became even more evident. Through the construction and animation of buildings and spaces, the Main Plaza became a kind of infrastructure that further stratified and mediated the layered relational fields of sky, earth, and underworld as well as those involving nobles and commoners. Although humans were clearly central to the agencies through which Monte Albán was constituted as a mountain of creation and sustenance, so were rain, earth, maize, deities, masks, buildings, bloodletters, and certainly the mountain itself which, as a liminal place, drew together and transformed relations among people and a multitude of other-than-human entities. The mountaintop, and particularly its Main Plaza, gathered new beings, including the Rain Deity, animate buildings, *nahuales*, and *xicani*, and transformed established entities such as humans, ancestors, rain, and earth. The acts through which these beings were assembled and through which they exchanged vitality included human and auto-sacrifice as well as rainfall, ancestor veneration, divination, feasting, animating offerings, *nahualism*, and the growth, harvesting, and consumption of maize.

As a mountain of creation and sustenance, Monte Albán was crucial to the fertility of maize and therefore to human life. In farm fields on the slopes of the mountain or in the valley below, the transferal of vitality visible in the growth of maize was often beyond people's control as crops could fail due to the vagaries of weather, pests, and disease. In their fields below the sacred mountain, farmers may have had some abilities to repay debts to the divine through the consumption of their bodies by the earth in death or through other sacrificial acts (Monaghan 1995, 2009). As a mountain of creation and sustenance, however, Monte Albán enabled people to more powerfully influence flows of vitality that were crucial to the growth of maize because of the close proximity of sky, clouds, earth, rain, and maize. The Main Plaza was a place of powerfully affective, multi-sensorial, and multi-temporal experiences involving rain, clouds, and mist; blood spilled in sacrifice to summon deities and ancestors; powerful substances such as jade offered to the earth; deity masks that merged humans and gods; and food consumed in feasting. From the mountaintop, participants, at least during the rainy season, could directly view the results of their entreaties to the gods as Monte Albán was engulfed in clouds or as rainstorms could be seen moving across the valley below. In the Zapotec world, the result was sustenance and life through the growing and harvesting of maize and other crops, making urbanization at Monte Albán as much an economic as a religious act. These economic effects may have been further amplified if the large populations drawn to the sacred mountain encouraged economies of scale with further economic consequences such as increases in craft specialization and the emergence of markets (Ortman et al. 2015).

The early years of Monte Albán not only involved changing relations between humans and divinities, but also the increasing stratification of social distinctions surrounding commoners and nobles. Urbanity at Monte Albán was, therefore, also a profoundly political-assemblage process. Ceremonies on the plaza valorized and legitimated the authority of ritual sponsors and religious specialists. Certain ceremonies such as those associated with the termination of the cistern were inclusive in bringing a large audience together, while also exclusive in differentiating participants based on variable capacities to communicate with the divine. In contrast, animating and sacrificial ceremonies in more restricted settings were primarily affective in constituting social distinctions related to status and access to the divine. Ritualized acts enhanced the ability of nobles to create debts and obligations, extract tribute in the form of goods and labor, and acquire exotic items by establishing relationships with prominent people from distant places and so contributed to political power.

The performance of these ceremonies on a mountain of creation and sustenance objectified, fixed, and regulated the sensorial and mnemonic assemblages that were brought together here, contributing to the creation of a political order, although one that was not unquestioned. Groups of non-nobles, such as the possible sodality depicted in the iconographic program of Building L-sub, shared with nobles certain abilities to engage with the divine including merging with the Rain Deity and communicating with ancestors. The boundaries between nobles and commoners were therefore less distinct than they were in later periods. This blurring of boundaries is

88 Arthur A. Joyce

borne out by continuities in mortuary practices and access to social valuables during the Danibaan and Pe phases (Joyce 2010:142–144; Martínez López et al. 2014). The assemblages centered on the Main Plaza during the Nisa phase changed hereditary rulers and communal organizations, alike. The political upheaval enacted an agential cut creating a much greater separation between the agencies of nobles and those of commoners and included attempts to erase memories of powerful corporate groups led by prominent commoners along with the increasing appropriation of the Main Plaza by rulers.

The layered relational fields centered on the Main Plaza extended and transformed spatialities throughout the valley and beyond in ways that constituted Monte Albán as an alterity (see Bauer, Chapter 8), a stratum with distinct identities and ways of being. There were limits, however, to the process. Assemblages focused on the Main Plaza as a mountain of creation and sustenance were most powerfully affective through their proximity to rain and clouds, the impressive monumentality and cosmic symbolism of the plaza as well as the drama of the ceremonies carried out there. Without direct participation, the affective power of the assemblages centered on the Main Plaza appears to have been diffuse and rapidly deterritorialized with distance, particularly for people in communities such as El Palenque and Daínzu that were periodically in conflict with Monte Albán. Yet Monte Albán was a powerful assemblage converter that appears to have triggered diffuse, but far-reaching ripples through the later Formative Oaxacan Highlands as numerous hilltop urban centers likely inspired by Monte Albán rapidly coalesced (Joyce 2010).

Monte Albán was therefore a vibrant urbanity whose infrastructure and acts enacted agential cuts that both stratified and mediated social differences and cosmic planes that included people, earth, rain, maize, deities, ancestors, and other animate beings over space and through time. It was a place of affective experience involving engagements with the divine through human sacrifice, rainfall, the growth and consumption of maize, the summoning of ancestors, and acts that brought buildings to life or merged human and deity. Such experiences defined and were defined by Monte Albán, a mountaintop rising above the Valley of Oaxaca whose distinctive atmosphere—an alterity of ancestors, earth, rain, clouds, wind, springs, and celestial bodies—was more directly and intensely experienced relative to other places in the valley. As a dense convergence of vital forces, the beings that they animated, and the acts through which these forces were transferred and transformed, Monte Albán constituted a new urban ontology that was simultaneously religious, political, economic, and social; artificially separable through a Cartesian lens, but for the Zapotec a "roiling maelstrom of affect" (Thrift 2008:171), an urban haecceity distinct from social life elsewhere in the valley and beyond: a city.

Acknowledgments

I would like to thank the Historical Society of Boston, particularly Don Yerxa, and the John Templeton Foundation for funding that supported the writing of this chapter. I thank Tim Pauketat and Susan Alt for inviting me to participate in the School for Advanced Research and Amerind seminars on which the present book is based, along with my fellow seminar participants. I also appreciate the input of Stacy Barber, Ollie Harris, Sarah Kurnick, Robert Markens, Tim Pauketat, Ed Swenson, Javier Urcid, and Tim Webmoor.

References

Acosta, Jorge R. 1949 El pectoral de jade de Monte Albán. *Anales del Instituto Nacional de Antropología e Historia* 3:17–25.

——— 1965 Preclassic and Classic Architecture of Oaxaca. In *Handbook of Middle American Indians*, vol. 3, edited by Robert Wauchope, pp. 814–848. University of Texas Press, Austin.

Barabas, Alicia M. 2006 *Dones, dueños y santos: Ensayo sobre religiones en Oaxaca*. Consejo Nacional para la Cultura y las Artes, el Instituto Nacional de Antropología e Historia y Miguel Ángel Porrúa, Mexico City.

Barad, Karen 2007 *Meeting the Universe Halfway*. Duke University Press, Durham and London.

Barber, Sarah B., and Mireya Olvera Sánchez 2012 A Divine Wind: The Arts of Death and Music in Terminal Formative Oaxaca. *Ancient Mesoamerica* 23(1):9–24.

Becker, Marshall J. 1993 Earth Offering Among the Classic Period Lowland Maya: Burials and Caches as Ritual Deposits. In *Perspectivas antropológicas en el mundo Maya*, vol. 2, edited by María Josefa Iglesias Ponce de León and Francesc Ligorred Perramon, pp. 45–74. Publicaciones de la S.E.E.M., Barcelona.

Bell, Catherine 1992 *Ritual Theory, Ritual Practice*. Oxford Press, New York.

Bennett, Jane 2010 *Vibrant Matter: A Political Ecology of Things*. Duke University Press, Durham, NC.

Blanton, Richard E. 1978 *Monte Alban: Settlement Patterns at the Ancient Zapotec Capital*. Academic Press, New York.

Blanton, Richard E., Gary M. Feinman, Stephen A. Kowalewski, and Linda M. Nicholas 1999 *Ancient Oaxaca*. Cambridge University Press, Cambridge.

Blomster, Jeffrey P. 2010 Complexity, Interaction, and Epistemology: Mixtecs, Zapotecs, and Olmecs in Early Formative Mesoamerica. *Ancient Mesoamerica* 21:135–149.

Cahn, Robert, and Marcus Winter 1993 The San José Mogote Danzante. *Indiana* 13:39–64.

Carter, Nicholas P. 2017 Epigraphy and Empire: Reassessing Textual Evidence for Formative Zapotec Imperialism. *Cambridge Archaeological Journal* 27(3):433–450.

Caso, Alfonso, Ignacio Bernal and Jorge R. Acosta 1967 *La cerámica de Monte Albán*. Memorias del Instituto Nacional de Antropología e Historia No. 13. Mexico City.

DeLanda, Manuel 2016 *Assemblage Theory*. Edinburgh University Press, Edinburgh.

Deleuze, Gilles, and Felix Guattari 1987 *A Thousand Plateaus: Capitalism and Schizophrenia*. Translated by Brian Massumi. University of Minnesota Press, Minneapolis.

Flannery, Kent V. and Joyce Marcus 2005 *Excavations at San José Mogote 1: The Household Archaeology*. Prehistory and Human Ecology of the Valley of Oaxaca, vol. 13. Museum of Anthropology, University of Michigan Memoirs, No. 40. Ann Arbor, MI.

——— 2015 *Excavations at San José Mogote 2: The Cognitive Archaeology*. Prehistory and Human Ecology of the Valley of Oaxaca, vol. 16, Museum of Anthropology, University of Michigan Memoirs, No. 58. Ann Arbor, MI.

Foster, George 1944 Nagualism in Mexico and Guatemala. *Acta americana* 2(1–2):83–103.

Freidel, David A., Linda Schele and Joy Parker 1993 *Maya Cosmos: Three Thousand Years on the Shaman's Path*. William Morrow, New York.

Furst, Jill L. 1995 *The Natural History of the Soul in Ancient Mexico*. Yale University Press, New Haven, CT.

Gillespie, Susan D. 1993 Power, Pathways, and Appropriations in Mesoamerican Art. In *Imagery and Creativity: Ethnoaesthetics and Art Worlds in the Americas*, edited by Dorothea S. Whitten and Norman E. Whitten Jr., pp. 67–107. University of Arizona Press, Tucson.

Grove, David C. 1999 Public Monuments and Sacred Mountains: Observations on Three Formative Period Sacred Landscapes. In *Social Patterns in Pre-Classic Mesoamerica*, edited by David C. Grove and Rosemary A. Joyce, pp. 255–295. Dumbarton Oaks, Washington, DC.

Guernsey, Julia 2010 A Consideration of the Quatrefoil Motif in Preclassic Mesoamerica. *RES: Anthropology and Aesthetics* 57/58:75–96.

Hamilakis, Yannis 2017 Sensorial Assemblages: Affect, Memory and Temporality in Assemblage Thinking. *Cambridge Archaeological Journal* 27(1):169–182.

Harris, Oliver J. T. 2017 Assemblages and Scale in Archaeology. *Cambridge Archaeological Journal* 27(1):127–139.

Harris, Oliver J. T., and John Robb 2012 Multiple Ontologies and the Problem of the Body in History. *American Anthropologist* 114(4):668–679.

Harrison-Buck, Eleanor 2012 Architecture as Animate Landscape: Circular Shrines in the Ancient Maya Lowlands. *American Anthropologist* 114(1):64–80.

Hermann Lejarazu, Manuel A. 2009 La serpiente de fuego o yahui en la Mixteca prehispánica: iconografía y significado. *Anales del Museo de América* 17:64–77.

Hutson, Scott R., and Travis W. Stanton 2007 Cultural Logic and Practical Reason: The Structure of Discard in Ancient Maya Houselots. *Cambridge Archaeological Journal* 17(2):123–144.

Joyce, Arthur A. 2000 The Founding of Monte Albán: Sacred Propositions and Social Practices. In *Agency in Archaeology*, edited by Macia-Anne Dobres and John Robb, pp. 71–91. Routledge Press, London.

——— 2010 *Mixtecs, Zapotecs, and Chatinos: Ancient Peoples of Southern Mexico*. Wiley-Blackwell Press, Malden, MA.

——— 2019 Animating Public Buildings in Formative-Period Oaxaca: Political and Ontological Implications. In *Sacred Matter: Animism and Authority in Pre-Columbian America*, edited by Steve Kosiba, John Janusek, and Thomas Cummins. Dumbarton Oaks, Washington, DC.

Joyce, Arthur A., and Sarah B. Barber 2015 Ensoulment, Entrapment, and Political Centralization: A Comparative Study of Religion and Politics in Later Formative Oaxaca. *Current Anthropology* 56(6):819–847.

Kowalewski, Stephen, Gary Feinman, Laura Finsten, Richard Blanton and Linda M. Nicholas 1989 *Monte Albán's Hinterland, part II: Prehispanic Settlement Patterns in Tlacolula, Etla, and Ocotlán, the Valley of Oaxaca, Mexico*. Memoirs of the University of Michigan Museum of Anthropology No. 23. Ann Arbor.

López Austin, Alfredo 1988 *Human Body and Ideology: Concepts of the Ancient Nahuas*, vol. 1. University of Utah Press, Salt Lake City.

——— 1989 *Hombre-Dios: Religión y política en el mundo Náhuatl*. 2nd edition Universidad Nacional Autónoma de México, Mexico City.

López Austin, Alfredo, and Leonardo López Luján (editors) 2009 *Monte sagrado: Templo mayor*. Instituto Nacional de Antropología e Historia y Universidad Nacional Autónoma de México, Mexico City.

López Luján, Leonardo 2005 *The Offerings of the Templo Mayor of Tenochtitlan*, revised ed. Translated by Bernard R. Ortiz de Montellano and Thelma Ortiz de Montellano. University of New Mexico Press, Albuquerque.

Marcus, Joyce, and Kent Flannery 1996 *Zapotec Civilization: How Urban Society Evolved in Mexico's Oaxaca Valley*. Thames and Hudson, London.

Markens, Robert 2013 El significado de la greca escalonada en la imaginería prehispánica de Oaxaca: Una base del poder político. *Cuadernos del Sur* 18(35):67–81.

——— 2014 Análisis del Conjunto Arquitectónico de las Tumbas 1 y 2 de Zaachila. In *Zaachila y su historia prehispánica: Memoria del 50° aniversario del descubrimiento de las tumbas prehispánicas de Zaachila, 1962–2012*, edited by Ismael Vicente Cruz and Gonzalo Sánchez Santiago, pp. 75–98, Secretaría de las Culturas y Artes de Oaxaca y el Ayuntamiento de Villa de Zaachila, Oaxaca.

Martínez López, Cira, and Robert Markens 2004 Análisis de la función político-económico del conjunto Plataforma Norte lado poniente de la Plaza Principal de Monte Albán. In *Estructuras políticas en el Oaxaca antiguo*, edited by Nelly M. Robles García, pp. 75–99. Instituto Nacional de Antropología e Historia, Mexico City.

Martínez López, Cira, Marcus Winter and Robert Markens 2014 *Muerte y vida entre los zapotecos de Monte Albán*. Serie Arqueología Oaxaqueña 5. Instituto Nacional de Antropología e Historia, Centro INAH Oaxaca, Oaxaca.

Minc, Leah D., R. Jason Sherman, Christina Elson, Marcus Winter, Elsa M. Redmond, and Charles S. Spencer 2016 Ceramic Provenance and the Regional Organization of Pottery Production during the Later Formative Periods in the Valley of Oaxaca, Mexico: Results of Trace-Element and Mineralogical Analyses. *Journal of Archaeological Science: Reports* 8:28–46.

Mock, Shirley B. (editor) 1998 *The Sowing and the Dawning: Termination, Dedication, and Transformation in the Archaeological and Ethnographic Record of Mesoamerica*. University of New Mexico Press, Albuquerque.

Monaghan, John 1990 Sacrifice, Death, and the Origins of Agriculture in the Codex Vienna. *American Antiquity* 55:559–569.

——— 1995 *The Covenants with Earth and Rain*. University of Oklahoma Press, Norman.

——— 2000 Theology and History in the Study of Mesoamerican Religions. In *Supplement of the Handbook of Middle American Indians. Volume 6. Ethnology*, edited by John Monaghan, pp. 24–49. University of Texas Press, Austin.

——— 2009 Sacrificio y poder en Mesoamérica. In *Bases de la complejidad social en Oaxaca, memoria de la cuarta mesa redonda de Monte Albán*, edited by Nelly M. Robles García, pp. 181–197. Instituto Nacional de Antropología e Historia, Mexico City.

Ortman, Scott G., Andrew H. F. Cabaniss, Jennie O. Sturm, and Luís M. A. Bettencourt 2015 Settlement Scaling and Increasing Returns in an Ancient Society. *Science Advances* 1(1):1e00066. DOI: 10.1126/sciadv.00066.

Pauketat, Timothy R. 2013 *An Archaeology of the Cosmos: Rethinking Agency and Religion in Ancient America*. Routledge, London and New York.

Peeler, Damon E., and Marcus Winter 1992 Mesoamerican Site Orientations and Their Relationship to the 260-day Ritual Period. *Notas Mesoamericanas* 14:37–62.

Redmond, Elsa M., and Charles S. Spencer 2006 From Raiding to Conquest: Warfare Strategies and Early State Development in Oaxaca, Mexico. In *The Archaeology of Warfare: Prehistories of Raiding and Conquest*, edited by Elizabeth N. Arkush and Mark W. Allen, pp. 336–393. University Press of Florida, Gainesville.

——— 2008 Rituals of Sanctification and the Development of Standardized Temples in Oaxaca, Mexico. *Cambridge Archaeological Journal* 18(2):239–266.

Sahagún, Fray Bernardino 1950–1982 *Florentine Codex: General History of the Things of New Spain*. Translated by Charles H. Dibble and Arthur J. O. Anderson, 12 vols. School of American Research and the University of Utah, Santa Fe, NM.

Schele, Linda, and Mary Ellen Miller 1986 *The Blood of Kings, Dynasty and Ritual in Maya Art*. Kimbell Art Museum, Fort Worth, TX.

Sellen, Adam T. 2002 Storm-God Impersonators from Ancient Oaxaca. *Ancient Mesoamerica* 13(1):2–19.

Sherman, R. Jason 2005 Settlement Heterogeneity in the Zapotec State: A View from Yaasuchi, Oaxaca, Mexico. PhD dissertation, Department of Anthropology, University of Michigan and University Microfilms, Ann Arbor, MI.

Sprajc, Ivan 2018 Astronomy, Architecture, and Landscape in Prehispanic Mesoamerica. *Journal of Archaeological Research* 26(2):197–251.

Stross, Brian 1998 Seven Ingredients in Mesoamerican Ensoulment. In *The Sowing and the Dawning: Termination, Dedication, and Transformation in the Archaeological and Ethnographic Record of Mesoamerica*, edited by Shirley B. Mock, pp. 31–39. University of New Mexico Press, Albuquerque.

Taube, Karl 1996 The Rainmakers: The Olmec and Their Contribution to Mesoamerican Belief and Ritual. In *The Olmec World: Ritual and Rulership*, edited by Jill Guthrie, pp. 83–103. Art Museum, Princeton University, Princeton, NJ.

——— 2000 Lightning Celts and Corn Fetishes: The Formative Olmec and the Development of Maize Symbolism in Mesoamerica and the American Southwest. In *Olmec Art and Archaeology: Social Complexity in the Formative Period*, edited by John E. Clark and Mary Pye, pp. 297–337. Studies in the History of Art, vol. 58. National Gallery of Art, Washington, DC.

——— 2004 *Olmec Art at Dumbarton Oaks*. Dumbarton Oaks Research Library and Collection, Washington, DC.

Tedlock, Dennis 1996 *Popol Vuh*. 2nd edition. Simon and Schuster, New York.

Thrift, Nigel 2008. *Non-Representational Theory: Space / Politics / Affect*. Routledge, New York.

Tricarico, Anthony 2015 Urban Agriculture within the Valley of Oaxaca: Investigations and Implications of Agricultural Terracing at Monte Albán, Oaxaca. Unpublished MA thesis, University of Central Florida, Orlando.

Urcid, Javier 1994 Un sistema de nomenclatura para los monolitos grabados y los materiales con inscripciones de Monte Albán. In *Escritura Zapoteca prehispánica*, edited by Marcus Winter, pp. 53–79. Contribución No. 4 del Proyecto Especial Monte Albán 1992–1994. Instituto Nacional de Antropología e Historia, Centro INAH Oaxaca, Oaxaca.

——— 2001 *Zapotec Hieroglyphic Writing*. Dumbarton Oaks Studies in Pre-Columbian Art & Archaeology 34. Dumbarton Oaks, Washington, DC.

——— 2005 *The Zapotec Scribal Tradition: Knowledge, Memory, and Society in Ancient Oaxaca*. Foundation for the Advancement of Mesoamerican Studies, Coral Gables, FL. (www.famsi.org/zapotecwriting/)

——— 2009 Personajes enmascarados: El rayo, el trueno y la lluvia en Oaxaca. *Arqueología Mexicana* 16(96):30–34.

——— 2011a Las oráculos y la guerra: el papel de las narrativas pictóricos en el desarrollo temprano de Monte Albán (500 a.C.–200 d.C.). In *Monte Albán en la encrucijada regional y disciplinaria: memoria de la quinta Mesa Redonda de Monte Albán*, edited by Nelly M. Robles García and Ángel Rivera Guzmán, pp. 163–240. Instituto Nacional de Antropología e Historia, Mexico City.

——— 2011b Sobre la antigüedad de cofres para augurar y propiciar la lluvia. *Arqueología Mexicana* 19(110):16–21.

——— 2014 Otra Narrativa de Jugadores de Pelota en Dainzu. In *Panorama arqueológico: Dos Oaxacas*, edited by Marcus Winter and Gonzalo Sánchez Santiago, pp. 43–62. Arqueología Oaxaqueña 4. Instituto Nacional de Antropología e Historia, Centro INAH Oaxaca, Oaxaca.

Urcid, Javier, and Arthur A. Joyce 2014 Early Transformations of Monte Albán's Main Plaza and Their Political Implications, 500 BC-AD 200. In *Mesoamerican Plazas*, edited by Kenichiro Tsukamoto and Takeshi Inomata, pp. 149–167. University of Arizona Press, Tucson.

Vogt, Evon Z. 1976 *Tortillas for the Gods: A Symbolic Analysis of Zinacanteco Rituals*. Harvard University Press, Cambridge.

Whalen, Michael E. 1988 Small Community Organization during the Late Formative Period in Oaxaca. *Journal of Field Archaeology* 15:291–306.

Winter, Marcus 1994 El Proyecto Especial Monte Albán 1992–1994: Antecedentes, intervenciones y perspectivas. In *Monte Albán: Estudios recientes*, edited by Marcus Winter, pp. 1–24. Contribución No. 2 del Proyecto Especial Monte Albán 1992–1994. Instituto Nacional de Antropología e Historia, Centro INAH Oaxaca, Oaxaca.

———— 2001 Palacios, templos y 1300 años de vida urbana en Monte Albán. In *Reconstruyendo la ciudad Maya: El urbanismo en las sociedades antiguas*, edited by Andres Ciudad Ruiz, M. J. Iglesia Ponce de Léon, and M. del Carmen Martínez, pp. 253–301. Sociedad Española de Estudios Mayas, Madrid.

Zedeño, María Nieves 2009 Animating by Association: Index Objects and Relational Taxonomies. *Cambridge Archaeological Journal* 19(3):407–417.

5

ASSEMBLING TIWANAKU

Water and stone, humans and monoliths

John Wayne Janusek

Cities create electric engagements. They generate affect, foment relations, and produce subjects. Louis Wirth (1938) noted that urbanism creates diversity and density as core dispositions for an emergent 'way of life.' Wirth's insight and later anthropological attention focus on social relations in the production of urbanism. In tune with my colleagues in this volume, I seek to explode this perspective. I approach cities as places of dense gathering and intense transaction among multiple classes of materials, places, and beings. In these transactions, humans were core protagonists—what Bennett calls *operators* (2010).[1] Yet urban transactions in Tiwanaku, the focus of this study, incorporated all sorts of beings, places, and things. People comprised subjects (Althusser 1971) and personae (Mauss 1967) in relation to a raft of places, assemblages, and nonhuman beings that urban centers incorporated or indexed. In Tiwanaku, such nonhuman places and beings included water, stone, hydrolithic assemblies, and sculpted monoliths.

Pre-Columbian cities institutionalized relations between humans and non-human landscapes and beings. The sprawling city of Teotihuacan in central Mexico (200–600 CE) established visual and proxemics linkages with surrounding mountains, springs, and celestial bodies, many of which appear as animate characters in strategically positioned sculptures and murals (Cowgill 2015; Headrick 2007). The Pyramids of the Sun and Moon on the axial Street of the Dead sedimented an authorized experience of human relations with these 'natural' features as a monumental urban assembly. Calendrical rituals recurrently vitalized this experience and instilled predominant ontological dispositions and subjectivities among urban inhabitants. Such transitive relations and enduring dispositions constituted what Pauketat (this volume) terms 'religion' in the pre-Columbian Americas.

Tiwanaku constituted a comparable urban phenomenon in the highest Andes. By 500 CE, it had emerged as a primary center from a multi-centered political community in the Lake Titicaca basin of South America (Figure 5.1) (Janusek 2015a).

After 600 CE it became a primary urban center in the south–central Andes, and by 700 CE a vibrant city centered on several monumental campuses that drew pilgrims, diplomats, ritualists, and others for recurring ritual events (Janusek 2004, 2008, 2015b; Kolata 1993, 2003; Vranich 2009, 2016). Ceremonies conducted during such events fomented Tiwanaku's urbanization while expanding its name and geopolitical influence, what Munn (1986) terms its emergent *fame*, across the Andes. Tiwanaku's hydrolithic assemblages and monolithic beings were central to this expansive fame (Janusek 2019; Janusek and Bowen 2018).

In this chapter, I explore Tiwanaku's centrality, fame, and prestige by exploring the flows of materials that generated the city and the vital engagements of elements and beings that promoted its expansive influence. Tiwanaku's renown trumpeted a vital political ecology that linked the center and its constituent materials and beings to the geophysical world around it (see Biersack 2006; Robbins 2012). Tiwanaku constituted a seductive ecoregime; a field of assembled celestial movements, water flows, imposing mountains, vital stone, fickle humans, and uncanny lithic personages as a coherent cosmopolitical cartography. I adapt Escobar's (1999) notion of nature regime as a particular engagement with the nonhuman, to a pre-Columbian situation in which 'nature' as a master category and ontological foil for all things 'nonhuman' *did not exist*. Andean worlds, in which water incubates generative creatures and mountains embody ancestral persons, refuse to abide by such an ontology and

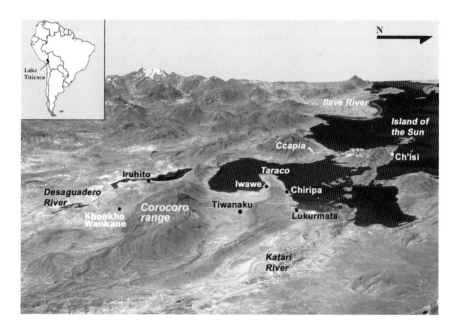

FIGURE 5.1 Oblique view of Tiwanaku in relation to local sites, landforms, and the southern portion of Lake Titicaca (image by J. Janusek)

96 John Wayne Janusek

its Judeo-Christian historical foundations (Abercrombie 1998; de la Cadena 2015; Salomon 1991).

During Tiwanaku's career as a primary center, its cartography was substantially territorialized (DeLanda 2006). Two paired monumental complexes, each consisting of multiple raised platforms with enclosed sunken courts, defined its core spatial parameters, while a host of proxemic and visual linkages to hydrologic, lithic, and celestial flows extrapolated their vital catchment beyond relatively proximate urban boundaries. Such linkages raise the question that urban ecologists critically pose for cities: Considering the far-flung vital ecologies any city requires for its ongoing production or growth, how should we delimit their expansive boundaries? Chicago's explosive growth in North America during the nineteenth century depended on water in Lake Michigan timber from forests in Wisconsin, and grains on prairies that stretched west toward the Mississippi (Cronon 1992. Similarly, Tiwanaku's geopolitical import depended on aquifers, mountains, celestial bodies, fauna, and humans (Janusek and Bowen 2018; Janusek and Williams 2016) located far beyond the boundaries of the city as it has been traditionally defined in archaeology (Childe 1950).

I have written papers on my investigations of the roles of sky, water, and stone in the emergence and ongoing production of Tiwanaku. In a comprehensive examination of Tiwanaku's monoliths, I argue that they were lithic beings who constituted a master geopolitical cartography that tethered their temple homes to particular montane places of origin (Janusek 2019). I have privileged humans as a particular kind of operator, in building temples, quarrying stone, constructing waterworks, and carving monoliths. In this chapter, I level the playing field among ontological classes by focusing on the elements, materials, and things that constituted Tiwanaku and its emergent geopolitical field. I mesh my ongoing research into the material production of Tiwanaku, which emphasizes the material animacy of pre-Columbian urbanism (Janusek 2019), with insights from political ecology and 'New Materialisms,' which inspire archaeologists to revisit cities as continually reassembled, politically charged, and vital material concentrations. I hesitate to propose a flat ontology, such as that espoused in much actor-network theory (Latour 2005), in which materials in an assemblage operate according to equal outcomes and values. Considering assemblages of beings and things as potentially political engagements, I seek to locate the 'key operators' in Tiwananku's assemblages, that is, the particular instantiations or relations that accrued inordinate value or gravity.[2]

I investigate Tiwanaku's ecoregime as an assembly of materials, beings, instantiations, and relations. Tiwanaku's emergence as a center simultaneously constituted transformations in landscapes and flows, as well as human, faunal, and floral communities. To understand this emergence, I 'follow the materials' (Weismantel and Meskell 2014) as they moved toward and through Tiwanaku and find that this perspective encourages us to reconsider the role of fleshly humans as but one class of operators in the production of a high-altitude Andean city 'dense' with things, affects, movements, and recombined materialities (see Pauketat, Chapter 1). This perspective encourages the questions posed by critical urban ecologists: What is a city, in light of its thriving, pulsating, diversified material constitution? Should archaeologists define cities strictly according to the extent of their human occupation, or consider their broader material catchments? The received perspective, as outlined by Childe (1950) and recently trumpeted by others (Smith 2009), instantiates a subjective experience of modern cities which, since the rise of capitalism in Europe, shutters attention to nonhuman flows and features. Pre-Columbian cities such as Tiwanaku operated according to starkly different relations and assemblies.

I articulate a political ecology that meshes insights derived from recent studies in new materialism (Barad 2007; Bennett 2010; Coole and Frost 2010; DeLanda 2006; Deleuze and Guattari 1987). I have three aims. First, I shift emphasis from stasis to movement, inert objects to fluid elements. Archaeologies of landscape have taken us far in focusing attention on dynamic human–environment relations, yet the concept of 'landscape' is burdened by a Western aesthetic that 'captures' places as static backdrops for a discerning, distanced, longing elite gaze (Cosgrove 1998; Jackson 1986). An emphasis on movement tempers this focus with an *archaeology of flows* that foregrounds perceptions of landscapes, elements, and things in light of their ongoing temporalities and inevitable transformations (Edgeworth 2011, Weismantel 2018).

Second, I shift emphasis from *interaction* to *trans-action*. If interaction privileges 'thing … balanced against thing in causal interconnection' (Dewey and Bentley 1949:108), like colliding billiard balls, *trans-action* emphasizes 'aspects and phases of action' rather than fixed objects. It treats entities as temporary instantiations of encounters. As Pauketat (Chapter 1) puts it, 'things and bodies are always emergent … they come into being as flows and movements mediate larger webs of relations.' Trans-action trains attention to the heterogeneous capacities that things in an assemblage harbor, only some of which are engaged in the encounters that bind them together as a particular assemblage in a particular place at a particular moment (Harris 2017). 'An assemblage owes its [emergent] capacity to the vitality of the materialities that constitute it' (Bennett 2010:34). Furthermore, new encounters with other things or beings may transform the character of constituent participants in an assemblage. In Tiwanaku, encounters of stone and water afforded each element new capacities, while human–monolithic encounters enacted spatio-temporally expansive transformations (Janusek 2019; sensu Munn 1986).

Third, I engage relations across ontological fields. In object-oriented accounts, chasms among ontological domains constitute unfathomable rifts (Morton 2013). Yet things of different ontological domains somehow manage to engage one another, if uncannily and asymmetrically. As Bennett notes (2010:2), citing W. J. T. Mitchell, 'objects are the way things appear to a subject … Things, on the other hand [signal] the moment when the object becomes the other,' intransigent, powerful, worthy of respect or destruction; *uncanny*. A U.S. citizen goes about life engaging things to activate her agency in the world. An Iphone, a computer, an automobile are useful objects at her disposal that may serve her needs. This is all good until her computer crashes or her car breaks down; suddenly, those useful, domesticated machines become animate things that 'act back,' denying her agency and amplifying their own uncanny power.

Globally, relations across ontological domains comprise uncanny relations of animacy and reciprocal power. As Sahlins puts it (2008:88), 'As enchanted as our universe may still be, it is also still ordered by a distinction of culture and nature that is evident to virtually no one else but ourselves.' In the Amazon, relations between humans and animals manifest as reciprocal, 'perspectival' relations of predator and prey (Conklin 2001; Viveiros de Castro 1998). From their incipient urban origins, Andean cities keyed geographical features and flows, their influence grounded in perceptual, material, and semiotic relations to nearby mountains and peaks, springs, streams, stone, clay, salt, and other earthly sources (Allen 2002; de la Cadena 2015; Dean 2010). These features and flows embodied animate, ancestral forces rendered central to the well-being of humans, crops, and herds. Ritual acts that featured libations, songs, prayers, and blood offerings were the contexts in which humans directly encountered and reciprocally transacted with the potent living forces of the geophysical world.

I next summarize Tiwanaku's Formative origins in the southern Lake Titicaca basin. I then describe the vast network that drew water toward and through Tiwanaku, highlighting the site's primary aquifer and Perimeter Canal. Following, I describe the stone employed to construct Tiwanaku's temples and monoliths, emphasizing the shift from sandstone to volcanic stone and exploring how the materiality of specific constructions created hydrololithic encounters. I then turn to the importance of humans in the center, their key places of encounter with assembled constructions, and their engagements with Tiwanaku's monolithic temple denizens. Finally, I focus on monoliths and their scaled instantiation as Presentation, Extended Arm, or Chachapuma beings. In conclusion, I consider humans and monoliths key operators in Tiwanaku, and their engagement and reciprocal animacy as particularly generative of Tiwanaku's pan-Andean fame and geopolitical influence.

Formative origins

The Late Formative (100 BCE–500 CE) started as a period of long-term drought in the southern Lake Titicaca basin (Abbott et al. 1997). The small, southern portion of the lake had disappeared, several prior Middle Formative centers (e.g., Chiripa on the Taraco peninsula) were abandoned, and new centers were settled below permanent mountain springs. Tiwanaku was one of these centers, settled at the south edge of a rich aquifer that carried spring, stream, and subterranean water from the Corocoro range to the south edge of the Tiwanaku Valley. It and other Late Formative centers created an emergent, multicentered political community that thrived during Late Formative 1 (100 BCE–300 CE). By 200 CE, this community centered on the paired centers of Tiwanaku and Khonkho Wankane, situated on either side of Corocoro (Figure 5.1). The sites shared a north–south axis, similar trapezoidal sunken temples, similar sandstone monoliths (a substyle shared by no other center; see Janusek and Ohnstad 2018), and a similar north–south orientation toward prominent peaks and celestial observations.

Relations to the horizon and sky directed core elements of construction and orientation at Khonkho and Tiwanaku. A Late Formative 1 focal sunken temple at each site directed movement and perceptual engagements on a predominant north–south axis. Movement through Khonkho Wankane funneled pilgrims from an extensive central plaza toward its Sunken Temple which, via strategically located portals, provided dramatic visual engagements with Mount Sajama and the auspicious rise of nighttime constellations to the south (Benitez 2013; Janusek 2015b). Tiwanaku's Sunken Temple offered a parallel engagement with Mount Kimsachata, the southern pole directly above its peak, and the same constellations. Monumental constructions after 300 CE dramatically reconfigured these connections. The Late Formative 2 Dual Court Complex at Khonkho and the Kalasasaya platform at Tiwanaku shifted human movement and celestial-horizon alignments decisively toward an east–west axis. This new axis privileged the centrality of solar (solstice and equinox) cycles for punctuating time and keeping calendars and, at Tiwanaku, meshed them with visual engagements to the distant ice-capped peak of Illimani to the east, and the ancient volcano Ccapia to the west. This axial shift generated Tiwanaku's meteoric rise as the Lake Titicaca basin's primary urban center.

Water

Tiwanaku's emergence as a primary center after 500 CE corresponded with a wetter climate (Abbott et al.1997; Binford et al. 1997). The shifting ecology of the Titicaca region inspired new temples and waterworks. It correlated with the construction of a monumental hydraulic network that afforded the expanding center its emergent form (Figure 5.2). The materiality of water—its seen, heard, and felt presence—as well as the recurring seasonality of its ebbs and torrents, were crucial components of the intensive affective experiences the center afforded. Flowing water created clear divisions in the city and directed human flows along specific paths.

Flowing strands of the network linked the center from Mount Kimsachata in the Corocoro range, 11 kilometers to the south, to the Guaquira River, just to the north. Tiwanaku's water derived from a subterranean aquifer that sloped down from Kimsachata toward the site (Argollo et al. 1996). Humans manipulated this aquifer to (1) direct the surface flow of water via streams toward the center, and (2) enhance the flow of water from a group of springs just northwest of the site (Janusek and Bowen 2018). Streams emerging from valleys on either side of Kimsachata diverted torrential rainy season flows away from the center.

The pivot of Tiwanaku's water network was its Perimeter Canal (Janusek and Bowen 2018; Janusek and Ortloff 2014; Ortloff and Janusek 2016). The monumental feature is apparent in aerial photos, satellite images, and attentive reconnaissance. Archaeologists have routinely referred to it as a 'moat' (Browman 1997; Janusek 2004:130–131; Means 1931:123–125) and have considered it a continuous feature that served either defense (Posnansky 1945:121–122) or to isolate 'elite'

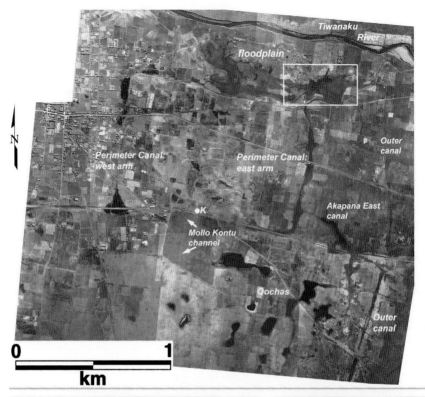

FIGURE 5.2 Top image: Composite 1930s aerial photo of Tiwanaku showing the Perimeter Canal and related hydrological features, including Mollo Kontu Canal, Akapana East Canal, Outer Canal, and Guaquira River. 'K' marks the spot near the intersection of the Mollo Kontu and Perimeter canals where the Kochamama monolith triad was found. Bottom image: Detail of the north portion of the network, emphasizing water flow from the northwest and northeast arms of the Perimeter Canal into the Guaquira floodplain, which incorporated dense raised-field farming systems (both images by J. Janusek).

space in an encompassing 'concentric cline of the sacred' (Kolata 1993:90–96). Critical analysis during the 2000's concluded, correctly, that the feature is discontinuous and that it slopes down to the south, toward the Guaquira river, on a 2 percent gradient (Bentley 2013:122; Isbell 2013:178–180). Throwing out the moat with the moat water, the analysts conclude that no such feature ever existed. I argue that, to the contrary, the feature once interpreted as a 'moat' was among Tiwanaku's most impressive monuments, a fluid reciprocal counterpart for its temples, and a channel for liquid flow that shaped the city and its movements.

The Perimeter Canal funneled water from Kimsachata's aquifer and drew it around either side of Tiwanaku's Northeast Monumental Campus. The proximal surface input was the Mollo Kontu Canal, a south–north trending canal that funneled water from south of that campus to the south-central portion of the Perimeter Canal (Janusek and Bowen 2018; Janusek and Ortloff 2014). The place where Mollo Kontu meets the Perimeter Canal has been heavily disturbed throughout generations of human activity. Following their respective paths, however, the place where they met is easy to pinpoint geographically. The Perimeter Canal bifurcated Mollo Kontu's water around either side of the Northeast Monumental Campus. One well-preserved arm drew water around its east side, so that it flowed just below the extensive residential compounds of Akapana East (Janusek 2004), and ultimately toward the raised fields that populated the south floodplain of the Guaquira River. The west arm, much of it under the town of Tiahuanaco, drew water around the west side of the campus, and ultimately toward a series of outlets that fed into raised field patches in the same floodplain. The Perimeter Canal was a monumental linchpin in an encompassing hydrologic infrastructural network that meshed aquatic capacities and human technical interventions.

The centrality of water flow in Tiwanaku calls into question approaches that treat 'the urban' as consisting strictly of human activity and habitation. It shifts our attention toward the critical approaches of urban ecologists who seek to understand cities as ongoing relational transformations of environments and their particular material affordances (e.g., rivers, lakes, trees, soils, stones, metals, etc.; see Cronon 1992; Gandy 2003; Kelman 2006). First, Tiwanaku's aquatic network extended far beyond its monumental-residential core. Water input depended on a geologically ancient aquifer that largely flowed beneath the surface from the Corocoro foothills. Yet humans intervened and redirected water above ground and in places where the subterranean aquifer percolated to the surface. Astute Tiwanaku hydrologists directed some streams toward the Perimeter Canal, and redirected others so that they flowed away from human constructions and occupations. Recent community excavations in a seasonal stream east of the site revealed massive cobbles and boulders, indicating that its flow was sometimes turbulent during pre-Columbian rainy seasons. Northwest of the center, humans fitted springs with volcanic stone faucets and sandstone conduits, creating a water temple that generated a rich aquatic environment. The marshy, waterlogged areas that hugged the east and west sides of Tiwanaku's urban core constituted locales ideal for pasturing llamas and alpacas.

Second, Tiwanaku's monumental-residential core incorporated landscapes, flows, and activities that refuse to square with traditional notions of 'the urban.' The southeast quadrant of the city incorporated a cluster of extensive sunken basins, or *qochas* (Figure 5.2) (Janusek 2008:183–184; Janusek and Bowen 2018). Historical and ethnographic research indicate that *qochas*, created by excavating shallow basins to collect and reserve rainy-season water, serve to enhance cultivation, provide water for camelids, and create micro-environments that support fish, waterfowl, and other species (Flores Ochoa 1987; Lémuz and Janusek 2016). Analysis of aerial photos taken during a rainy season in the 1930s indicates that these *qochas* constituted a coherent cluster interlinked by small surface canals and tied into Tiwanaku's encompassing hydrologic network (Ortloff and Janusek 2016). Water flowing into this network via Kimsachata's subterranean aquifer could have been shifted among *qochas* as desired.

Tiwanaku also incorporated raised field networks (Figure 5.2) (Janusek and Bowen 2018; Janusek and Ortloff 2014). Like *qocha* clusters, these networks served cultivation while simultaneously providing water for camelids and creating micro-environments for fish and waterfowl. Humans amassed beds of soil to plant crops surrounded by water-filled swales that collected water seasonally, if not perennially, to keep crop roots moist. At night, when temperatures frequently fell below freezing near harvest, the swales acted for humans; they created a warm 'heat envelope' that protected the growing crops (Kolata 1991, 1993). The same 1930s aerial photos mentioned above yield detailed evidence for raised fields within Tiwanaku. Raised fields line the Akapana East Canal that links the Mollo Kontu qocha cluster to the Perimeter Canal. Raised fields are ubiquitous in the floodplain below and just north of the monumental core. Water flowing around the northeast monumental campus, fed by the Mollo Kontu Canal and its distal Kimsachata aquifer, flowed through the Perimeter Canal and then split, each of its north ends, into a series of canals that nourished those fields and their swales, and ultimately percolated into the Guaquira River, which directed the water toward Lake Titicaca.

Dry to rainy season shifts and longer-term fluctuations demand infrastructural flexibility. The Perimeter Canal and its extended network incorporated cushions for those inevitable cycles. Computational Fluid Dynamics (CFD) analysis indicated that the Perimeter Canal was constructed to balance Tiwanaku's fluctuating water regime in order to stabilize the Northeast Monumental Campus while ensuring regular water flow toward Guaquira (Janusek and Bowen 2018; Janusek and Ortloff 2014; Ortloff 2014; Ortloff and Janusek 2016). Humans constructed canals that enhanced water's cyclical affordances and cushioned its less predictable, sometimes minimal, sometimes torrential, occurrences. Key was creating a stable relation between the relatively slow movement of Kimsachata's subterranean aquifer and the quicker flow of the Perimeter Canal and its surficial extensions. In the rainy season (December–March), the Perimeter Canal hastened seasonal runoff and heightened phreatic levels. During dry seasons, as phreatic levels subsided, tributary canals such as Mollo Kontu, Akapana East, and Tiwanaku's Outer Canal, kept the aquifer's phreatic boundary from sinking too low. The Perimeter Canal and its hydraulic tentacles served as an assembled fulcrum in a fluctuating hydrological ecology. It sought to balance watery fluctuations with Tiwanaku's monumental needs by ensuring that the Northeast Campus rested on solid ground while preventing the disappearance of the rich, deep aquifer during dry seasons and longer droughts.

Building Tiwanaku's Perimeter Canal produced massive amounts of silty clay. This heavy, thick soil was sifted to construct new temples in the Northeast Monumental campus. Excavations at Late Formative Khonkho Wankane indicated that soils excavated from the marsh surrounding the primary platform had been sifted to create strategically engineered strata that afforded long-term stability. Porous sandy strata drew water into the platform, punctuated by relatively impermeable, sloped and clay-rich soils that led water down from and off the platform. Drawing on this formative engineering expertise, Tiwanaku builders sifted and remixed soil from the Perimeter Canal to produce artisanal mixtures of silt, sand, and clay to ensure the endurance of Akapana over recurring rainy seasons (Medina 2008).

Stone

Stone also flowed into and through Tiwanaku, if following very different technologies, cycles, and communities of practice. Like water, stone was elemental to Tiwanaku's ongoing production and its emergence as a major Andean urban ceremonial center. During the Late Formative, the facades of Khonkho Wankane's and Tiwanaku's monumental complex consisted primarily of sandstone and related sedimentary materials. Key constructions such as the interior walls of Tiwanaku's Sunken Temple and the outer platform wall of the Kalasasaya platform (Figure 5.3), manifest a distinctive architectural canon in which tall, deeply set sandstone pilasters sunk deep into the earth buttressed wide sections of coursed, stratigraphically bonded, relatively small rectangular blocks. Sandstone constituted the bulk of Tiwanaku monumental stone construction throughout the Middle Horizon. Other materials were incorporated diacritically, to mark them as distinctive, special materials; for example, the tenoned heads perforating the interior court walls of the Sunken Temple consist of rare volcanic tuff. Nevertheless, the sandstone-focused construction technique dates at least as early as the Middle Formative (Cohen and Roddick 2007) and is resplendent in Khonkho Wankane's core temples (Janusek 2015a). Sandstone remained central to Tiwanaku construction after CE 500, in complement to the deployment of volcanic andesite.

Sandstone for Tiwanaku, as for Khonkho Wankane, derived from the sedimentary-rich Corocoro range that separated the centers. On Corocoro's south side, which furnished sandstone for Khonkho Wankane, several monolith quarries are known near the high summit plus 12 sandstone blocks that had been left behind while *en route* to Khonkho (Ponce 1971). The Kaliri quarry in the upper Kausani valley, some 13 kilometers southeast and over 400 meters above Tiwanaku, served as the expanding center's primary source of sandstone (Figure 5.4) (Janusek et al. 2013; Janusek and Williams 2016).

FIGURE 5.3 The reconstructed Kalasasaya complex, facing northwest. Its andesite balcony wall is at the center-left portion of the image (photography by Wolfgang Schüler)

The Kaliri quarry covered 12 hectares and incorporated areas dedicated to specific tasks. On climbing the Kausani Valley from the Tiwanaku Valley, Kaliri is the first sedimentary exposure that exhibits large, minimally exfoliated sandstone outcrops. Tiwanaku stone workers took advantage of linear geological fractures in the sandstone bedrock, prying out naturally fractured blocks in the north portion of the site and hauling them elsewhere for finer work. Pried blocks were hauled to places just north of the quarries to be split, hammered, pecked, and smoothed (Janusek and Williams 2016:102–103). The stones employed to work the sandstone consisted of durable cobble tools—green quartzite and porphyry that, while naturally present in Corocoro, were oddly not found in significant quantities at the site (Protzen and Nair 2013:177). The roughly carved blocks were then carted to an area further north to be more finely shaped and formed. This area is littered with sandstone flakes (Janusek et al. 2013:Figure 4.18).

The carved blocks were hauled down a well-trodden, and still viable, path that snaked through the Kausani Valley to the Tiwananku valley *pampa*, or plain. Before they were hauled, many had been fitted with ground notches on two—and in some cases, four—opposing edges so that they could be carried down with durable ropes (Janusek and Williams 2016:103). These 'rope holds' served as grips that allowed groups of workers to carry the blocks from the quarry, down the mountain, and ultimately toward Tiwanaku. Several sandstone blocks incorporated into Akapana's terrace facades display rope holds. While most blocks left behind on the Kausani road had been fitted with such rope holds, a few presented linear scrape marks,

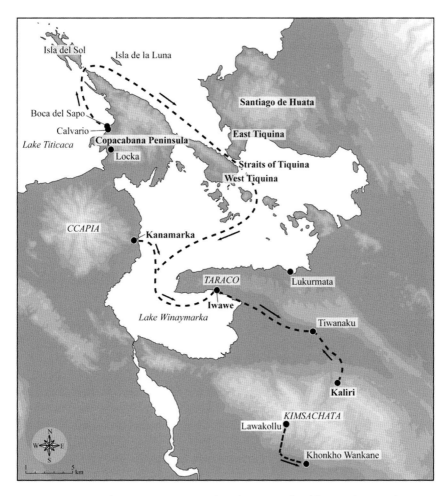

FIGURE 5.4 Map showing movement of sandstone to Khonkho Wankane and Tiwanaku on either side of the Corocoro range, and movement of volcanic stone to Tiwanaku from Ccapia and Copacabana (image by Patrick Ryan Williams and Jill Seagard, Field Museum)

indicating that they had been dragged rather than having been carted by ropes. It appears that at least two if not more cartage technologies were deployed to move Kaliri sandstone to Tiwanaku.

The stones were hauled by rope to the site of Chusicani, located where the valley meets the pampa, an intersection of altiplano micro-environments with great productive and ritual importance for the Aymara and their ancestors. Chusicani incorporates monumental platforms and clusters of quarried sandstone blocks that had been left behind while in transit. It was likely here that roughly formed blocks were prepared for the final journey over the valley floor toward Tiwanaku. Older members of the community recall having seen abandoned worked stones—commonly termed 'tired stones,' affording them animacy—on the pampas north and west of Chusicanai, en route to Tiwanaku. Most of these stones have by now been appropriated to build houses and other structures. Chusicani may well have housed the miners and masons who worked the Kaliri quarry. Perhaps they regularly brought their working materials back home with them every day, explaining why so few stone tools are known from Kaliri.

The movement of sandstone from Kaliri to Chusicani, and from Chusicani across the pampa to Tiwanaku, constituted an ongoing material cycle that was acutely apparent for anyone inhabiting or visiting Tiwanaku. The constant flow of sandstone to the center was a critical element of its emergent fame. Carting and carving impossibly massive sandstone blocks such as those employed to construct Akapana's basal terrace or Pumapunku's East Portico demanded particularly intensive ritual acts and feats of human effort. Tiwanaku leaders and ritual choreographers likely counted on calendrical ceremonies to capitalize on the bodily work of hundreds, if not thousands of willing, eager pilgrims.

Early in the Middle Horizon, Tiwanaku masons gained access to the volcanic stone located in outcrops across the small, southern portion of Lake Titicaca. The shift to incorporating volcanic stone to construct temples and carve monoliths, in particular of bluish-gray andesite, was a critical transformation that manifested Tiwanaku's emergent prestige and expanding geopolitical purchase in the south-central Andes. Workers quarried stones from the foot of Mount Ccapia, a visually stunning ancient volcano just across the lake, and from outcrops near the peninsula of Copacabana, further north, which provided access to the nearby Island of the Sun. Temple alignments toward Ccapia and ritual sites and offerings at Copacabana and on the shores of the Island of the Sun indicate that the Tiwanaku held these to be powerful, animate landforms. Much like transferring the materiality of Corocoro's sandstone, the movement of andesite constituted a material appropriation of the animate power of those landforms to embellish Tiwanaku's new temples and give form to its ancestral personages.

Quarrying volcanic stone from points across the lake produced new circuits of movement for stone and humans and demanded entirely new technologies of stone production (Figure 5.4). Chemical sourcing indicates that Ccapia was the primary source of volcanic andesite for Tiwanaku monumental production (Janusek et al. 2013; Janusek and Williams 2016). Many of Tiwanaku's iconic lithic works—the Solar Portal, the Ponce Monolith, and the massive orthostats of Kalasasaya's west balcony wall—were hewn of Ccapia andesite. Tiwanaku quarry masons likely took advantage of large andesitic boulder outcrops below Ccapia's foothills and near its lakeshores (Protzen and Nair 2013:179–180; Stübel and Uhle 1892:pt. 1, plate 2). Lakeshore sites such as Kanamarka were key locales for gathering, roughly sculpting, and then rafting andesite blocks from Ccapia toward beaches on the east side of the lake. Andesite blocks were then carted up the Tiwanaku valley, likely along the path of the Guaquira River that hews to its north edge. The north edge of Tiwanaku, just north of Kalasasaya, incorporates a ramp that connects Guaquira to the northeast monument campus. Andesite fine carving took place in an area just southeast of this ramp, near Kalasasaya. Several large stones with production scars cover this area of the site. They include a massive andesite block left in the process of being quartered, and another gridded with parallel carved troughs (Janusek and Williams 2016:108). Volcanic stones quarried from Copacabana and Ccapia, rafted across the lake, carted overland along the Guaquira, and then up the ramp to Tiwanaku, were deposited here for fine cutting.

After 600 CE, architects strategically incorporated volcanic stone into Tiwanaku sandstone-and-soil temples. Volcanic blocks were set into spaces prominent during major ritual events and that facilitated dramatic sensory engagements with key celestial movements, water sources, and terrestrial features. Pumapunku's massive east sandstone platform and sunken court supported several carved andesite portals and, covering its primary west staircase entrance, were lintels of Ccapia andesite carved to index the *totora*-reed thatch rooves that protected most Tiwanaku buildings (Janusek 2008:121; Janusek and Williams 2016:109; Ponce 1971:Figures 101–102). Akapana's cyclopean basal west terrace, framing its primary staircase entrance, incorporated regularly placed, bulky andesite orthostats (Janusek et al. 2013:71–73). The Putuni complex featured a primary east entrance and inner and outer facades consisting primarily of andesite, complementing a staircase platform, outer walls, and inner chambers of sandstone blocks (Janusek and Williams 2016:113–114).

Kalasasaya robustly embodies the transition from sandstone to paired sandstone-and-andesite construction (Figure 5.4). This temple likely critically instituted new spatial and building practices in Tiwanaku. Most of the structure was constructed during Late Formative 2 according to iconic Late Formative construction techniques, with facades of roughly carved sandstone blocks framed and buttressed by massive sandstone pilasters set deep into the earth. Kalasasaya's north and south walls feature this technology. Framing its east wall are soft diorite pilasters quarried from a source near Copacabana. This wall was built early in Kalasasaya's construction history. It was its west balcony wall, however, consisting of 11 massive Ccapia pilasters that framed wide segments of well-fitted andesite ashlars, all on a sandstone foundation, that constituted the late *coupe de grace* for andesite construction. This wall not only included a critical sequence of stone markers for observing the annual set points of the sun from solstice to solstice, but it also constituted the east portion of Tiwanaku's remarkable 'andesite corridor.'

Volcanic stone from particular landforms across the lake occupied critical temple locations. The east wall of Kalasasaya, as noted above, incorporated massive dioritic pilasters from sources near Copacabana, most likely by Locka, on the south side of the peninsula. Employing this stone, which is prone to crumbling, was possibly experimental. The massive maquette placed in the east enclosure of the Kantatayita complex, on the other hand, was strategically situated. A west enclosure paved with Ccapia blocks afforded entry into the temple and directed people toward the east enclosure, the temple's inner sanctum. The latter was an intimate room consisting of foundations comprised of large bluish-gray Ccapia andesite blocks. The green-hued, massive andesite maquette they enclosed had been carved to replicate a sunken court replete with staircases and a primary entrance (Posnansky 1945:124–125). It

108 John Wayne Janusek

may have served to choreograph and plan ceremonial performances and, periodically, to accept ritual offerings (Janusek 2008:126). While other blocks we examined in Kantatayita derived from Ccapia, only the maquette and one other block derived from a quarry on the Copacabana peninsula (Janusek and Williams 2016:115).

Tiwanaku's emergence as a primary center corresponded with the expansion of a monumental hydrologic complex articulated with a new program of stone quarrying, cutting, movement, and placement. The ongoing flow of water toward, though, and out of Tiwanaku—which varied dramatically seasonally and over longer-term cycles—complemented the flow of sandstone from Corocoro and andesite from across the lake. While we do not have a precise handle on the exact cycles of stone quarrying, movement, and carving, partially worked stones left behind at every important location in the movement of both types of stone materials indicate that it was recurring, if not ongoing, and likely constituted a dramatic experience of Tiwanaku. The complementary circuits, origins, textures, colors, technologies, and communities of practice attendant on sandstone and volcanic materials defined their respective significance in the center. Major ritual events, I suggest, featured and specified the respective materiality of the stones, in intimate engagement with water flow and celestial movements, as the latent chthonic forces they embodied as appropriated, animate particles of their beings.

Hydrolithic assemblies

Tiwanaku's monumental production rendered carved stone and flowing water potent, fluid, telluric elements that constituted the foundation of an ambitious ontological project. Particularly dramatic, assembled trans-actions of water and stone were ritualized—in Bell's (1992) sense that 'ritual is as ritual does,' as I like to put it—in contexts of human and, in some cases, monolithic, engagement. In some monumental projects, reciprocal trans-actions among specific varieties of water and stone valorized their vital material qualities. For example, a perennial spring some 250 miles south of Pumapunku was converted into a water temple (Figure 5.5). The Choquepacha fountain is at the base of a bluff and, even today, percolates to the surface valued 'sweet' (*mux'a* in Aymara) water from Kimsachata's subterranean aquifer to nourish herds in the marshy plain just west of Tiwanaku. Builders placed at least two carved andesite blocks, each carved at the center of its upper side with a small notch, to direct water down onto two aligned rows of sandstone blocks, each carved with central gutters that directed water toward the marshy plain beyond. The rest of the temple, including revetment blocks to prevent the bluff's erosion, consisted of sandstone. Choquepacha's assembly highlighted the primary articulation of sweet, telluric spring water and andesite. Sandstone played a secondary, if reciprocally important role.

Tiwanaku's southwest and northeast monumental campuses constituted shifting assemblages of soils, stones, water, humans, and monolithic personages, among other elements. Each of their constituent temples required continual transformation, reconstruction, and maintenance (Couture and Sampeck 2003;Vranich 2001,

FIGURE 5.5 Choquepacha Fountain, Tiwanaku's water temple, facing northwest and emphasizing its abundant water flow (photo by J. Janusek)

2009). Pumapunku and Akapana were particularly spectacular constructions that dramatized hydrolithic trans-actions. Both were terraced platforms fitted with elaborate stone revetments that buttressed carefully sifted and layered soils in Akapana, quarried from the nearby Perimeter Canal. In each, impeccably crafted sandstone channels directed water from upper terraces down into the structure, or over its lower terraces and ultimately toward the base terrace. Pumapunku incorporated obliquely aligned canals of impeccably fitted sandstone blocks that were cinched with bronze cramps. The cramps were poured as molten bronze and left to solidify in place (Lechtman 2003). As they solidified and contracted, they pulled the cramped stones tightly together. The channels directed water into drains that surrounded Pumapunku's base terrace, ultimately leading it toward the west marshes fed by Choquepacha. Akapana was riddled with circuitous sandstone channels that drained rainwater downward from its upper terraces via steep stone-lined drop structures, and out of the structure via arched, finely carved outlets built into its lower terrace (Figure 5.6). Water ultimately flowed down into sandstone-lined drains that fed so many deep, subterranean, cardinally aligned monumental canals that funneled it toward the Guaquira River to the north.

Pumapunku and Akapana assembled the cyclical, regenerative capacities of mountains. Their properties shifted from dry to rainy seasons. In the latter, the temples collected water, which, on ritual occasions, drained into elaborate basins down into their subterranean guts and out from their base terraces (Figure 5.6). The sound of gushing water would have been deafening; the structures would

FIGURE 5.6 View east from atop Pumapunku, highlighting the view of Mount Illimani (A) and view west from the balcony platform of Kalasasaya, highlighting a view of Mount Ccapia (B) (photos by J. Janusek)

have trembled dramatically (Kolata 1993:104–134). Yet Pumapunku and Akapana did not just *represent* potent, ancestral mountains such as Kimsachata and Ccapia, their assembly physically *indexed* those mountains. They were crafted of the same matter that constituted mountains and their geophysical landscapes; clay-rich soil that had eroded from Kimsachata; carved sandstone quarried in Corocoro's summit outcrops; andesite ashlars quarried from more distant volcanic outcrops across the lake; and Kimsachata water. The sensorial experience of water flowing through stone canals—its deafening sound, seismic rumble, sudden disappearance in basins and reappearance in basal arched drains—dramatically enacted for ritual participants the seasonally violent flow of water from mountains and, specifically, Kimsachata's streams that passed along the outskirts of Tiwanaku.

Monumental assemblies, Pumapunku and Akapana, honored and *perfected* powerful surrounding mountains such as Kimsachata and Ccapia. Their materiality appropriated the inherent animate power of those dramatic landforms and incorporated them into new, geometrically ordered assemblages that were planned, engineered, and constructed with human effort. These and other temples simultaneously *condensed* intimate engagements of water and stone, temple and sky, and human and monolithic personages. They constituted 'miniature' ecoregimes in a nested ecology of circuits and flows. Tiwanaku's monumental ecoregimes remain incomplete without considering the fleshly and lithic personages that rendered them vital.

Fleshly subjects

Humans were elemental for the dynamic assemblages that created Tiwanaku. They brought a vast range of capacities to bear—including embodied skills and political motivations—on the configuration and transformation of Tiwanaku's broad landscape. As project leaders, engineers, hydrologists, stonemasons, or builders, they made things happen, to paraphrase Bennett (2010:9), and at times were key forces catalyzing the ongoing assembly of Tiwanaku's monumental constructions. Yet these were not the only human operators. Pilgrims, diplomats, ritualists, traders, and others periodically came to Tiwanaku from far regions, drawn to its geopolitical influence, ritual prestige, and monolithic fame. They took new experiences back home with them, perhaps as transformed persons in Turner's (1975) sense of a pilgrim who 'returns to a different home,' fortifying Tiwanaku's distant allure. All such persons were key potential operators in Tiwanaku's ongoing production and expansion.

Movement toward, into, and through Tiwanaku was supremely ritualized. Some people traveled long distances—coming from the eastern and western Andean valleys and the northern Lake Titicaca basin—to participate in recurring Tiwanaku ceremonies (Blom 2005; Janusek and Blom 2006). Travel toward Tiwanaku likely was enacted as pilgrimage. Numerous small Tiwanaku monumental complexes in the altiplano maintain no permanent habitation and yet mark key routes of travel across ecological zones (for example Kachwirkala, Portugal 1998:82–87, and Simillake, Browman 1981:416). This is reminiscent of contemporary pilgrimage to Bolivia's Virgin of Copacabana, during which families traveling to the shrine—located on the south shore of Lake Titicaca—stop at a sequence of small ritual locales situated in mountain passes and other locations to pour libations and pray. Procession into Tiwanaku likely was punctuated by important gestures, libations, or other ritual actions of offering or purification.

Southwest campus

Tiwanaku cyclically gathered huge populations for ritual events, so the question of how visitors entered the city is critical. While this issue is rarely addressed (but see Vranich 1999), we can reconstruct probable entrances based on what we now know of its two primary monumental campuses and the location of waterworks and residential compounds. The south, east, and northwest portions of the city were home to dense residences, workshops, and local temples (Janusek 2004, 2008). Most pilgrims and visitors likely sought to enter Tiwanaku by directly approaching its southwest or northeast monumental campuses. One primary route led people toward Pumapunku and the southwest campus from the west. This would have entailed crossing over the marsh created by the Choquepacha spring, which likely was fitted with perishable bridges for particular events. Because Pumapunku extends westward as a large earthen esplanade over a bluff that bounds the west side of Tiwanaku, an approach from the west created a unique perspective that visually aggrandized Pumapunku as a spectacular massive earthen construction (Vranich 1999).

Movement onto the esplanade brought celebrants close to Pumapunku's primary west entrance. The sandstone staircase entrance was wide, suggesting many could enter at once. Covering the staircase were lithic portals fitted with Ccapia andesite lintels carved to index the totora-reed thatch rooves that covered domestic constructions. Guarding the entrance, and sitting on andesite pedestals on either side of the staircase, was a pair of grimacing chachapumas, each gripping an axe in the right hand and a trophy head in the left (Posnansky 1945:204–207). Scaling the stairway and passing through the portals, celebrants proceeded down a long, enclosed hallway that fed them toward Pumapunku's primary sunken court. Whether just before entering the hallway, or once entering the court, celebrants—on a clear day—captured a dramatic vista of the glacier-capped peak of Illimani directly to the east. In fact, popular human entry up onto Pumapunku likely corresponded with sunrise at auspicious times in the celestial calendar. Once in the court, celebrants had their first sensory engagement with the Pumapunku monolithic personage, who likely inhabited this place.

Kochamama triad and the northeast campus

The other primary entrance to Tiwanaku was its northeast monumental campus. Hydrological and productive systems, in particular the Perimeter Canal, precluded entry from all but its north and south sides. The north side was fitted with a ramp that facilitated the movement of roughly formed andesite blocks up from the Guaquira River. The area below the ramp is where the north extensions of the Perimeter Canal drain into the raised field networks that occupied the marshy river plain just north of the site. This was thus a sort of 'utility entrance' for people moving stone blocks, managing water flow, or working raised fields. The only possible substantial entrance to the campus was to the south, where the Mollo Kontu canal meets the Perimeter Canal; the only place where the Perimeter Canal is not visible on the surface today.

I hypothesize that the Mollo Kontu canal defined a primary route into the northeast monumental campus. The canal follows a straight line toward the Perimeter

Canal for 200 meters. A recent UNESCO-backed project that fitted drones with infrared cameras detected a linear, durable feature that runs parallel to the canal (Gallego Revilla and Pérez González 2018). It may turn out to be a canal wall, but I suspect the imagery detects a hard-packed road that adjoined the canal and led people toward and into the northeast monumental campus. If I am right, celebrants flowing toward the site followed and paralleled the flow of water from Corocoro. As they approached the Perimeter Canal, a triad of monolithic personages greeted them. Archaeologists at the turn of the twentieth century located three monoliths near this junction (Créqui Montfort and de la Grange 1904; Stübel and Uhle 1892). The triad consist of a tall, thin Presentation monolith flanked by two Extended Arm attendants. All three are of red sandstone quarried from Corocoro. Did this mono-lithic triad serve to greet—and perhaps intimidate— humans as they sought entry into the water-bounded campus? Their placement at a critical hydraulic junction and entrance intimates that this was the case. Water flowing from Kimsachata and humans following its flow toward Tiwanaku, jointly encountering a triad of imposing sandstone personages—also from near Kimsachata—at one of Tiwanaku's rare entrances, constituted a potent moment in the trans-action of its animate materialities.

The central Presentation monolith of the triad, Kochamama, depicts repetitive iconography indexing water and fish (Figure 5.7). Its iconography differs consid-erably from that of other Presentation monoliths. A repeating image is a circle bounded by 'rippled' lines, each of which sprouts multiple fish-headed appendages. Sprouting fish heads dominate Kochamama's iconography, likely emphasizing its relationship with the aquatic juncture it guarded. Further, two large fish-head assemblages rise up from its pedestal and along the sides of its lower legs. They rise from the depths of the earth in which Kochamama stands and, more precisely, from the Perimeter Canal the personage stood beside and, during rainy seasons, within.

Akapana and Kalasasaya

Once past this juncture humans processed through some of the northeast campus's core monumental constructions. Closest and to the northeast was the main entrance of the Akapana, consisting in a wide staircase surrounded by andesite pedestals that likely supported at least two basalt *chachpuma* sculptures, one of which was found in situ in 1989 (Kolata 1993:126–129; Manzanilla 1992). Akapana's staircase, much like Pumapunku's, drew processions of celebrants to the top of the platform, affording a majestic due east view of the glaciated peak of Illimani. A striking, bulky, three-piece portal of dark Ccapia andesite likely framed this view, or that of the entrance to a hypothetical sunken temple and inner sanctum—long since gutted—to which those who scaled Akapana ultimately led. As at Pumapunku, such ritual processions were timed according to particularly auspicious moments of solar rise (e.g., equinox, sol-stice, etc.) on the eastern horizon in relation to Illamani (Figure 5.8).

Procession through Akapana directed people toward the south entrance of the Sunken Temple and, to the west, the primary west entrance into Kalasasaya's

FIGURE 5.7 Hydraulic features in the Akapana platform. (A) A perforated stone water collector and canals in a residential complex atop Akapana. (B) Arched drainage outtakes at the base of Akapana's lowest terrace (photos by J. Janusek)

FIGURE 5.8 The Kochamama Monolith Triad, located just east of the intersection of the Mollo Kontu and Perimeter Canal. Left image shows the triad in situ (adapted from a postcard ca. 1912). Center image shows Kochamama's (central monolith) right torso iconography, bedecked with rippled icons sprouting fish-headed appendages, and a fish-headed appendage traversing its arm (adapted from Posnansky 1945, Figure 101b). Right image shows Kochamama's lower portion, with large down-facing fish heads hanging from its lower garment and one of two opposing fish-headed creatures slithering up from the personage's feet and pedestal (adapted from Wright 1907:258)

platform. Movement into Kalasasaya facilitated a visual engagement with Mount Ccapia to the northeast. The west portion of the platform, divided from the bulk of the platform by a low wall, served as a place to observe settings of the sun on the horizon from austral winter to austral summer solstice. A west 'balcony wall' buttressed by 11 imposing andesite pilasters—Tiwanaku's largest known volcanic blocks, all quarried from Ccapia—bounded this platform. As the setting sun shifted across the horizon, each block marked or 'captured' its descent at a key moment in the annual cycle, as viewed by a person standing on a platform at the east edge of the balcony. When it set over the wall's northernmost Ccapia block on the austral winter solstice (June 21), the sun also set over the peak of that ancient volcano (Figure 5.8). At dusk on that day, solar flow, the ancestral peak—the source of most andesite and of the block that captured the solstice sunset—the Kalasasaya platform, the persons gathered in ritual procession to experience the event, and the andesite Ponce monolith for which Kalasasaya served as a temple home, gathered in a spectacular relational moment of ritual transformation.

Andesite Corridor

Kalasasaya's west balcony corresponded with the construction of the Putuni platform just to the west in CE 600–700. Putuni enclosed a large courtyard and was the ceremonial space for an upper status residence nestled into its northwest portion (Couture 2002; Couture and Sampeck 2003). Together, Kalasasaya and Putuni constituted an architectural ensemble aligned toward Mount Ccapia to the west. Vranich convincingly proposes (2009, 2016) that a route of human movement tied the structures together in processional time. Fitted with a diminutive andesite monolith (Janusek 2019), the Putuni courtyard constituted a local space for commensal events that followed the majestic views and momentous ritual acts in Kalasasaya. Hosts, pilgrims, ritualists, diplomats, and others proceeded west along Kalasasaya's north side—from any of a few staircases, most people likely exiting back out from the main east staircase—turned left (south) and continued through a cramped corridor, flanked to the right by the Chunchukala, and exited into the vast, dramatic corridor that separated Kalasasaya from Putuni (Figure 5.9). To the left, celebrants finally experienced the sheer monumentality of Kalasasaya's balcony wall, and the breathtaking depth of its 11 sun-capturing andesite pilasters. To the right, they witnessed the impeccably crafted east wall of the Putuni platform, one of the finest in Tiwanaku. Seams between stones were flush, and imperfections grafted

FIGURE 5.9 The Andesite Corridor that frames Mount Kimsachata in the distance (facing south). It is created by Kalasasaya's balcony wall, to the left (east), and Putuni's east platform wall, to the right (west) (photo by J. Janusek)

with tiny, impeccable ashlars. Apart from the foundation on which Kalasasaya's pilasters rested, both walls consisted entirely of andesite, and all the blocks we sampled derived from Ccapia. The andesite corridor was one of a kind.

Tiwanaku's andesite corridor condensed the flows, materials, and relations that accrued ritual potency as Tiwanaku emerged as a primary center in the region. It *embodied* that potency. It effectively re-centered the south-facing views that that Late Formative Sunken Temple had celebrated prior to Akapana's construction (Benitez 2013; Janusek 2004, 2006). The corridor framed Mount Kimsachata to the south, Tiwanaku's cardinal focal point in the Corocoro range. It effectively decentered the Late Formative Sunken Temple by re-centering the south view in a corridor formed by new temples constructed of more durable, volcanic materials. The view south linked humans, sky, water, and stone. It framed the mountain over which the southern celestial pole spun nightly, from which Tiwanaku's rich aquifer, springs, and streams originated and, just nearby, where Tiwanaku's sandstone originated. The andesite corridor, bounded by the Kalasasaya-Putuni ensemble oriented east–west toward Ccapia, framed this engagement. It reconstituted Kimachata's vitality as an ancient, yet still-vital, source of celestial, aquatic, and lithic potency. Movement through the andesite corridor constituted another macro-moment.

Monolithic personages

Monoliths were the famed, powerful nonhuman beings that people came to apprehend when they thronged to Tiwanaku for calendrical ritual events. Monoliths were Tiwanaku's key nonhuman operators, and its platform and sunken court complexes constituted their temple homes. Presentation monoliths were Tiwanaku's most *famous* personages (sensu Munn 986). All but the Kochamama monolith, described above, were found in association with a monumental construction; the Pumapunku in the Pumapunku complex, the Fraile on the west side of Kalasasaya, the Ponce under Kalasasaya's sunken court, and the massive Bennett (~8 meters tall) lying prone in the Sunken Temple. Most consist of Corocoro sandstone; only Ponce consists of Ccapia andesite. Each is a large—in the case of Ponce and Bennett, enormous—standing personage wearing elaborate clothing (Figure 5.10). Each clutches to its chest a drinking chalice, or *kero*, with its right arm, and a tablet for ingesting consciousness-altering snuff, in its left (Torres 2001, 2018). The gesture identifies them as lithic personages offering the contents of those objects to their fleshly interlocutors (also Bandy 2013, Janusek 2006). Ceramic braziers placed around the bases of the monoliths dramatized their flickering vitality by night.

Monolithic personages occupied Tiwanaku's inner sancta. They were central to Tiwanaku's expanding prestige and geopolitical influence as a ceremonial city (Janusek 2006, 2019). Archaeologists describe monoliths as located in one or another of Tiwanaku's key monumental spaces. My research encourages an epistemic shift; rather than thinking of monumental complexes as housing this or that monolith, I retrain our frame to consider monumental complexes as *temple homes for* particular monoliths. This aligns far better with emergent understandings of

FIGURE 5.10 Three of Tiwanaku's five known presentation monoliths, shown to relative scale: Fraile (A), Bennett (B), and Ponce (C). Fraile consists of sandstone and stands 2.8 meters high (including its buried plinth); Bennett consists of sandstone and stands 7.3 meters high; and Ponce consists of andesite and stands 3.2 meters high (image B courtesy of Clare Sammells, A and C by J. Janusek)

other sculptures in the Andes, for example, the Lanzón monolith around which the early Formative temple of Chavín de Huantar, Peru, was constructed (Weismantel 2014), or the powerful wooden idol of Pachacamac—the 'World Creator'—who 'inhabited' his shrine at the time of Spanish conquest (Estete 1843[1534]).

Tempering the reciprocal gesture of Presentation Monoliths were the hierarchical relations that tied them to humans and other monolith classes. Monoliths always present *keros* and snuff tablets with two left hands, which, drawing on Inca analogy (Cummins 2002:64–65; Janusek 2019), suggests monoliths addressed their human interlocutors as lesser status 'recipients.' Extended Arm guardians flanked and guarded Presentation monoliths. The aforementioned sandstone Kochamama triad epitomizes this relation. Two andesite Extended Arm monoliths that likely originally flanked and attended the andesite Ponce indicate that monoliths condensed social hierarchies and ethnic differences. The Extended Arm Pachacama and Suñawa monoliths stand exactly the same height (2.2 meters). Yet, while Pachacama wears a bulbous turban, Suñawa wears a squared hat. This complementarity resonates with my dissertation findings, which indicated that Tiwanaku was a cosmopolitan city that incorporated diverse communities drawn from far regions (Janusek 2002, 2004). Research with bio-anthropologist Deborah Blom indicated that, for human bodies, communal diversity manifested as two broad styles of cranial modification, annular (conical) and squared (flattened) (Blom 2005; Janusek and Blom 2006). Complementary styles of woven headgear—conical and squared hats (Frame 1990)—accentuated the different styles of modified heads. Cranial modification and respective woven clothing constituted embodied practices of identification in Tiwanaku. Pachacama and Suñawa condensed two broad cranial styles and macro-community identifications as paired, subservient attendants to primary Presentation personages, Tiwanaku's most powerful other-than-human beings.

Chachapumas comprised a third class of monoliths. They guarded entrances to Tiwanaku's temples and directed processions toward Presentation and Extended Arm monoliths. Chachapumas—man-feline in Aymara—were paired, transitive beings. All consist of volcanic stone, whether bluish-gray andesite or black basalt. They embody standing, kneeling, or crouching personages carved with imagery of human sacrifice. Most hold an axe in one hand and a severed human head in the other; two hold a severed head in front of their torsos. Their fierce composure and sacrificial imagery suggest that they demanded a 'sacrifice' of the humans who entered Tiwanaku's inner sancta. This may well have involved specific offerings, not to mention acts of purification, but also perhaps a ritual, transformative 'death' for initiates in order to become fully capacitated Tiwanaku persons. Maurice Bloch notes (1992) that rites of passage globally, and coming of age specifically, require not just a 'liminal' phase of transformation, as Van Gennep argued, but also a dramatic sacrificial death and rebirth of the prior, 'raw' human being as a socialized, newly empowered person. Chachapumas ensured that those who entered Tiwanaku's inner sancta were appropriately crafted subjects.

Monoliths were Tiwanaku's key nonhuman operators and its famed monumental campuses their temple homes. Humans encountered lithic personages in recurring cycles of pilgrimage that facilitated charged, transformative ritual engagements. Those engagements featured trans-actions that reciprocally created fully animate lithic and empowered fleshly subjects. Chachapumas did sacrificial dirty work, ensuring that those who entered monolithic temple-homes consisted in appropriately purified and gestured ritual subjects. Extended Arm Attendants were lithic guardians, some of whom condensed the multiplex bodies of Tiwanaku's diverse communities. Presentation Monoliths were Tiwanaku's rock stars, and human pilgrims trumpeted their fame—ensuring their spatiotemporal expansion and geopolitical impact (sensu Munn 1986)—by enacting pilgrimage to visit them, making offerings for them, and sharing stories and tokens of those potent experiences upon their return home. Tiwanaku's urban reach transcended the city, its tentacles of influence were far-flung, and its modes of geopolitical influence were far more intricate and embodied than traditional political models can account.

Assembling Tiwanaku

Tiwanaku was a unique urban phenomenon in the pre-Columbian Andes. Its ritual-political gravity and peculiar material assembly trumpeted its identity as a place of ritual and social gathering. In this capacity, Tiwanaku differed from other well-known Andean cities. It differed dramatically from Wari, in the Ayacucho region to the northwest, which emphasized high walls and exclusionary spaces (Isbell and Vranich 2004). If Wari spatial practices kept people out, Tiwanaku sought to bring in diverse communities.

Tiwanaku's peculiar character and geopolitical renown crystallized in formative generations. Middle Formative centers such as Chiripa, which dated to 400–200 BCE, were centers of periodic ritual, social, and political gathering as much as they were centers of permanent occupation and geopolitical control (Hastorf 2003). During the ensuing Late Formative (200 BCE–500 CE), Tiwanaku was one of several centers in a multicentered political community until, after 150 CE, it and Khonkho Wankane, across the Corocoro range, constituted a primary 'pair' of centers for the next 200 years. Most of Tiwanaku's Formative occupations lie buried under later urban constructions. Khonkho Wankane was an incipient urban center (Janusek 2015a, 2015b) that drew communities for specific, calendrical events from across the southern Lake Titicaca region. Excavations indicate that Tiwanaku was a similar center (Janusek 2019; Ponce 1981). Khonkho and Tiwanaku were paired centers that shared much in common; their Sunken Temples facilitated the same celestial observations, they were populated with similar Mocachi-style anthropomorphic monoliths (Janusek and Ohnstad 2018), and they resided on the same north–south cardinal orientation across the Corocoro range.

A political ecology framework informed with new materialist insight affords an unexplored dimension for understanding Tiwanaku. Like most interpretations of cities in the Western tradition, including those of Louis Wirth and the Chicago School of Urban Sociology, most archaeological interpretations of Tiwanaku restrict themselves to the domain of human relations and activities. As noted, humans were key operators, but by far not the only—and perhaps not even the most important—operators in the city. Water from ritualized springs and imposing mountains ebbed and flowed in the city seasonally, always constituting a dynamic element of its form and cyclical events. Stones quarried from animate mountains and outcrops constituted complementary cycles of flow toward the city, likely the work of specialized communities of stonemasons. While sandstone quarried from Corocoro regularly made its way to Tiwanaku from a primary quarry near the animated personages of Turituini, andesite found its way to the center via totora raft across the south portion of Titicaca, up the lower Tiwanaku Valley, and ultimately across a ramp just north of Kalasasaya. Water and stone were not dead utilitarian resources. In Tiwanaku, they were vital matters that manifested the telluric power of the mountains, springs, and other animate earthly features they derived from and indexed.

Such a perspective explodes Tiwanaku's boundaries and expands insights into its core activities and expansive tentacles. Archaeologists for years have occupied themselves with the standard drive to determine Tiwanaku's urban extent—but largely unsuccessfully, since estimates range from 4 to nearly 7 square kilometers (Kolata 1993; Lémuz 2005). Whatever its extent, this perspective limits the city to an area of primary human occupation and cyclical gathering. We have seen that Tiwanaku incorporated a seasonally shifting water network that linked it to Kimsachata, to the south, and the Guaquira River, to the north. We have also seen that Tiwanaku's very construction hinged on stones quarried from Corocoro and from volcanic outcrops on Lake Titicaca's shores. The axiality and orientation of Tiwanaku's temples, even as they shifted, indexed a panoply of nighttime and daytime celestial movements and cycles. Taking these expansive material flows seriously and, for the sake of critical thought, bundling them as a conjoined urban production, I ask: What *were* Tiwanaku's urban boundaries? Minimally, its 'human occupation' constituted the core of its monuments, residences, and local material catchment. Maximally, Tiwanaku was an expansive urban phenomenon that included the vast ecologies and multiplex celestial, aquatic, and lithic flows it gathered. In the latter sense, the experience that drove Tiwanaku's fame and geo-political influence, Tiwanaku gathered flows and condensed vitalities from across the south–central Andes and material cosmos.

Political ecology armed with new materialist insight helps us make sense of the vast swaths of productive features in past urban landscapes such as Tiwanaku. Productive practices are not vital urban activities following traditional perspectives on urbanism (Childe 1950; Smith 2009). Primary productive careers of farming and pastoralism, according to Western urban ideals, are best located outside the city. Recent research acknowledging evidence for vast landscapes of garden and farming in pre-Columbian Mesoamerican cities considers them case studies in 'low-density' urbanism (Isendahl and Smith 2013; Scarborough et al. 2012). While archaeologists tout their sustainability, by not addressing the question, 'What is urban density,' they uncritically produce an assumption of density as 'purity.' The concept of low-density urbanism is a slippery slope down into the morass of narrow-minded thinking on urbanism; for urban ecologists, it applies equally to contemporary North American cities flanked by vast, sprawling suburbs and strip malls, which are decidedly not landscapes of primary production.

Pre-Columbian cities like Tiwanaku and Cuzco incorporated vast productive and hydrological systems. They were low-density cities. I prefer to call them, simply, *cities*, noting that most cities *everywhere* encompass vast outlying settlements (e.g., suburbs) or intermittent productive regimes (e.g., farms, gardens, fisheries). As part of its hydrologic network, Tiwanaku incorporated several areas dedicated to farming and herding. First, streams on either side of the site, both engineered to carry rainy-season overflow around the edges of the inhabited city, fed areas ideal for llama and alpaca grazing. Second, the southeast sector of the site consisted of an interlinked cluster of sunken basins, or *qochas*, dedicated to farming and herding. This network linked into Tiwanaku's encompassing hydraulic grid. Third, Tiwanaku incorporated raised field systems along primary canals and at the north edge of the city. Archaeologists interpret raised fields as the enterprise of 'rural' farmers in peri-urban landscapes; the Katari Valley's Koani Pampa in Bolivia, or the Huatta Pampa of Puno, Peru (Erickson 1999; Janusek and Kolata 2004; Kolata 1991). Rather, *qocha* and raised field systems were integral urban activities in Tiwanaku.

Stone and water created electric engagements in Tiwanaku's urban landscape. While each material maintained its temporality of ebb and flow, specific architecture and materials apostrophized their dramatic encounters. The terraced platforms of Akapana and Pumapunku incorporated labyrinthine sandstone-lined drainage networks that carried water down into and throughout the structures toward massive, deeply buried canals to lead subterranean water and waste toward the Guaquira River. Canals cinched with bronze cramps dramatized the sound and tectonic impact of water flowing through the temples built to ritualize stone-water engagements, creating powerful experiences during astronomically scheduled ceremonies. Water disappearing into carved basins on Pumapunku and Akapana and then reappearing as streams emerging from basal canal outlets, celebrated its dramatic flows and intricate circuits.

Volcanic stone became a valued lithic material once Tiwanaku leaders and architects incorporated and began quarrying volcanic outcrops across the south portion of Lake Titicaca. Andesite came to complement traditional sandstone construction via its inclusion in particularly valued, witnessed, or ritualized places; for example, Pumapunku's upper terraces, Akapana's impeccably carved west buttresses, Kalasasaya's west solar observatory and balcony wall, and Putuni's platform (Janusek and Williams 2016). Over generations, sandstone came to index the local Corocoro range and its ancient quarries in Corocoro, while andesite came to index the volcanic landscapes recently brought into Tiwanaku's expanding fold. Sandstone indexed Tiwanaku's local geopolitical past, and andesite its expansive geopolitical mission. Tiwanaku temples manifested these values and relations. For example, in Choquepacha andesite blocks guided water from the Kimsachata's subterranean, telluric aquifer onto sandstone gutters that then directed it out from the center via spaghetti-like canals on the west side of the city. Whether because andesite was quarried from near the shores of the nearby lake, or because both are bluish-gray in color, spring water and andesite assumed a valued relation in Tiwanaku.

Trans-actions between monoliths and humans constituted the most potent and transformative engagements in Tiwanaku. Presentation Monoliths were Tiwanaku's most powerful denizens. They stood at the whirling center of the myths, legends, and rituals that drew humans from vast communities to the center. Temples constituted their homes, and pilgrims, diplomats, ritualists, and others came to Tiwanaku periodically, their visit timed according to astronomically ordered seasonal cycles, to engage and supplicate them, whether via songs, prayers, libations, offerings, or sacrifices. This is not to say every person was allowed to approach Tiwanaku's lithic personages, or had the guts to do so, as was the case with pilgrims to the wooden idol of Pachacamac on the central Peruvian coast (Estete 1843[1534]). Regardless, making a pilgrimage to Tiwanaku—approaching the center, entering its bounded southwest (Pumapunku) and northeast (Akapana-Kalasasaya) campuses—constituted potent ritual acts.

Conclusion

Monoliths were Tiwanaku's centers of ritual gravity. As the Formative graded into the Middle Horizon, monolithic production shrank from multiple centers into one. After AD 500, erecting monoliths ceased at regional centers such as Khonkho Wankane, where they had stood during the Late Formative. Tiwanaku enacted a kind of centripetal monopoly on monolithic production and erection; from the beginning of the Middle Horizon through the very end of monolithic production at the beginning of the Late Intermediate Period, Tiwanaku is the only center that featured large-scale Presentation, Extended Arm, and Chachapuma monoliths. Small-scale Extended Arm and Chachapuma sculptures are known from local residential contexts and a few surrounding centers, indicating that stone sculptures constituted an emergent geopolitical cartography in the southern basin (Janusek 2019). Once inside a sunken enclosure, humans approached monoliths cautiously and conducted solemn ritual acts, whether libations, offerings, dramatic sacrifices, or more simply, prayer-like supplications.

Human encounters with monoliths centered on a reciprocal animacy that drove Tiwanaku's ritual-political fame. Monoliths and their lithic guardians demanded that humans approach them as ancient, honored, and powerful beings. Devout humans were appropriately gestured, attired, attentive, and in a proper ritual state fostered by *chicha* and/or mind-altering resins. Humans approached monoliths or at least drew near their residences with pragmatic projects in mind, whether supplicating for a healthy family, a rich harvest, a productive herd, a new house, or a successful business deal. If the details of these proposed projects are lost to us, the reciprocal animacy of lithic and fleshly beings that emerged from these encounters is clear. Humans approached monoliths as potent living beings just as monoliths reciprocally demanded that humans act as appropriately embodied, fully animate persons. People returned from these engagements empowered, vital citizens in Tiwanaku's ritual-political mission. As Victor Turner (1975) alluded long ago, they returned, deeply transformed, to a different home.

124 John Wayne Janusek

Tiwanaku emerged in a multi-centric field of formative centers in the Lake Titicaca basin. In the middle of the first millennium CE, it emerged as a city that garnered remarkable fame and wielded ritual-geopolitical influence across the Andes. In this chapter we have followed the materials to get at the center's political ecology and its gravity as the center of a transformative ecoregime intricately tied to its expanding environment. Tiwanaku comprised and condensed an ongoing assembly of fields (e.g., earth, sky), flows (e.g., water, stone), and beings (e.g., mountains, humans, monoliths) in order to create a vital cosmopolitical cartography. This living cartography demanded constant work. Ultimately, in the volatile shift that archaeologists term 'Tiwanaku collapse,' it disintegrated as material assemblies and flows rerouted and redirected dramatically in the face of climatic and macro-geopolitical shifts to generate decentralized, mobile pastoral communities.

Tiwanaku drew people from far regions for transformative experiences that created an expansive geopolitical regime. It did this by creating the foundations for cross-ontological trans-actions, hydrolithic engagements, and encounters between fleshly and lithic personages. Humans did not monopolize Tiwanaku politics. Tiwanaku's fame resided in the gritty materiality and auspicious encounters of its heterogeneous, relational beings. Their descendants remain potent in Bolivia today. Monoliths are still powerful persons that live by night, and people born in the town of Tiahuanaco are *kalawawa*, born of stone. Tiwanaku's water temple remains a potent place of ritual offering. Old subjectivities die hard. Stone and hydrolithic assemblies remain critical for Tiahuanaco's vitality in a global world order.

Notes

1 The term Bennett uses, drawing on Gilles Deleuze, is 'quasi-causal operator.' I have reduced this ponderous phrase, which clarifies that such operators are never *entirely* causal in an assemblage, to its core term.
2 See Joyce's (Chapter 4) discussion of 'agential cuts' for a parallel discussion.

References

Abbott, Mark, Michael W. Binford, Mark Brenner, and Kerry Kelts 1997 A 4500 14C yr high-resolution record of water-level changes in Lake Titicaca, Bolivia-Peru. *Quaternary Research* 47:169–180.

Abercrombie, Thomas 1998 *Pathways of Memory and Power: Ethnography and History among an Andean People.* University of Wisconsin, Madison.

Allen, Catherine 2002 *The Hold Life Has: Coca and Cultural Identity in an Andean Community*, 2nd edition. Smithsonian Books, Washington, DC.

Althusser, Louis 1971 Ideology and Ideological State Apparatuses. In *Lenin and Philosophy and Other Essays*, translated by Ben Brewster, pp. 127–186. Monthly Review Press, New York.

Argollo, Jorge, Leo Ticcla, Alan L. Kolata, and Oswaldo Rivera 1996 Geology, Geomophology, and Soils of the Tiwanaku and Catari River Basins. In *Tiwanaku and its Hinterland: Archaeology and Paleoecology of an Andean Civilization, Vol. 1.*, edited by Alan L. Kolata, pp. 57–88. Smithsonian Institution Press, Washington, DC.

Bandy, Matthew 2013 Tiwanaku Origins and Early Development: The Political and Moral Economy of a Hospitality State. In *Visions of Tiwanaku*, edited by Alexei Vranich and

Charles Stanish, pp. 135–150. Cotsen Institute of Archaeology Press, University of California, Los Angeles.

Barad, Karen 2007 *Meeting the University Halfway: Quantum Physics and the Entanglement of Matter and Meaning*. Duke University Press, Durham, NC.

Bell, Catherine 1992 *Ritual Theory, Ritual Practice*. Oxford University Press, Oxford.

Benitez, Leonardo 2013 What Would Celebrants See? Sky, Landscape, and Settlement Planning in the Late Formative Southern Titicaca Basin. In *Advances in Titicaca Basin Archaeology 2*, edited by Alexi Vranich and Arthur Levine, pp. 89–104. UCLA Cotsen Institute of Archaeology, Los Angeles.

Bennett, Jane 2010 *Vibrant Matter: A Political Ecology of Things*. Duke University Press, Durham, NC.

Bentley, Nicholas 2013 The Tiwanaku of A. F. Bandelier. In *Advances in Titicaca Basin Archaeology-2*, edited by Alexei Vranich and Abigail R. Levine, pp. 117–126. UCLA Cotsen Institute of Archaeology, Los Angeles.

Biersack, Aletta 2006 Reimagining Political Ecology: Culture/Power/History/Nature. In *Reimagining Political Ecology*, edited by Aletta Biersack and James B. Greenburg, pp. 3–40. Duke University Press, Durham, NC.

Binford, Michael W., Alan L. Kolata, Mark Brenner, John W. Janusek, Matthew T. Seddon, Mark Abbott, and Jason H. Curtis 1997 Climate Variation and the Rise and Fall of an Andean Civilization. *Quaternary Research* 47(2):235–248.

Bloch, Maurice 1992 *Prey into Hunter: The Politics of Religious Experience*. Cambridge University Press, Cambridge.

Blom, Deborah E. 2005 Embodying Borders: Human Body Modification and Diversity in Tiwanaku Society. *Journal of Anthropological Archaeology* 24(1):1–34.

Browman, David L. 1981 New Light on Andean Tiwanaku. *American Scientist* 69(4):408–419.

———— 1997 Political Institutional Factors Contributing to the Integration of the Tiwanaku State. In *Emergence and Change in Early Urban Societies*, edited by Linda Manzanilla, pp. 229–244. Plenum Press, New York.

Childe, V. Gordon 1950 The Urban Revolution. *Town Planning Review* 21(1):3–17.

Cohen, Amanda, and Andrew Roddick 2007 Excavations in the AC (Achachi Coa Kkollu) Sector. In *Kala Uyuni: An Early Political Center in the Southern Lake Titicaca Basin, Excavations of the Taraco Archaeological Project*, edited by Matthew S. Bandy and Christine A. Hastorf, pp. 41–66. Archaeological Research Facility, University of California, Berkeley.

Conklin, Beth 2001 *Consuming Grief: Compassionate Cannibalism in an Amazonian Society*. University of Texas Press, Austin.

Coole, Diana, and Samantha Frost 2010 Introducing the New Materialisms. In *New Materialisms: Ontology, Agency, Politics*, edited by Diana Coole and Samantha Frost, 1–43. Duke University Press, Durham, NC.

Cosgrove, Denis E. 1998 *Social Formation and Symbolic Landscape*. University of Wisconsin Press, Madison.

Couture, Nicole Claire 2002 The Construction of Power: Monumental Space and an Elite Residence at Tiwanaku, Bolivia. Unpublished PhD Dissertation. University of Chicago.

Couture, Nicole C., and Sampeck, Kathryn 2003 'Putuni: A History of Palace Architecture in Tiwanaku.' *Tiwanaku and Its Hinterland: Archaeology and Paleecology of an Andean Civilization, Vol. 2*, edited by A. L. Kolata, pp. 226–263. Smithsonian Institution Press, Washington, DC.

Cowgill, George 2015 *Ancient Teotihuacan: Early Urbanism in Central Mexico*. Cambridge University Press, Cambridge.

Créqui-Montfort, MM. de, and Sénéchal de la Grange 1904 Rapport sur une Mission Scientifique en Amérique du Sud (Bolivie, République Argentine, Chili, Pérou). *Nouvelles Archives des Missions Scientifiques* 12:81–129.

Cronon, William 1992 *Nature's Metropolis: Chicago and the Great West.* W. W. Norton, New York.

Cummins, Thomas B. F. 2002 *Toasts with the Inca: Andean Abstraction and Colonial Images on Quero Vessels.* University of Michigan Press, Ann Arbor.

Dean, Carolyn J. 2010 *A Culture of Stone: Inka Perspectives on Rock.* Duke University Press, Durham, NC.

DeLanda, Manuel 2006 *A New Philosophy of Society: Assemblage Theory and Social Complexity.* Continuum, London.

Deleuze, Gilles, and Felix Guattari 1987 *A Thousand Plateaus: Capitalism and Schizophrenia.* University of Minnesota Press, Minneapolis.

Dewey, John, and Arthur F. Bentley 1949 *Knowing and the Known.* Beacon Press, Boston.

De la Cadena, Marisol 2015 *Earth Beings: Ecologies of Practice across Andean Worlds.* Duke University Press, Durham, NC.

Edgeworth, Matthew 2011 *Fluid Pasts: Archaeology of Flow.* Bristol Classical Press, London.

Erickson, Clark 1999 Neo-Environmental Determinism and Agrarian 'Collapse' in Andean Prehistory. *Antiquity* 73(281): 634–642.

Escobar, Arturo 1999 After Nature: Steps toward an Antiessential Political Ecology. *Current Anthropology* 40(1):1–20.

Estete, Miguel de 1843[1534] La relación del Viaje que hizo el Señor capitán Hernando Pizarro por mandado de su hermano desde el pueblo de Caxamarca a Parcama y de allí a Jauja. In *Verdadera relación de la conquista del Perú*, edited by Francisco de Xerez. BAE 26:338–346.

Flores Ochoa, Jorge A. 1987 Cultivation in the *qocha* of the South American Puna. In *Arid Land Use Strategies and Risk Management in the Andes: A Regional Anthropological Perspective*, edited by David L. Browman, pp. 271–296. Westview Press, Boulder.

Frame, Mary 1990 *Andean Four-Cornered Hats.* Metropolitan Museum of Art, New York.

Gallego Revilla, José Ignacio, and María Eugenia Pérez González 2018 *Tiwanaku: Entre el Cielo y la Tierra.* UNESCO, Quito.

Gandy, Matthew 2003 *Concrete and Clay: Reworking Nature in New York City.* MIT Press, Cambridge, MA.

Harris, Oliver J. T. 2017 Assemblages and Scale in Archaeology. *Cambridge Archaeological Journal* 27(1):127–139.

Hastorf, Christine 2003 Community with the Ancestors: Ceremonies and Social Memory in the Middle Formative at Chiripa, Bolivia. *Journal of Anthropological Archaeology* 22(4):302–332.

Headrick, Annabeth 2007 *The Teotihuacan Trinity: The Sociopolitical Structure of an Ancient Mesoamerican City.* University of Texas Press, Austin.

Isbell, William H. 2013 Nature of an Andean City: Tiwanaku and the Production of Spectacle. In *Visions of Tiwanaku*, edited by Alexie Vranich and Charles Stanish, pp. 167–196. UCLA Cotsen institute of Archaeology, Los Angeles.

Isbell, William H., and Alexei Vranich 2004 Experiencing the Cities of Wari and Tiwanaku. In *Andean Archaeology*, edited by Helaine Silverman, 167–182. Blackwell, New York.

Isendahl, Christian, and Michael E. Smith 2013 Sustainable Agrarian Urbanism: The Low-Density Cities of the Mayas and Aztecs. *Cities* 31:132–143.

Jackson, John Brinckerhoff 1986 *Discovering the Vernacular Landscape.* Yale University Press, New Haven.

Janusek, John Wayne 2002 Out of Many, One: Style and Social Boundaries in Tiwanaku. *Latin American Antiquity* 13(1):35–61.

———— 2004 *Identity and Power in the Ancient Andes: Tiwanaku Cities through Time.* Routledge, London.

———— 2006 The Changing 'Nature' of Tiwanaku Religion and the Rise of an Andean State. *World Archaeology* 38(3):469–492.

———— 2008 *Ancient Tiwanaku.* Cambridge University Press, Cambridge.

———— 2015a Of Monoliths and Men: Human-Lithic Encounters and the Production of an Animistic Ecology at Khonkho Wankane. In *The Archaeology of Wak'as: Explorations of the Sacred in the Precolumbian Andes*, edited by Tamara L. Bracy, pp. 335–368. University of Colorado Press, Boulder.

———— 2015b Incipient Urbanism at the Early Andean Center of Khonkho Wankane, Bolivia. *Journal of Field Archaeology* 40(2):127–142.

———— 2019 Cosmopolitical Bodies: Living Monoliths, Vital Tectonics, and the Production of Tiwanaku. In *Sacred Matter: Animacy and Authority in the Precolumbian World*, edited by Steven Kosiba, John W. Janusek, and Thomas Cummins, Dumbarton Oaks, Harvard University, Washington, DC.

Janusek, John Wayne, and Deborah E. Blom 2006 Identifying Tiwanaku Urban Populations: Style, Identity, and Ceremony in Andean Cities. In *Urbanization in the Preindustrial World: Cross-Cultural Perspectives*, edited by Glenn Storey, pp. 233–251. University of Alabama Press, Tuscaloosa.

Janusek, John Wayne, and Corey Bowen 2018 Tiwanaku as Telluric Landscape: Water and Stone in a Highland Andean City. In *Powerful Landscapes in the Ancient Andes*, edited by Justin Jennings, and Edward R. Swenson, 209-246. Albuquerque: University of New Mexico Press.

Janusek, John Wayne, and Alan L. Kolata 2004 Top-Down or Bottom-Up: Rural Settlement and Raised Field Agriculture in the Lake Titicaca Basin, Bolivia. *Journal of Anthropological Archaeology* 23(4):404–430.

Janusek, John Wayne, and Arik Ohnstad 2018 Stone Stelae of the Southern Basin: A Stylistic Chronology of Ancestral Personages. In *Images in Action: The Southern Andean Iconographic Series*, edited by William H. Isbell, Mauricio I. Uribe, Anne Tibali, and Edward P. Zegarra, pp. 75–106. UCLA Cotsen Institute of Archaeology Press, Los Angeles.

Janusek, John Wayne, and Charles Ortloff 2014 Water Management at Tiwanaku: Revisiting the Urban 'Moat' and its Hydraulic Features. Paper presented at the 54th Annual Meeting of the Institute of Andean Studies, January 11, University of California, Berkeley.

Janusek, John Wayne, Patrick Ryan Williams, Mark Golitko, and Carlos Lemuz 2013 Building Taypikala: Telluric Transformations in the Lithic Production of Tiwanaku. In *Mining and Quarrying in the Ancient Andes: Sociopolitical, Economic and Symbolic Dimensions*, edited by Nicolas Tripcevich and Kevin Vaughn, pp. 65–98. Springer, New York.

Janusek, John Wayne, and Patrick Ryan Williams 2016 Telluric Technē and the Lithic Production of Tiwanaku. In *Making Value, Making Meaning: Technē in Pre-Columbian Mesoamerica and Andean South America*, edited by Cathy L. Costin, pp. 95–128. Dumbarton Oaks Research Library and Collection, Washington, DC.

Kelman, Ari 2006 *A River and its City: The Nature of Landscape in New Orleans.* University of California Press, Berkeley.

Kolata, Alan L. 1991 The Technology and Organization of Agricultural Production in the Tiwanaku State. *Latin American Antiquity* 2(2):99–125.

———— 1993 *The Tiwanaku.* Blackwell Press, New York.

128   John Wayne Janusek

———— 2003 Tiwanaku Ceremonial Architecture and Urban Organization. In *Tiwanaku and Its Hinterland: Archaeology and Paleoecology of an Andean Civilization, Vol. 2*, edited by Alan L. Kolata, pp. 175—201. Smithsonian Institution Press, Washington, DC.

Latour, Bruno 2005 *Reassembling the Social: An Introduction to Actor-Network-Theory*. Oxford University Press, Oxford.

Lechtman, Heather 2003 Tiwanaku Period (Middle Horizon) Bronze Metallurgy in the Lake Titicaca Basin: A Preliminary Assessment. In *Tiwanaku and Its Hinterland: Archaeology and Paleoecology of an Andean Civilization, Vol. 2*, edited by A .L. Kolata, pp. 404–434. Smithsonian Institution Press, Washington, DC.

Lémuz Aguirre, Carlos 2005 Normalizacion de datos de asentamiento en la Cuenca Sur del Lago Titicaca. Report submitted to the Direccion Nacional de Arqueologia de Bolivia (DINAR), La Paz.

Lémuz Aguirre, Carlos, and John Wayne Janusek 2016 Desarrollo de las tecnologías prehispánicas y su correlacion con las reconstrucciones ambientales de los periodos Formativo y Tiwanaku en la Cuanca del Lago Titicaca. Paper presented at the Coloquio Internacional Sobre Contaminación Actual e Histórica en los Ecosistemas Acuáticos Andinos, La Paz, May 5.

Manzanilla, Linda 1992 *Akapana: Una Pirámide en el Centro del Mundo*. Universidad Nacional Autónoma de México, Instituto de Investigaciones Antropológicas, Mexico City.

Mauss, Marcel 1967 *The Gift: Forms and Functions of Exchange in Archaic Societies*, translated by Ian Cunnison, W. W. Norton & Co., New York.

Means, Philip Ainsworth 1931 *Ancient Civilizations of the Andes*. C. Scribner's Sons, New York.

Medina Huanca, Marcial 2008 Unidad de Excavación N1008-E2014, Akapana. research summary prepared for the report, *Proyecto Arqueológico Akapana 2008*. Submitted to the Bolivian Viceministry for the Development of Cultures, The National Unit of Archaeology, and the Municipal Government of Tiwanaku.

Morton, Timothy 2013 *Hyperobjects: Philosophy and Ecology after the End of the World*. University of Minnesota Press, Minneapolis.

Munn, Nancy D. 1986 *Fame of Gawa: A Symbolic Study of Value Transformation in a Massim Society*, revised edition. Duke University Press, Durham, NC.

Ortloff, Charles 2014 Groundwater Management in the 300 BCE–CE 1100 Pre-Columbian City of Tiwanaku (Bolivia). *Hydrology: Current Research* 5:2. Open access doi.org/10.4172/2157–7587.1000168.

Ortloff, Charles, and John Wayne Janusek 2016 Hydraulic Engineering of the Tiwanaku. In *Encyclopaedia of the History of Science, Technology, and Medicine in Non-Western Cultures*, edited by H. Selin, pp. 2267–2281, Springer-Verlag, Heidelberg.

Ponce, Carlos Sanginés 1971 Examen Arqueológico. In *Procedencia de las areniscas utilizadas en el temple Precolombino de Pumapunku* (Tiwanaku), edited by Carlos Ponce Sanginés, Arturo Castaños Echazu, Waldo Avila Salinas, and Fernando Urquidi Barrau, no. 22, pp. 13–206. Academia Nacional de Ciencias de Bolivia, La Paz.

———— 1981 *Tiwanaku: Espacio, tiempo, y cultura*. Los Amigos del Libro, La Paz.

Portugal Ortiz, Max 1998 *Escultura Prehispanica Boliviana*. UMSA, La Paz.

Posnansky, Arthur 1945 *Tihuanacu: Cradle of American Man, Vol. II*. J. J. Augustin Publisher, New York.

Protzen, Jean-Pierre, and Stella Nair 2013 *The Stones of Tiahuanaco: A Study of Architecture and Construction*. Cotsen Institute of Archaeology Press, University of California, Los Angeles.

Robbins, Paul 2012 *Political Ecology*, 2nd edition. Blackwell, New York.

Sahlins, Marshall 2008 *The Western Illusion of Human Nature*. Prickly Paradigm Press, Chicago.

Salomon, Frank 1991 Introductory Essay. In *The Huarochirí Manuscript: A Testament of Ancient and Colonial Andean Religion*, edited by Frank Salomon and George Urioste, pp. 1–38. University of Texas Press, Austin.

Scarborough, Vernon L., Arlen F. Chase, and Diane Z. Chase 2012 Low-density Urbanism, Sustainability, and IHOPE-Maya: Can the Past Provide More than History? *UGEC Viewpoints* 8:24–28.

Smith, Michael E. 2009 V. Gordon Childe and the Urban Revolution: A Historical Perspective on a Revolution in Urban Studies. *Town Planning Review* 80(1):3–29.

Stübel, Alphons, and Max Uhle 1892 *Die Ruinenstätte von Tiahanaco im Hochlande des alten Perú: Eine Kulturgeschichtliche Studie aug Grand selbsständiger Aufnahmen*. Verlag von Karl W. Hiersemann, Leipzig.

Torres, Constantino 2001 Iconografia Tiwanaku y en la parafenalia inhalatoria de los Andes centro-sur. *Boletin de Arqueologia PUCP* 5:427–454.

———— 2018 Visionary Plants and SAIS Iconography in San Pedro de Atacama and Tiahuanaco. In *Images in Action: The Southern Andean Iconographic Series*, edited by William H. Isbell, Mauricio I. Uribe, Anne Tibali, and Edward P. Zegarra, pp. 333–372. UCLA Cotsen Institute of Archaeology Press, Los Angeles.

Turner, Victor 1975 *Dramas, Fields, and Metaphors: Symbolic Action in Human Society*. Cornell University Press, Ithaca, NY.

Viveiros de Castro, Eduardo 1998 Cosmological Deixis and Amerindian Perspectivism. *Journal of the Royal Anthropological Institute* 4(3):469–488.

Vranich, Alexei 1999 Interpreting the Meaning of Ritual Spaces: The Temple Complex of Pumapunku, Tiwanaku, Bolivia. Unpublished PhD Dissertation. University of Pennsylvania.

———— 2001 La pirámide de Akapana: reconsiderando el centro monumental de Tiwanaku. In *Huari and Tiwanaku: modelos vs. evidencias, segunda parte*, edited by Peter Kaulicke and William H. Isbell, 295–308. Boletín de Arqueología vol. Pontíficia Universidad Católica del Peru, Lima.

———— 2009 The Development of the Ritual Core of Tiwanaku. In *Tiwanaku: Papers from the 2005 Mayer Center Symposium at the Denver Art Museum*, edited by Margaret Young-Sanchez, 11–34. Denver Art Museum, Denver.

———— 2016 Monumental Perceptions of the Tiwanaku Landscape, in *Political Landscapes of Capital Cities*, edited by Jessica Joyce Christie, Jelena Bogdanović, and Eulogio Guzmán, pp. 181–212.

Weismantel, Mary 2014 Inhuman Eyes: Looking at Chavín de Huantar. In *Relational Archaeologies: Humans, Animals, Things*, edited by Christopher Watts, pp. 21–41. Taylor and Francis, New York.

———— 2018 Cuni Raya Superhero: Ontologies of Water on Peru's North Coast. In *Powerful Places in the Ancient Andes*, edited by Justin Jennings and Edward R. Swenson, 175-208. University of New Mexico Press, Albuquerque.

Weismantel, Mary, and Lynn Meskell 2014 'Substances:' Following the Material through Two Prehistoric Cases. *Journal of Material Culture* 19(3):233–251.

Wirth, Louis 1938 Urbanism as a Way of Life. *American Journal of Sociology* 44(1):1–24.

Wright, Maria Robinson 1907 *Bolivia: El Camino Central del Sur-America, Una Tierra de Ricos Recursos y de Variado Interés*. Jorge Barrie and Sons, Philadelphia.

6

IMMANENCE AND THE SPIRIT OF ANCIENT URBANISM AT PAQUIMÉ AND LIANGZHU

Timothy R. Pauketat

Cities are assemblages, of course, and assemblages are comprised of diverse constituents (Kostof 1992). They are also 'made up of more than just physical things' and realized at different relational scales (Harris 2017:129). And they happen in different dimensions: visible and invisible, human and non-human, earthly and celestial, material and immaterial, animate and inanimate, real and imaginary, past and future, and living and dead (see Chapter 1).

Typical modernist or functionalist approaches to early cities consider few of these dimensions in their explanations, instead emphasizing the organizational features and purposes of urban places (e.g., Marcus and Sabloff 2008). By contrast, relational or affect-based approaches highlight the psycho-social qualities attendant to the atmospheres, spaces, and materials of cities (Amin and Thrift 2002; Thrift 2008). Mostly, though, they change the questions we ask about urbanism. They ask after that which 'territorialized' and 'stratified' relational fields such that cities resulted (see Chapter 1). They ask about the multi-dimensionality and strata of cities. And they ask how and why the histories of cities differ from or parallel others.

Addressing such questions is the goal of this chapter, and I pursue those questions by comparing two very different non-modern cities in two very different relational environments: Paquimé in northwest Mexico and Liangzhu in southeast China. As you will see, the 'immanence' of water, considered as a set of affective qualities or properties, is what unites these cases and promises some general insight into early urbanism (see also Alt, Janusek, Fleisher, and Harmanşah, Chapters 2, 5, 7, 9). In the end, watery affects also blur the lines between those causes and effects that we might label urban and those we might call religious.

Urbanism as affects and assemblage

I have previously discussed affective qualities using the concept of 'bundling' (Pauketat 2013a, 2013b):

Imagine riding with friends through an open, isolated prairie at dusk in the springtime. Regardless of the antecedent relations, if any, between the friends, the ride, the mode of locomotion (say, a horse-drawn carriage), the open prairie, the prairie grasses, 'a few birds wheeling here and there,' and the soft glow of the Moon against a deepening blue sky, your motion through that field will bundle aspects of the experience, perhaps a memory of some sort linking some or all of the perceived things and emotions. … Extending the time frame some, a letter to a friend, a photograph of the ride, or a passage in a book that recounts the same is also a bundle.

(Pauketat 2013a:35, citing Dickens 2004)

In this example, the ride does more than momentarily assemble things—be they people, a carriage, the prairie, or a blue sky (all of which are variably individuated or territorialized assemblages in their own right). It assembles affects (the gait and smell of the horse, the motions of prairie grasses and breezes, the wheeling birds, and the luminous moon) with motions, emotions, and memories, all of which are realized in realms ranging from the atmospheric to the neurological (Boivin 2008; Boivin and Owoc 2004; Hamilakis 2017; Strang 2014). And that is just a buggy ride.

Cities and urbanisms, as assemblages, are all the more affective in their basic properties and dynamics. Thus, while it might be tempting to define urbanism simply as any dense concentration of people, architecture, infrastructure, and materiel, my present point is better served by recognizing it to be an impossibly complicated affective entanglement. Nigel Thrift (2004:57; 2008:171) has done just this, calling urbanism a 'roiling maelstrom of affect.' Certainly, urbanism is a palpable phenomenon; people routinely note how some quality of this or that city makes them feel or remember simply by virtue of living in or moving through it (Certeau 1984). This is because urban spaces have their own atmospheres, incorporating everything from the smells of dark alleys and backlots to awesome vistas of monumental districts. Put these together, and we may appreciate that urban areas are always comprised of layer upon layer of affect, and might even be usefully considered as stratified, inter-assemblage 'haecceities' (Chapter 1, citing Deleuze and Guattari 1987). That is, urbanity might be said to be a condition, quality, or dimension of certain relational fields.

As opposed to urbanism generally, cities are things, not dimensions. A city is urbanism territorialized. Yet any city's qualities or affective modes are functions of the way urbanism is bundled and bounded locally, and they might range from 'phantasmagorical' to neglected or decaying (Benjamin 1999; Murray 2008:153). And while some pieces of urban assemblages might be 'detached and included in another without totally transforming the part itself' (Harris 2017:129, citing DeLanda [2006:10]), the same cannot be said of the urban assemblage as a whole, much less the wider relational field within which the assemblage is realized (following Deleuze and Guattari 1987:8; Gell 1998). This is because 'everything is positioned or moves in relational fields vis-à-vis other positioned and moving [substances, materials, phenomena, and] entities in ways that contribute to the overall mediation of that field' (Pauketat 2013a:42).

132 Timothy R. Pauketat

Consequently, assemblages generally and urban ones specifically, undergo internal transformations as part of their territorialization (à la Deleuze and Guattari 1987), in the spirit of Karen Barad's (2007) notion of 'intra-action'. Such transformations vary by degree and kind. However, generally speaking, to assemble or bundle is to 'reconfigure if not transform entire webs of relationships' (Pauketat 2013a:39). Cities do precisely this, always in the face of formidable human, material, and phenomenal forces seeking to 'deterritorialize' them on a continuous basis (see Van Dyke, Fleisher, and Bauer, Chapters 3, 7, and 8). Thus, cities are fragile and, when they endure, surprising (Yoffee 2016).

Immanence and water

My argument about the material affects of places and the causes of urbanism draws on the immanence of water. Immanence is any all-pervasive, rhizomatic, thickly affective, and thoroughly entangled quality of things. Air and wind, for instance, are comprised of invisible gases that flow through the atmosphere and pervade or enable intra- and interactions. They are immanent. So, too, is water immanent, assuming as it does myriad forms and states of matter, alternately contained by or containing air, earth, and living organisms. As such, immanence transgresses dimensions of being to be incorporated into any number of things at any number of scales.

Immanence also implies religiosity. That such is the case seemed 'odd' to Gilles Deleuze and Felix Guattari (1987:282), who observed that religion 'works by immanence.' In the present case, I argue that water is immanent in ways that afford it affective and religious power—making it a literal and figurative spirit of ancient urbanism. Water, among other such spirits, enabled the stratification of relational fields in ways that help us to understand the causal relationships between urbanism and religion (see Chapter 1). The stratification of watery relations via infrastructure is what made the cities of Paquimé and Liangzhu cities. On the flip side, dramatic differences between the cities, and ultimately their urban histories, are rooted in fundamentally dissimilar wet and dry climates and landscapes.

Long ago, Aristotle (2004) offered a hylomorphic theory of substances and things whereby the latter emerged from the former via the imposition of form. And without excusing the problematic emphasis by some on the human mind in this process (as reviewed by Ingold 2013:20–26), we can nevertheless appreciate the distinctions between substance and things that have led various archaeologists to recognize the power of elemental matter and phenomena or the emphasis in non-Western ontological realms on the seemingly immaterial, animate, and inalienable qualities of things (Alberti and Bray 2009; Bird-David 1999). Colin Richards (1996) and Robert Hall (1989, 1997), for instance, both emphasized water's ability to flow, pond, and reflect and refract light, leading people to perceive it as a horizontal and vertical demarcation of non-human atmospheric and cosmic realms.

Such properties and qualities are immanent (and rhizomatic), which is to say pervading and existing within and throughout relational fields and the bodies, entities, or things thereof. Water's immanence, in fact, could be discussed in terms of its trans-dimensional and multi-scalar flows: transpiration and hydrological, organic, and physiological processes (Edgeworth 2011; Scarborough 2003; Strang 2014). Veronica Strang (2014) sums up the pervasive qualities, phenomenality, and dimensionality of water:

> We are all familiar with water's material properties: its fluidity, its transformative capacities, its conductivity and its connectivity. Its molecular structure is such that these properties pertain at every level: thus its 'behaviour' in becoming ice, liquid or steam in a domestic kitchen is echoed in its freezing and thawing at the edge of a polar ice cap, or in its evaporation from oceans and forests. Its capacity to hydrate casts water as an essential 'matter of substance' for even the smallest microbial organisms. It is vital in human, animal and plant bodies, irrigating cells, enabling the circulation of nutrients, and carrying away waste. It is similarly essential to all ecosystemic processes, whether local, regional, continental or planetary in scale. Water materially connects the tiniest microbe with human bodies, with ecosystems and with world hydrological systems, composing the relationships between them (Helmreich 2009; Vernadsky … [1998]). This connection is both spatial and temporal: water's fluid movements may be as fleeting as the tiny capillary shifts through which water crosses a plant membrane, or as glacial as the accumulation of meltwater in underground aquifers. Water is therefore an ideal medium for considering material and ideational flows between scales and for revealing how the properties of things are omnipresent in and active upon engagements between things and persons.
>
> (Strang 2014:134).

But such flows are even more immanent than Strang suggests, especially given that water in its various states assembles or is assembled by other non-human phenomena: light, heat, barometric pressure, terrain, gravity, and altitude. Water vapor and water bodies refract light. Heat boils and atomizes water and the liquid becomes atmospheric humidity. Water vapor eventually condenses, falling to the ground and eroding the terrain as it flows downslope.

The results of all this watery circulation, or lack thereof, possess affective qualities that become the basis of other things and associations perceived by people: rivers, lakes, deserts, mists, clouds, storms, floods, and rainbows. They are also the basis of causal relationships beyond the things commonly known by people around the world. Clouds form in the sky over mountains. Rain falls from clouds to be absorbed by plants. Halos of light appear around full moons prior to warm fronts. Full moons tug at tides.

In part, such knowledge is a function of the "enchanting" affects of water and other natural phenomena (following Gell 1998). People come to know and anticipate such affects, the latter leading to human interventions and, ultimately, infrastructure. For example, some such knowledges, anticipations, and interventions are the basis of agriculture, which involves some level of meteorological and biological

134 Timothy R. Pauketat

awareness. Others are the foundations of, say, time-keeping practices and calendrical systems (Aveni 2001). Still others are more nearly economic or political, such as the building of irrigation systems or the control of water temples and water gods (see infrastructure as defined by Yoffee 2016). The latter, of course, are also religious, by which I mean that they coordinate cosmic order with terrestrial and perceptual movements, especially of the human sort (see Chapter 1). I would argue that the stratified combination of the above, especially as built around infrastructures that were self-perpetuating to some extent, is the epitome of urbanity.

Of these, I would also argue that the most causally significant affects and infrastructures are the most fundamental, elemental, and immanent. This is because, as Strang (2014) observes, water flows between existential scales and dimensions, enabling relations and associations within and between states of matter, bodies, and wider atmospheric and environmental zones. And for such reasons, and at some point in the past or present, people worldwide revere with religious fervor non-human flows and movements; such is the basis of animism and other forms of human spirituality (Bird-David 1999). It goes without saying that water and other elemental qualities bundled with it are among those things that inform human spirituality.

This is especially true in the cases of Paquimé and Liangzhu, and a closer examination of both will permit me to argue for the place of water's immanence with respect to the two cities' historical development. Following a review of the archaeological knowns from both places and their regions, I highlight the ways in which the instantiation of places, and later engagements of people in those places, were trans-scalar and trans-dimensional relationships that varied owing to the affective linkages through which they were assembled, and ultimately converted, by water. I also highlight the ways in which water, or the absence thereof, in the two cases led to divergences in urban form and history. I conclude by outlining how such emplaced urbanisms, either Paquimé's extremely dry urbanism or Liangzhu's excessively wet urbanism, might be understood as religious conversions of immanent relationships.

Paquimé

Paquimé is the first 'city' in northwestern Mexico's Chihuahua Desert, though its urban period dates late (1250–1450 CE) in North America's pre-Hispanic era (Figure 6.1). Archaeologists debate the developmental history and urban qualities of Paquimé, sometimes also called Casas Grandes. Some archaeologists would prefer simply calling the complex a pueblo (i.e., town) or a 'community' rather than a city, primarily because of its relatively small human population (for contrasting views, see Cordell 2015:205; Lekson 1999; Minnis and Whalen 2015b). The maximum human population living at Paquimé, some 2,000 to 3,000 human beings, was never great compared to Mesoamerican contemporaries to the south (Cordell 2015:199–200). Then again, Paquimé's population and urbanism was not limited to people or to this central site (see below).

In any case, sometime around 1250 CE, a compact, multi-storied civic-ceremonial complex was built over an earlier pithouse village in the Río Casas Grandes Valley, a

Ancient urbanism at Paquimé and Liangzhu **135**

particularly well-watered portion of Northwest Mexico's 'Chihuahua culture' area, nestled up against the Sierra Madre Occidentals, and ideal for agriculture (Kelley and Searcy 2015:18; Minnis and Whalen 2015a). The construction event or events that produced the multi-storied pueblo are difficult to track with current archaeological evidence but are part of the basis for distinguishing an earlier Viejo period from a later Medio period, the climax of Paquimé. It remains tempting to correlate this construction event or phase with Mesoamerican contact or with the arrival at Paquimé of a fallen star, a 1.5 metric-ton meteorite, later found wrapped in cloth and buried alongside an adult male in an adobe-block tomb at Paquimé (DiPeso 1974; Tassin 1902). Casas Grandes iconography does feature the imagery of the Morning Star, also known as the planet Venus, which in Mesoamerica is commonly bundled with human and solar forms (Mathiowetz 2011; Thompson 2007). In fact, Morning Star imagery appears practically *de novo* in the form of Paquimé's famous Medio-period 'Ramos Polychrome' pots (VanPool and VanPool 2007).

Moreover, there is a central design to the city, with a north–south axis running through a cruciform-shaped, stone-faced platform south through a room block. On either side of this centerline are slightly off-cardinal rooms, colonnaded entrances, walls, ball courts, and other platforms. Some adobe walls are aligned 3 to 7 degrees east of true north, mostly to the east of the centerline, and others are aligned 3 to 5 degrees west of true north, mostly to the west of the centerline (DiPeso 1974).

Doubtless, the construction of Paquimé was historically related to geopolitical and climatic changes taking place across the American Southwest/Northwest Mexico in the thirteenth century CE. To the north, the generational periodicity of Mogollon and Puebloan pilgrimage sites, including Chaco and its successors (Chapter 3), had come untethered from people concomitant with a series of population migrations (Newsome and Hays-Gilpin 2011). Insular communities and solar-aligned Pueblos with large plazas and locally dense human populations developed at about the same time as Paquimé, a pattern that in some ways has lasted to today. To the south, across what would become the 'Casas Grandes region', other small adobe apartment complexes were under construction to house a year-round population of maize and other cultigen farmers at the beginning of the Medio period (DiPeso 1974; Schaafsma and Riley 1999; Whalen and Minnis 2001, 2012). Some probably housed immigrants from Mogollon regions to the north, if not elsewhere (Shafer 1999).

Three centuries later, the highest adobe walls had crumbled, while others were 'still standing 30 feet above the 20-foot-high mound' of ruins (Wilcox 1999:98). Spanish explorers described the city in the mid-sixteenth century, reporting

> many houses of great size, strength, and height. These houses are six or seven stories high, … [and] contain large and magnificent patios paved with enormous, beautiful stones. There are hand carved stones that supported the magnificent pillars made of heavy trunks brought from far away. The walls of the houses are stuccoed and painted in many shades and colors.
>
> (VanPool and VanPool 2007:3)

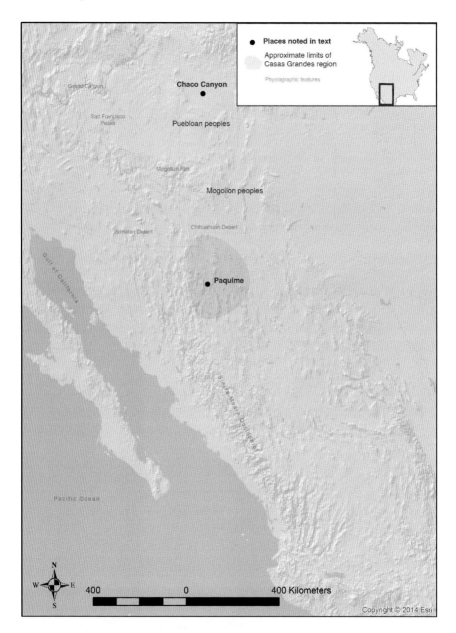

FIGURE 6.1 Physiographic map of the Casas Grandes region (map by T. Pauketat)

The painted imagery on the various walls probably included oversized versions of serpent and macaw beings, some anthropomorphized, in rich hues of green, red, brown, and white as also seen on the Ramos Polychrome pots (Figure 6.2).

Paquimé's extensive rectilinear room blocks and walled-in courtyards covered about 20 hectares, the core of which was studded with stone-faced mounds and

FIGURE 6.2 Ramos Polychrome pottery jar, 20 cm tall, showing polychrome serpent and associated imagery (Amerind Foundation, photo by T. Pauketat, Courtesy Amerind Foundation, Dragoon, Arizona)

official Mesoamerican-style ballcourts. In total, there were up to 2,000 rooms in the city (Cordell 2015:199; DiPeso 1974). Some spaces were private, opening into living rooms and storerooms. Other interior rooms were easily accessed via hallways and off patios and plazas (Wilcox 1999). These would have been cool and dimly lit compared to the dry and warm desert outside. Blue sky would have poured into the open-air patios at the heart of most roomblocks, linking the earthly adobe interiors to the rain and skylight from above.

Workshops and aviaries were arrayed around such patios. The latter contained adobe and stone pens for raising macaws and turkeys that were kept for their feathers, not as a food source (Figure 6.3). Over 800 of these birds—300 macaws and 500 turkeys—were found ritually killed and buried underneath Paquimé's floors and courtyards, some with artifacts suggesting to archaeologists their connection to water and the trans-dimensional 'Flower World' of Mexico and the greater Southwest/Northwest—a netherworld of fragrant flowers, birds, butterflies, and sunshine—practically embodied by Paquimé itself (Hays-Gilpin and Hill 2000; Mathiowetz 2011; McGuire 2012).

Additional evidence of that which Paquimé venerated is found among the high hills and mesas of the region. Some of these elevated shrines connected to Paquimé (Pitezel 2007, 2011; Swanson 2003). One such shrine, Cerro de Moctezuma, sat atop a mesa a few kilometers east of and overlooking the city. A reservoir and a small Medio-period settlement, El Pueblita, are situated near the shrine (Pitezel 2007, 2011). A cave, with a walled entrance, is located downslope beneath the shrine (Pitezel 2007). Excavations into the shrine revealed the wing bones of water birds (Pitezel 2011), and the structure was rectangular with four stonewalled quadrants set

FIGURE 6.3 Paquimé residential room block, view to north with unexcavated mound to right, 2009 (HJPD, GNU Free Documentation and Creative Commons Attribution-Share Alike 3.0 Unported license)

inside a circle; one wall segment seems to orient the whole construction to north. Moreover, in profile, the shrine appears as a 'stepped-cloud' (Swanson 2003:763–764). Overlooking Paquimé and physically connected to it by an ancient road, this and the other shrines in the region assembled the dispersed seen and unseen watery and solar powers of the world and were, in turn, assembled by Paquimé.

Cerro de Moctezuma's form and water-bird wing bones (likely from fans), as well as the pervasive imagery of horned or plumed serpents in and on Paquimé's pottery-vessel walls, presumably evoked associations of the Flower World, water, and beings thought to 'live in water' (VanPool and VanPool 2007:30–32). Macaws and macaw imagery were pervasive across Paquimé, and were historically bundled by Puebloan and Mesoamerican people with watery affects via their red and green feathers (DiPeso et al. 1974; Mathiowetz 2011; VanPool and VanPool 2007).

Other monuments and public works related birds and water to human residents. These include walk-in wells, a water-supply canal (*acequia madre*) that channeled water into the city's cisterns, a subsurface water supply and drainage system that linked major room blocks together, and seven platforms. One multi-terraced platform elevated an adobe building on its summit and featured a ramp down into a cistern. The cruciform platform, mentioned earlier, constituted an immanent attachment to the sun and the Morning Star (Venus, which may be seen immediately before the sun rises (Thompson 2007), as well as to the outlying Cerro de Moctezuma shrine (Figure 6.4). Other platforms take the forms of a beheaded bird and a serpent. All centered—which is to say tightly bundled or highly circumscribed—otherwise-dispersed spiritual forces inside Paquimé proper. And

FIGURE 6.4 Paquimé infrastructural features: left, subfloor drains in roomblock; right, sunrise over cruciform mound (Courtesy Amerind Foundation, Dragoon, Arizona)

Source: DiPeso 1974, vol. 2: figures 34 and 110.

all probably stratified the relational field of spiritual forces into distinct subfields of power. This is especially true of the water-supply features, which formed one or more layers of infrastructure (see below).

There was also an astonishing number—3.9 million—of marine shell artifacts and discarded detritus piled in some rooms of Paquimé, especially odd given that the city sits in the middle of a desert. Besides their obvious derivation from ocean water, the shells further indicate Paquimé's immanent relationships with water. More than likely, people travelled long distances to West Mexico and the Pacific Ocean to acquire the shells (Whalen 2013). Various archaeologists have suspected that such travel may indicate periodic pilgrimage circuits not unlike those yet known in northwestern Mexico (Nelson 2010). That, in turn, points to a cosmic or cosmopolitan centering process, where the city—to be assembled as a city— necessarily embodied all of the powers of a greater regional or transregional web of relations. That web—and ultimately the comings and goings of people in and out and, ultimately, away from Paquimé—led to a kind of urban history unlike that of other cities in the world.

The point seems amplified by the ruins of Paquimé. Christine VanPool and Todd VanPool (2007) estimate that up to 15,000 pots have been taken by looters from the rooms of Paquimé and its outliers since the 1500s. Many of these were

140 Timothy R. Pauketat

the extraordinary Ramos Polychrome pots featuring elaborate cloud, serpent, macaw, and humanoid iconography (Mathiowetz 2011; VanPool and VanPool 2007). These pots, perhaps similar to avian burials, may have mediated the closure of powerful rooms or roomblocks much as did the burial of human bodies (DiPeso 1974:Figure 432, vol. 2). In the end, and if anything like descendants, other-than-human forces were among those that impelled people to depart (Kuwanwisiwma 2002).

Liangzhu

Among the earliest cities in Asia, if not the world, is late Neolithic-period Liangzhu (ca. 3100–2600 BCE). Liangzhu sits in the low-lying coastal plain of southeast China, 60 kilometers south of Lake Tai and 25 kilometers north of the Qiantang River (Liu et al. 2016). The city might be described as an organized concentration of natural and artificial mounds and waterways surrounded by habitation areas, earthen walls, cemeteries, artificial dams, and rice fields (Liu et al. 2016; Qin 2013; Renfrew and Liu 2018). The complex sprawls across an 'area of about 50 sq km in the plains, surrounded by mountains and hills … The elevation of this area is about 2–3 meters above sea level on average, and there are just a few natural, small hills around 20–30 meters in height' in the vicinity, with the Dazhe Mountains (Dazheshan) on the horizon north of the city center (Qin 2013:586–587).

In that geographic position, this earliest of Chinese cities was sited on an open plain only 10 meters or so above sea level, surrounded by low mountains on all but the northeast and southeast sides (Figure 6.5). The view to the northeast from the center of the city is, in fact, afforded by a zero-degree horizon all the way to the Pacific Ocean (some 200 kilometers in the direction of modern-day Shanghai). Moreover, the view in that direction is framed by the Dazhe Mountains, to the north, and the Yang Mountains to the east. In between, the northern extreme rising positions of the sun (summer solstice) and full moon (northern minimum and maximum positions) would have been visible (see Appendix). The sun would rise in this maximum northern position once a year, while a northern maximum full moon would rise a few degrees to the north of that—appearing to emerge out of the base of the Dazhe Mountains—during one or two out of every 18.6 years (Pauketat 2013a). Halfway through its long 18.6-year cycle, or 9.3 years later, the northernmost full moonrise would have emerged in a minimum position midway between the Dazhe and Yang Mountains (see below).

Each year, of course, the full moon also rises in a southeastern extreme position, and in that direction the maximum southern full moon would appear to rise out of and then trace the summit of the Daxiong Mountains as it arcs across the southern night sky every 18.6 years. Likewise, a minimum southern moonrise would appear 9.3 years later. Interestingly, this also the direction of the Qiantang River, which is a day's walk (25 kilometers) away across the flat rice-growing plain (Figure 6.5). Not incidentally, the Qiantang River and the Hangzhou Bay into which it flows are known today for the world's largest tidal bore, a wave up to 9 meters high locally,

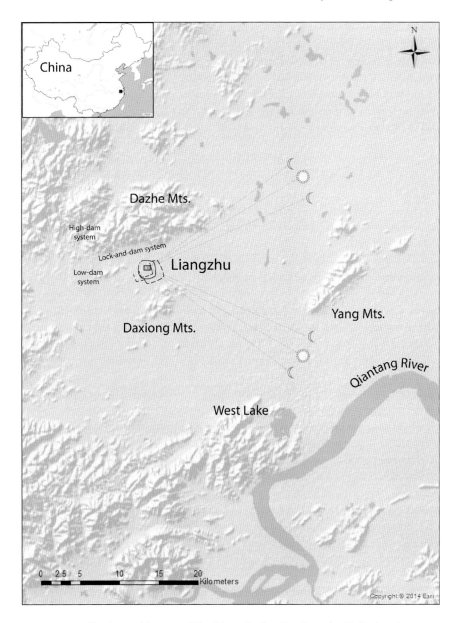

FIGURE 6.5 Physiographic map of the Liangzhu locality (map by T. Pauketat)

called the Silver (or Black) Dragon. This singular wave, a result of the peculiar configuration of Hangzhou Bay at the river's mouth, probably became a perceptible phenomenon in the fourth millennium BCE, with the dropping of sea levels to within a meter of the current level (L. Li et al. 2017; Wang et al. 2012; Zong 2004). At that time, before the founding of Liangzhu, the Silver Dragon would have roared up the river with each full and new moon, with the most impressive displays happening during the perigean spring tides in both the autumn and spring seasons. The visual, audible, and palpable affects of this phenomenon today draw thousands of tourists a year to the banks of the Qiantang (Lynch 1982).

From all indications, early Liangzhu-period rice agriculturalists, who had moved into the region from diverse homelands in preceding centuries, conceived, laid out, and built their monumental center from the lowlands 'as a radical creation' around 3100–3000 BCE (Liu et al. 2018:13638). This was a time of 'rapid increase in population' that followed a veritable historical moment when the region appears to have been 'chosen, settled, and developed … with a distinct purpose in mind' (Qin 2013:578–579). Current interpretations by Bin Liu and associates (2018) hold that a stupendous rectangular platform of earth, Mojiaoshan, 10 meters tall and covering 30 hectares, was raised in short order around 3000 BCE. Radiocarbon dates suggest that this took place at or shortly after the construction of massive earthen dams and water control features in the foothills of the Dazhe Mountains to the north of the city (Liu et al. 2018; Renfrew and Liu 2018).

Mojiaoshan appears to have been positioned both to face the Dazheshan peaks as well as to parallel the east–west movements of the sun and moon throughout the year. Atop it were additional earthen platforms, each elevating palatial, rammed-earth, pole-and-thatch buildings. Lesser platforms in the surrounding cityscape elevated other presumed public-ritual structures and cemeteries (Figure 6.6). Surrounding Mojiaoshan was a great 60-meter-wide rammed earth wall that enclosed a 300-hectare rectanguloidal area. An additional 800 hectares of city space and the wider world were outside (Liu et al. 2016). Eight 'water gates' enabled people in boats to pass into the inner city, navigating a network of canals, wetlands, rice paddies, and wooden decks or piers therein (Liu et al. 2016:17). In the 'outer city' are additional earthen walls and canal segments. All told, and excluding the earthen dams and other water control features north of the city, the walls, mounds, and canals of Liangzhu 'required the use of over 8,400,000 m^3 of soil', much of it from the Dazheshan to the north, and 'required the mobilization of a huge amount of human labor and probably took several hundred years to complete' (Liu et al. 2016:16).

Given Liu and associates' (2016) appraisal of the time needed to complete these projects, it is interesting to note that the outer-city walls and canals betray a secondary or earlier off-cardinal orthogonal city grid. Liu and colleagues (2016, 2018; Renfrew and Liu 2018) interpret these outer features as contemporary and suggestive of a complex stratified cityscape that developed in the Middle and Late Liangzhu period. However, the features might also have been the vestiges of an off-cardinal Early Liangzhu-period city superimposed by the later, cardinally aligned Moijiaoshan and inner wall. If so, then the early iteration(s) of Liangzhu would have been oriented to about 67 degrees of azimuth, the angle of minimum north full moonrise (Appendix). That angle is very nearly matched, in fact, by one off-cardinal rectangular platform south of Mojiaoshan (midway between two projected earthen walls and a ditch). If part of an early off-cardinal early city plan, then

Ancient urbanism at Paquimé and Liangzhu 143

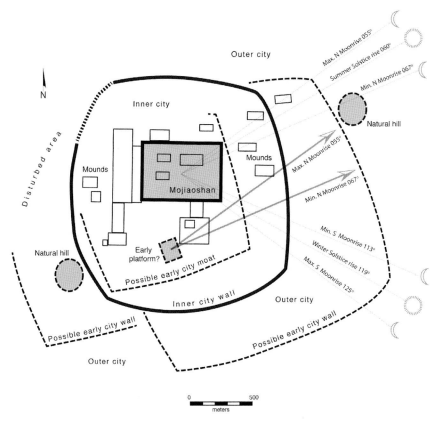

FIGURE 6.6 Schematic plan map of Liangzhu city's major earthen and watery features

Source: Adapted and reinterpreted from Liu et al. 2016.

that plan would have positioned Liangzhu between the Dazhe, Yang, and Daxiong Mountains to the north, east, and south, respectively, as well as to the long 18.6-year cycle of the moon and the perigean tidal bore of the Qiantang River.

Perhaps Liangzhu city, in other words, witnessed one or more major city-wide urban redesigns, with the early configurations built relative to one set of landscape and celestial features, most notably the moon, and a later one aligned to cardinal directions as established by the annual movements of the sun (see He 2013). Either way, the proximity of the city to the rainwater rushing off Dazheshan to the north and the Qiantang tidal bore to the southeast should not be overlooked, especially given the massive water-control features around the city and the significance of water to Neolithic wet-rice farmers. That is, Liangzhu's rice fields and farmers were positioned betwixt rains, landscape features, and locomotive cosmic bodies (both sun and moon), the city itself then packaging all of these affects and powers as itself.

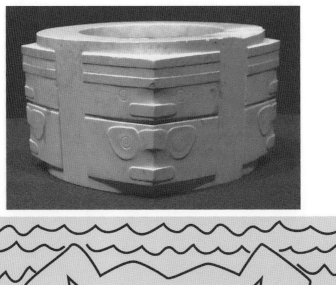

FIGURE 6.7 Engraved images of a mask or essence of a Liangzhu water spirit (top, close-up of a *cong* object, 10 cm wide, Shanghai Museum, photo by T. Pauketat; bottom, close-up of engraved lines on black pottery vessel)

Source: Adapted from Zhejiang 2015: 206.

Such a positionality was seemingly assembled not only via the city's infrastructure, but through the crafting of carved jade *bi*, *cong*, and *yue* objects (Zhejiang 2015). Such objects were probably regalia that, when held or worn, clothed human beings with spiritual powers. Among the imagery featured on the *cong* objects, as well as etched on Liangzhu's black pottery, are monstrous faces and anthropomorphic or zoomorphic characters, the latter including water spirits and beings—dragons, alligators, birds, snakes, clouds (Figure 6.7). The jade objects were locally carved in workshops from raw nephrite originating in the mountains north and west of Liangzhu (Qin 2013:592–593; Zhejiang 2015). A hybrid 'sacred man and animal' image, said to wear a feathered headdress, might also depict a cumulonimbus storm cloud. The pottery etchings, too, may have evoked the powers of watery dragon spirits in Liangzhu's commensal settings, flooding human senses with the spiritual force embodied by the Qiantang tidal bore.

Discussion

As Paquimé's non-human artifacts and images reveal, and as Liangzhu's Silver Dragon and water-spirit imagery attest, people were most assuredly not the only, if even the primary, mediators of these two urbanisms. Initially, as noted above, climate-related sea-level rise, weather shifts, or related geopolitical episodes encouraged people to relocate both to flat coastal lands around Lake Tai and to a relatively lush Chihuahua-desert oasis. Thus, the rice-growing potential of the Liangzhu locality's well-watered landscape, just a few meters above sea level after 3300 BCE, most certainly pulled farmers into the Taihu Plain well before the construction of the city's great earthen platforms and hydraulic earthworks. Likewise, the maize-growing potential of the Casas Grandes region, well south of the extant populations of Mogollon and Puebloan peoples, may have been sufficient to attract farmers to the Casas Grandes region (Kelley and Searcy 2015:27; Minnis and Whalen 2015a).

Next, we might recognize the historical effects of a stratum of human–non-human relations via the staple crops of the regions that might have been necessary, if by itself insufficient, to explain urbanism. That is, rice, which needs to sprout up from standing water and then mature in dark, organic, water-saturated earth, in turn requires of people water-retention and irrigation, large-scale cooperation, and significant labor investment. Yet it can be dried and stored for long periods and transported or mobilized to feed many. Maize has similar storage and transport potential when dried or ground into meal, though it is a water-sensitive plant easily suffocated by standing water. Unlike rice, it depends on the evaporation of water in sunshine, and would perish with too much precipitation at the wrong times.

The people in both regions likely knew most of this, but that is not to say that agriculture was their intention, nor is it to locate causality primarily in human mediation. The tendrils of such rhizomatic agricultural webs would have extended out from rice and maize fields, such that agriculture would have constituted its own stratum of interaction (DeLanda 2016:139; Deleuze and Guattari 1987:20). Agriculture attached, articulated, and assembled the world out there by territorializing and layering affects—including those connected to all-pervasive substances such as water—vis-à-vis all the things in between. Such was the substratum of urbanism, and affective substances—especially water—would have immanently linked everything else, including pots, craft items, human beings, buildings, and monuments.

At Paquimé, pottery territorialized the complex relationships of the Casas Grandes world, with the painted earthenware appearing to give form to spiritual lifeforces within the domestic sphere. Maize, of course, is often processed or cooked in water and in pots made, obviously, from earth and water by human hands. At various stages in the cooking process, steam is driven off from the grain, adding maize's sweet scents to the kitchen area. Such affects, again, would have constituted immanently fluid attachments, with an undeniable affectivity, to the wider agricultural stratum. Once consumed, the starchy foods were digested, energizing human bodies and generating human wastes that might be returned to the field.

In the case of Paquimé, of course, water's immanence is characterized not so much by its presence as by its absence. In northern Chihuahua, the periodicity of precipitation events and the water requirements of maize made the lighter, aerated soils of the region ideal for agriculture if less than ideal for dense human habitation. People needed to go to water, or water needed to go to them. Fittingly, the urbanism that emerged—characterized by immanent, watery, spiritual relations with periodic non-human forces—also necessitated a more active engagement with water. That is, the absence of water impelled people to come and go with greater frequency, and to invest in a relatively elaborate water supply and drainage system—acequias, cisterns, conduits, and wells—and ultimately to leave the Casas Grandes region.

The genealogy of infrastructure is especially key, since it would have further stratified Medio-period Paquimé—creating a series of assemblages less directly tethered to daily human activities. For all intents and purposes, such infrastructure transgressed both scales and dimensions of relational fields by affording non-human forces some greater degree of primacy in human lives. That is, Paquimé's water features allowed fundamentally powerful substances, such as water, to more clearly coordinate and order human lives. When such forces are as immanent as water, the historical effect must have been especially profound. This is precisely why archaeologists can identify founding moments in the first place—reconfigurations or 'conversions' of entire relational fields.

At Liangzhu, finely made black-slipped earthenware recapitulated the watery origins of earthen construction materials and rice fields. The ceramic containers were made from clay dug from subsoils, as were the city's earthen monuments, and the very presence of such a pot in a household may have assembled the user or viewer at a higher order (e.g., Emerson and Pauketat 2008; Kus and Raharigaona 2004). Unlike Paquimé, Liangzhu's late Neolithic reality did not entail human movements of the same periodicity or sort. Water was everywhere in southeast China. Pots and dams at Liangzhu were about containing it more than moving it to people. In such a relational realm, water transport—moving some amount of supplies and possessions in boats through or around the city—can become a potentiality that would have added another layer of infrastructure atop those of the impressive earthen dams and water-control features north and west of Liangzhu, which were under construction at or before the founding of the city (M. Li et al. 2016; Liu et al. 2018).

Such infrastructural developments arguably gave the city, even as periodically renewed and realigned, a developmental potentiality (to host a dense human population, among other things), an enhanced durability (to last up to 700 years), and a legacy effect (with the jade-crafting industry shaping Chinese history for a millennium to follow). As an aside jade, too, may have been immanently linked to mountains and water, but segmented from most people in ways that engendered social stratification over the long run, as seen in the burials of human remains in and around the city.

Both cities, Paquimé and Liangzhu, remained intensively and immanently tethered to water. The very designs of the two cities reviewed here attest to that which is possible when immanence is elevated to prominence. But there were obvious differences that mattered. For instance, Liangzhu's embedded or sequential cardinal and off-cardinal grids folded together the substantial and phenomenal qualities of earth, sun, *and moon* with water. I have elsewhere noted the potential affects of the latter with regard to the temporality and organizational scale of human experience (Pauketat 2013a, 2013b). Such cosmic assemblages may promote expansive ontological sensibilities among people, as opposed to the more narrow focus on annual solar relationships, such as at Paquimé (Pauketat 2011).

Unlike waterlogged Liangzhu, Paquimé was dry. Water there was unevenly distributed. It moved to people (via rainstorms and human infrastructure) or vice versa via conduits, wells, springs, and pots. Moreover, it was mostly invisible, its affects experienced as absence and evaporation. Indeed, rains soaked into maize fields and disappeared. Wet adobe walls evaporated rapidly. Water gurgled beneath room floors and pooled in damp cisterns and walk-in wells, out of sight, awaiting people to visit it, dip it, and carry it to their rooms or those of caged birds, who would have gulped it from small bowls and squawked loudly. Paquimé's open-air and avian atmosphere primarily gathered the sun and stars, as common to the later Puebloan people to the north (Newsome and Hays-Gilpin 2011). The sun-loving, water-sensitive maize plant, in turn, might encourage more frequent human movements to and from fields, homes, and wells.

The result: Paquimé recapitulated the region's transpiration cycle, which brought noisy thunder and rain to the land in dramatic cloudbursts in between dry spells. Water was intermittently immanent, and much energy was expended moving it and people from here to there, giving the place a kind of 'hustle and bustle' atmosphere (VanPool and VanPool 2007:647). Both people and water came and went. Is it any wonder that the city might be depopulated and forgotten in relatively short order (200 years) by people who were entangled with alternately wet and dry landscapes.

By the same token, given its immersion in water at all scales and experiential dimensions, is it any wonder that Liangzhu might be rebuilt, time and again, in place for up to 700 years? At Liangzhu, a person walked in water, fished from water, planted rice in water, and transported oneself and one's supplies across water. There was possibly less hustle-and-bustle about the place, which instead possessed a spatiality that Amin and Thrift (2002) would describe as 'distanciated'—extended across the open impounded waters, canals, and rice paddies in and around the city—if not also a temporality extended by the long 18.6-year cycle of the moon. The omnipresent liquidity of Liangzhu, with its floating detritus and aquatic organisms, living and dead, certainly must have altered the look, smell, sounds, and feel of that city and, from there, its history.

It seems unlikely, owing to such assemblage differences, that Paquimé could have been comparable to Liangzhu, or to other cities, in critical respects. If Liangzhu city's liquidity gave it a distanciated feel, Casas Grandes' (and Puebloan) urbanism was, for all intents and purposes, distanciated in time as well as regional space. Thus,

148 Timothy R. Pauketat

we should not necessarily expect parallel urban experiences, histories, or fragilities between the two. And yet one final parallel seems apparent.

Assemblage conversions, religious conversions

In the two urban cases, everything from water tables, crops, mountains, celestial objects, and atmospheric phenomena need to be understood as potentially causal to the agricultural strata or webs of relations that undergirded urbanism. However, none of them were, by themselves, necessarily sufficient to generate cities. By the same token, neither were people, alone, sufficient to invent cities. So how did they come about and, ultimately, how might a New Materialist perspective contribute to an understanding of urbanism?

Disassembling the Paquimé and Liangzhu cases by tracing their water, among other immanent relations, even in a cursory fashion, sheds some light on the critical relationships that help to explain how an agricultural society, broadly defined, might have been radically reconfigured or *converted* into an ordered, urban one (see Chapter 1). The conversion of an entire inter-assemblage relational field is a good way to think about what happened at both Paquimé and Liangzhu. Meredith Chesson (2019) might label the process 'fast urbanism', contrasting it with the 'slow urbanism' of burgeoning village-based landscapes (see also Birch 2013). In fast urbanism, formerly discrete realms or strata were assembled at rates and relational scales tantamount to an instantaneous folding or intensification of relations.

In coastal China during the third millennium BCE, we must not overlook the assemblage-conversion potential of the moon, directly, and indirectly via the Qiantang tidal bore. But, to what extent did the Silver Dragon produce Liangzhu? Or, more likely, to what extent did it bundle the moon with this place, its people, and its rice crops? Given the moon's monthly and perigean periodicity, the experience of lunar time for the people of Liangzhu may have become regimented and firmly emplaced in the Taihu Plain, a function of the cosmic relationship of the moon to water, as observed by the people of Liangzhu via the repetitive and locomotive tidal bore. At the same time, rice crops would necessarily have been planted and harvested with respect to both the solar year and the flash floods that poured off of Dazheshan to the north. Liangzhu sat in the middle of this all and might have become a city, not by any particular human desire, except as informed by earth-historical coincidence.

The monumental walls, dams, canals, and platforms achieved urbanity—a transdimensional assemblage that brought terrestrial and cosmic realms together in space and time—with every construction, reconstruction, or visitation by people. That is, whatever its genesis and whatever its builders and craftspeople did or did not think that they were doing, Liangzhu's monumentality and imagery—its earthen substantiality, its cosmic positionality, its watery, monstrous spirits, and its human-labor intensity—made Liangzhu 'a radical creation'. Each construction was a massive intervention by people in the spirit realm, and an infrastructural intervention by spirits in the human realm. Mojiaoshan in particular crystallized the relations between the sky above, the water-shedding, timber-rich, and jade-producing mountains to the north and west, the east–west progression of the sun at its mid-year equinoxes, the vast rice fields to the west and east, and the Silver Dragon to the south. Such a construction likely had any number of consequences unintended by people, of which urbanism and a more formalized religion were primary.

That which distinguishes Paquimé from other pueblos to the north and likens it to Mesoamerican urbanism is not simply the number of its rooms or density of its human population, but its immanent infrastructure and regional integration. Water was channeled into, along, and under the multi-storied complex to cisterns and platforms. These were facilities built by people, yes, but they afforded water (and the transpiration cycle generally) an all-encompassing, yet intimate and religious, intervention in the history of people. Moreover, major Medio-period construction and infrastructure projects were also cosmic mediations that constituted a radical trans-dimensional assemblage of substances, phenomena, and beings from otherwise distinct planes of existence: sky, mountain, and maize field. For all intents and purposes, Medio-period Paquimé was an intensely reassembled, large-scale, and trans-dimensional array of fundamental, elemental, and affect-rich associations between soils, crops, clouds, rain, and water-control infrastructure.

Mircea Eliade (1987) would have called the moments wherein human and non-human realms were re-assembled 'hierophanies' (see also Van Dyke, Chapter 3). For him, these were religious happenings, and I have argued that the rhythms or movements of such relations—especially but not exclusively celestial movements and cosmic temporalities—are that which, when embodied by or amidst people, produce the ordered spaces and practices commonly called religion (Pauketat 2013a). I would now argue that such *orders*, when bundled with people via an infrastructural hierophany, were also *religious conversions*. For present purposes, the value in recognizing such conversions lies in their urbanizing affects and effects. Through them, large-scale, inter-assemblage or inter-strata relationships might be assembled at higher orders of existence.

Here, it is critical to recognize that affects of very different sorts can be entangled such that they in turn afford new territorializations, mediations, things, or agencies. Moreover, more than people drove the process. Infrastructural hierophanies, I argue, converted both pre-Paquimé and pre-Liangzhu agricultural landscapes into urban ones. Urbanism, then, was the assemblage of different, distinct strata in ways that require us to rethink cause and effect. This is because when larger-than-life forces with radically dissimilar locomotive movements and affects (such as the sun, moon, mountains, etc.) are tightly and immanently bound (through water) to human–plant social fields, then radical assemblage conversion—the city—results (Figure 6.8).

Conclusion

There may be utility in appreciating that the rate and scale of such conversions elsewhere, perhaps tied to the particular qualities of that assembled in other parts of the

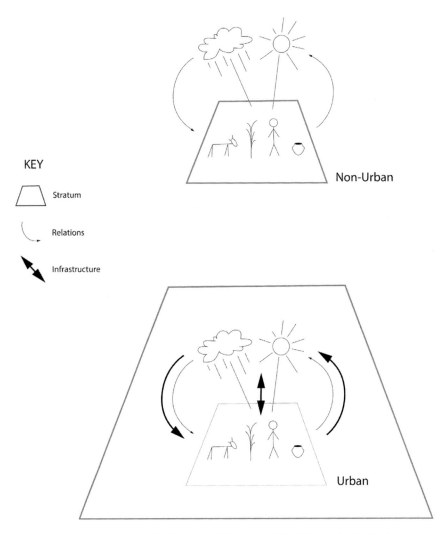

FIGURE 6.8 Non-urban and urban assemblages, simplified (image by T. Pauketat)

world, might have been more or less than the rate and scale witnessed at Liangzhu and Paquimé. Such historical variability might result from differential dispositions of relatively stable landscape features or other entities, such as mountains, rivers, celestial objects, tidal bores, or seasonally migrating flocks of birds. It may revolve around the perceptive or physical motions of specific beings, or the affects of phenomena in relationship to cosmic or atmospheric objects, as with squawking birds or surging tidal bores and the moon, or the piling up of platforms or pyramids parallel to the annual movements of the sun. Or they might be contingent on the carefully positioned material offerings left behind by people to propitiate spirits.

Ancient urbanism at Paquimé and Liangzhu **151**

When we complicate the picture, we can begin to appreciate how such assemblage conversion—the superpositioning or layering of a series of such semi-distinctive relational fields through their intersection with just such higher-order or trans-dimensional mediators—may be that which achieved what Fustel de Coulanges (1980) sensed when he declared that the founding of any ancient city 'was always a religious act' (see Chapter 1). Indeed, that which territorialized urbanizing fields of relations to produce cities, and which kept these stratified assemblages from fragmenting along their many cleavage planes, probably included the immanent and religious relationships of, say, water vis-à-vis earth, sky, crops, and people. Of course, such relationships did not last forever; the possible repeated renewals of Liangzhu and the brief duration of Paquimé attest to the fragility of urbanisms resting largely on the fluxes and flows of substances, materials, and phenomena.

But these two early and dissimilar cities—one in a desert and the other in a lush coastal plain—expose some possible answers to the questions of what early urbanism is and where it comes from. Non-human forces were critical in territorializing the relational fields that would give rise to Paquimé and Liangzhu long before people showed up to fulfill the urban potential of the location. Infrastructure, the intervention of people into such forceful fields and vice versa, brought immanent relations to the foreground. But it was the folding together of distinct earthly and celestial strata—a kind of infrastructural hierophany—that made possible the conversion of pre-urban assemblages into cities.

Acknowledgements

This chapter is a direct result of archaeological research conducted from 2014 to 2017 under the auspices of the John Templeton Foundation, grant 51485 (T. Pauketat and S. Alt, co-PIs), and a fellowship with the National Endowment for the Humanities (FA-58536-15). The JTF funded our first seminar at the School for Advanced Research in Santa Fe, NM, with additional support provided by the SAR. The Amerind Foundation supported our second seminar, held in February 2018 in Dragoon. My visits to Liangzhu were as part of groups associated with the Shanghai Archaeology Forum in 2013 and 2017. Special thanks to Liu Bin, director of the Liangzhu project, and Li Min, for his years of prodding me to take Liangzhu seriously. I am certain that my treatment of both Liangzhu and Paquimé leave much to be desired by those actually doing the hard work of archaeological investigation at both sites, and for that I beg their indulgence. Finally, I am also grateful for the discussions and advice of seminar participants, all of whom are contributors to the present volume, especially Susan Alt and Oliver Harris. Along with B. Jacob Skousen and an anonymous review, they provided critical comments on earlier versions of this chapter.

Appendix

Calculations of the rising and setting positions of the sun and moon's lower tangency at 3000 bce (following Wood 1980:61–64 with declination values interpolated from Hawkins 1966:table 3)

Begin by determining an uncorrected angular elevation of the horizon (h). The value of h is calculated by taking the inverse tangent of the vertical distance between the foresight (horizon) and the backsight location elevations divided by the horizontal distance between the two locations (foresight elevation—backsight elevation). This uncorrected value of h is then corrected to account for the effects of the earth's curvature, refraction, lower limb tangency, and parallax (for the moon only).

For the sun, the following equation is used:

corrected h = uncorrected h—refraction correction + 0.25 (lower limb tangency)—visible distance (km) x 0.0045.

For the moon, the following equation is used:

corrected h = uncorrected h—refraction correction + 0.25 (lower limb tangency correction) + 0.95 (parallax correction)—visible distance (km) x 0.0045.

Then, the formula used is:

$$\cos A = \frac{\sin \delta - \sin \phi \sin h}{\cos \phi \cos h}$$

where A is the rising or setting azimuth of the sun or moon, h is the corrected angular elevation of the horizon, δ (delta) is the declination of the sun or moon, and ϕ (phi) is the latitude. The calculations for Liangzhu follow:

Calculations	Max North Moonrise	Summer Solstice rise	Min North Moonrise	Min South Moonrise	Winter Solstice rise	Max South Moonrise
Declinations at 3000 BCE*	29.182	24.03	18.882	18.882	24.03	29.182
Sine declination	0.4876	0.4072	0.3236	0.3236	0.4072	0.4876
Latitude of Liangzhu	30.39	30.39	30.39	30.39	30.39	30.39
Cos latitude	0.8226	0.8226	0.8226	0.8226	0.8226	0.8226
Sin latitude	0.5059	0.5059	0.5059	0.5059	0.5059	0.5059
Distance to mountain peak/foresight (meters)	8000	0	0	0	3500	3500
Elevation of mts./foresight, plus 25-meter high trees on mountains only	94	0	0	0	95	66
Elevation of central Liangzhu	10	10	10	10	10	10

Vertical / horizontal distances	0.0118	0	0	0	0.0243	0.0189
Angular elevation (a.e.) of Liangzhu: Inverse tan of vertical distance / horizontal distance	0.6732	0	0	0	1.3920	1.0805
Corrected h for Liangzhu: refraction correction of 0.35, ala Wood fig. 4.5, and lower limb tangency of 0.25 + corrected for parallax 0.95	1.5232	–	0.85	0.85	–	1.9305
Corrected h for Liangzhu: refraction correction of 0.35, plus .25 lower limb tangency for sun (a la Wood 1980:fig. 4.5)	–	–0.1	–	–	1.292	–
Cos a.e.	0.99965	0.99999	0.99989	0.99989	0.999746	0.99943
Sin a.e.	0.0266	–0.0017	0.0148	0.0148	0.0226	0.0337
Cos A (Azimuth, see Wood 1980:62)	0.5766	0.4961	0.3843	0.3843	0.4813	0.5724
Inverse cos (3000 BCE positions)	54.79	60.26	67.40	67.40	61.23	55.08
Azimuth positions	**54.79**	**60.26**	**67.40**	**112.60**	**118.77**	**124.92**

*Note: derived from Hawkins 1966 (table 3) and Wood 1980 (table 4.1).

References

Alberti, Benjamin and Tamara L. Bray 2009 Animating Archaeology: Of Subjects, Objects, and Alternative Ontologies. *Cambridge Archaeological Journal* 19(3):337–343.

Amin, Ash, and Nigel Thrift 2002 *Cities: Reimagining the Urban*. Polity Press, Cambridge.

Aristotle 2004 *The Metaphysics*. Translated by H. Lawson-Tancred. Penguin, New York.

Aveni, Anthony F. 2001 *Skywatchers (revised edition)*. University of Texas Press, Austin.

Barad, Karen 2007 *Meeting the Universe Halfway: Quantum Physics and the Entanglement of Matter and Meaning*. Duke University Press, Durham, NC.

Benjamin, Walter 1999 *The Arcades Project*. Translated by H. Eiland and K. McLaughlin. Harvard University Press, Cambridge, MA.

Birch, Jennifer (editor) 2013 *From Prehistoric Villages to Cities: Settlement Aggregation and Community Transformation*. Routledge, London.

Bird-David, Nurit 1999 'Animism' Revisited: Personhood, Environment, and Relational Epistemology. *Current Anthropology* 40(supplement):67–91.

Boivin, Nicole 2008 *Material Cultures, Material Minds: The Impact of Things on Human Thought, Society and Evolution*. Cambridge University Press, Cambridge.

Boivin, Nicole, and Mary Ann Owoc (editors) 2004 *Soils, Stones and Symbols: Cultural Perceptions of the Mineral World*. UCL Press, London.

Certeau, Michel de 1984 *The Practice of Everyday Life*. University of California Press, Berkeley.

Chesson, Meredith S. 2019 The Southern Levant during the Early Bronze Age I-III. In *The Social Archaeology of the Levant: From the Past to the Present*, edited by A. Yasur-Landau, E. Cline and Y. M. Rowan, pp. 163-182. Cambridge University Press, Cambridge.

Cordell, Linda S. 2015 Ancient Paquimé: A View from the North. In *Ancient Paquimé and the Casas Grandes World*, edited by P. E. Minnis and M. E. Whalen, pp. 192–207. University of Arizona Press, Tucson.

DeLanda, Manuel 2006 *A New Philosophy of Society: Assemblage Theory and Social Complexity*. Bloomsbury, London.

———2016 *Assemblage Theory*. Edinburgh University Press, Edinburgh.

Deleuze, Gilles, and Felix Guattari 1987 *A Thousand Plateaus: Capitalism and Schizophrenia*. Translated by B. Massumi. University of Minnesota Press, Minneapolis.

Dickens, Charles 2004 *American Notes*. Penguin Books, London.

DiPeso, Charles C. 1974 *Casas Grandes: A Fallen Trading Center of the Gran Chichimeca. Vols. 1–3*. Amerind Foundation and Northland Press, Dragoon and Flagstaff, AZ.

DiPeso, Charles C., J. B. Rinaldo and G. J. Fenner 1974 *Casas Grandes: A Fallen Trading Center of the Gran Chichimeca. Vols. 4–8*. Amerind Foundation and Northland Press, Dragoon and Flagstaff, AZ.

Edgeworth, Matt 2011 *Fluid Pasts: Archaeology of Flow*. Bristol Classical Press, London.

Eliade, Mircea 1987 *The Sacred and the Profane: The Nature of Religion* (originally published 1959). Harcourt Brace and Company, San Diego.

Emerson, Thomas E., and Timothy R. Pauketat 2008 Historical-Processual Archaeology and Culture Making: Unpacking the Southern Cult and Mississippian Religion. In *Belief in the Past: Theoretical Approaches to the Archaeology of Religion*, edited by D. S. Whitley and K. Hays-Gilpin, pp. 167–188. Left Coast Press, Walnut Creek, CA.

Fustel de Coulanges, Numa Denis 1980 *The Ancient City*. Johns Hopkins University Press, Baltimore.

Gell, Alfred 1998 *Art and Agency: An Anthropological Theory*. Oxford University Press, Oxford.

Hall, Robert L. 1989 The Cultural Background of Mississippian Symbolism. In *The Southeastern Ceremonial Complex*, edited by P. Galloway, pp. 239–278. University of Nebraska Press, Lincoln.

——— 1997 *An Archaeology of the Soul: Native American Indian Belief and Ritual*. University of Illinois Press, Urbana.

Hamilakis, Yannis 2017 Sensorial Assemblages: Affect, Memory and Temporality in Assemblage Thinking. *Cambridge Archaeological Journal* 27(1):169–182.

Harris, Oliver J. T. 2017 Assemblages and Scale in Archaeology. *Cambridge Archaeological Journal* 27(1):127–139.

Hays-Gilpin, Kelley, and Jane H. Hill 2000 The Flower World in Prehistoric Southwest Material Culture. In *The Archaeology of Regional Interaction: Religion, Warfare, and Exchange across the American Southwest and Beyond*, edited by M. Hegmon, pp. 411–428. University of Colorado Press, Boulder.

Hawkins, Gerald S. 1966 *Astro-archaeology*. Smithsonian Institution Astrophysical Observatory, Research in Space Science Special Report 226, Cambridge, MA.

He, Nu 2013 The Longshan Period Site of Taosi in Southern Shanxi Province. In *A Companion to Chinese Archaeology*, edited by A. P. Underhill, pp. 255–277. Blackwell, London.

Helmreich, Stefan 2009 *Alien Ocean: Anthropological Voyages in Microbial Seas*. University of California Press, Berkeley.

Ingold, Tim 2013 *Making: Anthropology, Archaeology, Art and Architecture*. Routledge, London.

Kelley, Jane H., and Michael T. Searcy 2015 Beginnings: The Viejo Period. In *Ancient Paquimé and the Casas Grandes World*, edited by P. E. Minnis and M. E. Whalen, pp. 17–40. University of Arizona Press, Tucson.

Kostof, Spiro 1992 *The City Assembled: The Elements of Urban Form through History*. Thames and Hudson, London.

Kus, Susan M., and Victor Raharigaona 2004 Materials and Metaphors of Sovereignty in Central Madagascar. In *Rethinking Materiality: The Engagement of Mind with the Material World*, edited by E. DeMarrais, C. Gosden and C. Renfrew, pp. 239–248. McDonald Institute for Archaeology, Cambridge.

Kuwanwisiwma, Leigh J. 2002 *Hopit Navotiat*, Hopi Knowledge of History. In *Prehistoric Culture Change on the Colorado Plateau*, edited by S. Powell and F. E. Smiley, pp. 161–163. University of Arizona Press, Tucson.

Lekson, Stephen H. 1999 *The Chaco Meridian: Centers of Political Power in the Ancient Southwest*. AltaMira Press, Walnut Canyon, CA.

Li, Lan, Cheng Zhu, Zhen Qin, Michael J. Storozum and Tristram R. Kidder 2017 Relative Sea Level Rise, Site Distributions, and Neolithic Settlement in the Early to Middle Holocene, Jiangsu Province, China. *The Holocene* doi: 10.1177/0959683617729442:1–9.

Li, Min, Bin Liu, Ningyuan Wang, Jianfeng Lang and Yi Wei 2016 Water Management at the Liangzhu Prehistoric Mound Center, China. Paper Presented at the Irrigation in Early States: New Directions, Oriental Institute, University of Chicago, March 3–4.

Liu, Bin, Ningyuan Wang and Minghui Chen 2016 A Realm of Gods and Kings: The Recent Discovery of Liangzhu City and the Rise of Civilization in South China. *Asian Archaeology* 4:13–31.

Liu, Bin, Ningyuan Wang, Minghui Chen, Xiaohong Wu, Duowen Mo, Jianguo Liu, Shijin Xu and Zhuang Yijie 2018 Earliest Hydraulic Enterprise in China, 5100 Years Ago. *PNAS* 114(52):13637–13642.

Lynch, David K. 1982 Tidal Bores. *Scientific American* 247(4):146–156.

Marcus, Joyce, and Jeremy A. Sabloff (editors) 2008 *The Ancient City: New Perspectives on Urbanism in the Old and New World*. School for Advanced Research Press, Santa Fe, NM.

Mathiowetz, Michael D. 2011 The Diurnal Path of the Sun: Ideology and Interregional Interaction in Ancient Northwest Mesoamerica and the American Southwest. PhD dissertation, Department of Anthropology, University of California, Riverside.

McGuire, Randall H. 2012 Mesoamerica and the Southwest/Northwest. In *The Oxford Handbook of Mesoamerican Archaeology*, edited by D. L. Nichols and C. A. Pool, pp. 513–524. Oxford University Press, Oxford.

Minnis, Paul E., and Michael E. Whalen 2015a Ecology and Food Economy. In *Ancient Paquimé and the Casas Grandes World*, edited by P. E. Minnis and M. E. Whalen, pp. 41–57. University of Arizona Press, Tucson.

———— 2015b Introduction: The Joint Casas Grandes Expedition in Historical Context. In *Ancient Paquimé and the Casas Grandes World*, edited by P. E. Minnis and M. E. Whalen, pp. 3–16. University of Arizona Press, Tucson.

Murray, Martin J. 2008 The City in Fragments: Kaleidoscopic Johannesburg after Apartheid. In *The Spaces of the Modern City: Imaginaries, Politics, and Everyday Life*, edited by G. Prakash and K. M. Kruse, pp. 144–178. Princeton University Press, Princeton, NJ.

Nelson, Ben A. 2010 The Connected World of the Mimbres. In *Mimbres Lives and Landscapes*, edited by M. C. Nelson and M. Hegmon, pp. 9–15. School for Advanced Research Press, Santa Fe, NM.

Newsome, Elizabeth A., and Kelley Hays-Gilpin 2011 Spectatorship and Performance in Mural Painting, 1250–1500: Visuality and Social Integration. In *Religious Transformation in the Late Pre-Hispanic Pueblo World*, edited by D. M. Glowacki and S. Van Keuren. University of Arizona Press, Tucson.

Pauketat, Timothy R. 2011 Getting Religion: Lessons from Ancestral Pueblo History. In *Religious Transformation in the Late Pre-Hispanic Pueblo World*, edited by D. M. Glowacki and S. Van Keuren. University of Arizona Press, Tucson.

———— 2013a *An Archaeology of the Cosmos: Rethinking Agency and Religion in Ancient America*. Routledge, London.

———— 2013b Bundles in/of/as Time. In *Big Histories, Human Lives: Tackling Problems of Scale in Archaeology*, edited by J. Robb and T. R. Pauketat. School for Advanced Research Press, Santa Fe.

Pitezel, Todd A. 2007 Surveying Cerro de Moctezuma, Chihuahua, Mexico. *Kiva* 72(3):353–369.

———— 2011 From Archaeology to Ideology in Northwest Mexico: Cerro de Moctezuma in the Casas Grandes Ritual Landscape. Unpublished PhD dissertation, Department of Anthropology, University of Arizona, Tucson.

Qin, Ling 2013 The Liangzhu Culture. In *A Companion to Chinese Archaeology*, edited by A. P. Underhill, pp. 574–596. Blackwell Publishing, London.

Renfrew, Colin, and Bin Liu 2018 The Emergence of Complex Society in China: The Case of Liangzhu. *Antiquity* 92(364):975–990.

Richards, Colin 1996 Henges and Water: Towards an Elemental Understanding of Monumentality and Landscape in Late Neolithic Britain. *Journal of Material Culture* 1(3):313–336.

Scarborough, Vernon L. 2003 *The Flow of Power: Ancient Water Systems and Landscapes*. School of American Research Press, Santa Fe.

Schaafsma, Curtis F., and Carroll L. Riley (editors) 1999 *The Casas Grandes World*. University of Utah Press, Salt Lake City.

Shafer, Harry J. 1999 The Mimbres Classic and Postclassic: A Case for Discontinuity. In *The Casas Grandes World*, edited by C. F. Schaafsma and C. L. Riley, pp. 121–133. University of Utah Press, Salt Lake City.

Strang, Veronica 2014 Fluid Consistencies: Material Relationality in Human Engagements with Water. *Archaeological Dialogues* 21(2):123–150.

Swanson, Steven 2003 Documenting Prehistoric Communication Networks: A Case Study in the Paquimé Polity. *American Antiquity* 68(4):753–767.

Tassin, Wirt 1902 The Casas Grandes Meteorite. *Proceedings of the U.S. National Museum* 25(1277):69–74.

Thompson, Marc 2007 Pre-Columbian Venus: Celestial Twin and Icon of Duality. In *Religion in the Pre-Hispanic Southwest*, pp. 165–184. AltaMira Press, Lanham, Maryland.

Thrift, Nigel 2004 Intensities of Feeling: Towards a Spatial Politics of Affect. *Geografiska Annaler* 86B(1):57–78.

———— 2008 *Non-Representational Theory: Space | Politics | Affect*. Routledge, London.

VanPool, Christine S., and Todd L. VanPool 2007 *Signs of Casas Grandes Shamans*. University of Utah Press, Salt Lake City.

Vernadsky, Vladimir I. 1998 *The Biosphere*. Springer-Verlag, New York.

Wang, Zhanghua, Chencheng Zhuang, Yoshiki Saito, Jie Chen, Qing Zhan and Xiaodan Wang 2012 Early Mid-Holocene Sea-Level Change and Coastal Environmental Response on the Southern Yangtze Delta Plain, China: Implications for the Rise of Neolithic Culture. *Quaternary Science Reviews* 35:51–62.

Whalen, Michael E. 2013 Wealth, Status, Ritual, and Marine Shell at Casas Grandes, Chihuahua, Mexico. *American Antiquity* 78(4):624–639.

Whalen, Michael E., and Paul E. Minnis 2001 *Casas Grandes and Its Hinterland: Prehistoric Political Organization in Northwest Mexico.* University of Arizona Press, Tucson.

———— 2012 Ceramics and Polity in the Casas Grandes Area, Chihuahua, Mexico. *American Antiquity* 75(3):527–551.

Wilcox, David R. 1999 A Preliminary Graph–Theoretic Analysis of Access Relationships at Casas Grandes. In The Casas Grandes World, edited by C. F. Schaafsma and C. L. Riley, pp. 93–104. University of Utah Press, Salt Lake City.

Wood, John E. 1980 *Sun, Moon and Standing Stones.* Oxford University Press, Oxford.

Yoffee, Norman 2016 The Power of Infrastructures: A Counternarrative and a Speculation. *Journal of Archaeological Method and Theory* 23(4):1053–1065.

Zhejiang, Sheng 2015 *Power in Things: New Perspectives on Liangzhu.* Wen wu chu ban she, Beijing.

Zong, Yongqiang 2004 Mid-Holocene Sea-Level Highstand along the Southeast Coast of China. *Quaternary International* 117(1):55–67.

7

THE GATHERING OF SWAHILI RELIGIOUS PRACTICE

Mosques-as-assemblages at 1000 CE Swahili towns

Jeffrey Fleisher

For the Swahili of the eastern African coast, mosques are crucial to the constitution of a town, as Middleton (1992:60) describes: "A settlement without a mosque is not a 'founded' town." The Swahili term for "founded town" is *mji uliubunika*, which means literally "a city that has been constructed/designed/composed." In this way, the construction of a mosque is synonymous with constructing a town, and this chapter seeks to understand the ontological underpinnings of this construction. Key to this analysis is a close study of the evolution of ca. 1000 CE coral-built mosques that emphasizes construction materials and their links to particular coastal ecologies. Put simply: The materials of early mosques (built of sand, coral, and wood) lead us to the foreshore/nearshore environment adjacent to these coastal settlements, and thus they can be understood as an assemblage built from these particular locales. Following Ingold (2012:431), I seek to shift interpretations of mosques solely as "objects" to "the material flows and formative processes wherein they come into being." In this way, I seek to reframe the construction of mosques at this particular period "as a process of growth, or ontogenesis."

One of the ways mosques come into being is through how they *gather*. Researchers of the Swahili have understood the way mosques can serve as a locus of human gathering, as Muslim adherents travel to the mosque multiple times a day or, at the very least, every Friday (e.g., Wynne-Jones 2016:84–85; Fleisher 2010a). But such a perspective offers up mosques as containers, and people alone as agents. What I attempt to describe in this chapter is the variable ways in which mosques may be understood as "things" (Ingold 2012; Hodder 2012) in which the quality of things ("thingness") is "in their connections, and in their flows into other forms" (Hodder 2012:8). My conceptualization here draws on recent efforts to draw out the assemblages and entanglements of things, and to understand the stabilizing and destabilizing processes that characterized them (DeLanda 2006; see also Hodder 2012; Deleuze and Guattari 1987; Latour 2005; Pauketat 2013).

The period in which these mosques were constructed, ca. 950–1000 CE, represents an historical inflection point in the chronology of the coastal Swahili; it is a period when a few smaller villages transformed into larger towns, and other towns were constructed de novo. I have argued elsewhere (Fleisher 2010b) that this was a period of urban development, with nascent urban centers drawing countryside population into locales that were becoming more cosmopolitan and interconnected to the Indian Ocean world (LaViolette 2008). Long-distance trade intensified during this period and, thus, relationships within and among towns and other ports along the northern Indian Ocean rim were expanding and becoming more heterogeneous. It is the first period in which the Swahili began to journey far from the eastern African coast, and their material culture can be found in places as distant as the coast of Yemen (Rougeulle 2015). Thus, the ports of these Swahili towns, conterminous with the fore/nearshore, were locales of great fluidity and movement, connecting these nascent towns with hundreds (if not thousands) of other coastal village and towns. As assemblages, we might regard these zones as places of deterritorialization—places subject to processes that "destabilize spatial boundaries or increase internal heterogeneity" (DeLanda 2006:13).

In contrast, I argue, mosques were assemblages in which we can see processes of territorialization, processes that "define or sharpen the spatial boundaries of actual territories" (DeLanda 2006:13). In conceptualizing mosques-as-assemblages, we can consider how they entangle materials, humans, affects, texts, postures, performances, directionality—to name just a few. But my effort here is not to just make the case for mosque-as-assemblage, but rather to situate a particular mosque-assemblage in time and space (the Swahili coral-built mosques of 1000 CE) to ponder the way they were territorializations of particular substances, materials and phenomena connected to the ecology of the fore/nearshore. In this way, I argue, the Swahili were seeking to create a new type of stability in an increasingly fluid and changing world, while remaining firmly connected to it. To do this, I follow the materials that composed mosques to their place of origin, the fore/nearshore that was adjacent and connected to all Swahili towns.

This approach also offers the possibility of engaging with Swahili conceptual frameworks to think about the eastern African past. In the last 30 years, there has been great effort to recover the African roots of ancient Swahili towns and to recognize the local agency involved in founding, building, and administering them (Nurse and Spear 1985; Allen 1993; Horton 1996). This work has transformed how the Swahili past has been studied and has cast off decades of racist, colonialist rhetoric about the foreign origins and development of the Swahili. And yet, the history of the precolonial Swahili past that is now told focuses primarily on global, comparative frameworks—those of subsistence economies, merchant entrepreneurs, and cities and states (e.g., Wright 1993; Kusimba 1999). Although the work of placing Swahili settlements among other global examples of complex societies has been important, the emphasis on such qualities risks erasing crucial conceptual frameworks that likely shaped these places and their histories. As Stahl (2005:11) notes, the emphasis on cross-cultural elements that are understood as "hallmarks of cultural progress" are often deployed "to demonstrate that Africa too had a proud history of innovation and social complexity, one that rivaled other world areas in age and could therefore provide a platform for generating respect for African cultural history." This is important work, to be sure but, in the effort to situate African examples among other global examples, the distinctive qualities found were always "assessed in relation to … the universal qualities of a [Western] past" (Stahl 2005:12).

One alternate way forward, as proposed here, is to consider the meaning and nature of material assemblages, informed by Swahili conceptual frameworks. I echo TallBear"s (2017:191–192) plea to take seriously "indigenous metaphysics": "an understanding of the intimate knowing relatedness of all things" (see also Deloria 2001). This work on Native American conceptions resonates here because of the importance of spirits, as TallBear (2017:191–192) describes: "The co-constitutive entanglements between the material and the immaterial—that is, indigenous peoples' social relations also with 'spirit' beings (for lack of a better term) … constitute a boundary crossing that is difficult for interspecies and new materialist thinkers." There have been hints of the importance of spirits in previous work on the Swahili (e.g., Kusimba 1999:86; Horton and Middleton 2000:190–194), but only in reference to particular forms of power, and never pursued through an understanding of the vitality of things. My effort here is to write a particularly local narrative of the emergence of Islamic practice by attending to material assemblages from the archaeological record, as well as ethnographic understandings of the possible entanglements of those assemblages with the spirit world.

This chapter gives a brief overview of the ancient Swahili, describing the dominant themes in this archaeological region. I then explore the development of mosques and Islam on the coast, situating the emergence of the first coral-built mosques by 1000 CE and their constituent materials. Following these materials, I describe the rich assemblage that composes the fore/nearshore, explore its natural resources and rhythms, the activities of the Swahili in it (fishing, shell collecting, disembarking and embarking), and the possible nonhuman actants that may have lived there, sea spirits, beings that live alongside the Swahili, possessing them at times. Finally, I ponder the nature of these entanglements, as possible demonstrations of devotion or a quieter means of building in local powerful forces in the context of a foreign religious locale.

The Swahili: A brief overview

Today, the remains of dozens of coral-built towns dot the eastern African coast (Figure 7.1) from Somalia to Mozambique, extending to offshore islands in Zanzibar, the Comoros, and Madagascar. These towns were home to the ancestors of the contemporary Swahili, a Muslim urban society that has inhabited the thin coastal strip since approximately 600 CE. Historical, linguistic, and archaeological research on the Swahili (Nurse and Spear 1985; Kusimba 1999; Horton and Middleton 2000; Pearson 1998; Wynne-Jones 2016) has documented the development of these towns from small fishing and farming villages in the middle of the first millennium CE to their emergence as more densely populated towns in the early second millennium.

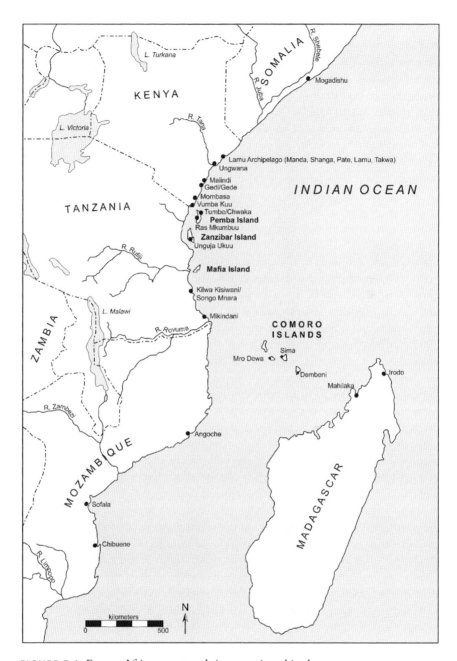

FIGURE 7.1 Eastern African coast and sites mentioned in the text

162 Jeffrey Fleisher

Between 600–800 CE settlements on the coastal corridor increased dramatically, with small fishing and farming communities established along the entire coast and offshore islands. These settlements were materially indistinguishable from those in the more distant interior and thus indicate that that the coast was first settled from the interior rather than by visitors from abroad. By 950–1000 CE a number of these communities had established themselves as trade ports (Fitton 2017), evidenced by larger numbers of imported ceramics, glass, beads, and metals from the Persian Gulf and broader northern Indian Ocean rim. From 1000 CE significant changes occur in Swahili towns: Some villages become more densely populated and expand significantly while others are founded anew; the first congregational mosques of coral are constructed suggesting the conversion of more and more residents to Islam; long-distance trade increases; the Swahili begin traveling beyond coastal regions, to live and participate in trade entrepots as far as the Yemeni coast (Rougeulle 2015). In general, by 1000 CE, the Swahili world expanded outward, as they become more maritime oriented, and actively engaged in the larger Indian Ocean world.

Swahili towns are known ethnographically as places that managed continental trade: Merchants in towns brokered the exchange of goods from between the African continent and ports along the Indian Ocean rim, trading gold, ivory, animal skins, and other goods for imported ceramics, beads, and cloth (Middleton 1992). The archaeology of Swahili towns has traditionally focused on these merchant functions: How the emergence of towns was tied to exchange patterns in the larger Indian Ocean world system (Kusimba 1999; Horton and Middleton 2000; LaViolette 2008). In an earlier archaeology, this focus led many researchers to interpret the early Swahili as a colonial imposition, the result of Persian or Arab migrations and towns as colonial outposts of a distant Islamic world (Kirkman 1964; Chittick 1974). However, the last 30 years of research has documented the unambiguous local origins of Swahili towns and people, including their stratigraphic relationship to first millennium settlements associated with regional local ceramics and the linguistic origins of Swahili as a Bantu language.

More recent research has focused on the relationship between Swahili towns and their associated landscapes, drawing out the social, political and economic networks that existed in the immediate countryside (Wynne-Jones 2007; Fleisher 2010b; Pawlowicz 2012) and the more distant hinterlands (Kusimba and Kusimba 2005; Walz 2010). Renewed attention to the towns themselves has helped to reveal more about daily life in Swahili towns, and how particular places and spaces were constructed and used by town residents (Horton 1996; Fleisher 2014; Wynne-Jones 2013, 2016).

Mosques and evolution of Islam on the Swahili coast

From mud to coral: Mosques from 780 to 1000

In this section I explore what is known about the evolution of Islam in Swahili towns, charting developments from 780 to 1500 CE and the emergence of the first coral-built mosques at 1000 CE. What we understand about the development of Islamic practice

Gathering of Swahili religious practice **163**

comes primarily from the development of mosques and mosque architecture. The physical centrality of mosques in Swahili settlements, often located at the heart of the town, as well as the permanence of the building materials used, are thought to reflect its enduring social significance (Gensheimer 1997; Horton & Middleton 2000) and the power of Islam as a force in organizing daily life (Wilson 1982; Wright 1993).

Mosques have been interpreted as indicators of the presence of particular Islamic sects (Horton 1996:419–423), as proxy measures for the size of Islamic communities within the town, and their chronological development used to illustrate the development of Islamic adherence (Garlake 1966; Horton 1991). Archaeologists have also suggested that mosques had a symbolic role within a larger landscape, seeing investment in elaborate examples as signifying the religious commitment of elite town dwellers, providing an important focal point for a regional population (LaViolette & Fleisher 2009; Fleisher 2010b; Wynne-Jones 2016:162–163). Likewise, Fleisher (2010a) has argued that particular architectural features in central mosques, such as displays of imported bowls, may represent the power and authority of local leaders to act as patrons to urban residents. Wynne-Jones (2016:84–85, 162–163) has suggested that the mosque "indexes the communal identity of the community," serving as a key marker of the practices of an Islamic community.

The best known pre-1000 CE mosques are those recovered by Horton through his remarkable excavations in the central sector of Shanga, a Swahili town located in the Lamu archipelago in northern Kenya. The site was inhabited continuously from 750 to 1425 CE. At that site, it appears Islam was practiced by a small group of people as early as 780 CE, just over 150 years after the death of Mohammed. Horton's (1996) excavations revealed structures from these centuries that are most likely the remains of early wattle-and-daub mosques, built to accommodate a small group of devotees. These mosques may have been built for visiting Islamic merchants from the Persian Gulf but also likely included local inhabitants in the first instance. Merchants would have had to stay in Swahili towns for a period of time to carry out their trades, but also to wait for the monsoon winds to shift: Indian Ocean monsoon winds alternate yearly, shifting from northeasterly to southwesterly winds. These regular changes allowed Muslim merchants from the Persian Gulf and other Indian Ocean ports to sail easily back and forth to the eastern African coast. These earliest mosques, however, were located at Shanga's central area, alongside other community structures, in an area that was likely controlled by the local community. The fact that these early mosques were not located at the margins of the settlement suggests that some local residents were actively involved in their construction and use. Islam, however, remained a minority religious practice in Swahili towns until approximately 1000 CE. At Shanga, the small earthen mosques were replaced with a larger one: the first Friday mosques intended for larger and more permanent communities.

The example of mosque evolution from Shanga is crucial to this interpretation. Horton's excavations there in the 1980s revealed a stratified sequence of mosques at the center of the settlement, including nine re-buildings from 780–1000 CE (Figure 7.2). The first phases, from 780–920 CE, included small mosques of wattle-and-daub (Buildings A-E), with close-set rammed posts and mud walls.

SHANGA
Development of Mosques

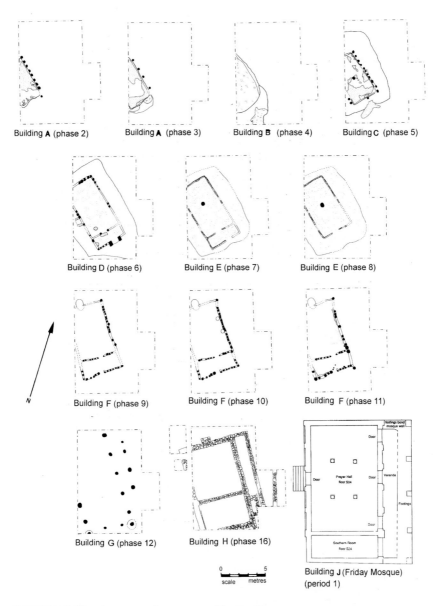

FIGURE 7.2 Development of mosques at Shanga, Kenya
Source: Adapted from Horton 1996 with permission.

A small *mihrab*, a prayer niche that indicates the direction of Mecca, is evident by 850 CE (Building F), confirming the interpretation that these were, in fact, early mosques. After Building F, Horton documents a period of transformation, in which the mosque is rebuilt first as a wooden structure (Building G), with large posts, and then the first mosque built of coral (Building H), in approximately 920 CE. Building H was built with *Porites*, a form of coral that was mined from coastal reefs and the foreshore (Figure 7.3). This coral was shaped into small blocks, mortared with mud, and faced with white plaster, made from reduced coral.

FIGURE 7.3 Excavated mosques at Shanga, showing earlier wattle-and-daub mosques and later *Porites* mosque above

Source: From Horton 1996 with permission.

As Horton (1996:399) notes, although the construction material changes, the "architectural forms remain largely unchanged" from the earlier structures. This mosque was in use for less than a hundred years and then replaced by a larger mosque at approximately 1000 CE. This mosque was also built of *Porites* coral, utilizing material from the previous mosque. Horton refers to this as the first "Friday mosque," arguing that it was a "building large enough to accommodate the majority of the male adult population" of the settlement, and thus indicating that the settlement now contained a majority Islamic population. This mosque forms the basis for the Friday mosque that endured at Shanga until 1425, when the site was ultimately abandoned. Throughout these 400 years, the mosque was enlarged and embellished to accommodate an ever-expanding town population.

An alternative mode of the advent of an Islamic community comes from archaeological research on northern Pemba Island (Figure 7.4), which has revealed the changing demographics that led the emergence of Islamic towns. In the earliest phase, 800–1000 CE, the region was settled extensively—small villages dotted the landscape from the coast to the interior. A few larger villages, located at the coasts, were evidently better connected to the long distance trade; in these villages were found imported pottery, glass, and metals from the Persian Gulf and Indian Ocean ports (Fleisher and LaViolette 2013; Juma 2004). Around 1000 CE, however, the settlement pattern shifted dramatically, with a significant reduction in the number of villages in the countryside, and the creation of new coastal settlements—often near or adjacent to earlier ones—that were more compact but densely populated. I have argued that these settlement changes—such as the foundation of new towns on Pemba Island—was effected through the movement of countryside communities to a new center, a process through which a town was "composed" (Fleisher 2010b:280).

Previous arguments about the emergence of towns often emphasized their growth as linked to the development of regional and long-distance trade (Kusimba 1999; Horton 1996), suggesting that settlement growth expanded outward from the towns in response to increasing economic opportunities with overseas merchants. The data from Pemba Island, however, suggest that the foundation of towns created a demographic pull from the surrounding countryside, and that this "may have been based partly on the desire of regional populations to form a religious community" as Islam became the dominant religious affiliation (Fleisher 2010b, see also Wynne-Jones 2016). This can be seen in the construction of coral-built Friday mosques, structures that continued to be rebuilt in larger and more elaborate forms in Pemba's stonetowns (LaViolette and Fleisher 2009), a pattern repeated at most other Swahili towns. Wright (1993:671–672) has articulated a similar argument, suggesting that the practice of Islam was one of the key means through which towns and villages became entwined, "bind[ing] villages and smaller centers more closely to emerging towns."

The foundation of a Swahili town is seen as coterminous with the foundation of a central, congregational mosque (*msikiti wa Ijumaa*, "the mosque of gathering together" or "Friday mosque"; Middleton 1992:60). In Arabic, the word for "Friday,"

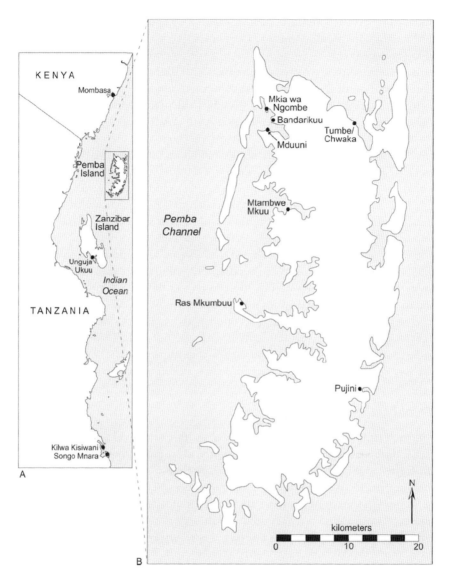

FIGURE 7.4 Pemba Island, Tanzania

which comes from the root word of "gathering," takes its name from the practice in which the entire community gathers on that holiest day of the week. Many scholars of "Islamic cities" regard the construction of the Friday mosque as the key element of urban life (Lapidus 1969; Hourani and Stern 1970; Eickelman 1974; Abu-Lughod 1987), a "locale in which the life of the Prophet could be lived out to the fullest" (Wheatley 1972:622). On Pemba Island, the settlement shift from countryside to town was marked by the construction of the first permanent, centrally located mosques during the early to mid-eleventh century CE. In this way,

168 Jeffrey Fleisher

Swahili towns were "founded" (*mji uliubunika*), composed of residents from the surrounding countryside, gathered in settlements but also through the construction of the mosque itself.

Based on this material record of the evolution of Islamic practice, most researchers have focused on the "why" of Islamic conversion, and offered interpretations that focus on the pragmatics of accepting Islam by local Swahili communities (Kusimba 1999; Horton 1991, 1996; Pouwels 1987, 2000). Such research suggests that the conversion to Islam would have facilitated exchange relationships with Muslim merchants, binding them to particular communities to which they would return year after year. In this scenario, the yearly visits by Muslim merchants from overseas would have not only exposed the Swahili to Islam and Islamic practice, but would also have reinforced the benefits of conversion, as local merchants attempted to attract and retain these overseas visitors. Others have suggested that the conversion to Islam was a form of protection from enslavement (Trimingham 1964). We know that slaves were routinely shipped from eastern Africa to the Middle East by the ninth and tenth centuries CE (Popovic 1999) and, thus, the suggestion is that Swahili communities converted to Islam to protect themselves from enslavement and to become active participants in that same trade. While all of these pragmatic interpretations may be valid, they do not offer any insight into why mosques were built and rebuilt at particular times and in particular materials. To interpret the rich material record of mosques solely through architectural styles/features and mosque size is to overlook choices that were made in materials and construction.

Coral-built mosques at 1000 CE

Although Horton stresses the importance of the first Friday mosque at Shanga—in that it documents the emergence of majority Islam in the town—I want to shift the focus and think more about the materials of mosque construction rather than their size, and focus on the first coral-built mosques. All of the pre-900 CE mosques at Shanga were made of the same earthen materials and built in the same ways as houses and other structures. At around 950–1050 CE, however, there emerged a series of mosques at coastal sites that have a new series of materials (Horton 1991; Horton and Middleton 2000:59–61)[1]: *Porites* coral walls, mangrove wood roof beams, all built on a raised platform of white beach sand. At Shanga, this correlates to Building H and succeeding first Friday mosque. Similar types of mosques are found at towns that were founded de novo, such as the site of Chwaka on Pemba Island (Figure 7.5), where these were the first mosques constructed; other examples are known from the Kenyan and Tanzanian coast and islands. The shift to *Porites* coral in the construction of mosques—the first evidence of more permanent architecture along the coastal corridor—is generally regarded as evidence of the importation of new construction technologies and/or a greater investment in the symbolic permanence of Islamic practice by building in stone. A number of sites on the eastern and western shores of the Red Sea are built in worked coral, such as Berenike (Sidebotham and Wendrich 2000) and Suakin (Greenlaw

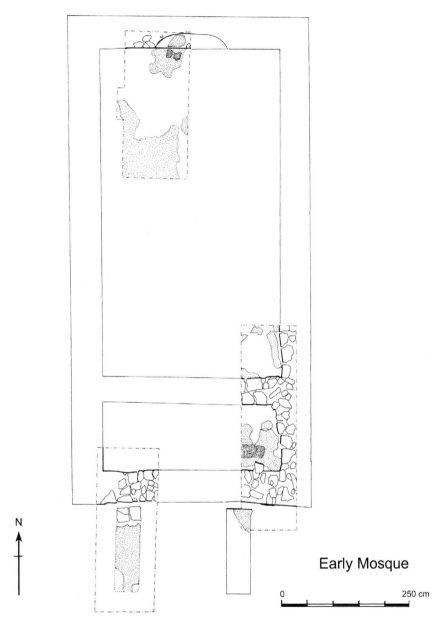

FIGURE 7.5 Plan of early *Porites* mosque at Chwaka (plan by M. Horton)

1995), suggesting that this building technology may have been introduced from that region. The greater investment of this new technology in primarily mosques offers indications of the renewed symbolic importance of mosques in communities that were rapidly converting to Islam. Such arguments, however, fail to examine the full range of materials used to construct early, Swahili coral mosques.

In describing the archaeology of mosque materials, I suggest that the advent of *Porites* coral mosques represented an intentional shift toward materials from the sea and a shift away from materials of the land: from wattle-and-daub to *Porites* coral, mangrove wood, and white beach sand. This transformation of materials, marking the key centuries of local Islamic conversion, represents a physical (re)construction of the space and place of Islamic practice into one shaped by elements of the fore/nearshore. The investment in these materials cannot be explained by an imported building technology alone and should be understood as a process of assembling a form and space of religious practice that intentionally entangled elements of the fore/nearshore with daily Islamic practice.

Although prior wattle-and-daub mosques were built on the ground surface, the first *Porites* coral mosques were constructed on raised levels, built up with more than one meter of white beach sand. This sand would have been brought from the foreshore, basket by basket, to create a new, leveled surface. In all the mosques from this period, archaeological research has confirmed the presence of these deep, white sandy deposits. These deposits were often very "clean," with few to no artifacts found in this fill. The *Porites* coral used to construct the foundation and walls was exceedingly difficult to obtain and shape. Unlike coral rag (a rubbly limestone quarried on land from the remains of ancient coral reefs and which is present on the surface and easily quarried on the coast and islands), *Porites* coral comes from either the reef, from which it must be physically cut, or from coral blooms that wash up on the foreshore. Once acquired, this material must be shaped when wet, as it remains soft and workable only when fresh or wet. These early mosques were constructed not of haphazard fragments of *Porites* but rather neatly shaped, square and rectangular blocks. Finally, the roof of these early *Porites* mosques was likely constructed of a wood frame made of mangrove wood and then roofed over in palm or other types of thatch. Mangrove wood, like *Porites* coral and beach sand, was found in the swampy flats of the foreshore as well, growing in dense stands that are inundated tidally but become accessible when the tide goes out. Harvesting mangrove wood is difficult: The dense, above-ground root systems of mangrove trees makes maneuvering through a mangrove swamp complicated and mangrove wood itself is physically dense and difficult to cut. For all these materials, the difficulty in obtaining, moving, and fashioning them suggests that they were not chosen purely for ease or for functional purposes—the sourcing of materials for these mosques thus focused on an extremely limited part of the coastal environment. This sourcing left aside a number of more-easily obtained alternatives: In most areas, for example, there was ample coral rag, a more easily acquired form of coral, found on the island landscape itself, at the surface; alternatives to beach sand were numerous (and not necessary to create a level surface); there were many places on the coast that were covered in dense tropical forest, with a rich assemblage of trees that could have been used for construction. The archaeological remains of these mosques are thus pointing us toward the fore and nearshore, to which I now turn.

The fore/nearshore and Swahili towns

Resources and rhythms

The earliest coral-built mosque materials point us to a particular environment related to Swahili towns, that of the foreshore and nearshore. The foreshore is the part of the shore found between the high-water and low-water marks. In some places it can simply be a section of beach that is revealed when the tide recedes, but in many places in eastern Africa, because of coastal geology, a low tide reveals deep and wide flats with pools, coral outcrops, and other features. The nearshore extends further than the foreshore and includes areas that are always inundated but remain shallow most of the time; at most coastal towns the nearshore extends to a coral reef, where the ocean waves break.

In the literature on Swahili towns, this zone is most often discussed as a port, a place of entry and disembarkment for local travelers and fisherman, and for long-distance traders (Fitton 2017). Fitton's (2017) recent study of a number of nearshore locales in first-millennium CE Swahili sites has shown that these were likely active zones, busy with craft activities, houses, and possibly mosques (see also Fitton and Wynne-Jones 2017). Ports made certain travel possible—both along the coastal corridor but also when long-distance traders would arrive. And yet, the foreshore/nearshore has its own rhythms, guided by low and high tides, seasonal monsoons (with winds blowing from the northeast or southwest), lunar cycles that bring spring and neap tides, tropical cyclones, and the movement and growth cycles of fish, shellfish, and coral. These cycles served to reveal and conceal resources, thus structuring the daily lives of those living on the coast: when shellfish could be collected, when nets would be stretched across foreshore inlets, when boats could be poled out to the reef to spear fish or to collect and reset traps.

Through an analysis of fish and shellfish remains from Swahili sites (Quintana Morales and Horton 2014), we know that the foreshore/nearshore zone was exploited extensively. Fish consumed at the sites came from most parts of the fore/nearshore: muddy flats, sea grass beds, mangroves and mangrove channels, and the coral reef. These were fished with a wide range of techniques: nets, spears, basket and fence traps, and hook and line (Quintana Morales and Horton 2014). The analysis of fish remains suggests that prior to 1000 CE, most or all fish were coming from these close-by areas. After 1000 CE, larger, deep-water fish remains are found in fish assemblages (especially shark), suggesting that Swahili fisherman were employing new fishing and sailing technologies outside of the fore/nearshore. At the same time, the broader faunal assemblages indicate a shift toward more protein from domesticated animals—cows, goats, and chickens.

The fore/nearshore also included extensive zones of mangrove stands, where trees grew in the muddy, tidally inundated areas extending out from the shore. Mangroves provided important building material for houses and boats, and also an aquatic community in which crabs and other animals live. Coastal dwellers regularly traverse mangrove swamps, through which paths are cut to allow people to move between close islands or to store and access small dugout canoes. Research in eastern African mangrove swamps (Punwong et al. 2013) demonstrates how these resources were increasingly exploited from the first to the second millennium CE.

The fore/nearshore was thus an assemblage of fish, shells, reef, water, boats, nets, humans, mud, mangrove, and much more. The coastal settlement by early Swahili speakers, and their increasing use and incursions into the fore/nearshore must have had a territorializing effect, as they become increasingly entangled with this assemblage. As we have seen, the space from the reef to the mangrove swamps and shore was a rich biotic community, one with fish to be trapped, speared, and netted, wood to be harvested, and shells to be collected. And yet, the activities and actants within ports and fore/nearshores are often considered to be "places of intense deterritorialization" in contrast to inland towns (Jervis 2017; Delanda 1997). Ports, as gateway settlements, are more fluid due to the comings and goings of visitors, merchants, and others, as well as the constantly pulsating rhythms of the sea, sand, mud, and fish. The final group of actants who may have inhabited the late first-millennium fore/nearshore are sea spirits, entities that may have played a role in stabilizing the identity of this environmental assemblage.

Other possible residents of the fore/nearshore: Sea spirits

Contemporary ethnographies of the Swahili offer another possible group of residents in the fore/nearshore: sea spirits. I am aware of the anachronism in using twentieth-century ethnography to think about possible actants in the 1000 CE coastal region, a move that threatens to create a narrative in which a distinction is drawn between "pre-Islamic" and "Islamic" practices, as if these were separable. However, based on historical linguistic reconstruction, there is some indication that for early Swahili communities "the focus of their daily religious 'observance' was on spirits" (Pouwels 2000:254), although we understand little to nothing about them. Following Bennett (2010:17), I see this discussion as a moment of "methodological naiveté" that might allow me to "render manifest a subsistent world of nonhuman vitality."

Although there is ample documentation in the ethnographic literature of widespread belief in different forms of spirits (Caplan 1975; Giles 1987; Middleton 1992; Lambek 1981), archaeologists have not engaged with this material to date. Much of the ethnographic work is concerned with spirit possession and the practices that are involved in identifying, diagnosing, and treating/resolving cases of spirit possession. In this literature, spirits are noted for their similarity to humans even though they are recognized as somewhat different; they are not, therefore, understood as "supernatural" nor worshipped in ways similar to religious practice. As Lambek (1981:28) notes, "people interact with [spirits] on a social level … their ontological status is more similar to humans than to God or the angels." Whereas God is "empirically unobservable" and thus approached through the Koran and religious practice, spirits are "empirically real … based upon sensory experience and empirical validation of

Gathering of Swahili religious practice **173**

certain propositions concerning their natures." As such, there are numerous ways in which spirits are entangled in particular landscapes. Sprits are also associated with particular foods and other substances that they eat and require to be exorcised from a human body. It is, however, the ecological aspects of spirits that I want to emphasize here, in particular the distinction often drawn between "sea" and "land" spirits, a distinction that is found in most ethnographic discussions of Swahili spirits (but see Middleton 1992:170ff). In this discussion, I draw primarily from the ethnographic work of Pat Caplan (1975) on Mafia Island, Tanzania, Michael Lambek's (1981) work on Mayotte in the Comoros Islands, and John Middleton's (1992) research on Lamu in Kenya and in Zanzibar.

I use Caplan's general term of "sea spirits" for a category of spirits that have various names along the coast (*majini* in Mafia, *patros* in Mayotte, *pepo* in Zanzibar). These spirits live in underwater villages, areas "adjacent to the coast, often at points where there are mud flats or mangrove swamps, that is, where the boundaries between land and sea become ill defined" (Lambek 1981:36). These spirits are local: They are "said to be indigenous … and live in underwater villages along the coasts, in places often linked to early settlements" (Lambek 1993:51). Offerings to such spirits, Caplan (1975:101) notes, can be made by "floating little boats out to sea." In contrast, "lands spirits" "live on dry land, usually in the bush, and their homes or shrines [*mapango*, lit. 'caves' but also rocks and trees] are known." The distinction between sea and land spirits is significant. On Mayotte, sea spirits (*patros*) are like humans, have families and village organization similar to humans but contrast with them in many ways: they are invisible, immortal, and can possess humans. They have what Lambek (1981) calls "cultural" differences: different language, music, styles of dancing, and eat "substances that humans consider inedible or unworthy of eating" such as cologne, blood, uncooked liver. Land spirits (*trumba*), in contrast, are "deceased humans, not a separate species." This distinction is made clear through what each consumes—land spirits consume "that which is defined locally as forbidden or foreign" (wine and spirits, packaged cigarettes, honey brew) but consumable.

Both land and sea spirits have contradictory relationships to Islam and Islamic practice. All ethnographers recognize that, in general, orthodox Islamic practitioners condemn the cults involved in spirit possession. However, Islam itself recognized the existence of various spirits and offers ways to deal with them. And so, while the Swahili attempt to keep separate the world of spirits and that of Islam, there are few efforts by Islamic leaders to deny the existence of spirits. As Lambek (1981:32) notes "what is challenged is never the existence of spirits, but the respectability of possession activities." In Mayotte, therefore, spirits must be "kept away from Islamic ritual … because possession is disruptive to ritual order." In this way, "spirits are in some sense challenging to the fundamental sociopolitical assumptions and implications of Islamic ideology" (Lambek 1981:33). In a somewhat different take from Mafia Island, although Caplan argues that spirit guilds are generally condemned, "sea spirits…are thought in some vague way to be more 'Koranic'" than land spirits, with some informants arguing that sea spirits are "moslems" and

174 Jeffrey Fleisher

land spirits "pagans." Such linkages to Islam, Caplan argues, are based on similarities in ritual practice: "rituals to propitiate sea spirits or to initiate a person possessed by one into a guild involve features that are also common to orthodox Islamic ritual, these include the use of the Koran, incense, rose-water, and the Arabic language" (Caplan 1975:101).[2]

Discussion

What can we learn by geo-locating the primary building materials of these first Friday mosques within the fore/nearshore? For one, we can now expand the purview of what I identified as a key feature of mosques—that they gather. In addition to the people and communities that they gather for prayer, we now understand additional ways that these mosques serve to gather elements of the fore/nearshore at ca. 1000 CE. This expands our understanding of the mosque-as-assemblage and serves to entangle the mosque into a broader assemblage that encompasses the varied elements of this ecology—water, fish, shellfish, reefs, boats, nets, humans, mud, mangrove, sea spirits.

There are a number of ways to interpret this entanglement. It is possible that these new mosques were demonstrations of devotion,[3] new affective fields in which the Swahili transformed a form of gathering of a living assemblage by territorializing it in a new and transformative way. If we imagine what it took to acquire and work the construction materials, we get a sense of the labor involved. Acquisition for all three materials—*Porites*, mangrove, and beach sand—would have been challenging, managing not only the marine environment, but the physical difficulty of cutting *Porites* and mangrove wood, and transporting the hundreds of baskets of beach sand from the shore to the mosque site. It is not just that it was difficult to acquire these materials, but also there was a material engagement that put people *within* this particular ecology, working to extract and shape the materials needed for the mosque—imagining this type of engagement can get lost when we just consider them as "resources." This includes: the laborers walking to the beach to scoop sand at the water's edge, the craftsmen diving in the lagoon for *Porites* coral blooms or to the reef to cut *Porites*, and wood cutters wading through the dark, muddy waters of the mangrove swamps to find appropriate timber. The labor itself could have a been a form of devotion, but the materials used and the assemblage that they extended into these new religious structures may have served to draw the powerful forces of the fore/nearshore—sea spirits and sustenance and renewal—into the first community mosques. In their orientation, mosques pointed toward Mecca, but in their construction they were entangled with the fore/nearshore.

There is, however, an alternate narrative of these mosques, a version in which the entanglements of mosque and fore/nearshore are quieter. It is possible that raising these early mosques, as constitutive constructions, were acts that not only "represented" the advent of majority Islam in towns but also the way that Swahili people sought to negotiate between spiritual concerns from home and abroad. Rather than making obvious, public gestures to the powerful forces of the fore/

nearshore such as sea spirits, which would have been anathema to visiting Muslim merchants and religious figures, it was built into the floor, the walls, and the roofs of mosques. These materials, I argue, would have had the effect of encasing towns-people in materials associated with powerful places and forces. This might, in some ways, be viewed as a quietly syncretic act, one that actively wove "local" conceptions into a foreign and more "global" order of bodies, prayers, and gathering.

Although it is impossible to understand the particular ways that the early Swahili were attempting to engage with the fore/nearshore in these early mosques, the attention to materials in this chapter does offer an initial sense of the complexities of the emergence of urban life and Islamic practice on the Swahili coast. Rather than simply documenting the "adoption" or "conversion" to Islam, we can begin to see how the early Swahili sought to build up new forms of religious practice, gathering together communities and materials in meaningful ways. These "mosques-as-assemblages" were likely comforting and intensely "local" in their form, providing a counterbalance to the advent of the practices of Islam within—learning and carrying out daily prayers in a foreign language while facing a distant and unseen place, Mecca. As such, they had a territorializing effect, serving to "increase the internal homogeneity of" the mosque-as-assemblage, a process that contrasted sharply with the highly fluid, destabilizing assemblage of the fore/nearshore. In this way, I argue, the Swahili may have been seeking to create a new type of stability in an increasingly fluid and changing world, while remaining firmly connected to it.

Afterword

7 Iterating and rebuilding mosques, from "building in" to "building out"

By way of conclusion, I explore briefly the changes that occur in the construction and materials of Swahili mosques after 1050 CE, changes that serve to emphasize the particular materiality of the first coral mosques. Thus far, I have highlighted the construction materials used in the earliest coral Friday mosques at Swahili sites, and have argued that they represent an intentional building in of the fore/nearshore assemblage. Changes in the materials and construction of mosques in later centuries serve to further highlight the particularity of these mosques and suggest a shift from "building in" to "building out," a change reflected in the make up of the urban form. At some sites, the initial *Porites* coral mosques continued to be used for centuries, with some expansions and alterations. However, many of these mosques were ultimately dismantled and new, larger mosques, made of coral rag, were erected in their place. At Chwaka on Pemba Island, the eleventh-century *Porites* mosque was replaced in the fourteenth or fifteenth centuries with a grand, highly embellished coral rag mosque (see Figures 7.6 and 7.7). This new mosque contained barrel vaults and domes, and a highly decorated mihrab made of carved *Porites* coral. In such new mosques, which became the standard in architecture along the entire Swahili coast after the thirteenth century, *Porites* coral was used only as embellishments

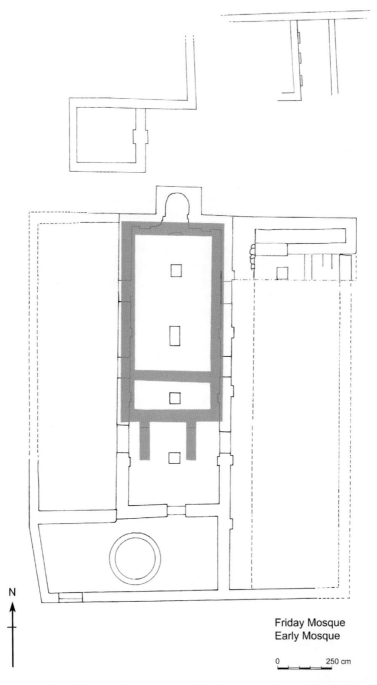

FIGURE 7.6 Plan of later Friday mosque with early mosque inset, Chwaka, Pemba Island (plan by M. Horton)

FIGURE 7.7 Friday mosque at Chwaka excavated; wall stump of early *Porites* mosque visible in lower left corner of photo

for the mihrab, and in doorjambs and sills, to create squared corners. This period, from the thirteenth to fifteenth centuries CE, was one in which building in coral rag expanded dramatically along the coast: mosques, houses, tombs, and town walls were now constructed in coral rag. In these centuries, we thus see the emergence of what are called "stonetowns," places built extensively in coral rag. As discussed, coral rag is plentiful along the coast, quarried on the mainland and islands.

The shift from building in *Porites* to using coral rag was thus both a material change but also one of scale, from the intensive construction of early mosques in *Porites* to the extensive construction of whole towns in coral rag (including the mosque). The first *Porites* mosques built *in* the fore/nearshore changed to mosques of coral rag construction in later centuries, allowing for building *out*—out to tombs, out to large, complex multistoried houses, out to additional mosques in the settlement. Rather than the "gathering" of materials and space in the early *Porites* mosques, coral rag construction was, I argue, an attempt at covering town space, rather than simply a rededication and transformation of the "gathered" mosque. This was not only a significant material transformation, but also a rethinking of the framing of urban space and form.

The changes that occurred in building materials after the thirteenth century CE serves to highlight the particularity of the first coral-built Swahili mosques, and the materials that were used in their construction. The changes made to mosques after the thirteenth century indicates the decreasing importance of materials from the fore/nearshore in the construction of these religious structures—Porities coral was replaced with coral rag, foundation fills contained a greater variety of sands and soils, and roofs were often embellished with domes and vaults made of coral rag. These later mosques bundled different elements—distant architectural forms and ideas (domes, barrel vaults, squinches), imported vessels, and other elements that served to widen the networks that mosques marked. This was a period when rebuilding was common in many coastal towns, and reconstructing a mosque meant transforming its materials and meanings. The context of this rebuilding was shifting trade connections from ports in the Persian Gulf to those in the Red Sea, increasing competition on the coast itself (as powerful centers emerged in northern, central and southern zones), and greater influence of sharifs (religious leaders from abroad) who came to question the heterodox nature of coastal Islam.

While the earliest mosques can be seen as "building in" local forms of religious practice, the later mosques were built to be more demonstrative and powerful, funneled through the imagery and practice of commensality (Fleisher 2010a) and more orthodox forms of Islam. The stripping away of elements of the sea might have been an effort by the Swahili of creating distinctions between the religiosity of Islam and the practices related to the powerful forces of the fore/nearshore, the sea spirits. We can see this tension enduring in the ethnographic literature on sea and land spirits, where the practices of engagement with them are banished from the mosque and generally are at odds with Islamic practice. Although the existence of spirits is not in doubt, they are seen as potentially disruptive of the Islamic order and ideology. The changes to mosques over the centuries suggest that this contemporary tension is not new, and was likely an ongoing debate in Swahili towns for centuries.

I close this chapter with a description of a deposit made at the Friday mosque at Chwaka, on Pemba Island (Figure 7.8). This grand coral rag mosque was built in the fourteenth or fifteenth centuries, a reconstruction over the foundation of an earlier *Porites* mosque. The mosque, along with the town itself, went out of active use in the late fifteenth or early sixteenth century, after which time it slowly decayed and collapsed. In excavating this mosque in 2002, we revealed a deposit left in the mihrab, an offering made in the holiest place in the mosque, likely sometime in the seventeenth or eighteenth centuries. The deposit contained a local

FIGURE 7.8 Deposit in the mihrab of the Chwaka Friday mosque: (a) general view; (b) close-up (photos by M. Horton)

ceramic vessel with two large pieces of other vessels covering it, a grinding stone, and shell. Horton's (2004) interpretation of this deposit suggests that each element refers to different spirits: "This pot contained the spirit (hence, it had to be covered and contained) and this is part of the tradition of the burial of fingo pots found all along the coast, which contained prophylactic magic to protect special places such as doorways or gateways. The offering of the shell is because this was seen as a sea spirit, while the grinding stone referred to a domestic spirit." Horton argues that by placing the offering in the mihrab, the residents were approximating a cave, places where contemporary offerings were known to be made to spirits. In this offering, made in the late second millennium, we can see the ongoing practices of gathering and composing within mosques and material assemblages that entangle the practices of Islam and the practices related to spirits. This offering punctuates another moment of a longer-term history of religious practices that stretches from the foundation of towns, the establishment of majority Islam, and the ongoing negotiation between Islamic practice and the practices related to spirits of the sea and the land.

Acknowledgments

Research at Chwaka on Pemba Island was funded by the National Science Foundation (BCS0138319, Adria LaViolette, PI) and carried out between 2002 and 2006. This research would not have been possible without the support of the late Maalim Hamad Omar, Director, Department of Archives, Museums, and Antiquities, Zanzibar; our colleagues in archaeology in Dar es Salaam, Zanzibar, and Pemba; and the communities on Pemba that supported our research throughout the years. A version of this chapter was presented to my anthropology colleagues at Rice University, and I am thankful for their insights and comments; in particular, my thanks to Natali Valdez for pointing me to Kim TallBear"s work and other great advice. Many of the ideas in this chapter have been rumbling around for quite some time, and I want to thank Tim Pauketat and Susan Alt for providing the amazing opportunity to write it up and discuss with a wonderful group of scholars. I also thank Adria LaViolette, Stephanie Wynne-Jones, and Mark Horton for many inspired conversations about early versions of it.

Notes

1 Fitton and Wynne-Jones (2017) have recently identified a possible *Porites* mosque at the site of Unguja Ukuu on Zanzibar that may date to 900 CE or slightly earlier—this would represent a particularly early example of the mosques discussed here.

2 Swahili spirits are tied in complicated ways to Islamic spirits. In the Quran, there are entire *suras* devoted to discussion of "jinn," a class of supernatural creatures that, with humans and angels, are the three creations of Allah (this is where we get our westernized, Orientalized "genie"). Like the sea spirits of the Swahili, jinn are both similar and different from humans—they can be good and evil, they have social lives and they practice religion. One of the main Swahili terms for spirits, *jini* is a transformation of the Arabic "jinn." But

in Swahili, the plural form of jini is *majini*, which also means "in the water," reasserting and building a connection between Swahili sea spirits and those understood through Islamic teaching alone.

3 I thank James Faubian for this suggesting this insight.

References

Abu-Lughod, Janet L. 1987 The Islamic City—Historic Myth, Islamic Essence, and Contemporary Relevance. *International Journal of Middle Eastern Studies* 19: 155–176.

Allen, James de Vere 1993 *Swahili Origins: Swahili Culture and the Shungwaya Phenomenon.* J. Currey, London.

Caplan, Pat 1975 *Choice and Constraint in a Swahili Community: Property, Hierarchy and Cognatic Descent on the East African Coast.* Oxford University Press, London and Nairobi.

Chittick, H. Neville 1974 *Kilwa: An Islamic Trading City on the East African Coast.* Memoir. Vol. 5. British Institute in Eastern Africa, Nairobi and London.

DeLanda, Manuel 1997 *A Thousand Years of Nonlinear History.* Swerve, New York.

——— 2006 *A New Philosophy of Society: Assemblage Theory and Social Complexity.* Continuum, London.

Deleuze, Gilles, and Félix Guattari 1987 *A Thousand Plateaus: Capitalism and Schizophrenia.* Minnesota University Press, Minneapolis.

Deloria, Vine Jr. 2001 American Indian Metaphysics. In *Power and Place: Indian Education in America*, edited by Vine Deloria Jr. and Daniel R. Wildcat, pp. 1–6. Fulcrum, Golden, CO.

Eickelman, Dale 1974 Is There an Islamic City? The Making of a Quarter in a Moroccan Town. *International Journal of Middle East Studies* 5: 274–294.

Fitton, Thomas 2017 Pushing the Boat Out: A Study of Spatial Organisation and Harbour Spaces in the Early Swahili Ports of the Zanzibar Archipelago, 550–1100 CE. PhD thesis, University of York.

Fitton, Thomas, and Stephanie Wynne-Jones 2017 Understanding the Layout of Early Coastal Settlement at Unguja Ukuu, Zanzibar. *Antiquity* 91(359): 1268–1284.

Fleisher, Jeffrey B. 2010a Rituals of Consumption and the Politics of Feasting on the Eastern African Coast, AD 700–1500. *Journal of World Prehistory* 23(4): 195–217.

——— 2010b Swahili Synoecism: Rural Settlements and Town Formation on the Central East African Coast, A.D. 750–1500. *Journal of Field Archaeology* 35: 265–282.

——— 2014 The Complexity of Public Space at the Swahili Town of Songo Mnara, Tanzania. *Journal of Anthropological Archaeology* 35: 1–22.

Fleisher, Jeffrey B., and Adria LaViolette 2013 The Early Swahili Trade Village of Tumbe, Pemba Island, Tanzania, AD 600–950. *Antiquity* 87(338): 1151–1168.

Garlake, Peter S. 1966 *The Early Islamic Architecture of the East African Coast.* Biea Monograph. Oxford University Press, London.

Gensheimer, Thomas 1997 At the Boundaries of the Dar-Al-Islam: Cities of the East African Coast in the Late Middle Ages. Unpublished PhD thesis, University of California.

Giles, Linda 1987 Possession Cults on the Swahili Coast: A Re-Examination of Theories of Marginality. *Africa* 57: 234–258.

Greenlaw, Jean-Pierre 1995 *The Coral Buildings of Suakin: Islamic Architecture, Planning, Design and Domestic Arrangements in a Red Sea Port* [in English]. Kegan Paul International, London; New York; Bognor Regis, Sussex, England.

Hodder, Ian 2012 *Entangled: An Archaeology of the Relationship between Humans and Things.* Wiley-Blackwell, London.

182 Jeffrey Fleisher

Horton, Mark C. 1991 Primitive Islam and Architecture in East Africa. *Muqarnas* 8: 103–116.

——— 1996 *Shanga: The Archaeology of a Muslim Trading Community on the Coast of East Africa.* Memoir, vol. 14. British Institute in Eastern Africa, Nairobi.

——— 2004 Islam, Archaeology, and Swahili Identity. In *Changing Social Identity with the Spread of Islam: Archaeological Perspectives*, edited by D. Whitcomb, pp. 67–88. Oriental Institute, Chicago.

Horton, Mark C., and John Middleton 2000 *The Swahili: The Social Landscape of a Mercantile Society.* Blackwell, Oxford.

Hourani, Albert, and Samuel M. Stern 1970 *The Islamic City.* Bruno Cassirer, Oxford.

Ingold, Timothy 2012 An Ecology of Materials. *Annual Review of Anthropology* 41: 427–442.

Jervis, Ben 2017 Assembling the Archaeology of the Global Middle Ages. *World Archaeology* 49(5): 666–680.

Juma, Abdurahman 2004 *Unguja Ukuu on Zanzibar: An Archaeological Study of Early Urbanism.* Studies in Global Archaeology, vol. 3. Societas Archaeologica Upsaliensis, Uppsala.

Kirkman, James S. 1964 *Men and Monuments on the East African Coast.* Lutterworth, London.

Kusimba, Chapurukha M. 1999 *The Rise and Fall of Swahili States.* AltaMira Press, Walnut Creek, CA.

Kusimba, Chapurukha M., and Sibel B. Kusimba 2005 Mosaics and Interactions: East Africa, 2000 B.P. to the Present. In *African Archaeology: A Critical Introduction*, edited by Ann B. Stahl, pp. 392–419. Blackwell, Oxford.

Lambek, Michael 1981 *Human Spirits: A Cultural Account of Trance in Mayotte.* Cambridge University Press, Cambridge.

——— 1993 *Knowledge and Practice in Mayotte: Local Discourses of Islam, Sorcery and Spirit Possession (Anthropological Horizons).* University of Toronto Press, Toronto.

Lapidus, Ira M. 1969 Muslim Cities and Islamic Societies. In *Middle Eastern Cities: A Symposium on Ancient, Islamic, and Contemporary Middle Eastern Urbanism*, edited by Ira M. Lapidus, pp. 47–79. University of California Press, Berkeley.

Latour, Bruno 2005 *Reassembling the Social: An Introduction to Actor-Network-Theory.* Oxford University Press, Oxford.

LaViolette, Adria 2008 Swahili Cosmopolitanism in Africa and the Indian Ocean World, A.D. 600–1500. *Archaeologies: Journal of the World Archaeological Congress* 1: 24–49.

LaViolette, Adria, and Jeffrey B. Fleisher 2009 The Urban History of a Rural Place: Swahili Archaeology on Pemba Island, Tanzania, 700–1500 AD. *International Journal of African Historical Studies* 42(3): 433–455.

Middleton, John 1992 *The World of the Swahili: An African Mercantile Civilization.* Yale University Press, New Haven.

Nurse, Derek, and Thomas Spear 1985 *The Swahili: Reconstructing the History and Language of an African Society AD 800–1500.* University of Pennsylvania Press, Philadelphia.

Pauketat, Timothy R. 2013 Bundles of/in/as Time. In *Big Histories, Human Lives: Tackling Problems of Scale in Archaeology*, edited by John Robb and Timothy R. Pauketat, pp. 35–56. School for Advanced Research Press, Santa Fe.

Pawlowicz, Matthew 2012 Modelling the Swahili Past: The Archaeology of Mikindani in Southern Coastal Tanzania. *Azania* 47(4): 488–508.

Pearson, Michael 1998 *Port Cities and Intruders: The Swahili Coast, India, and Portugal in the Early Modern Era.* Johns Hopkins University Press, Baltimore.

Popovic, Alexandre 1999 *The Revolt of African Slaves in Iraq in the 3rd/9th Century.* Markus Wiener, Princeton, NJ.

Pouwels, Randall L. 1987 *Horn and Crescent. Cultural Change and Traditional Islam on the East African Coast, 800–1900.* Cambridge University Press, Cambridge.

―――― 2000 The East African Coast, c. 780–1900 C.E. In *The History of Islam in Africa*, edited by Nehemia Levtzion and Randall L. Pouwels, pp. 251–272. Ohio University Press, Athens.

Punwong, Paramita, Robert Marchant, and Katherine Selby 2013 Holocene Mangrove Dynamics from Unguja Ukuu, Zanzibar. *Quaternary International* 298: 4–19.

Quintana Morales , Eréndira, and Mark C. Horton 2014 Fishing and Fish Consumption in the Swahili Communities of East Africa, 700–1400 CE. *Internet Archaeology* 37. doi: 10.11141/ia.37.3.

Rougeulle, Axelle (ed.) 2015 *Sharma: Un entrepôt de commerce medieval sur la côte du Hadramawt (Yémen, ca 980–1180)*. British Foundation for the Study of Arabia, Monograph No. 17. Archaeopress, Oxford.

Sidebotham, Steven. E, and Willemina Wendrich 2000 *Berenike 1998: Report on the 1998 Excavations at Berenike and the Survey of the Egyptian Eastern Desert, Including Excavations in Wadi Kalalat*. CNWS, Leiden.

Stahl, Ann B. 2005 *African Archaeology: A Critical Introduction*. Blackwell, Malden, MA.

TallBear, Kim 2017 Beyond the Life/Not Life Binary: A Feminist-indigenous Reading of Cryopreservation, Interspecies Thinking and the New Materialisms. In *Cryopolitics: Frozen Life in a Melting World*, edited by Joanna Radin and Emma Kowal, pp. 179–202. MIT Press, Cambridge, MA.

Trimingham, J. Spence 1964 *Islam in East Africa*. Clarendon Press, Oxford.

Walz, Jonathan R. 2010 *Route to a Regional Past: An Archaeology of the Lower Pangani (Ruvu) Basin, Tanzania*, 500–1900 C.E. University of Florida, Gainesville.

Wheatley, Peter 1972 The Concept of Urbanism. In *Man, Settlement and Urbanism*, edited by Peter J. Ucko, Ruth Tringham and G.W. Dimbleby, pp. 601–637. Duckworth, London.

Wilson, Thomas H. 1982 Spatial Analysis and Settlement Patterns on the East African Coast. *Paideuma* 28: 201–219.

Wright, Henry T. 1993 Trade and Politics on the Eastern Littoral of Africa, AD 800–1300. In *The Archaeology of Africa: Food, Metals and Towns*, edited by Thurstan Shaw, Paul J.J. Sinclair, Bassey Andah and Alex Okpoko, pp. 658–670. Routledge, London.

Wynne-Jones, Stephanie 2007 Creating Urban Communities at Kilwa Kisiwani, Tanzania, AD 800–1300. *Antiquity* 81: 368–380.

―――― 2013 The Public Life of the Swahili Stonehouse. *Journal of Anthropological Archaeology* 32: 759–773.

―――― 2016 *A Material Culture: Consumption and Trade in Precolonial East Africa*. Oxford University Press, Oxford.

8

URBANISM AND THE TEMPORALITY OF MATERIALITY ON THE MEDIEVAL DECCAN

Beyond the cosmograms of social and political space

Andrew M. Bauer

Introduction

The intersections of religion and urbanism are perhaps no more evident anywhere in the world than on the Deccan plateau of southern India, where during the Medieval Period (ca. 500–1600 CE), multiple political capitals were founded, planned, and rebuilt with clear attention to cosmological principles and canons (Figure 8.1). Indeed, there are numerous examples of how urban design was directed toward the creation of city layouts that were symbolic of religious affiliations, beliefs, and practices. The thirteenth-century city layout of Warangal, for instance, has been considered a massive cosmogram that shares "characteristic features with mandala and yantra schemes" (Michell 1992a: 16). Similarly, the royal center of the fifteenth-century imperial capital of Vijayanagara paralleled the structural arrangement of contemporary Hindu temples and linked the authority of the ruler with the divine hero-king Rama (e.g., Fritz 1986; Fritz and Michelle 1987). And the later sixteenth-century capital of the Qutb Shahis—Hyderabad—was built to approximate the form of Warangal, but with its alignments offset slightly so that the city's central features at its axial intersections—the commanding Charminar with its four minar towers and upper-story mosque—were oriented toward the qibla to Mecca, "a suitable orientation for a city designed to commemorate the beginning of the second Islamic millennium" (Eaton and Wagoner 2014: 227). In short, urban forms of the medieval Deccan were often religious forms.

Given the cosmographic architecture of the Deccan, it is unsurprising that previous scholarship has focused on the designs of political capitals, documenting how formal architectural traditions would intersect with canonical prescriptions in organizing urban space. However, to call attention to the multiple instances where urban forms might be considered cosmograms is to say little about the historical processes of urbanization or the quotidian activities that reshaped urban

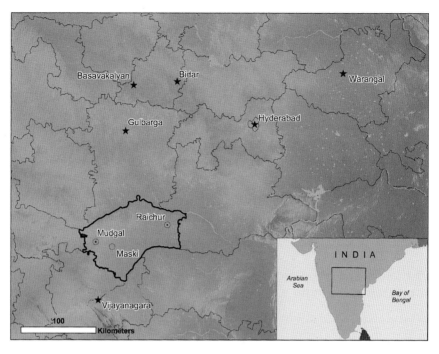

FIGURE 8.1 Location of sites and capital centers noted in text (Raichur District outlined in bold)

space through social practice. Moreover, missing from much of the scholarship on medieval Deccan cities is attention to the hundreds of "secondary" and "tertiary" centers of the region, where a vast proportion of inhabitants resided. These places were no less "urban" in their assemblages of diverse populations of people, things, and practices, but many do not appear to have been "designed" anew with religious tenets in mind. Addressing these places calls for attention to the landscapes of daily life and the diversity of materials, practices, and things that shaped and reshaped urban contexts. It is this concern for landscape, and the various other-than-human things that also constitute social places, through which it will be productive to consider the processes of urbanization on the Deccan.

In this chapter I augment existing scholarship by integrating a concern for the processes that gave form to settlements during the Medieval Period through an analysis of the occupation of the site of Maski (Raichur District, Karnataka). In doing so, I argue for an approach to medieval urbanization on the Deccan that looks beyond the city plans of imperial capitals or monumental centers to track the ways that the production of spatial forms and their corresponding sociality was constituted by a range of materials, things, and people that ultimately produced urban conditions across much of the region. While this chapter does not challenge the significance of the objectives highlighted in the excellent scholarship that has hitherto linked religious symbolism to urban spaces on the Deccan, the case of Maski—as a smaller

186 Andrew M. Bauer

and historically less prominent medieval center—calls attention to settlement processes and practices that have largely evaded analyses to date. More specifically, I examine the implications of considering the material dynamics of the massive granitic hill and the vestiges of a longer history of prehistoric occupation there as mediators in the development of medieval settlement: Affecting experiences of social space as the active slopes and unforgiving terrain of the boulder-strewn hills practically shaped how residential places were crafted and influenced perceptions of socio-spatial alterity. The production of a variety of urban relationships at sites such as Maski was not simply an outcome of medieval political or economic activities on the Deccan, nor the result of deliberate city planning or cosmographic design; rather these relationships emerged as a variety of people, materials, and things came to mutually affect each other in producing new kinds of social places. Then, again, this is not to suggest that the production of social space at medieval Maski was apolitical in character—a point that I elaborate below.

The landscape of religion and urbanism in medieval South India

Writing about a region where archaeologists have long questioned the utility of distinctions between "profane" and "sacred" or "prosaic" and "ritual" in characterizing interpretations of past social practices and cultural spaces, it seems hardly appropriate to frame a chapter around the role of religion in processes of urbanization. In the Medieval Period of southern India, basic agricultural production practices for many inhabitants were simultaneously oriented toward both devotional and subsistence ends, and during the previous Iron Age (ca. 1200–300 BCE) the production of pastoral herding resources was linked with a number of commemorative mortuary practices, challenging the degree to which the distribution of mortuary monuments can be accurately partitioned as constitutive of a ritual landscape that was distinct from a realm of quotidian economic activities (e.g., Bauer 2015; Morrison 2009). Thus, it is worth noting upfront that I am generally in agreement with calls to question post-Enlightenment paradigms that conceptualize religion as a stable analytical category that qualitatively stands apart from a suite of other social practices that are generative of cultural and historical contexts (see Baires 2017; Deloria 2003; Fowles 2013; Pauketat 2013). Indeed, Steadman's (2009: 21) topical survey of various archaeologically documented "religions" is careful to note at the outset that many of the contexts discussed in her book likely had no word for "religion" as such.

Then again, one would be mistaken to ignore entirely the salience of institutionalized ritual activities and ideologies in any investigation of Medieval Period urbanization or spatial production. In point of fact, as Eaton and Wagoner (2014: xii) have aptly noted, the historiography of the region has often been (overly) reliant on religious identification to frame the Deccan's social history as a binary "Hindu-Muslim encounter" (see, for example, Nilakanta Sastri 1955). Yet, in the multicultural urban contexts of the medieval Deccan, where various sects of Hinduism, Jainism, and Islam were practiced, many inhabitants identified with formalized religious traditions that were differentiated through material practices and discursive ideologies. To be clear, religious practices were not universally shared, stable, or unchanging, and fusion and fluidity between different ideologies and practices did occur (e.g., Asher and Talbot 2006; Eaton and Wagoner 2014; Fisher 2017; Novetzke 2016; Stoker 2016; Talbot 1995). While one must be careful to not reify religious differences or to privilege them a-priori as the primary axes of social identification and affiliation—as should be evident below—it is nevertheless the case that religious practices were entangled with the production of political relationships: some rulers prescribed official "state religions," and others deliberately sought to promote and perpetuate particular ideological canons, such as the divinity of the king (e.g., Asher and Talbot 2006; Fritz 1986; Fritz et al. 1984; Heitzman 1991; Stein 1977; Subbarayalu 2012).

Thus I am generally sympathetic to the suggestion that archaeologists should avoid treating "religion as a monolithic and structuring thing" (Baires 2017: 59) but am equally cautious not to eschew entirely the analytical utility of identifying practices as religious or ritual—regardless of how we imagine a dialectical relationship between the two (e.g., Fogelin 2007). If we take religious practice to be "ritualized venerations" (sensu Pauketat 2013: 2) of some form of other-than-human power, then there might be good reasons for considering the possibility of religion as a "structuring thing" (*contra* Baires 2017: 59), not because we have to subscribe to a universal understanding of "religion" as structural, but because inhabitants of some historical contexts understood religious ideologies as significant to their material practices that might have nevertheless been "simultaneously religious, political, social, and intellectual" (Deloria 2003: 194). For instance, the political efficacy of devotional ideologies operated much differently in Chola period historical contexts when Hindu rulers were equated with deities than in previous periods when they were not (Stein 1977; Subbarayalu 2012: 201), and differently still in later Mughal historical contexts (e.g., Alam and Subrahmanyam 2011: 124–164; 2018; Subrahmanyam 2017). To frame all cultural practices equally as religious and political potentially loses analytical purchase on how religious practices (e.g., veneration of the king as an other-than-human power) differentially contributed to shaping specific socio-historical contexts, just as making all things equally political risks their "trivialization by the inclusion of all and sundry cultural phenomena as somehow political in character" (Johansen and Bauer 2011: 9).

Deccan cities: Cosmograms and canons

Previous scholarship has treated the relationships between religion and Medieval Period urbanism in South India in two principal ways through an empirical focus on monumental ritual centers or the capital cities of empires. On one hand, city plans and urban spaces have often been interpreted to reflect and embed cosmographical principles in daily life (e.g., Fritz 1986; Fritz et al. 1984; Michell 1992a; Eaton and Wagoner 2014). On the other, temple and pilgrimage sites and their associated rituals have been argued to facilitate the aggregation of a diverse range

188 Andrew M. Bauer

of people, specialized crafts, and merchant activity, effectively taking on the role of "central-places" in the lexicon of economic geography and providing the impetus for the development of "urban" spatial contexts that were constituted by associations of diverse people and services (e.g., Heitzman 1987). The focus of the first is typically on form and stresses planning rooted in religious prescriptions, cultural structures, or politicized ideological claims. The focus of the latter is on historical process, and stresses that urban environments emerge more as a result of individual agents' participation in a wide set of simultaneously ritual and economic donative practices.

There are multiple instances where the production of urban environments on the medieval Deccan can be linked with religious ideologies and canons. George Michell's (1992a) analysis of Warangal, the capital of the Kakatiya empire (ca. 1163–1323 CE) from the early thirteenth century until its sacking by the Delhi sultanate, serves as an excellent example. Michell (1992a) demonstrates that Warangal is enclosed by three concentric fortification rings (1.2 km, 2.4 km, 12.5 km in diameter, respectively), at the center of which is a square enclosure where a temple complex and probable royal residence were located near the intersection of two principal axial alignments that bisected the city cardinally. The inner most ring is composed of faced granitic stone more than six meters high and is frequently termed the Warangal Fort, which is broken by four gateways of a standard pattern at four cardinal points:

> Each example consists of a rectangular barbican divided into two enclosures that project 60 m out from the fortifications. Four square bastions protrude from the external corners of the barbican; an additional, fifth bastion, projects from the side wall to protect the external doorway located there.
>
> (Michell 1992a: 7)

Moreover, "the outermost doorways of the gateway in the stone fortifications are positioned to one side of the barbicans so that a turn to the right is required on leaving the innermost zone" (Michell 1992a: 14–15).

As a consequence of these turns, movement through the four gateways displays a form of rotational symmetry, such that the "underlying structure of movement in the city would have consisted of three superimposed svastikas at different scales, each corresponding to one ring of fortifications" (Figure 8.2, Michell 1992a: 14). Michell (1992a) interprets the city plan as corresponding to theoretical models of cities that are described in various mythological texts and Hindu shastras, including the "svastika town" form. Indeed, some texts specifically associate a svastika town as being especially "fit for habitation of kings" (Michell 1992a: 15; see also Dutt 2009).

Other medieval Deccan cities and large-scale architectural configurations were constructed to conform to religious canons. At Hyderabad, for instance, Eaton and Wagoner (2014) have recognized a similar footprint to that of Warangal, but with an axial alignment toward Mecca. And at Vijayanagara, it has been argued that the royal center paralleled the orientation of contemporary Hindu temples and established

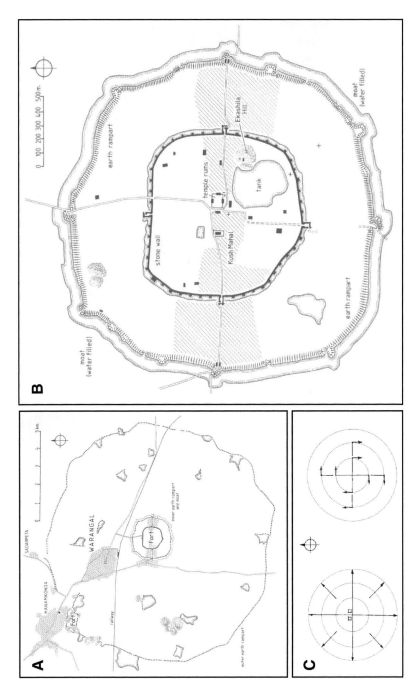

FIGURE 8.2 City plan of Warangal (A–B) and patterns of movement (C) into and out of the city (by kind permission from George Michell)

links between the authority of the ruler and the divine hero-king Rama, insightfully speaking to royal strategies for ideologically maintaining imperial authority (e.g., Fritz 1986; Fritz et al. 1984; Sinopoli and Morrison 1995).

It is important to stress that the development of many of these places, however, diverged from the spatial imaginaries of elites and specialists who helped shape their conformation. Indeed, while several of the gates of Warangal still structure movement into and out of the central fort area, other gates have been entirely bypassed. And many segments of the original axial roads are no longer extant. These historical phenomena remind us that the efficacy of embedding cosmographic principles in urban space was nevertheless dependent on the perception, recognition, and use of a variety of historically differentiated actors.

Many of the Deccan's medieval urban centers were populated by a diverse range of inhabitants, including Muslims who had migrated from northern India, recent immigrants from Southwest Asia, the Arabian Peninsula, and Africa, as well as native populations devoted to various Hindu sects and temples (e.g., Asher and Talbot 2006: 164–166; Eaton 1978). In the case of Hyderabad, for instance, one might question the degree to which many of its inhabitants recognized their orientation toward Mecca as they traversed the city's primary thoroughfare; despite the fact that Islam was the official religion of the state, the Qutb Shahs incorporated numerous Brahmins into their administration and the capital centers of Golkonda and later Hyderabad likely included various practicing Hindus from outlying regions (e.g., Asher and Talbot 2006: 164–172). The ethnic and religious diversity of the medieval Deccan thus calls into question the degree to which any city layout would have been uniformly recognized for its ideological significance by all city dwellers, given the range of culturally and historically conditioned subjectivities in perceiving space (e.g., Kosiba and Bauer 2013; Lynch 1977; A. Smith 2003; see also below).

Moreover, despite their large-scale cosmological orientations, some medieval urban centers belie perceptions that their rulers and inhabitants strictly adhered to the canons of a single religion or sect. Although frequently referred to as a "Hindu city," Vijayanagara rulers and elites are well documented to have developed a unique "courtly-style" of architecture (e.g., Michell 1992b) that also drew heavily on Persian traditions and elements that were manifest in the capital centers of their rival states, the Bahmani and subsequent Deccani Sultanates to the north. Many monumental public structures at Vijayanagara included domes and arches adopted from building canons associated with Islam. The creation of these features were perhaps deliberate efforts to produce more incorporative perceptual spaces in a city that also included a great number of Muslims, whose mosques and tombs were also salient constituents of the landscape (e.g., Fritz et al. 1984; Fritz and Michell 2015; Sinopoli 2003).

Wagoner (1996) has argued that the cultural "Islamicization" of Vijayanagara courtly style was itself a political strategy through which "indigenous elites attempt[ed] to enhance their political status and authority through participation in the more 'universal' culture of Islam" (854). This was reflected in courtly dress as well as in building styles, and attests to the desire of the court "to participate in a cosmopolitan culture that extended far beyond the confines of south India" (Asher and Talbot 2006: 72). Thus, at Vijayanagara, we see the production of urban space as an emergent historical product of diverse cultural practices and political strategies (see also Sinopoli 2003). While the spatial imaginaries of designers or architectural specialists evoked cosmological schemes, they can hardly serve as the sole explanation for the historical processes and configurations through which the urban environment took shape and conditioned human experience.

Ritual practices and defining "urbanization" in South India

This is not to say that religious tenets and practices were not critical to the historical production of urban environments in medieval South India—a strong argument can be made that in some contexts they were. Heitzman's (1987) impressively detailed studies of urban growth at various Chola Period (849–1279 CE) ritual centers of Tamil Nadu have characterized a process of "temple urbanism." Heitzman (1987) charts an historical sequence wherein ritual pilgrimage and donative practices related to temple worship linked hinterland shepherds with merchants and demonstrated the "interpenetration of rustic, ritual, and commercial economies" in processes of urbanization in medieval South India (806; see also Heitzman 1991). More specifically, he argues that once established through an endowment, temples facilitated the concentration of a range of mercantile, craft, and agricultural production activities. Because temple rituals required a diversity of "foodstuffs and precious goods" they facilitated the development of commercial networks and artisanal specialists who "congregated in larger numbers around the lands of the religious institutions" (Heitzman 1987: 816, see also Nagaswamy 1978: 135–140).

Yet, Heitzman (1987) is also careful to point out that despite such concentrations of people and activities, settlements associated with temple urbanism appear to have followed spatial plans similar to their contemporary "rural" villages. House clusters were segmented into blocks by caste or occupational specialization, and these blocks were separated by extensive agricultural fields and gardens, such that "[t]he arrangements for the support of expanding temple personnel ... preserved an agrarian economy in the heart of the multiplying neighborhoods" (Heitzman 1987: 816–817).

Heitzman's analysis of the Chola centers of Tamil Nadu raises several fundamental and definitional questions that have long been concerns among archaeologists who study uranism: namely, what constitutes an "urban" context. For many archaeologists, urban places are those that show relatively dense spatial aggregations of heterogeneous economic activities or occupational specializations (e.g., Childe 1950, Cowgill 2004, Sanders and Webster 1988). In the terms of economic geography that would develop from the work of Walter Christaller, they could be equated to functional central places; they provide high numbers of goods and services. As Heitzman's analysis of Chola centers demonstrates, however, these "services" need not be restricted to purely "economic" or administrative domains (see also Marcus 1973). Hence, it is unsurprising to see a long history of debate over whether some early cities or central places were primarily "mercantile," "administrative," or "regal-ritual" (sensu Fox 1977) in their primary "function" (cf. Chase et al. 1990; Marcus 1973; Sanders and Webster 1988).

In this context, Cowgill's (2004) review of the archaeology of urbanism is careful to avoid a definition for a "city" that rests on absolute population size or the number or types of diverse services or functions that might be provided in such places. Cowgill (2004) understands urban spaces and cities to be relative— defined in distinction to that which might be considered non-cities in a given cultural and historical period. Inhabitants of cities are those whose "activities, roles, practices, experiences, identities, and attitudes differ significantly from those of other members of the society who identify most closely with 'rural' lands outside of such settlements" (527). In other words, for Cowgill (2004), urbanism might be considered "a way of life" (sensu Wirth 1938) and the identification of cities is contingent on the recognition or production of socio-spatial alterity. Needless to say, the definition of "urban" or "city" is highly variable in archaeological practice and has historically been treated flexibly enough to accommodate less dense settlement clusters, such as those described for Chola period South India noted above, as well as the ceremonial centers of the Classic Period Maya (e.g., Coe 1984).

The politics of urban landscapes

Given the long history of archaeological scholarship on urbanization, and the various definitions that might be applied to the recognition of "cities" (cf. Adams 1966; Childe 1950; Cowgill 2004; Emberling 2003; M. Smith 2003; Sanders and Webster 1988), it is not my concern to rely on the medieval Deccan to retread definitional grounds. Instead, I highlight an important aspect of the creation of urban environments that has received considerable treatment among geographers more generally: namely, the production of social space. As noted above, the cities of the medieval Deccan brought together diverse populations of people, practices, and things. Temples, mosques, palaces, potters, smiths, administrators, farmers, herders, and priests, and the various materials and animals with which they were constituted and entangled, were generative of new kinds of heterogeneous spaces, places, and landscapes.

It has now become nearly axiomatic that space is not a neutral container for action and practice. Since the inception of urban studies with the Chicago School of Sociology, which would (not unproblematically) frame city dwellers as competitors for resources and distinctive racial, ethnic, and socio-economic neighborhoods as an outcome (e.g., Park and Burgess 1922), a long history of research has called attention to the recursive relationships between urban spaces and various forms of social distinctions and inequalities. Indeed, Harvey's (1990: 204) insistence that social relationships are profoundly spatial phenomena takes on remarkable significance in the diverse contexts of urban environments (see also Harvey 1996; Lynch 1977). Space is now recognized as a relational and social product (e.g., A. Smith 2003; Lefebvre 1990), and landscape has taken on new meanings in archaeological scholarship that has recast the production of space as political (Bauer 2011; Kosiba and Bauer 2013; Johansen 2011; A. Smith 2003).

To recognize space as a relational and social product begs the question of its production. How is it, for instance, that spaces and places become meaningfully differentiated and efficacious to the generation of multiple kinds of social affiliations and distinctions? One approach might usefully draw on Ingold's understanding of landscape as "a congealed form" of what he terms a "taskscape—the entire ensemble of tasks, in their mutual interlocking" (Ingold 2000: 199, 195). "Just as the landscape is an array of related features, so—by analogy—the taskscape is an array of related activities" (Ingold 2000: 195). While cultural meanings of tasks and activities are not congealed to particular places in any fixed, universal, or singular sense, it is evident that experiences of associations among meaningful tasks and their articulations with material environments is one mode through which places become simultaneously socially, materially, and symbolically differentiated: people do different things in different places, come to know and understand environments, and the recursive relationship between practice and environment becomes constitutive of both (meaningful) landscapes and differentiated subjectivities (see also Bauer 2011; Rizvi 2011).

Yet, as Smith (2003) has noted,

> not all individuals have the same capacity to engage in the production of spaces on the level of experience or of perception. There are constraints on the constructions of landscapes, both the physical spaces and the meanings associated with them.
>
> (70)

Hyderabad's commanding Charminar with its four minar towers, for instance, was not an equal product of all of the city's inhabitants, nor was it likely uniformly evocative to all of the city's residents. For Smith (2003), this recognition requires attention to social differences, inequalities, and "the social organization of production ... and power that allows things to get built" (Smith 2003: 67). Indeed, the recursive production of social relationships and differentiated perceptions and intelligibility of places makes urban environments well suited to an investigation of spatialized politics.

For example, in their recent provocation to consider the "charisma" *of* and *in* cities, Hansen and Verkaaik (2009), recognize city environments as entities that are not fully knowable. Their cacophonies of sounds, mixtures of smells, and diverse gatherings of "buildings, infrastructure ... and anonymous crowds" afford mythologies of cities that render them and their distinctive places (e.g., neighborhoods, barrios, slums) opaque to many of their inhabitants. Far from precluding political action, however, such spaces of illegibility present opportunities for certain figures to emerge as charismatic actors. The potentiality of these actors to operationalize this urban "infra-power" arises precisely "on the basis of their capacit[ies] to interpret, manage and master the opacity of the city" (Hansen and Verkaaik 2009: 5), such as "politicians, gangsters, business tycoons, and the everyday hustler [who] assume leadership [or] claim hidden and dangerous abilities and powers" (Hansen and Verkaaik 2009: 9).

A concern for what Hansen and Verkaaik term urban "infra-power," and the diverse social environments that enable it, means casting attention on the various human inhabitants of cities, but also the heterogeneous materials that give shape to places and their sensorial properties as emergent phenomena. Indeed, Hansen and Verkaaik (2009: 22) consider infrapower to be a largely rhizomatic (sensu Deleuze and Guattari 1987) form of social connectivity that emerges via "properties or potentialities of people and their environment through actions and events." It is important to emphasize, as Dawdy (2016a:33) stresses, that addressing the social and political contexts for such connectivity in cities also means coming to terms with the "materiality of urban life—its tangle of brick and mortar, concrete monuments, vacant lots, speed bumps, litter, street front shops, parking lots, and sewer drains." Urban structures and buildings are not merely the realized product of architects and designers (e.g., Latour and Yaneva 2008), and the production of materially and symbolically differentiated places and spaces (and all of the various perceptions and affects they afford) that both enable and constrain human practices and politics are not just created by human networks, capital, and labor—they are also created by clay that crumbles, stones that endure, materials that decay, vegetation that grows, and animals that graze (see also Bauer 2015).

It is this concern for landscape, and the various other-than-human things and materials that also constitute social places, through which it will be productive to consider the processes of urbanization at Maski. As one of the Deccan's many medieval urban centers that does not appear to have been "designed" anew with religious prescriptions in mind, it is a location where it will be possible to highlight urbanization processes other than what attention to the Deccan's principal capital and ritual centers has hitherto stressed. Indeed, the long-term history of occupation at Maski—from at least the Neolithic Period onward—suggests a different approach to urbanism.

The Maski Archaeological Research Project and medieval Maski

The site of Maski is situated in the western half of Karnataka's Raichur district in southern India (Figure 8.1). It is well known in Indian archaeology for a Brahmi inscription at the base of a massive granitic inselberg ("island mountain," Figure 8.3) that names the Mauryan emperor Asoka (ca. 268–232 BCE) as a "follower of the Buddha" (e.g., Patil and Patil 1998: 34), allowing scholars to identify Asoka as the "author" of a number of minor rock edits that are located on the Southern Deccan and that attest to cultural developments and interactions across broad areas of the subcontinent during the Early Historic Period (ca. 300 BCE–500 CE; e.g., Ray 1986). Mid-twentieth-century excavations into the sediments around the base of the large granitic hill by the Archaeological Survey of India's B. K. Thapar revealed a long history of occupation, including materials associated with all of the canonical archaeographic periods of southern India—for example, Neolithic, Iron Age, Early Historic, and Medieval (Thapar 1957; see also Bauer and Johansen 2015; Johansen and Bauer 2015).

Intensive pedestrian survey across a 64 square-kilometer study area centered on Maski by the Maski Archaeological Research Project (MARP) began in 2010 and has now systematically documented nearly 60 percent of the region. This recent work recorded a high number of additional prehistoric settlements, as well as extensive occupation during the Medieval Period and an associated expansion of agricultural land use across much of the peneplain of the survey zone (Figure 8.3; e.g., Bauer 2018; Johansen and Bauer 2015). Medieval settlement sites cover approximately 60 hectares of the study area, close to 25 hectares of which is aggregated in numerous, discontinuous, densely packed occupational terraces that are nestled against and set amongst the rocky slopes of the large and salient granitic inselberg hill known locally as the Durgada Gudda (e.g., Bauer 2018; Johansen and Bauer 2015). In addition to the occupation on the Durgada Gudda, another large concentration of settlement occurs in a partially fortified site on the plain just north of the hill that is also about 25 hectares in size and known locally as Sulidabba. The remainder of the medieval sites are primarily small "farmsteads" or field stations (< one hectare in size) that are spread across the peneplain, the western portion of which is comprised by red sandy soils and the eastern portion by the more moisture-retentive and "fertile" clay-rich vertisols or *regur* (the so called "black cotton soil").

It is noteworthy that regur's "fertility"—itself an emergent phenomenon of relationships among cultivars, clay, sunlight, moisture, and microbes—and its widespread distribution on the Raichur Doab has led to several historical arguments about the unique social history of the region related to persistent efforts at medieval military conquest. The reason for the political salience of the Raichur Doab, many have argued, was its desirability as an economic and agricultural resource base

FIGURE 8.3 The Maski Durgada Gudda inselberg

rooted in its physical geography. Stated explicitly by Eaton and Wagoner (2014: 242), "Raichur's pivotal role in the evolution of military technology and architecture in the Deccan derives in large part from its location ... in the heart of a coveted zone exceptionally rich in agriculture and minerals."

Many scholars have commented on how often "control" of the region surrounding Raichur shifted among competing polities during the medieval and early modern periods. Eaton and Wagoner (2014: 272–273) have aptly characterized it as an "extremely unstable" area, having "changed hands" four times in the sixteenth century alone, and often considered a liminal space between competing dynastic polities even earlier—first between the Chalukays and Cholas, later between the Kakatiyas, Yadavas, and Hoysalas, and ultimately between the Vijayanagara Empire and Bahmani Sultanate and its successor Deccan Sultanates. Indeed, historical scholarship indicates that between CE 1005 and CE 1565, more than 20 military campaigns occurred in the Raichur Doab, including a battle at Maski in CE 1021 (Bauer and Johansen in press). Competition for the Raichur Doab has rightly led scholars to characterize it as remarkably significant to medieval social history, and specifically to the development of forms of cultural and religious pluralism that uniquely characterized the ancient Deccan. It was in this "frontier" space (Eaton 2005: 16), or "contested border region between prevalent powers in the Deccan" (Gommans 1998: 6), where claims of sovereignty by Muslims, Shaivites, and Vaishnavites overlapped, rulers erected innovative defensive architecture and moved troops, and varied populations of military personnel, agriculturalists, and merchants settled. Indeed, by the end of the sixteenth century the Deccan likely showed the influence of a more diverse population of Persians, Arabs, Africans, and South Asians than did even north India (e.g., Asher and Talbot 2006: 163–166).

Given this historical context, here I primarily focus on the Medieval Period sites that MARP identified on the Durgada Gudda as a way of drawing a productive comparison to the better-studied architectural configurations of the capital centers of the Deccan noted above. Medieval settlement on the hill is constituted by a number of closely spaced and differentiated occupational contexts that are set amongst the hill terraces, talus slopes, colluvial valleys, and adjacent pediment slopes that characterize the inselberg (Figure 8.3). Separated by architectural divisions, terrace retention walls, and, in many cases, the boulder-strewn topography of the inselberg, many of these occupational contexts were analytically distinguished by MARP as separate "sites" (e.g., MARP-28, MARP-30, MARP-59, MARP-102) so as to explicitly capture architectural and artificial variations among them during the first phase of regional recording (e.g., Bauer and Johansen 2015; Johansen and Bauer 2015). However, taken as a whole, they constitute a number of differentiated places of ostensibly contemporaneous settlement that were densely occupied between the eleventh and sixteenth centuries, comprising a concentrated occupational area on and around the Durgada Gudda. In short, there is evidence for both dense and extensive occupation, a diversity of social tasks and activity spaces (e.g., metal working, temple worship, house construction, trash disposal, etc.), and constructed paths to both connect and channel movement among a number of

Urbanism and the medieval Deccan   **197**

differentiated places. Moreover, the Medieval Period occupation concentrated at the Durgada Guddda outcrop can be clearly contrasted with a number of smaller Medieval Period settlements associated with agricultural expansion that are scattered across the region's broader peneplain (Figure 8.4). In relational terms, the concentration of settlement on and around the Maski inselberg thus appears remarkably distinct from other peneplain medieval settlements.

There is even some evidence that one of MARP's sites served as an administrative center for the imperial ambitions of the Chalukyas of Kalyana (ca. AD 973–1163), who were formally seated nearly 200 kilometers to the north at Basavkalyan. Patil and Patil (1998: xix) have suggested, based on inscriptional data associated

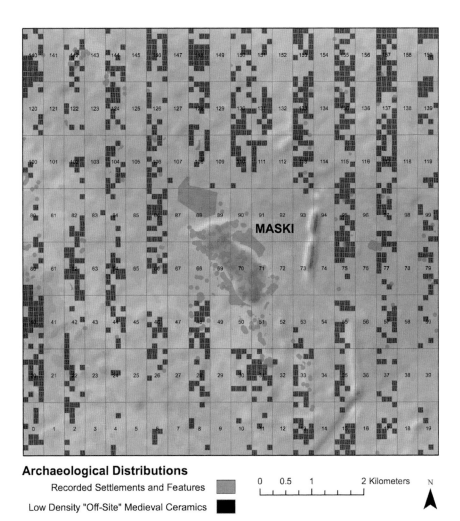

FIGURE 8.4 MARP study region, showing the distribution of recorded sites and low-density Medieval Period ceramics suggestive of land use

with site MARP-102, that the location known as Mosangi (as it is referred to in inscriptions) should be considered a regional center of the Chalukyas. Indeed, numerous eleventh-and twelfth-century stone inscriptions from the region suggest strong imperial claims were made to the place by the Chalukyas, and that some members of the elite dynasty regularly visited and perhaps held court at Maski. Although an argument that Maski was an administrative center of any kind requires further evaluation, the archaeological and inscriptional record make clear that Maski was a significant place during the period, and that both settlement and agricultural activities expanded at that time. For instance, MARP documentation of "off-site" artifact distributions associated with agricultural field stations and manuring activities suggest that much of the survey region appears to have come under cultivation during the period (Figure 8.4; see also Bauer 2018; Johansen and Bauer 2015).

To be clear, the occupation of Maski does not approximate the spatial extent or population density that would characterize the Deccan's medieval capital centers of Bidar, Gulbarga, Hyderabad, Vijayanagara, or Warangal. Moreover, only a limited number of contexts show the kinds of formalized defensive architecture that would constitute many of the well-documented citadels and forts of the medieval Deccan, such as those at nearby Raichur and Mudgal (e.g., Eaton and Wagoner 2014). Yet, there can be little doubt that Maski was a place of settlement aggregation during the Medieval Period. The archaeology attests to dense and extensive settlement around the hill, the presence of at least one former temple, and differentiated spaces for residential activities that could be distinguished from the smaller settlements that were dispersed across the agricultural peneplain. Moreover, the inscriptional record indicates the presence of several Hindu temples and a diversity of regional occupants who included practitioners of Jainism, Hinduism, and Islam, the latter of which are also attested to by medieval and early modern period Islamic graves (e.g., Patil and Patil 1998).

Given this spatial and historical context, Maski represents a good location to examine processes of urbanism and settlement aggregation that might highlight aspects of spatial production that have hitherto been ignored by scholarship on the commanding imperial capitals of the Deccan. How, for instance, do urban forms appear different at Maski than at Vijayanagara or Warangal? How might we explain settlement aggregation and the generation of social space in such a regional center? And how might our understanding of Maski's development inform investigations of spatial production at the well-studied capital centers?

The temporality of materiality in producing social space at Maski

The questions above beg attention to a much deeper and less linear historical process than what was presented as a static view of the medieval centers and settlement on and surrounding the granitic inselberg at Maski. As many archaeologists have recently stressed, the archaeological record, like all landscapes, is a diachronous product that is constituted by materials and phenomena that stubbornly resist their classification as belonging to a singular "past" period. Whether it be a reliquary box that contains "vestiges" of the past but that exists in and constitutes the present (e.g., Olivier 2011), the "heterogeneous time" induced by the patina of New Orleans ruins that disrupt linear narratives of the city (e.g., Dawdy 2016b), or even the methane-producing irrigation reservoirs that were built more than five hundred years ago in South India but that continue to contribute to agricultural and greenhouse gas production today (e.g., Bauer and Bhan 2018)—materials have temporalities that complicate singular periodizations and unilinear conceptions of process. It is this temporality of materiality that forecloses a simple understanding of the urban environment of Maski and, importantly, its history of production, as a process rooted solely in the Medieval Period. As Kathleen Morrison (2009) has lucidly pointed out, places have a way of persisting—not because their meanings are stable, but because their material constituents perpetuate them as distinct and perceptible places. It is this concern with the temporal qualities of materials and the persistence of place that will allow a productive contrast between the development of settlement at Maski with that of the "newly" designed capital cities of the medieval Deccan.

The production of medieval residential places on the Maski Durgada Gudda began well before the Medieval Period. Systematic survey of the hill documented ceramics, chipped stone, and ground stone axes characteristic of the Neolithic Period (ca. 3000–1200 BCE) spread across parts of one of the upper terraces of the southern portion of the hill. A wide diversity and remarkably high number of granitic petroglyphs primarily depicting herd animals (e.g., cattle) and wild fauna (e.g., tigers and peacocks) are also associated with this occupation. Following the Neolithic Period, there is evidence that inhabitants of the region established at least temporary settlements on the same upper terrace as did previous inhabitants and, furthermore, augmented and expanded on the suite of petroglyphs with new techniques and animal motifs (e.g., horses and later elephants).

As they are still evident today, numerous Neolithic Period rock art motifs would have been visible to Iron Age inhabitants of the site, influencing the production and location of later petroglyphs and perhaps settlement places. The Iron Age (ca. 1200–300 BCE) occupation of the upper terraces was, however, more extensive than in the prior Neolithic Period and also extended onto a number of adjacent and lower terraces (e.g., MARP-30, MARP-82, MARP-155; MARP-241; Johansen and Bauer 2015). At the same time, Iron Age inhabitants appear to have also modified the upper terraces of the Durgada Gudda with retention walls composed of modified granitic cobbles in select locations to maintain slope, sediment, and settlement conditions and, at others, such as on the uppermost terraces of MARP-82, they crafted cobble walls that delineated distinct residential places and probable house clusters (Figures 8.5, 8.6, and 8.8C).

As Johansen and Bauer (2015) have noted, Iron Age settlement configurations on the extant terraces probably generated distinctive social spaces among residential groups of a broader community of hill inhabitants. For instance, some upper terraces have evidence for restricted access, such as a cobble enclosure wall, and show "clear and unfettered visual access to the residential spaces" of the lower terraces; yet,

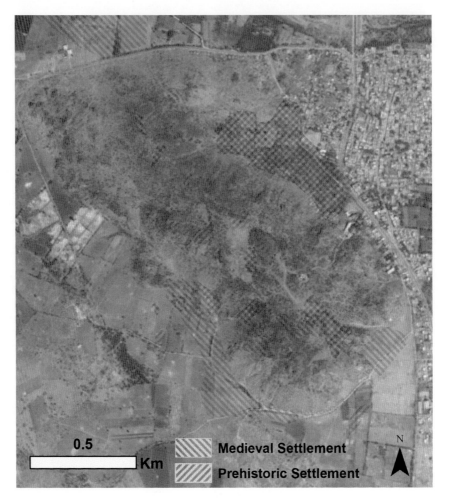

FIGURE 8.5 Distribution of prehistoric and Medieval Period settlement terraces overlain on high-resolution satellite imagery of the Durgada Gudda (crosshatched areas were occupied in both prehistoric and medieval periods)

inhabitants "residing below would have seen little more than the looming perimeter wall above and tendrils of smoke from cooking hearths" (Johansen and Bauer 2015: 4). In short, by the Iron Age there is evidence that settlement practices began to spatially inscribe particular kinds of social differences, likely reinforcing emerging forms of social distinctions that are also attested through archaeological evidence in the monumental mortuary record and by evidence for consumption differences across excavated domestic contexts (e.g., Bauer 2015; Bauer and Johansen 2015; Bauer and Trivedi 2013; Johansen 2011; Sinopoli 2013).

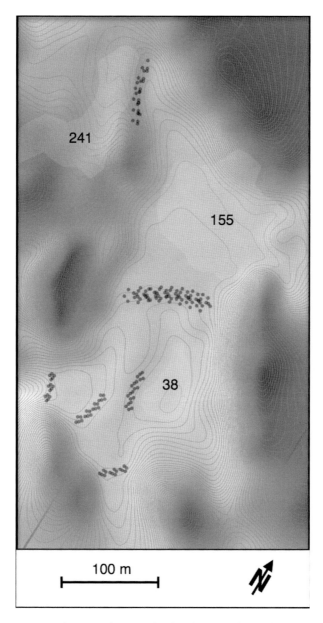

FIGURE 8.6 Topographic map showing the distribution of several recorded settlement terraces and associated retention walls amongst the uppermost rock slopes of the Durgada Gudda (1-meter contour interval)

The production of Iron Age landscapes at Maski thus attests to cultural practices of settlement organization as significant to the creation and maintenance of particular kinds of socio-spatial alterity. Yet, it is important to recognize that Iron Age settlement places on the Durgada Gudda were not simply the product of human designs or cultural forms. The long-term geomorphology of the inselberg hill and the erosional and weathering processes that produced the hill's unique topography and terraces, which are separated by exposures of massive residual granitic boulders and difficult to traverse core stone slopes, heavily contributed to the maintenance of social space at this site complex. Indeed, the various residential terraces, separated by steep boulder slopes and narrow paths of movement across the boulder-strewn hill, highly structured the flow of people, animals, and things through prehistoric settlement spaces (see also Bauer 2015 and Johansen 2011 for comparison). Frequently there are no more than two narrow approach paths to upper residential terraces (e.g., MARP-82, MARP-241). While the unforgiving rock slopes did not *determine* the establishment of human settlement on the hill, they did facilitate the perpetuation of residential distinctions. As settlement expanded onto multiple hill terraces the residual boulders and core stones that constituted the Maski hills similarly became constitutive of spatial divisions within a broader community of residents, forming visual barriers between different terraces and making others difficult to physically access. The degree to which steep rock slopes and larger granitic boulders were reshaped to accommodate settlement appears to have been limited. Rather, prehistoric occupants ostensibly augmented exposed smaller boulders with other stones and cobbles to craft retention walls and architectural alignments, while the larger and more salient core stones and steep slopes and deep ravines served to divide and differentiate residential terraces (see Johansen 2011 for comparison).

Given that the Maski Durgada Gudda inselberg is composed of Precambrian granitic rock and is the result of millions of years of weathering and planation (cf. Bauer 2015; Büdel 1982; Radhakrishna and Vaidyanadhan 1997; Thomas 1994), it is tempting to see the hill and its current form as a nearly timeless product of a deep geological past. And yet at Maski, as well as on other granitic residual hills of the Southern Deccan, slope and sediment processes have been rather active over the last five thousand years of human occupation. Occupational refuse has increased sedimentation in some locales while soil erosion has intensified in relation to land clearance and herding activities in others (e.g., Bauer 2014; 2015). Moreover, some core stone boulders, soil, and sediment have moved downslope through processes of mass wasting (Figure 8.7). As noted above, prehistoric inhabitants worked to maintain slope and sediment conditions in some locations by building retention walls. This, however, was by no means a singular activity. Similar to processes of entanglement described by Hodder (2012), inhabitants were compelled to actively maintain these features as erosional processes perpetually destabilized them and altered their coursings (see also Bauer 2015).

In this sense, one might consider the processes of materially generating the built forms and places of the Maski Durgada Gudda as a process of "growth" (sensu Ingold 2000). Drawing on a number of provocative calls to resist Aristotelian

FIGURE 8.7 Colluvium from upper settlement terrace of MARP-82

hylomorphism that separates matter and form (e.g., Deleuze and Guattari 1987), Ingold has challenged archaeologists to reconsider the crafting process (e.g., Ingold 2000, 2012, 2013). Buildings are not simply the result of bringing together "lineaments and matter" (Ingold 2013: 50). For Ingold, the fashioning of artifacts and built forms should be considered comparable to a process of growing crops or raising animals, in which practical interactions among a multitude of materials and biophysical processes dynamically shape material outcomes. Artifacts "emerge—like the forms of living beings—within the relational contexts of the mutual involvement of people and their environments" (Ingold 2000: 77). Extending this analogy to spatial production at Maski, it becomes possible to frame the "built environment" as an emergent product of human practices, material weathering, and the active slope processes that perpetually refashioned settlement places.

Medieval Period social space on the Maski Durgada Gudda could be considered the result of a similar process. Settlement was even more extensive than that of the Iron Age, but similarly expanded onto adjacent hilltop terraces in addition to the pediment slopes that surround the bottom of the hill, where excavations have revealed the presence of earthen domestic structures (Bauer and Johansen in press). Among the hilltop residential terraces, occupational areas evident by extant stone structures and architectural alignments continued to be divided by rock slopes and residual granitic exposures. Although these spaces have not yet been fully mapped in detail, it is evident that many of the terraces included room blocks whose foundations were composed of faced and modified stones that range in size from boulders to cobbles. Moreover, some of the terraces themselves are often delineated with retention walls of various sizes; some that are composed of faced boulders and others of cobbles that are still preserved to heights of more than a meter.

In crafting these distinctive settlement places, Medieval Period practices of spatial production had to contend with the active residual products of millions of years of weathering and erosion[1] and, on some terraces, the remains of thousands of years of previous settlement refuse and detritus. For instance, the Medieval Period domestic deposits on site MARP-30 overlie and partly incorporate the remains of earlier Iron Age occupation (e.g., Bauer and Johansen 2015). Moreover, multiple large Medieval Period boulder and cobble coursed walls follow the contours of the surrounding granitic rock slopes at many locations. In some cases, these walls limit access to particular settlement places and, in others, they appear to protect residential locations against rockslides or the downslope movement of occupational colluvium of previously settled terraces above. For present purposes, it is important to stress that many of the medieval architectural alignments and terrace walls extant on the surface of the Durgada Gudda are not oriented to cardinal directions, but rather work with the curves and the topography of the rock slopes of the hill and thus are angled and arced in numerous directions. In that sense, many of the Medieval Period urban spaces on the Maski inselberg—differentiated by architectural materials, retention walls, rock slopes, and intra-hill ravines that were partly constitutive of symbolically and materially delineated residential clusters and places—are seemingly very different than the spatial forms that have been mapped among the medieval Deccan's great capital centers discussed above. Social space on the Durgada Gudda does not appear to be the product of stringent planning that strictly organized architectural divisions geometrically or laid out paths of movement and architectural orientations according to cosmological principles.

To be clear, some medieval structures and architectural alignments on the Durgada Gudda do face cardinal directions and suggest that their builders had a concern

FIGURE 8.8 Examples of room blocks (A,B), spatial divisions (C), and defensive walls (D) on the Durgada Gudda

for such prescribed orientations. However, careful analyses also suggest that these structures often belie the rule of such prescriptions. For instance, MARP recorded a series of north-facing fortification walls and associated "fort" room blocks that generally show cardinal orientations on the northern peaks of the Durgada Gudda. However, documentation of these features also indicates that many of the wall segments of these constructions incorporated extant boulders and core stones that altered their cardinal alignments and, in some cases, generated sinuous edges and "corners" (Figure 8.8A,B,D). In short, the spatial products of medieval settlement on Maski's Durgada Gudda were highly influenced by the extant distribution of sedimented terraces and boulder-strewn slopes, which were themselves the product of long-term geomorphological processes of weathering, erosion, and thousands of years of previous settlement and the resultant detritus. This is not to suggest that the resultant social landscape was determined by the presence of rock slopes and sediment, but rather that inhabitants crafted settlement places in concert with them and a concern for their dynamics.

The production of medieval urban environments on the Deccan

In the pages above I have sketched two very different descriptions of spatial production processes during the Medieval and Early Modern Periods of southern India. In the case of the Deccan's better-documented capital centers—such as those of

Hyderabad, Vijayanagara, and Waranagal— large-scale urban configurations appear to have been designed with clear attention to cosmographical or religious principles. In contrast, at Maski salient architectural remains of medieval settlement on the Durgada Gudda often lack such recognizable forms and orientations. Rather, many settlement places appear to have been accretionary products crafted in concert with careful attention to the dynamics of previous occupational refuse and the slope processes that affected sediment deposition and rockslides, which further gave shape to residential places and were likewise constitutive of spatial divisions within the broader settlement. It is tempting to view these different spatial configurations with the often-cited distinction between "planned" and "organic" urban development (cf. A. Smith 2003; M. Smith 2007). Moreover, corresponding to these distinctions, one might similarly argue that some forms were the product of overt political and religious claims (e.g., spatial links between the divine hero-king Rama with imperial rulers at Vijayanagara), while others (e.g., the architectural configurations on the Durgada Gudda) were apolitical in character, merely the accretionary product of profane quotidian activities. While the processes of landscape production on the Maski Durgada Gudda exemplify settlement practices that were ostensibly different than the layouts of the Deccan's capital centers, I would like to draw out a more fundamental point that destabilizes what the binaries of "planned" versus "organic" or "political" versus "apolitical" imply. In all of these cases social landscapes emerged with the active and practical participation of materials that conditioned places as products of and potentialities for political practice.

As noted above, urban environments are frequently characterized by a diversity of spaces and places that are not equally legible to all inhabitants. I am reluctant to apply to the medieval Deccan the infra-power that Hansen and Verkaaik (2009) attribute to contemporary (and primarily postcolonial) cities, but many of their characterizations of urban conditions find strong parallels among the diversified cultural and political contexts of the region described above. If, for instance, the "opacity" of cities becomes an opportunity for the emergence of charismatic actors, enabling some to establish influence through "special forms of knowledge, networks, [or] connectedness" (Hansen and Verkaaik 2009: 9), then one might accept that such possibilities were similarly enabled at some of the great capital cities of the medieval Deccan. No doubt, many quarters and corners of Vijayanagara and Hyderabad were differentially legible to inhabitants as the product of a diverse assemblage of human populations, materials, and building practices that were unfamiliar to some newly settled occupants. As Fritz and colleagues (1984) are careful to point out, the concentration of distinctive shrines in eastern areas of Vijayanagara indicate the presence of a Jaina community in at least one sector of the site and "numerous Islamic tombs, a cemetery, and two mosques … indicate a Muslim quarter" (12). While one should question the degree to which these spaces were exclusively occupied by inhabitants that identified as practitioners of Jainism or Islam, it is nevertheless probable that, as products of distinct assemblages of materials, tasks, and activities, they would have been differentially inhabited and "known" to the city's diverse inhabitants who were socialized in other contexts.

The capacities of Deccan rulers to assemble laborers, materials, craftspeople, and ritual specialists to generate and site buildings and monuments according to cosmographic principles and religious canons may have been the ultimate act in providing legibility to an uncertain historical context in which territorial conflict was relatively regular. And yet, as previously stressed, it is unlikely that the Deccan's religious symbolism would have been uniformly perceived by the diverse inhabitants who would have come to live in these cities. Moreover, the large-scale architectural configurations that mirrored cosmological designs or prescriptions at sites such as Vijayanagara or Warangal do not imply that all urban spaces and places at these "planned" cities readily conformed to such spatial logics. At Warangal, for instance, examination of the ringed perimeter walls demonstrate that some wall segments were diverted around extant rocky hills, while also taking advantage of slope morphology to create large water-retention reservoirs. In other words, the city form is far from a perfect rendering of the cosmogram that it apparently mimics, and thus its production might also be considered a process of "growth" similar to that of the settlement places at Maski.

The same argument can be made at Vijayanagara. Indeed, Vijayanagara's

> fortifications ingeniously utilize the natural terrain wherever possible: Walls run along the tops of rocky ridges, or traverse flat land at the shortest possible distance between granite outcrops. This partly explains the angular configuration of the walls, particularly on the north, but also partly on east and west. To the south the land is mostly flat; here the walls are more linear, though rarely straight.
>
> (Fritz et al. 1984: 10; see also Brubaker 2015)

In other words, the defensive architecture that enclosed the urban core, materially and symbolically constituting it as a place, was itself a partial product of the surrounding granitic hills. Imperial strategies to funnel the movement of people, animals, and goods through control points and valley gateways (e.g., Sinopoli and Morrison 1995) were shaped by the physical efficacy and imposing affectivity of the difficult-to-traverse and towering granitic hills and rock slopes, as well as the crafting of high defensive walls (Figure 8.9).

In this way, one might recognize parallels between how other scholars have viewed the production of geopolitical borders and spatial barriers as a product of heterogeneous constituents. Jason De León (2015) and Juanita Sundberg's (2011) analyses of the US–Mexico border, for instance, document how mountains and deserts also shape the conformation of the border and associated law-enforcement practices of policing it. And yet, as De León (2015) stresses in that case, there is considerable evidence that the configuration of difficult-to-traverse terrain as a critical part of the US–Mexico border assemblage "was intentionally set in motion by

FIGURE 8.9 Example of Vijayanagara gateway (A) and associated cross-valley wall (B) that limited the paths of movement into the urban core

policy strategists" whose designs "purposefully funneled [migrants] into the desert through various enforcement practices" (De León 2015: 60).

In a similar vein, it is important to stress that the defensive architecture of Vijayanagara's urban core was by no means an accident of an undirected historical assemblage or emergent human–nonhuman configuration. While one might agree with Ingold (e.g., 2012, 2013) and others (e.g., Deleuze and Guattari 1987) in their resistance to hylomorphic doctrines of matter and form, one should not ignore the political effects of constraining movement into and out of the city as an important strategic aspect of how imperial authority (and the royal coffer) was maintained at Vijayanagara. Rulers and craft specialists assembled defensive features and worked with the area's residual hills to affect practices of movement that were part of political objectives to influence perceptions of the empire and to render the people, materials, and things that entered and left legible to a variety of imperial mediators (e.g., soldiers, tax collectors, local strong persons, etc.; see Sinopoli and Morrison 1995). It is, of course, possible to consider the production of these defensive walls as a process of growth; however, that should not imply that growth cannot be directed by influential human actors or "mediants" (sensu Appadurai 2015) who might have vested interests in mind (see also Joyce, Chapter 4).

In contrast to the cosmographic urban forms noted above, many of the salient architectural remains of medieval settlement on the Maski Durgada Gudda lack the recognizable and formalized architectural traditions and orientations of the Deccan's great capital centers. Settlement places appear to have been crafted with modified cobbles and boulders in concert with careful attention to the dynamics of slope processes and rock slopes, which gave shape to residential places and were likewise constitutive of spatial divisions within the broader settlement. Whether these spatial divisions aligned with other kinds of social distinctions, such as those of status, occupation, rank, or religious affiliations, remains to be further investigated.

However, it is important to underscore that the activities that partly constituted the Maski landscape need not be divorced from activities associated with religion and ritual, despite not being as overtly indexed as at the capital centers. To reiterate a point noted at the outset of this chapter, previous scholarship has stressed that ostensibly quotidian activities such as agricultural and pastoral production practices could be deeply entangled in religious beliefs and practices in medieval South India (e.g., Morrison 2009). At Maski, for instance, inscriptions associated with temple donations make clear that a variety of land use and agricultural production were implicated in devotional practices, particularly as ritualized gifts redistributed land and reconstituted the meaning and value of specific assemblages of soil, water, and cultivars during a period of agricultural expansion in which new soils came into production (e.g., Bauer 2018). Thus, it is likely that the meaningful tasks and activities that partly gave shape to urban forms around Maski were simultaneously related to devotional ideologies for some inhabitants. However, other aspects of spatial production were also operative.

The distinctive residential terraces generated on the Maski Durgada Gudda were likely significant to the production and maintenance of social differentiation as their inhabitants differentially came to "know" different residential places. It is not difficult to imagine that those who lived and labored in earthen structures around the base of the hill had a much different experience than those who did so among stone buildings on an upper terrace. While some inhabitants likely felt comfortable traversing the steep rock slope boulders to reach well-known places, others probably did not. Some of these places would similarly have been much easier to defend in the event of a military attack or raid. Farmstead communities who lived on the plain, those who lived around the base of the Durgada Gudda, and those who lived on the upper terraces of the hill behind defensive walls, would likely have had much different fears and anxieties related to the well-documented military conflict that occurred in the region throughout the Medieval Period. Moreover, the distinctive clusters of medieval settlement likely enabled some inhabitants to forge relationships and social networks that traversed these spatial divisions, while at the same time that other inhabitants might have served as local leaders.

Thus, the boulders and rock slopes that separated residential terraces on Maski's Durgada Gudda were more than variegated materials that constituted obstacles to the implementation of regularized planning or the imposition of design forms; rather they "mediated" (sensu Latour 2005) the production of social space and emergent social affiliations and distinctions. They also provided opportunities for particular humans to instrumentally establish relationships that transcended such spatial divisions. Thus, the ostensibly "unplanned" urban landscapes of medieval Maski should not be considered somehow apolitical, in contrast to the manifestation of religious canons in a political landscape at the capital centers—though the politics that they entailed need not be recognized as identical. It is important to note that at places such as Maski, social affiliation and distinctions generated through residential spatial practices may very well have cut across the lines of rank or religion that scholars of medieval South India are so accustomed to highlighting. For instance, it is entirely possible that practitioners of various sects of Jainism, Hinduism, and Islam were settled on the less defensible peneplain around Maski throughout the long period of contestation over the Raichur Doab. These inhabitants potentially shared concerns or anxieties (e.g., over defense, soil conditions, access to water, etc.) that might have contributed to community formation, problematizing the degree to which we should consider religious affiliations and political affiliations as essentially coterminous in this historical context.

Conclusion: Beyond the cosmograms of Deccan social and political space

The insightful work of art historians, architects, and archaeologists has shown that monumental forms and styles that drew heavily on religious cosmologies and canons constituted many of the medieval Deccan's great capital centers. These studies have been wonderfully illustrative of how rulers and elites assembled diverse materials and craft specialists to generate urban contexts that could be understood through particular religious ideologies, symbolism, and practices. Moreover, in some instances the production of these landscapes appears to have been part and parcel of political strategies for constituting or maintaining authority, such as the positioning of Warangal's royal palace at the center of a cosmogram or linking Vijayanagara's royal zone with the Vishnu avatar Rama (e.g., Michell 1992a; Fritz et al. 1984). In that sense, the incisive work of these previous studies sheds important light on how politics was coupled with the manipulation of landscape in its concomitant experiential, perceptual, and conceptual dimensions (e.g., Harvey 1990; Smith 2003; Lefebvre 1990). Yet, it is important to remember that one needs to be socialized to "see" (e.g., Bourdieu 1984), and many of these urban forms would probably not have been understood uniformly by all of the cities' diverse inhabitants; or, more precisely, they were likely intelligible in different ways. Thus, the politics of landscape production at these places was not limited to the ideological work of embedding cosmograms in the built environment.

The medieval settlement on the Durgada Gudda of Maski ostensibly lacks many of the formalized monumental spaces that are so well documented at the region's capitals. The archaeological remains recorded to date suggest that settlement practices crafted residential places in concert with dynamic slopes and the residual rocks and terraces that make up the hill. The material legacies of both long-term processes of weathering and erosion and the accumulation of sediment and detritus of thousands of years of previous settlement gave shape to spatial forms as these materials became meaningful and settlement expanded onto adjacent but distinctive hill terraces. These materials— the durable core stones of granitic bedrock and the artifacts and colluvium of prior settlement—were as much a part of the social landscape of medieval Maski as a temple newly constructed in the eleventh century.

The temporalities of these materials, shaping both durable spatial divisions on the hills and inciting quotidian practices of slope and building maintenance, remind use that meaningful settlement places at Maski were not simply the result of elite conceptual building templates imposed onto an infinitely malleable material world of rock, regolith, or rubble. However, this is not to suggest that landscape production on the Maski inselberg should be differentiated from that of the Deccan's great capital centers as somehow less political in practice. The residential places produced by Maski's assemblage of architectural terraces, rock slopes, and difficult-to-traverse boulders were partly creative of socio–spatial differences as residential communities were constituted. Attention to the multiple temporalities of material dynamics, slope processes, and residual rocks that gave shape to urban forms, and differentiated residential places and activity and affect at Maski, need not be limited to such "secondary" or "tertiary" centers of the medieval Deccan. Urban forms at Maski do not merely demonstrate a different logic of spatial production (sensu M. Smith 2007) than those at the Deccan's imperial capital centers; rather, they highlight that social places are crafted with the active and practical participation of dynamic materials, a point that it is critical to remember also applied to the ostensibly newly planned constructions at the Deccan's capitals. However, this should not imply that the crafting of places was necessarily undirected by political objectives.

212 Andrew M. Bauer

The crafting of fortifications and access routes at sites like Warangal and Vijayanagara likely rendered the people, materials, and things that entered and exited the cities more legible to imperial agents (e.g., Sinopoli and Morrison 1995). To recognize this control of movement as an imperial strategy is also to call attention to the significance of rock slopes and hills, their physicality and temporal dynamics, as partly constitutive of the political landscape. Doing so also moves us beyond a concern for the ideological claims made through constructing cosmograms and toward an interest in how materials and political strategies were aligned to shape the politics of daily life and imperial practices. Yet, while spatial production even at sites such as Warangal and Vijayanagara might be considered a process of "growth" in which materials played a dynamic role, we should not forget that growth can often be directed with political aims in mind. Assemblages need not be the emergent product of aimless human–nonhuman configurations. Thus, alongside any new archaeological concerns for materials and their dynamics in giving shape to a conjoined human–nonhuman social history scholars must also be attuned to how materials are entrained (sensu Bauer and Kosiba 2016) in cultural fields of value and significance, which means not straying too far from an anthropocentric lens.

Acknowledgments

I owe many thanks to the Archaeological Survey of India for the kind privilege and permission to conduct the research at Maski presented above (F.1/8/2009-EE). I would also like to extend gratitude to the American Institute of Indian Studies for their generous assistance and continuous support for the project, and particularly Dr. Pradeep Mehendiratta, Purnima Mehta, and Dr. Vandana Sinha. Special thanks are also owed to friends, colleagues, and project co-directors of the Maski Archaeological Research Project, including Peter Johansen and those of the Karnataka Department of Archaeology, Museums, and Heritage, T. S. Gangadhar, Dr. R. Gopal, Dr. Gavisiddaiah, and N.L. Gowda. This chapter would not have come together without the kind invitation of Tim Pauketat and Susan Alt to participate in an Amerind Foundation seminar on religion, new materialisms, and ancient urbanism. I am deeply grateful to Tim and Susan for including me in those discussions, and for the helpful feedback from all who attended. Lastly, sincere thanks are also owed to several anonymous reviewers, Tim Pauketat, and Mannat Johal for recommendations that improved the quality of this chapter. Of course, any responsibility for errors or opinions remains with the author.

Note

1 Of course, inhabitants of medieval Maski would not have conceptualized the age and chronology of these processes through the paradigms of contemporary geomorphology. Yet, it is worth noting that Hindu cosmologies conceived of multiple worldly cycles that

unfolded over millions of years, which were quite lengthier than the chronologies of traditions among the "Peoples of the Book" at the time (see Trautmann 2009: 35–38).

References

Adams, Robert McC. 1966 *The Evolution of Urban Society: Early Mesopotamia and Prehispanic Mexico.* Aldine, Hawthorne, NY.

Alam, Muzaffar, and Sanjay, Subrahmanyam 2011 *Writing the Mughal World.* Permanent Black, New Delhi.

——— 2018 Mediterranean Exemplars: Jesuit Political Lessons for a Mughal Emperor. In *Machiavelli, Islam and the East: Reorienting the Foundations of Modern Political Thought,* edited by Lucio Biasiori and Giuseppe Marcocci, pp. 105–129. Palgrave Macmillan, Cham, Switzerland.

Appadurai, Arjun 2015 Mediants, Materiality, Normativity. *Public Culture* 27(2): 221–237.

Asad, Talal 2003 *Formations of the Secular: Christianity, Islam, Modernity.* Stanford University Press, Stanford, CA.

Asher Catherine, B., and Cynthia Talbot 2006 *India Before Europe.* Cambridge University Press, Cambridge.

Baires, Sarah 2017 *Land of Water, City of the Dead: Religion and Cahokia's Emergence.* University of Alabama Press, Tuscaloosa.

Bauer, Andrew M. 2011 Producing the Political Landscape: Monuments, Labor, Water, and Place in Iron Age Central Karnataka. In *The Archaeology of Politics: the Materiality of Political Practice and Action in the Past,* edited by Peter G. Johansen and Andrew M. Bauer, pp. 83–113. Cambridge Scholars Publishing, Newcastle upon Tyne.

——— 2014 Impacts of Mid- to Late-Holocene Land Use on Residual Hill Morphology: A Remote Sensing and Archaeological Evaluation of Human-Related Soil Erosion in Central Karnataka, South India. *The Holocene* 24: 3–14.

——— 2015 *Before Vijayanagara: Prehistoric Landscapes and Politics in the Tungahbadra Basin.* Manohar and American Institute of Indian Studies, New Delhi.

——— 2018 Remote Sensing Soils and Social Geographies of Difference: The Landscape Archaeology of Regur from Iron Age through Medieval Period Northern, Karnataka, Southern India. *Journal of Field Archaeology* 43(1): 31–43.

Bauer, Andrew M., and Mona Bhan 2018 *Climate Without Nature: A Critical Anthropology of the Anthropocene.* Cambridge University Press, Cambridge.

Bauer, Andrew M., and Peter G. Johansen 2015 Prehistoric Mortuary Practices and the Constitution of Social Relationships: Implications of the First Radiocarbon Dates from Maski on the Occupational History of a South Indian "Type Site." *Radiocarbon* 57(4): 795–806.

Bauer, Andrew M., and Peter G. Johansen in press The Maski Archaeological Research Project (2010-2018): Initial Results from a Multi-Period Interdisciplinary Project on the Raichur Doab. *Current Science.*

Bauer, Andrew M., and Steve Kosiba 2016 How Things Act: An Archaeology of Materials in Political Life. *Journal of Social Archaeology* 16(2): 115–141.

Bauer, Andrew M., and Mudit Trivedi 2013. Contextualizing Megalithic Places: Survey, Mapping, and Surface Documentation in the Environs of Hire Benakal (Koppal District, Karnataka). Man and Environment 38(2): 46–61.

Bourdieu, Pierre 1984 *Distinction: A Social Critique of Taste.* Harvard University Press, Cambridge, MA.

——— 1990 *The Logic of Practice.* Stanford University Press, Stanford, CA.

Brubaker, Robert P. 2015 *Vijayanagara: Warfare and the Archaeology of Defense*. Manohar, New Delhi.

Büdel, Julius 1982 *Climatic Geomorphology*. Princeton University Press, Princeton, NJ.

Chase, Diane Z., Chase, Arlen F., and William A. Haviland 1990 The Classic Maya City: Reconsidering the "Mesoamerican Urban Tradition." *American Anthropologist* 92(2): 499–506.

Childe, V. Gordon 1950 The Urban Revolution. *The Town Planning Review* 21(1): 3–17.

Coe, Michael D. 1984 *The Maya*. Thames and Hudson, New York.

Cowgill, George L. 2004 Origins and Development of Urbanism: Archaeological Perspectives. *Annual Review of Anthropology* 33: 525–549.

Dawdy, Shannon L. 2016a Profane Archaeology and the Existential Dialectics of the City. *Journal of Social Archaeology* 16(1): 32–55.

——— 2016b *Patina: A Profane Archaeology*. University of Chicago Press, Chicago.

De Certeau, Michel 1984 *The Practice of Everyday Life*. University of California Press, Berkeley.

De León, Jason 2015 *The Land of Open Graves: Living and Dying on the Migrant Trail*. University of California Press, Berkeley.

Deleuze, Gilles, and Felix Guattari 1987 *A Thousand Plateaus: Capitalism and Schizophrenia*. University of Minnesota Press, Minneapolis.

Deloria Jr., Vine 2003 *God Is Red: A Native View of Religion*. Fulcrum Publishing, Golden, CO.

Dutt, Binode B. 2009 *Town Planning in Ancient India*. Isha Books, Delhi.

Eaton, Richard M. 2005 *A Social History of the Deccan, 1300–1761: Eight Indian Lives*. Cambridge University Press, Cambridge.

Eaton, Richard M. 1978 Sufis of Bijapur, 1300-1700. Princeton University Press, Princeton.

Eaton, Richard M., and Phillip B. Wagoner 2014 *Power, Memory, Architecture: Contested Sites on India's Deccan Plateau, 1300-1600*. Oxford University Press, Oxford.

Emberling, Geoff 2003 Urban Social Transformations and the Problem of the "First City": New Research from Mesopotamia. In *The Social Construction of Ancient Cities*, edited by Monica L. Smith, pp. 254–268. Smithsonian Institute Press, Washington, DC.

Fisher, Elaine M. 2017 *Hindu Pluralism: Religion in the Public Sphere in Early Modern South Asia*. University of California, Oakland.

Fogelin, Lars 2007 The Archaeology of Religious Ritual. *Annual Review of Anthropology* 36: 55–71.

Fowles, Severin 2013 *An Archaeology of Doings: Secularism and the Study of Pueblo Religion*. School for Advanced Research Press, Santa Fe.

Fox, Richard G. 1977 *Urban Anthropology*. Prentice Hall, Englewood Cliffs, NJ.

Fritz, John M. 1986 Vijayanagara: Authority and Meaning of South Indian Imperial Capital. *American Anthropologist* 88(1): 44–55.

Fritz, John M., and George Michell 1987 Interpreting the Plan of a Medieval Hindu Capital, Vijayanagara. *World Archaeology* 19(1): 105–129.

——— 2015 *Hampi Vijayanagara*. Deccan Heritage Foundation, London.

Fritz, John M., George Michell, and M. S. Nagaraja Rao 1984 *Where Kings and Gods Meet: The Royal Centre at Vijayanagara, India*. University of Arizona Press, Tucson.

Gommans, Jos 1998 The Silent Frontier of South Asia, c. AD 1100–1800. *Journal of World History* 9(1): 1–23.

Hansen, Thomas B., and Oskar Verkaaik 2009 Introduction—Urban Charisma: On Everyday Mythologies in the City. *Critique of Anthropology* 29(1): 5–26.

Harvey, David 1996 *Justice, Nature and the Geography of Difference*. Blackwell, Oxford.

——— 1990 *The Condition of Postmodernity*. Blackwell, Cambridge, MA.

Heitzman, James 1991 Ritual Polity and Economy: The Transactional Network of an Imperial Temple in Medieval South India. *Journal of the Economic and Social History of the Orient* 34(1–2): 23–54.

———— 1987 Temple Urbanism in Medieval South India. *Journal of Asian Studies* 46(4): 791–826.

Hodder, Ian 2012 *Entangled: An Archaeology of the Relationships Between Humans and Things.* Blackwell, Malden, MA.

Ingold, Tim 2000 *Perceptions of the Environment: Essays on Livelihood, Dwelling and Skill.* Routledge, London.

———— 2012 Toward an Ecology of Materials. *Annual Review of Anthropology* 41: 427–442.

———— 2013 *Making: Anthropology, Archaeology, Art, and Architecture.* Routledge, New York.

Johansen, Peter G. 2011 Practicing Social Difference, Production Social Space: The Political Architectonics of Iron Age Settlement Places. In *The Archaeology of Politics: The Materiality of Political Practice and Action in the Past,* edited by Peter G. Johansen and Andrew M. Bauer, pp. 245–282. Cambridge Scholars Publishing, Newcastle upon Tyne.

Johansen, Peter G., and Andrew M. Bauer 2011 Reconfiguring "Politics" in the Reconstruction of Past Political Production. In *The Archaeology of Politics: The Materiality of Political Practice and Action in the Past,* edited by Peter G. Johansen and Andrew M. Bauer, pp. 1–28. Cambridge Scholars Publishing, Newcastle upon Tyne.

———— 2015 Beyond Culture History at Maski: Land Use, Settlement and Social Differences in Neolithic through Medieval South India. *Archaeological Research in Asia* 1: 6–16.

Kosiba, Steve, and Andrew M. Bauer 2013 Mapping the Political Landscape: Toward a GIS Analysis of Environmental and Social Difference. *Journal of Archaeological Method and Theory* 20: 61–101.

Latour, Bruno 2005 *Reassembling the Social: An Introduction to Actor-Network-Theory.* Oxford University Press, Oxford.

Latour, Bruno, and Albena Yaneva 2008 "Give Me a Gun and I Will Make All Buildings Move": An ANT's View of Architecture. In *Explorations in Architecture: Teaching, Design, Research,* edited by Reto Geiser, pp. 80–89. Birkhauser, Basel.

Lefebvre, Henri 1990 *The Production of Space.* Basil Blackwell, Oxford.

Lynch, Kevin (ed.) 1977 *Growing Up in Cities: Studies of the Spatial Environment of Adolescence in Cracow, Melbourne, Mexico City, Salta, Toluca and Warsaw.* MIT Press, Cambridge, MA.

Marcus, Joyce 1973 Territorial Organization of the Lowland Classic Maya. *Science* 180(4089): 911–916.

Michell, George 1992a City as Cosmogram: The Circular Plan of Warangal. *South Asian Studies* (8): 1–18.

———— 1992b *The Vijayanagara Courtly Style: Incorporation and Synthesis in the Royal Architecture of Southern India, 15th–17th Centuries.* Manohar and the American Institute of Indian Studies, New Delhi.

Morrison, Kathleen D. 2009 *Daroji Valley: Landscape History, Place, and the Making of a Dryland Reservoir System.* Manohar, New Delhi.

Nagaswamy, R. 1978 South Indian Temples as an Employer. In *Studies in Ancient Tamil Law and Society,* edited by R. Nagaswamy. Institute of Epigraphy, State Department of Archaeology, Government of Tamil Nadu, Madras.

Nilikanta Sastri, K. A. 1997 [1955] *A History of South India: From Prehistoric Times to the Fall of Vijayanagar.* Oxford University Press, New Delhi.

Novetzke, Christian L. 2016 *The Quotidian Revolution: Vernacularization, Religion, and the Premodern Public Sphere in India.* Columbia University Press, New York.

Olivier, Laurent 2011 *The Dark Abyss of Time: Archaeology and Memory.* Rowman and Littlefield, Lanham, MD.

Park, R. E., and Burgess, E. W. 1922 *Introduction to the Science of Sociology.* University of Chicago Press, Chicago.

Patil, Channabasappa S., and Vinoda C. Patil 1998 *Inscriptions of Karnataka vol. IV: Inscriptions of Raichur District*. Directorate of Archaeology and Museums, Mysore.

Pauketat, Timothy R. 2013 *An Archaeology of the Cosmos: Rethinking Agency and Religion in Ancient America*. Routledge, New York.

Radhakrishna, B. P., and R. Vaidyanadhan 1997 *Geology of Karnataka*. Geological Society of India, Bangalore.

Ray, Himanshu Prabha 1986 *Monastery and Guild: Commerce under the Satavahanas*. Oxford University Press, Delhi.

Rizvi, Uzma Z. 2011 Subjectivities and Spatiality in Indus Urban Forms: Mohenjo Daro, the Body and the Domestication of Waste. In *The Archaeology of Politics: The Materiality of Political Practice and Action in the Past*, edited by Peter G. Johansen and Andrew M. Bauer, pp. 221–244. Cambridge Scholars Publishing, Newcastle upon Tyne.

Sanders, William T., and David Webster 1988 The Mesoamerican Urban Tradition. *American Anthropologist* 90(3): 521–546.

Sinopoli, Carla M. 1993 *Pots and Palaces: The Archaeological Ceramics of the Nobleman's Quarter of Vijayanagara*. Manohar, New Delhi.

——— 2003 Echoes of Empire: Vijayanagara and Historical Memory, Vijayanagara as Historical Memory. In *Archaeologies of Memory*, edited by Ruth M. Van Dyke and Susan E. Alcock, pp. 15–33. Blackwell, Hoboken, NJ.

——— 2013 Exploring Ceramic Variability in Iron Age South India. In *South Asian Archaeology 2007, Proceedings of the 19th International Conference of The European Association of South Asian Archaeology, vol. I: Prehistoric Periods*, edited by D. Frenez and M. Tosi, pp. 233–241. Archaeopress–BAR International Series, Oxford.

Sinopoli, Carla M., and Kathleen D. Morrison 1995 Dimensions of Imperial Control: The Vijayanagara Capital. *American Anthropologist* 97: 83–96.

Smith, Adam T. 2003 *The Political Landscape: Constellations of Authority in Early Complex Polities*. University of California Press, Berkeley.

Smith, Michael E. 2007 Form and Meaning in the Earliest Cities: A New Approach to Ancient Urban Planning. *Journal of Planning History* 6(3):3–47.

Smith, Monica L. (ed.) 2003 *The Social Construction of Ancient Cities*. Smithsonian Institute Press, Washington, DC.

Steadman, Sharon R. 2009 *Archaeology of Religion: Cultures and Their Beliefs in Worldwide Context*. Left Coast Press, Walnut Creek, CA.

Stein, Burton 1977 The Segmentary State in South Indian History. In: *Essays on South India*, edited by Richard G. Fox. Duke University Press, Durham, NC.

Stoker, Valerie 2016 *Polemics and Patronage in the City of Victory: Vyasatirtha, Hindu Sectarianism, and the Sixteenth-Century Vijayanagara Court*. University of California Press, Oakland.

Subbarayalu, Y. 2012 *South India under the Cholas*. Oxford University Press, New Delhi.

Subrahmanyam, Sanjay 2017 *Jesuit Advice for a Mughal Emperor: A Seventeenth-Century Exchange of Ideas*. Talk presented at the Stanford Humanities Center, November 6, 2017.

Sundberg, Juanita 2011 Diabolic Caminos in the Desert and Cat Fights on the Rio: A Posthumanist Political Ecology of Boundary Enforcement in the United States–Mexico Borderlands. *Annals of the Association of American Geographers* 101(2): 318–336.

Talbot, Cynthia 2001 *Precolonial India in Practice: Society, Region, and Identity in Medieval Andhra*. Oxford University Press, New York.

——— 1995 Inscribing the Other, Inscribing the Self: Hindu-Muslim Identities in Pre-Colonial India. *Comparative Studies in Society and History* 37(4): 692–722.

Thapar, B. K. 1957 Maski 1954: A Chalcolithic Site of the Southern Deccan. *Ancient India* 13: 4–142.

Thomas, Michael F. 1994 *Geomorphology in the Tropics: A Study of Weathering and Denudation in Low Latitudes*. Wiley, New York.

Trautmann, Thomas 2009 *The Clash of Chronologies: Ancient India and the Modern World*. Yoda Press, New Delhi.

Wagoner, Phillip B. 1996 "Sultan Among Hindu Kings": Dress, Titles, and the Islamicization of Hindu Culture at Vijayanagara. *Journal of Asian Studies* 55:851–880.

Wirth, Louis 1938 Urbanisms as a Way of Life. *American Journal of Sociology* 44:3–24.

9

CITIES, THE UNDERWORLD, AND THE INFRASTRUCTURE

The ecology of water in the Hittite world

Ömür Harmanşah

Introduction: Cities and desire

In *Invisible Cities* , Italo Calvino poetically describes how the urban space is shaped, on the one hand, by the emotions and desires of a city's inhabitants that materialize into architectural form and, on the other hand, by the flows of cultural imagination, spatial metaphors, and storytelling:

> With cities, it is with dreams: everything imaginable can be dreamed, but even the most unexpected dream is a rebus that conceals a desire, or its reverse, a fear. Cities, like dreams, are made of desires and fears, even if the thread of their discourse is secret, their rules are absurd, their perspectives deceitful, and everything conceals something else.
>
> (Calvino 1978:44)

For Calvino, the city does not easily give away its meaning like an accidentally discovered ancient inscription of its deep history, because that history cannot be reduced to a stable archive of inscribed symbolic meanings or linguistic metaphors. Cities are assemblages that are always in a state of becoming. Letizia Modena has argued that Calvino's poetic writing as a theory of cities and civic life emerge from his intimate and deliberate engagement with academic work and critical histories of cities in the 1960s, when modern urban life was at a moment of crisis (Modena 2011: 1). The urban imagery provided in Marco Polo's stories recounted to the Mongol Emperor Kublai Khan in Calvino's *Invisible Cities* can be so powerful and accurate that architecture students around the world are often given assignments to visualize or materialize Calvino's fictional and utopian landscapes, as I was in my first year *Basic Design* studio at Middle East Technical University's School of Architecture.

The urban forms, spatial practices, and urban imaginaries, which are visualized powerfully and implied poetically in *Invisible Cities,* are vibrant and fluid in the real world, while they are continuously negotiated, and always remain unfinished. The reference to dreams and desires necessarily infers that the past, present, and future are syncopated in the daily rhythms of urban space and leave their traces within the folds of architectural spaces. This multi-temporal and materially complex grounding of the city can be characterized best through "assemblage thinking" and defined as an assemblage of traces and artifacts of human practice. This assemblage of the urban is composed of not only historical human agents but also more-than-human materialities that shape urban space, such as technologies of production, infrastructures, and the environment, each of which is itself an entity subject to historical process (Farías and Höhne 2016: 18; DeLanda 2016: 33). As an intersection point in networks of movement in regional ecologies, the city is a hybrid of cultural processes, social contexts of production and exchange, as well as more-than-human processes such as geomorphic histories (histories of deforestation, erosion, alluviation, etc., whose agents are both human and nonhuman). For this very reason, the city constitutes an assemblage of heterogenous temporalities and materialities enfolded in its nooks and crannies.

Walter Benjamin has demonstrated fast-paced vibrancy of the city in his unfinished long-term project *Passagenwerk* (*Arcades Project*), wherein cities are portrayed as *phantasmagorias*, eventful places of illusion and quick change within the framework of its deeper, more stable, structures (Heynen 1999: 100–102; Benjamin 2002). However, the affective experience of urban space always includes coming across the fragmentary remains of the past, its ruins, its debris, and its ghosts. This vibrancy of the city can then be read as a *messy, only partially governed* and *largely illegible* material world of human and nonhuman agencies involved in processes of urban placemaking (De Certeau 1984). This illegible, experimental, and affective character of urban space can be contrasted to the quantifiable and legible spaces of the planner, the sovereign, the utopian, and the divine authority, all of whom have claimed the design of cities. Affect is not divorced from its larger scale politics and the discursive structures of the public sphere.

If this is so, how do archaeologists and architectural and urban historians account for the fast pace of change in the shape and meaning of urban spaces, and the rhythm of everyday life while juxtaposing this with the longer-term utopic visions, planning gestures, and ordering desires of the political elites, that is, the so-called building programs (Vidler 2011: 16–17)? To such hybrid genealogy of urban spaces and their varied temporality, one must surely add collective senses of belonging and memory associated with urban environments, shared experiences that weave together what we call the fabric of the city, and the material flows through and between the cities and their countryside. For archaeologists who work on ancient cities of the Middle East, it is a notoriously difficult task to parse the archaeological and historical record for such complexity of evidence, since conventional histories of the ancient Near Eastern city are governed by a deep-rooted historicism that methodologically rules out or marginalizes such attempts persistently.

It is ironic that some of the most important overviews of the Near Eastern city are written by philologists and ancient historians with a heavy emphasis on the

220 Ömür Harmanşah

testimony of textual evidence (see, e.g., Postgate 1992, esp. Chapters 2 and 4; Van de Mieroop 1997; Leick 2003; Yoffee 2005). In these studies, the city takes the form of an abstract historical phenomenon and a social–bureaucratic institution rather than a concrete architectural ensemble or built environment embedded in an evolving regional landscape. Near Eastern cities are discussed as large-sized settlements that served as economic or ceremonial centers or administrative capitals at the origins of social complexity, division of labor, and trade (Postgate 1992: 73–74). However, in the accounts of the Near Eastern city, the treatment of architectural space, landscape, and technologies of construction (let alone the concepts of urban fabric, social memory, everyday practice) are either kept to a minimum or not mentioned at all. Note for example the single chapter dedicated to "urban landscape" in Marc Van de Mieroop's *Ancient Mesopotamian City* (1997). While Gwendolyn Leick's *Mesopotamia: The Invention of the City* (2003) presents chapters on several Near Eastern cities from Uruk to Babylon, the cities are presented largely as mythical, literary, and historical constructs rather than real urban landscapes. While archaeological studies of Near Eastern cities often provide a healthy counter-balance to historical narratives (e.g., Ur 2017; Stone et al. 2004), these studies remain too focused on the technologies of documenting the features of urban topography and the archaeological surface that they are often methodologically incompatible with studies of urban and architectural space in the classical world or elsewhere (compare to Favro 1999, Massey, Allen and Pile 1998).

In Near Eastern Studies, textual sources from the elite contexts are often given priority in writings on cities, whereas one would expect that a balanced understanding of the city as an architectonic reality, a material artifact, and a site of everyday experience would be possible through a balanced study of architectural technologies, histories of the built environment, and histories of regional landscapes alongside with archival evidence. It is mostly due to this prioritization of texts (which one might call the "authority of the archive") that there is a widespread and popular assignment of the authorship of public spaces solely to the stereotypical masculine agents of the Near Eastern past—the political actors, the kings, the gods, the despots. One rarely comes across any discussion on architectural knowledge, building technologies, or the social life of buildings and urban spaces in the study of the ancient Near East (for a brilliant exception, see Linzey 1995). The urban historian's challenge is then to negotiate evidence from different temporal scales, from everyday life practices to short-term building projects, from long-term change in building technologies to the slow-paced geological rhythm of the urban environment. Such temporal heterogeneity is inherent in urban life and urban time in ancient cities, evident in the calendar of ritual practices and urban festivals, or the timescales of infrastructures and the like.

It has been argued that Gilles Deleuze and Felix Guattari "insist how the city is a circulatory conduit, a flux that is always material (in all possible senses, including symbolic and discursive flows), but never fixed" (Kaika and Swyngedouw 2000: 120). To understand the materiality of urban space as an assemblage of material flows in its perpetually unfinished character is a productive way to address the vibrancy and materiality of city life discussed above. This is possible through an integration of archaeological methodology on ancient urban spaces, an eco-critical study of urban landscapes and a new materialist perspective. Leaning in this direction, in this chapter, I investigate water infrastructures in the Hittite cities of the Anatolian Bronze Age and demonstrate the theoretical possibilities that new materialism and political ecology offer to the study of ancient urban landscapes.

In the Hittite world, water is conceptualized as fluid, unbounded matter that connects different worlds and landscapes (see Erbil and Mouton 2012; Harmanşah 2015, 2018). Water was used in a variety of ritual contexts including libation, purification, and divination. First, emerging from the orifices of Anatolian karst geologies, water is believed to connect the divine Underworld and the surface of the earth through caves, sinkholes, springs, and river sources. According to Hittite and Hurrian ritual texts, this connection is maintained along the so-called "Divine Road of the Earth," which are sacred geological features such as caves, sinkholes, and ponors. Secondly, water is maintained or "territorialized" in large-scale water reservoirs in urban and rural landscapes, both creating spaces of everyday use and offering platforms of ritual action at the same time (Wittenberg and Schachner 2012; Beckman 2013). I argue that this continuous flow from the Underworld— the crowded world of chthonic deities and dead ancestors—to everyday landscapes of urban and rural environments, and the entanglement of specific sacred, secular, political, and ceremonial practices that take place around bodies of water, all together constitute an intriguing example of a heterogeneous infrastructure, an assemblage. This massive network that connects visible and invisible worlds, sites of collection and streams of flow, is articulated precisely at sites where the two realms intersect: the portals known in Hittite religion as "the Divine Road of the Earth." These extraordinary sites are places where the geological/natural and the mimetic/cultural coincide, while their formal, material, and functional differentiation is blurred.

I take the study of cities as the study of *unstable* and *unfinished* forms. Therefore the Deleuze-Guattarian nomadic notion of an assemblage (Nail 2017; Harris 2017; DeLanda 2016) as a headless confederation of human and nonhuman actors and affective bodies (Bennett 2010: 21–24) fits well with my understanding of material infrastructure, and through which I analyze and discuss Bronze Age infrastructures of water on the Anatolian plateau. This urban/rural/chthonic infrastructure, through which waters flow, contains spaces of sensorial experience and affect. I argue that these spaces take shape not only by virtue of the life-giving properties of clear spring water as holy substance, but also through the special attention given by Hittite builders to the architectonic and figural aesthetics of water monuments, which carry explicit mimetic links to Anatolian karst geologies. However, before we become immersed in the discussion of Hittite waters and watery landscapes, I aim in the next section below to locate my approach in the context of the study of cities and urban space in the ancient Near Eastern world.

222 Ömür Harmanşah

Near Eastern cities in perspective

Studies of ancient cities have been dominated by discourses of imperial projects and the will of political agents, who find support in divine interventions (Van de Mieroop 1999; Joffe 1998; Matthiae 1994; Mazzoni 1994, various contributions in Mazzoni [ed] 1994). According to these studies, cities are founded and built *ex novo* by gods or their earthly representative kings (Novák 2005; Westenholz 1998). This is a common trope one finds across the early Mesopotamian history from the way cities are portrayed in Sumerian city lamentations to the foundation of Agade by Sargon, or the multiple accounts of Assyrian emperors on their urban foundations, portrayed as political innovations and benevolent gifts to their subjects (Harmanşah 2013a: 25–28). In the deeper history of Mesopotamian urbanism, the idea of the divine foundation of cities is well-known from the epic poetry of the late third and early second millennia BCE, especially from the context of city lamentations of the early second millennium BCE (Tinney 1996). In these poems, the earliest cities of the Mesopotamian past have been founded by the "precious designs" (*giš-hur*) of divinities and supplied by their divine powers or essences (*me*). While the Sumerian concept *giš-hur* pointed to an actual drawing and a divinely ordained design, the highly complex notion of *me* was understood as an intrinsic power that both brought divine presence and order to a material entity (a city, a temple, the king's body) (Harmanşah 2013b: 380–381). This divine presence would make those bodies/artifacts to shine with iridescence, an intense visual affect that constituted its power in the material world (similar, for example, to how Byzantine icons were imagined in the eye of the believers). The "*mes*" of a city are often defined as its rituals, festivals, the functioning of its infrastructure, and the robust beauty of its walls, aspects of the city vital to its functioning and sustainability. These epic poems were sponsored by erudite Mesopotamian rulers who themselves carried out massive architectural renovations. This coalition of divine and political agencies in shaping the urban form introduced the idea of city life as civilized and controlled. The politically charged mythology of the ancient Mesopotamian city *overcodes* the actual dynamics of the production of space. This, as one might identify, is the fundamental political rhetoric of the state-sponsored epic poetry of city lamentations, and it functioned as a dominant discourse on urban space at the time.

Inspired by mythologies of kingship, ancient historians have portrayed royal cities predominantly as spectacles of the state, flourishing like mushrooms in the empty spaces of the territorial control (as they are portrayed in ancient texts), rather than as entities that emerge from historically specific processes of long-term settlement change or (geo-)histories of regional landscapes. These cities are in fact specifically portrayed as "disembedded" capitals in a universalist model developed in the 1970s and applied to many pre-modern urban societies (Joffe 1998, see discussion in Harmanşah 2013a: 4). Advocates of this model suggest that the urban foundations were "disembedded" from existing patterns of political structure and settlement hierarchy within a territorial state in order to create a new power base and reorient the political–military–bureaucratic structure of a territorial state. In

Cities, the Underworld, and infrastructure **223**

the disembedded capitals model, the founding of a city is conceptualized as a short-term historical event that is initiated through the eccentric decisions of narcissistic rulers.

In *Cities and the Shaping Memory in the Ancient Near East*, I critiqued the historicism that privilege the building of imperial capitals and their colonial claims on the takeover of a previously empty land (*terra nullius*), while I suggested that the process of urbanization in the Upper Mesopotamia in the Early Iron Age must be understood in the regional and deeper historical context of settlement ecologies and in the context of what went on in the countryside (Harmanşah 2013a). Following the collapse of the major urban centers of the Late Bronze Age at the climax of a global economic crisis in the Eastern Mediterranean world, a new process of urbanization was attested in the Upper Syro-Mesopotamian region during the Early Iron Age (ca. 1175–850 BCE). During those centuries of new political configuration, Assyrian and Syro-Hittite states shared the architectural practice of building urban centers, either as new capital cities, frontier towns, regional administrative centers, or military fortresses. While the "Land of Aššur"—that is, the core territories of the Assyrian Empire on the Middle Tigris basin—was continuously reconfigured with the building programs and shifting administrative centers at Kalhu (Nimrud), Dur-Šarrukēn (Khorsabad), and Ninua (Nineveh), Assyrian administrators also built cities such as Tušhan in the frontier zones as centers of regional control. Likewise, several Syro-Hittite cities emerge in the Iron Age landscape with a relatively new sense of public space, new types of public monuments and commemoration that explicitly claimed a Hittite–Luwian heritage, and the widespread architectural technology of carved orthostats.[1] Archaeological survey evidence strikingly demonstrates that the foundation of Assyrian and Syro-Hittite cities in the Early Iron Age corresponds with the wide scale resettlement of marginal landscapes and the foundation of new villages and hamlets (Harmanşah 2013a: 35–39). Therefore, we must see urban foundations as part of a broader settlement trend, a perspective offered to us by an archaeological understanding of landscape histories, in contrast to the historicist perspective that focuses on hubristic decision-making by the monarchs. Similarly, urban foundations were always accompanied by wider-scale transformation of landscapes, including cultivation of orchards, resettlement of displaced communities, improvement of agricultural production, construction of canals and aqueducts and opening of new quarries for large-scale building projects.

Therefore, I aim to make three main points on ancient cities of the Near East. The first point is to suggest that the making of cities is always part and parcel of larger ecologies of settlement and land use, regionally and historically specific processes of landscape change, and regimes of climate. They are not "disembedded" from the complex assemblage of settlement trends, geo-histories and climates, that is, what Faruk Tabak calls "general trends and common destinies," which involve multiple human and nonhuman actors, long-term economic conjectures, political shifts, and environmental instabilities (Tabak 2008: 10–24). Climatic and environmental fluctuations are always deeply entangled with collective interventions of human communities to the environment (cutting of forests, large-scale irrigation, extreme extraction, resource depletion, etc.), and these hybrid nature/culture processes that are recorded in the geomorphological record of landscapes also carry a heavy impact on how, when, and why cities emerge in a particular landscape.[2] This argument goes beyond Fernand Braudel and the Annales School of History's concept of the *longue durée*,[3] in which the idea of the long-term in the writing of history is usually characterized as cyclical, and the environment still remains a relatively silent backdrop (Chakrabarty 2009: 204). Contemporary debates on the global environmental crisis, climate change, and the new geological epoch known as the Anthropocene urge us, however, to think more creatively about alternative ontologies of time, other than the short-sighted scope of the political event, and to extend our understanding of the past by thinking through the lens of other temporalities such as deep time or geological time. Living in a historic moment of global climate change and the end of the Holocene, we are seeing an increasing amount of scholarly work on the agency of ecologies and climate(s) on historical processes (e.g., Degroot 2014, 2015a–b; Tabak 2008). Just as the Anthropocene debate has vehemently questioned the primacy and agency of the human species and its subordination of nature, and re-situated the human in a more democratic web of relationships with other living and nonliving entities on the planet, we must rethink the status of the city in history, not as the central focus of settlement histories but as only one actor among the many (Davies 2016: 7). This point also helps us to address the slow violence of historical accounts that has surreptitiously written out the non-elite and nonhuman agencies from histories of space and allocated the environment a passive background role. One of the critical realizations of Anthropocene thinking is the complete collapse of the conviction that the nonhuman, geological time is ahistorical or relatively unchanging or immutable.

My second point is that an effort is needed to dismantle further the constructivist concept of urban or architectural space of industrial modernity, which is often projected anachronistically to archaeological or historical contexts: the idea that space can be *designed before it was lived in*. This is a worldview that Tim Ingold has discussed as "the building perspective" (Ingold 2000: 153), overlapping with the characterization of architectural space in the modern movement (Heynen 1999). This view is in contrast to understanding space as an artifact of social relations of spatial production as Henri Lefebvre has argued (Lefebvre 1991), or the residue of what Michel de Certeau calls "spatial practices" (De Certeau 1984), or Ingold's "dwelling perspective" (Ingold 2000). Following this phenomenology of space, the act of building itself is a form of dwelling, to use the Heideggerian vocabulary. The production of space emerges out of the human processes of dwelling, or inhabiting, rather than being conceived a priori to it. An architectural analogy to this would be the relationship of a mole or a rabbit to its burrow. The burrow is an index of the act of passage, and it is a space that is performatively carved into the soil by the body of the animal in order to dwell in it. It is both a space of passage and a space of dwelling, and therefore the shape of the space is none other than the index of the body (Simonds 2012).

Cities, the Underworld, and infrastructure **225**

My third and final point concerns the affective and sensorial aspects of urban life and the question of the everyday as a creative, improvisational, and irreducibly material aspect of living in a city. This vibrancy of the city ranges from its smellscapes to its architectural textures and surfaces dampened by weathering, from the haptic experience of its public spaces to senses of urban temporality and collective remembering, and from sites of place-making to material practices that continuously transform and reconfigure those places. Although archaeologically difficult to trace, such aspects of urban living give us access to a third scale of spatial relationships that are materially and spatially grounded.

In the following sections I discuss the infrastructure of water in Hittite cities of the Anatolian Bronze Age. This case study allows me to present an alternative understanding of the production of urban space as a hybrid of geological features and architectural structures that are entangled in a mimetic relationship. Hittite water monuments, reservoirs, and dams not only allude to karst geological formations such as caves, springs, and sinkholes in their architectonic form, but they also connect seamlessly to these geological structures through the material flow of water, understood as a single network, a unique human–nonhuman assemblage, involving both mortal and immortal actors. Hittite cities as architectural programs appear as unique creations that do not simply use local topography and geology as a base and resource for its construction but, instead, urban spaces were imagined as natural extensions of existing geological structures. Political spectacles and religious practice were part and parcel of how urban water monuments were configured in the public sphere.

In the rest of this chapter, I tackle most comprehensively the second point, through an analysis of the ecologies of water as infrastructure: an unusual assemblage of hydro-geological places, urban ponds and waterworks, libation rituals, and arm-shaped vessels. I focus on the urban and rural landscapes on the Anatolian peninsula during the Late Bronze Age, when this landscape of karst uplands and lowlands was unified politically for the first time under a territorial empire (Hawkins 1996, 1998). In the sections below, I discuss the unusual associations between karst geologies and the mimetic architectonics of built monuments in urban and rural environments that provide sites of access to the Underworld, ritual practice associated with ancestors, as well as liminal sites of political significance. I consider water infrastructure as a nature/culture assemblage that brings together religious practices (in the form of water-based rituals) and political spectacles (in the form of commemorative monuments).

Ancestors, the Underworld and the infrastructure: The materiality of water in the Hittite world

Despite having written a monograph on Iron Age cities in Northern Mesopotamia and the politically charged practice of founding cities (Harmanşah 2013a), the concept of *infrastructure* remained an *uncomfortable* subject for me in the context of ancient cities. This is perhaps due to the fact that *infrastructure* is commonly understood as a technical matter related to the design of cities, an organizational *material* network, a subsurface system of invisible structures that underlies, serves, and knits together the dynamics of city life that otherwise takes place on the surface (Gandy 2011: 58). When functioning properly, infrastructures are usually invisible to us, hidden deep underground or behind walls that make them inaccessible to the sight and experience of everyday citizens (Gupta 2015: 557). Recent social scientific and humanities-based work have, however, allowed cultural and ecological criticism to engage with infrastructures, as exemplified by Akhil Gupta's intriguing question, "What can anthropology contribute to the study of electricity, and what can electricity contribute to the study of anthropology?" (Gupta 2015: 555). As Félix Guattari has written, "The contents of subjectivity have become increasingly dependent on a multitude of machinic systems" (Guattari 1992: 16), but has this not have been the case all along?

Understanding infrastructure as a technosphere, or a heterogenous confederation of bodies—fluid matter, and fossil fuels, a hybrid technical system of living and nonliving matter, and as a site of ecological politics—has been one of the most creative fields of research opened up in front of us thanks to the debates on the Anthropocene (Günel 2018). The fragmented nature of archaeological data on urban infrastructures proper (that have long been strictly deemed as functional, such as canals, reservoirs, streets and boulevards, sewage systems, city walls, or garbage dumps or the urban armatures of Roman cities) have rarely made it possible to speak about infrastructures extensively as a whole, as an intricate network rather than in fragments (see also Chapters 4 and 6).

The functionalist concept of infrastructure as an urban network of rationalization, cleansing and material disciplining of city life is a product of late nineteenth- and early twentieth-century modernity in urban planning, in the context of massive urban projects such as Baron Hausmann's transformation of Paris or the construction of Ringstrasse in Vienna. It is important to see this as part of the emergence of the modern states and their disciplining and sanitization of industrial cities. Urban historians have pointed out the political underpinnings of such surgical operations of the state, using all sorts of medical metaphors to heal and tame the diseased bodies of urban life (Gandy 1999, 2004, 2011; Vidler 2011). Projecting our learned infrastructural thinking towards antiquity requires us to be critical of techno-scientific visions of infrastructures as purely technical and functional, although we frequently suffer from such heavily modernist readings of ancient cities. This techno-scientific power discourse on infrastructure is also where the narratives of human hegemony over nature becomes embodied prominently and breeds the colonial discourse of despotic hydraulic urbanism of the Middle East. So where, then, lies infrastructure in the world of preindustrial urban life? Was it really a material network for healing and provisioning urban inhabitants, a lifeless entity, a totalitarian structural design that is imposed or a set of ad hoc solutions to everyday problems that arise from being urban?

While I attempt to distance myself from such entanglements of modernity, in this chapter I focus on Hittite cities from the Late Bronze Age Anatolian plateau,

Cities, the Underworld, and infrastructure 227

by focusing on *water* as vibrant matter, a structuring and structured element with a certain level of agency and autonomy that connected not just urban structural networks but more accurately and much more comprehensively the entire mineral world (see Chapters 2, 5, 6, and 7, this book). I will first discuss the Hittite capital Hattuša/Boğazköy, and then take the reader south to the rural frontier of Pedassa, where I have been directing an archaeological survey and landscape history project since 2010, titled Yalburt Yaylası Archaeological Landscape Research Project (Harmanşah 2018; Harmanşah, Johnson, Marsh and Durusu Tanrıöver 2017). I will argue that the water infrastructure projects of the Anatolian Late Bronze Age appropriated the vibrant ontology of water in the socio-religious imagination of Anatolian communities and their mimetic use of karst geologies, while at the same time these projects aimed at shaping and transforming urban and rural frontier landscapes through a delicate politics of water ecologies.

Archaeological work in Hittite Anatolia has shown us that earthen dams, stone-lined water reservoirs, and stone-built sacred pool monuments constituted some of the most prominent landscape features in the Hittite world during the Late Bronze Age in Central Anatolia (Figure 9.1). Such water monuments materialize in various architectural forms and building technologies and constitute prominently visible elements of urban and rural infrastructures in supplying water for drinking, irrigation, bathing, and so forth. What I will try to demonstrate, however, is that these water bodies and water structures participated in the wider mineral world

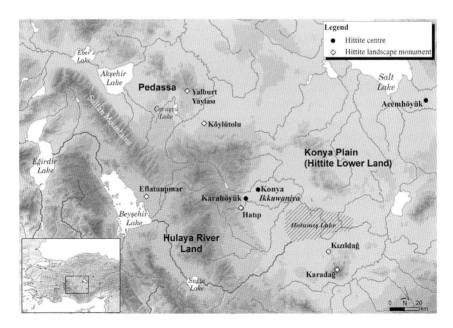

FIGURE 9.1 Map of the Anatolian peninsula during the Hittite Empire, with sites mentioned in the text (map by Ömür Harmanşah)

of the flow of water in visible and invisible domains of the earth, linking effectively the everyday to the Underworld, the mythical subterranean world where certain divinities and dead ancestors reside. Sacred pool monuments existed in an animated and mimetic relationship with karstic features of Anatolian geology and are characterized as the Divine Road of the Earth in texts from the Hittite world, identifying springs, caves and sinkholes, or the geological orifices through which water flows, as sites of interaction with the inhabitants of the Underworld.

I argue in the end that the Hittite bodies of water and water monuments can be understood as *infrastructures* that functioned as an intricate network of natural geologies and man-made mimetic monuments—and that this infrastructure makes sense as an "assemblage" with agency to use Jane Bennett's vital materialist term, a living, throbbing confederation of water bodies with material complexity and agency, both divine in nature and built as infrastructure all at the same time. I also speak about a certain *geopolitics* of water, where *geo* stands for geology not geography, where Hittite kings, gods of the Underworld, holy springs, rivers and mountains, dead ancestors, architectonics of water reservoirs, dams, canals, and pools, arm-shaped libation vessels all take part as agents in this confederacy.

Water from the ponds of Hattuša to the monuments at the borderlands

Water infrastructure in Hittite cities has recently been the subject matter of archaeological research in the capital cities of the empire (Hüser 1996, 2007; Seeher 2006, 2010; Schachner and Wittenberg 2012; Wittenberg and Schachner 2012) and in Hittite rural landscapes (Emre 1993; Harmanşah, Johnson, Marsh and Durusu Tanrıöver 2017), while the studies of water in Hittite religion and literature are also expanding (Erbil and Mouton 2012; Mouton 2018). Among the Near Eastern polities of the Bronze Age, the Hittites are unique in their investment of labor both for agricultural, practical, and cultic uses of water in both urban and rural contexts. The political ecology of water in Hittite Anatolia, especially in the context of its karst upland geologies, is characterized by such powerful hybridization of religious and practical infrastructures. At Boğazköy, the capital city of the Hittite Empire known as Hattuša, the German archaeological team discovered over the last few decades a complex network of hydrological installations (ponds, dams, and wells) that had woven the city with an infrastructure of water in connection with numerous water sources across the site (Schachner 2017: 36; Seeher 2010).

Notable among these are the so-called Eastern Ponds (*Ostteiche*) and two stone-built structures associated with them. The stone chambers were excavated during the 1988 field season by the German team in the area known as the *Südburg* or "Southern Citadel," the site of an Iron Age fortress, (Neve 1993: 67–80; Hawkins 1995; Seeher 2006) (Figure 9.2). The discovery and eventual reconstruction of the two vaulted chambers provoked major excitement among the archaeologists and historians of Hittite Anatolia and philologists of the Luwian language. The vaulted structures were built with finely dressed megalithic stone masonry with the Hittite

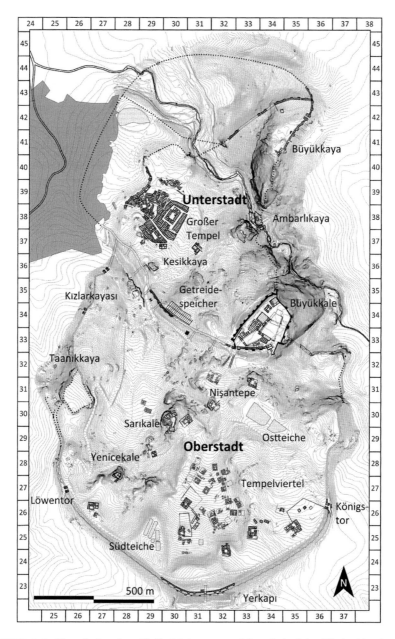

FIGURE 9.2 Hattuša (modern Boğazköy), ceremonial capital of the Hittite Empire. Plan of the excavated remains (Courtesy of German Archaeological Institute, Istanbul. Archive of the Bogazköy Expedition, Deutsches Archäologisches Institut. Graphic execution: D. Krüger)

FIGURE 9.3 Hattuša (Boğazköy), Chamber 2 at Südburg Sacred Pool Complex with hieroglyphic Luwian inscription (photo by Ömür Harmanşah)

masonry technique of fitting such blocks with smoothed curved edges. Chamber 1 to the southwest was undecorated and uninscribed, and therefore functionally made little sense to the archaeologists, while Chamber 2 to the northeast featured a lengthy hieroglyphic Luwian inscription carved on the walls of one of the chambers (Figure 9.3). This inscription commemorates the deeds of Šuppiluliuma II, one of the last kings of the empire at the end of the thirteenth century BCE.

Investigating the broader archaeological context of the two vaulted chambers, the German team realized that the stone-built chambers were in fact built *into* or more accurately *under* the northwestern corners of two extensive water reservoirs,

FIGURE 9.4 Hattuša (modern Boğazköy), Südburg Sacred Pool Complex, reconstruction sketch by Peter Neve (Courtesy of German Archaeological Institute, Istanbul. Archive of the Bogazköy Expedition, Deutsches Archäologisches Institut)

now known as the Eastern Ponds (Seeher 2006) (Figure 9.4). The Eastern Ponds are large reservoirs cut into the impervious soil on the edge of a mountain slope and lined with sloping stone wall like a glacis built in limestone and plastered with a watertight clay in the bottom. Earthen dams covered with stone surfaces separated

232 Ömür Harmanşah

and delimited the two ponds. The interpretation of the ponds by the German arch-aeological team swings back and forth between the cultic/ritual function to the purely functional. According to a recent paper by Wittenberg and Schachner (2012) and based on geomorphological fieldwork, the reservoirs were found to have been filled by the perennial inflow of rising groundwater and springs that were abundant across the urban site, rather than being supplied by any kind of piped water from outside the city. The architectural relationship of the two stone-built chambers to the Eastern Ponds have not been clarified by Wittenberg and Schachner, except for their suggestion that they may have been "used as outlets (sluices)" (Wittenberg and Schachner 2012: 317). I will return to this interpretation below to argue instead that these chambers function as portals into the Underworld, as testified by the hieroglyphic Luwian inscription of Chamber 2.

According to the full edition of the Südburg inscription by David Hawkins (1995), the inscription of Chamber 2 commemorates the king's military successes and foundation of new cities in the western and southwestern frontiers of the Hittite Empire. Hittite kings of the thirteenth century BCE concentrated much of their efforts in political diplomacy and military campaigns towards those frontiers, conquering lands, founding cities, and signing border treaties with neighboring vassal states. The inscription is accompanied by two relief images of ceremonially garbed male individuals that contextualize and literally bracket the inscription in the space of the stone chamber. The roughly finished smaller image that has been restored successfully by the archaeologists to the entrance of the Chamber, depicts a deified king image (Harmanşah 2015: Figure 4.2). Based on the ambiguous inscrip-tion accompanying the image "Suppiluliuma, Great King," Hawkins (1995: 19) has put forth the idea that the image "represents the ancestor Suppiluliuma I, acting as the protecting deity of the monument." The second relief image is carved on the wall at the far end of the chamber that seals the chamber up against the earth, and depicts a male deity, perhaps the Sun God of the Water, which is a god of the Underworld (Erbil and Mouton 2012: 55, note 9; see Harmanşah 2015: Figure 4.2). Wearing a solemn ceremonial garb, this deity holds a curved staff and is topped with a double-winged sun. Excavators discovered an unusual rectangular hole fea-ture at the base of the image of the deity on the floor of the chamber, although the function of this hole has not been determined.

The Luwian inscription of Chamber 2 ends with the following phrase in line 18: "Here a Divine Road of the Earth in that year (I) constructed." I will not go into the philological details here, but David Hawkins associated the signs DEUS. VIA+TERRA with the well-known cuneiform expression DINGIR.KAŠKAL. KUR of the Hittite and Hurrian texts, usually translated as "The Divine Road of the Earth" (Hawkins 1995: 44). As I have discussed elsewhere, the Divine Road of the Earth in Hittite and Hurrian texts refers to the geological orifices through which water flows: karst features of springs, natural tunnels, river gorges, caves, or sinkholes, linking the circulation of water above and below the earth (Harmanşah 2015: 64–65). In Hittite religion and mythology, the Divine Road therefore represents a conduit through which communication with the ancestors could be established. Through these portals, Hittite divinities appeared and disappeared in the Underworld. Furthermore, one finds the Divine Road of the Earth in the descriptions of frontiers in Hittite treaties, understood as ritually significant places. and they were also listed among divine witnesses to inter-polity treaties, and frequently portrayed as recipients of cultic libations.

This is actually the first time the term "Divine Road of the Earth" has been associated with a specific monument that referred to itself as such. Given the broader rich literary background of the term in Near Eastern texts, and considering the cave-like architectural form of the two stone-built chambers, it is tempting to argue that the Südburg structures are mimetic in nature and were literally conceptualized as built artificial tunnels that were designed to access the Underworld. The architectonics of the Divine Road structures such as this sacred pool complex offers a mimetic link to geological features such as caved springs and establishes a semantic relationship to the ritual significance of karstic springs, river tunnels, and sinkholes as cult places. A similar stone chamber is known from the site of Gavurkalesi, Southwest of Ankara, and was similarly interpreted as a monument to dead ancestors and "a deified entrance to the underworld" (Sørensen and Lumsden 2016: 68; Lumsden 2002).

In 2000, this time Jürgen Seeher and his team made another exciting discovery for the water infrastructure of Hattuša, and this discovery further perplexed all thinkers of Hattusha's urban space and its functionality (Seeher 2002: 59–78). This time, on the on the southwestern edge of the Upper city, the team excavated a separate group of five water reservoirs, now known as the Southern Ponds (Figure 9.5). Rectangular in shape, these oblong reservoirs are grouped together at a topographic edge, have semicircular ends, and are rather deep compared to the Eastern Ponds, reaching down to 7 to 8 meters. The construction of these deep reservoirs, all seem to date to sometime early in the fifteenth century BCE. Schachner and Wittenberg (2012) based on their year-round groundwater measurements and close monitoring at the ponds, have very recently and convincingly shown that the ponds must have been filled not by piped water, but through the perennial seepage from the underlying aquifer, and the surfacing of rising groundwaters during the winter and spring months, sufficient for consumption in the summer.

In the southern ponds, Jürgen Seeher's excavations revealed an impressive deposit of a very distinctive assemblage of vessels, found by the small dam that separated Ponds 1 and 5. The excavator himself associates this deposit with the rising fill in the bottom of the ponds and the end of their life cycle. However, when one studies the deposit closely, the unusual assemblage can be intimately linked to the meaning and function of water reservoirs. The assemblage contained mainly two kinds of very specialized vessels: fragments of about 90 spindle bottles and a large corpus of 190 arm-shaped libation vessels, a.k.a "libation arms" (Schoop 2009) (Figure 9.6). Ulf Schoop, who has studied the pottery in detail, dates this assemblage to a single dumping event around 1400 BCE based on C-14 dating. The libation arms and spindle bottles are representatives of the so-called "Red Lustrous Wheelmade Ware," a technology known largely from Eastern Mediterranean contexts, and the

FIGURE 9.5 Hattuša (Boğazköy) Southern ponds, computer reconstruction. Courtesy of German Archaeological Institute, Istanbul (Archive of the Bogazköy Expedition, Deutsches Archäologisches Institut)

FIGURE 9.6 Arm-shaped terracotta libation vessels from Hattusha's Southern Ponds. a.k.a. "libation arms" commonly identified with ^{GIŠ}ŠU.NAG.NAG=*kattakurant*— of Hittite texts (Archive of the Bogazköy Expedition, Deutsches Archäologisches Institut)

Neutron Activation Analysis strongly suggests that these vessels were imports from Northern Cyprus. The "arm-shaped vessels" of the archaeological record has been identified with GIŠ.ŠU.NAG.NAG or *kattakurant*—of Hittite ritual texts, a cut off or amputated arm-shaped vessel that is extensively used for libations of wine and other sacred liquid offerings to gods at sacred sites, such as *huwaši* stones or sacred pools (Heffron 2014: 168 n.22). Yağmur Heffron (2014) associates both zoomorphic vessels in the shape of various animals and such libation arms, which we might call anthropomorphic or perhaps more accurately prosthetic, with the performative cultic practice of "to drink a god"—suggesting a direct ingestion of divine substance through the hollow bodies of animated vessels.

In sum, in addition to this emergent and vital material connection to ritual practice, we can also consider the obvious fact that the Eastern Ponds and the Southern Ponds at Hattuša are actually spatially and topographically bracketing a vast built landscape of temple structures in Hattuša's spectacular Upper City. The South Ponds dominate the great plateau of clustered temple structures, while the East Ponds linked to a series of ritually significant rock outcrops such as Nişantaş. We would therefore need to understand that the water reservoirs must have been linked to ceremonial functions in one way or another. A similar kind of urban bracketing and spatial configuration is known from the impressive organization of a series of dams and reservoirs around the rationally planned city of Sarissa, modern Kuşaklı, founded in the late sixteenth century BCE, roughly contemporary with the southern ponds in Hattuša (Figure 9.7). By virtue of its rapidly planned layout, Kuşaklı possesses more of a sense of infrastructural appearance to our modernist eyes. Several water reservoirs and dams were planned in close relationship with each of the gates into the citadel (Müller Karpe 2015). However, judging from its prominent sacred spring sanctuary overlooking the city with its sacred pond, the Šuppitaššu sanctuary excavated by Tuba Ökse (1999), allows us to be skeptical of any positivist, functionalist understanding of water as a neutral natural substance, serving the needs of the city and its gardens.

The first part of my argument concerning water in the Hittite world, then, is the seamless coordination and earnest collaboration between what we moderns consider as the mineral substance of water and the geological landscape elements through which it flows. The latter includes the aquifers and rivers, on the one hand (the "natural" category), and the architectonic water structures built in urban and rural contexts (the "man-made" category), on the other. The architectonic structures include water reservoirs, earthen dams, stone pools, and man-made caves and grottoes, which establish an explicit mimetic relationship with the karst geological features of the Anatolian plateau and suggest a complete disrespect of the Hittites to our beloved Cartesian distinctions of nature and culture. They also suggest that what is geological and what is architectonic essentially function as an assemblage, or a hybrid collective with a relational ontology (see also Chapters 3, 5, 6).

The second part of the argument concerns the geopolitically distinctive conduits, or breaking points where the Underworld and the human world come together: That is the sites known as the Divine Road of the Earth, where Hittite imperial political

236 Ömür Harmanşah

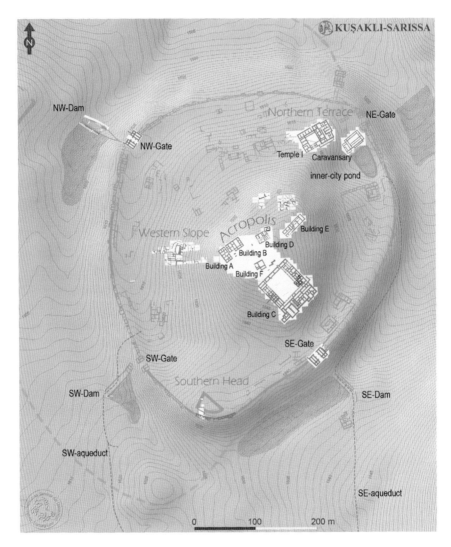

FIGURE 9.7 Sarissa, modern Kuşaklı. City plan with dams and water reservoirs (Courtesy of Andreas Müller Karpe and the Kuşaklı Project, Philipps-Universität Marburg)

statements are inserted. In Chamber 2 of the Südburg Sacred Pool Complex, we find the king Šuppiluliuma II's ambitious commemorative inscription, appropriating the powers of a particularly vital node in that assemblage. The best comparable example to Südburg in this matter comes from the site of Yalburt Yaylası, a Hittite Empire period sacred pool monument built on top of an abundant mountain spring northwest of the modern city of Konya (Figure 9.8), where I have been directing a regional survey project since 2010 (Harmanşah 2018). The monument sits in the middle of an impressive (albeit eroded) landscape filled with deep sinkholes, karst

Cities, the Underworld, and infrastructure   **237**

FIGURE 9.8 Yalburt Yaylası Mountain Spring monument: The Hieroglyphic Luwian inscription of Tudhaliya IV (1237–1209 BCE) (© Yalburt Yaylası Archaeological Landscape Research Project, Courtesy Ö. Harmanşah)

depressions, and abundant springs. It was discovered during the excavations for a rural infrastructure project in Fall 1970, when the local government was excavating the spring to distribute its waters to the nearby villages through underground piping. It was subsequently excavated by the Ankara Museum of Anatolian Civilizations and reconstructed based on its lengthy hieroglyphic Luwian inscription of the Hittite great king Tudhaliya IV (1237–1209 BCE) (Johnson and Harmanşah 2015). In his inscription, Tudhaliya IV commemorates his violent military campaigns to the southwest of the Anatolian peninsula, the Lukka lands and Wiyanawanda. Here, again, we find the striking juxtaposition of what was most likely considered as the Divine Road of the Earth, a sacred spring, a water reservoir built for the benefit of nearby fields and a Hittite settlement as well as an imperial commemorative monument, appropriating and colonizing what is considered the seamlessly connected confederation of the mineral world of water flows.

In a pioneering study of the Divine Road phenomenon in the Hittite texts, Edmund Gordon (1967) has demonstrated that the Divine Road of the Earth is an ambiguous thing: appearing as both a karstic geological feature of a watery orifice and as a built structure that mimetically relates to such a feature, a specific deity, and a politically charged site that delineated imperial borderlands and served in certain cases as places to sign inter-polity treaties. From here, then, we might speak of the great assemblage of water bodies in the Hittite world is also a political ecology of flows, movements and borderlands. The Anatolian Bronze Age water infrastructures

238   Ömür Harmanşah

operate on many levels of the hybridization of the political and the everyday, the divine and the human, the sacred and profane, the natural and cultural, to the point that these binary distinctions completely lose their meanings.

Conclusions: Water as assemblage

Jane Bennett (2010:23–24) describes assemblages as "living, throbbing confederations that are able to function despite the persistent presence of energies that confound them within." Unlike networks, they have "uneven topographies" that are formed by a heterogeneity of bodies and affects that cross paths. But perhaps most significantly they are headless confederations, not governed by any particular agent since none of the actants with their material bodies are powerful enough to govern the trajectory of the group. Bennett famously discussed the well-known North American blackout event on August 14, 2003, when the massive electric grid composed of a volatile mix of a heterogeneity of actants collapsed. She describes the grid as a volatile mix of actants: coal, sweat, electromagnetic fields, computer programs, electron streams, profit motives, heat, lifestyles, nuclear fuel, plastic, fantasies of mastery, static, legislation, water, economic theory wire and wood—collapsed as a result of a cascade of events, for reasons still quite unknown.

If infrastructures constitute modern urban life as interconnected, hybrid, and disenchanted, networky systems of material flow in the industrial metropolis, whether it is electricity, water, sewage, or speedy cars that are contained within the city limits, *water in Hittite cities*, I argue, was by definition the opposite: In its reservoirs, sacred grottoes, and stone-built pools, or the animated, embodied libation vessels, water appeared as a substance that connected the urban landscape to the wider geological and mythical (or we could say mytho-geological) worlds that are both visible and invisible, emergent and disappearing, all the time. The powerful vitality of this assemblage or collective, was then appropriated or colonized by the imperial power discourse at the critical nodes that brought that vitality into contact with the world of everyday life. The Hittite state's explicit engagement with what we might call hydro-social life, both in its ritual as well as agricultural and economic aspects, can be understood as a biopolitics of water. The vital materialist perspective, therefore, supported by material-culture studies, new materialism, agency, and actor-network theory open for us to consider ancient infrastructures as alternative, radically different ontologies.

What can the discussion of the infrastructure of water in Hittite cities contribute to debates on ancient cities, religion, and new materialism? In the Hittite ontology of the world, the distinction between the geological structures and built structures and monuments of water does not seem to be clear (at least according to the linguistic and archaeological evidence), as clearly exemplified by the divine portals into the netherworld. The nature/culture distinction that is so vehemently upheld by scholars is not just unhelpful and inaccurate in this case, but also irrelevant. The mimetic water monuments, however, were not considered simply formal imitations of caves, sinkholes, or ponds; they were not *identical* to the geological structures. Adopting both the material, the spatial, and the temporal properties of geological structures, these monuments were charged with religious potency, slow temporality, robust material agency, and vital animacy of karst geologies. Building on such cultural/material significance, water monuments are also incorporated into the political discourse of the empire through the inscription of imperial narratives on their walls, their well selected location in borderland landscapes and core urban centers, and the visually powerful display of imperial architectural technologies. This seamless blending of politics and religion in the infrastructure of water in Hittite cities and borderland landscapes speaks to the seamless continuity between the geological and urban infrastructures, where water acted as the connecting fluvial element with its special materiality (similar in a way to Akhil Gupta's characterization of the materiality of electricity), fluid, magical and mediated (Gupta 2015). The flat ontology of Deleuze–Guattarian assemblages is helpful in understanding the vast infrastructure networked by the flow and presence of water.

Notes

1 On the historical intersection of orthostat programs as an architectural technology and the foundation of cities in the Early Iron Age among the Syro-Hittite cities, see Mazzoni (1995a, 1995b, 1997, 2002) and Harmanşah (2007). On the specific case of Carchemish/Karkamish, see Denel (2007) and Gilibert (2011).
2 Specifically for Near Eastern settlement histories, see Wilkinson (2003), Wilkinson (2010), Izdebski et al. (2016). On the relationship between historical change and climate, see Degroot (2014, 2015a, 2015b).
3 Braudel (1972). See discussion in Shaw (2001) and Horden and Purcell (2000), Manning (1998), Hexter (1972).s

References

Beckman, Gary 2013 Intrinsic and constructed space in Hittite Anatolia. In *Heaven on Earth: Temples, Ritual, and Cosmic Symbolism in the Ancient World,* edited by Deena Ragavan, pp. 153–173. Oriental Institute Seminars 9. The Oriental Institute of the University of Chicago, Chicago.

Benjamin, Walter 2002 *The Arcades Project.* Translated by Howard Eiland and Kevin McLaughlin. Harvard University Press, Cambridge, MA.

Bennett, Jane 2010 *Vibrant Matter: A Political Ecology of Things.* Duke University Press, Durham, NC.

Braudel, Fernand 1972 *The Mediterranean and the Mediterranean World in the Age of Philip II.* Harper and Row: New York. Translation of La Méditerranée et le monde Méditerranéen à l'Époque de Philippe II. Librairie Armand Colin: Paris, 1966.

Calvino, Italo 1978 *Invisible Cities.* Translated by William Weaver of *Le città invisibili* (Guilio Einaudi Editore 1972). Harcourt, San Diego.

Chakrabarty, Dipesh 2009 The Climate of History: Four Theses. *Critical Inquiry* 35(2): 197–222.

Davies, Jeremy 2016 *The Birth of the Anthropocene.* University of California Press, Oakland.

De Certeau, Michel 1984 *The Practice of Everyday Life.* Translated by S. Rendall [of Arts de faire]. University of California Press, Berkeley.

Denel, Elif 2007 Ceremony and Kingship at Carchemish. In *Ancient Near Eastern Art in Context: Studies in Honor of Irene J. Winter by Her Students*, edited by Jack Cheng and Marian H. Feldman, pp. 179–204. Brill Publishers, Leiden.

Degroot, Dagomar 2014 'Never Such Weather Known in these Seas': Climatic Fluctuations and the Anglo-Dutch Wars of the Seventeenth Century, 1652–1674. *Environment and History* 20(2): 239–273.

——— 2015a Exploring the North in a Changing Climate: The Little Ice Age and the Journals of Henry Hudson, 1607–1611. *Journal of Northern Studies* 9: 69–91.

——— 2015b Testing the Limits of Climate History: The Quest for a Northeast Passage During the Little Ice Age, 1594–1597. *Journal of Interdisciplinary History* 45:4 (Spring): 459–484.

DeLanda, Manuel 2016 *Assemblage Theory*. Edinburgh University Press, Edinburgh.

Emre, Kutlu 1993 The Hittite Dam of Karakuyu. In Essays on Anatolian Archaeology, edited by Takahito Mikasa, pp. 1–42. Harrassowitz Verlag, Wiesbaden.

Erbil, Yiğit, and Alice Mouton 2012 Water in Ancient Anatolian Religions: An Archaeological and Philological Inquiry on the Hittite Evidence. *Journal of Near Eastern Studies* 71(1): 53–74.

Farías, Ignacio, and Stefan Höhne 2016 Humans as Vectors and Intensities: Becoming Urban in Berlin and New York City. In *Deleuze and the City,* edited by Hélène Frichot, Catharina Gabrilesson and Jonathan Metzger, pp. 17–32. Edinburgh University Press, Edinburgh.

Favro, Diane 1999 Meaning and Experience: Urban History from Antiquity to the Early Modern Period. *Journal of the Society of Architectural Historians* 58(3): 364–373.

Gandy, Matthew 1999 The Paris Sewers and the Rationalization of Urban Space. *Transactions of the Institute of British Geographers New Series* 24: 23–44.

——— 2004 Rethinking Urban Metabolism: Water, Space and the Modern City. *City* 8(3): 363–379.

——— 2011 Landscape and Infrastructure in the Late Modern Metropolis. In *The New Blackwell Companion to the City*, edited by Gary Bridge and Sophie Watson, pp. 57–65. Wiley-Blackwell, New York.

Ghosh, Amitav 2016 *The Great Derangement: Climate Change and the Unthinkable*. The University of Chicago Press, Chicago.

Gilibert, Alessandra 2011 *Syro-Hittite Monumental Art and the Archaeology of Performance: Stone Reliefs at Carchemish and Zincirli in the Earlier First Millennium BCE*. Walter de Gruyter, Berlin.

Gordon, Edmund I. 1967 The Meaning of the Ideogram d KASKAL.KUR = 'Underground Water-Course' and Its Significance for Bronze Age Historical Geography. *Journal of Cuneiform Studies* 21: 70–88.

Guattari, Félix 1992 Regimes, Pathways, Subjects. In *Incorporations*, edited by Jonathan Crary and Sanford Kwinter, pp. 16–37. Zone Books, New York.

Günel, Gökçe 2018 Review Essay: New Perspectives on Energy. *PoLAR: Political and Legal Anthropology Review.* https://polarjournal.org/2018/05/14/review-essay-new-perspectives-on-energy/ (Accessed May 25, 2018).

Gupta, Akhil 2015 An Anthropology of Electricity from the Global South. *Cultural Anthropology* 30(4): 555–568.

Hamilton, Clive, Christophe Bonneuil and François Gemenne (eds) 2015a *The Anthropocene and the Global Environmental Crisis: Rethinking Modernity in a New Epoch*. Routledge, London and New York.

Hamilton, Clive, Christophe Bonneuil and François Gemenne 2015b Thinking the Anthropocene. In *The Anthropocene and the Global Environmental Crisis: Rethinking*

Modernity in a New Epoch, edited by C. Hamilton, C. Bonneuil and F. Gemenne, pp. 1–13. Routledge, London and New York.

Harmanşah, Ömür 2007 Upright Stones and Building Narratives: Formation of a Shared Architectural Practice in the Ancient Near East. In *Ancient Near Eastern Art in Context: Studies in Honor of Irene J. Winter by Her Students*, edited by Jack Cheng and Marian H. Feldman, pp. 69–99. Brill Publishers, Leiden.

——— 2013a *Cities and the Shaping of Memory in the Ancient Near East*. Cambridge University Press, Cambridge.

——— 2013b The Cattlepen and the Sheepfold: Cities, Temples, and Pastoral Power in Ancient Mesopotamia. In *Heaven on Earth: Temples, Ritual, and Cosmic Symbolism in the Ancient World*, edited by Deena Ragavan. pp. 371–392. Oriental Institute Seminars 9. The Oriental Institute of the University of Chicago, Chicago.

——— 2015 *Place, Memory, and Healing: An Archaeology of Anatolian Rock Monuments*. Routledge, London.

——— 2018 Geologies of Belonging: The Political Ecology of Water in Central Anatolia. In *Water and Power in Past Societies*, edited by Emily Holt, pp. 259–277. Suny Series, The Institute for European and Mediterranean Archaeology Distinguished Monograph. State University of New York Press, Buffalo, NY.

Harmanşah, Ömür, Peri Johnson, Ben Marsh and Müge Durusu-Tanrıöver 2017 Lake-Places, Local Hydrology and the Hittite Imperial Projects in the Ilgın Plain: Yalburt Yaylası Archaeological Landscape Research Project 2015–2016 Seasons. In *The Archaeology of Anatolia: Recent Discoveries (2015–2016) vol.* II, edited by S. R. Steadman and G. McMahon, pp. 302–320. Cambridge Scholars Press, Newcastle upon Tyne.

Harris, Oliver J. T. 2017 Assemblages and Scale in Archaeology. *Cambridge Archaeological Journal* 27(1): 127–139.

Hawkins, J. David 1995 *The Hieroglyphic Inscription of the Sacred Pool Complex at Hattusa (SÜDBURG)*. Studien zu den Boğazköy-Texten Beiheft 3. Harrassowitz, Wiesbaden.

——— 1996 The Hittites and Their Empire. In *Royal Cities of the Biblical World*, edited by Joan G. Westenholz, pp. 69–79. Bible Lands Museum, Jerusalem.

——— 1998 Hattusa: Home to the Thousand Gods of Hatti. In *Capital Cities: Urban Planning and Spiritual Dimensions*, edited by J. G. Westenholz, pp. 65–81. Bible Lands Museum, Jerusalem.

Heffron, Yağmur 2014 The Material Culture of Hittite 'God-drinking.' *Journal of Ancient Near Eastern Religions* (14)2: 164–185.

Heynen, Hilde 1999 *Architecture and Modernity: A Critique*. MIT Press, Cambridge, MA.

Hexter, J. H. 1972 Fernand Braudel and the *Monde Braudellien. Journal of Modern History* 44: 480–539.

Horden, Peregrine, and Nicholas Purcell 2000 *The Corrupting Sea: A Study of the Mediterranean History*. Blackwell, Oxford.

Hüser, Andreas 1996 Wasser für Sarissa. *Antike Welt* 5: 93–97.

——— 2007 *Hethistiche Anlagen zur Wasserversorgung und Entsorgung*. Kuşaklı Sarissa Band 3. Verlag Marie Leidorf, Rahden/Westf.

Ingold, Timothy 1993 The Temporality of Landscape. *World Archaeology* 25(2): 152–174.

——— 2000 *The Perception of the Environment: Essays in Livelihood, Dwelling and Skill*. Routledge, London.

Izdebski, Adam, Jordan Pickett, Neil Roberts and Tomas Waliszewski 2016 The Environmental, Archaeological and Historical Evidence for Regional Climatic Changes and their Societal Impacts in the Eastern Mediterranean in Late Antiquity. *Quaternary Science Reviews* 136 (March): 189–208.

Joffe, Alexander H. 1998 Disembedded Capitals in Western Asian Perspective. *Comparative Studies in Society and History* 40: 549–580.

Johnson, Peri, and Ömür Harmanşah 2015 Landscape, Politics, and Water in the Hittite Borderlands: Yalburt Yaylası Archaeological Landscape Research Project 2010–2014. In *The Archaeology of Anatolia: Recent Discoveries (2013–2014)*, edited by Sharon Steadman and Gregory McMahon, pp. 255–277. Cambridge Scholars Press, Cambridge.

Kaika, Maria, and Erik Swyngedouw 2000 Fetishizing the Modern City: The Phantasmagoria of Urban Technological Networks. *International Journal of Urban and Regional Research* 24(1): 120–138.

Latour, Bruno 2018 *Facing Gaia. Eight Lectures on the New Climatic Regime*. Wiley, Cambridge and Medford.

Lefebvre, Henri 1991 *The Production of Space*, translated by D. Nicholson-Smith. Blackwell, Oxford.

Leick, Gwendolyn 2003 *Mesopotamia: The Invention of the City*. Penguin Books, NY.

Linzey, M. P. T. 1995 The Duplicity of Imhotep Stone. *Journal of Architectural Education* 48 (4): 260–267

Lumsden, Stephen 2002. Gavurkalesi: Investigations at a Hittite Sacred Place. In *Recent Developments in Hittite Archaeology and History,* edited by K. Aslıhan Yener, Harry A. Hoffner and Simrit Dhesi, pp. 111–125. Eisenbrauns, Winona Lake, IN.

Manning, Stuart W. 1998 From Process to People: Longue Durée to History. In *The Aegean and the Orient in the Second Millennium. Proceedings of the 50th Anniversary Symposium Cincinnati, 18–20 April 1997*, edited by Eric H. Cline and Diane Harris-Cline, pp. 311–325, Université de Liège, Histoire de l'art et archéologie de la Grèce antique, University of Texas at Austin Program in Aegean Scripts and Prehistory. Aegaeum 18: Annales d'archéologie égéenne de l'Université de Liège et UT-PASP. Liège.

Massey, Doreen, John Allen and Steve Pile 1998 *City Worlds*. Routledge, Hoboken, NJ.

Matthiae, Paolo 1994 Da Nimrud à Khorsabad: storia di un modello tra progetto e realizzazione. In *Nuove fondazioni nel Vicino Oriente antico: realta e ideologia*. Atti del colloquio 4–6 dicembre 1991; Dipartimento di Scienze Storiche del Mondo Antico, edited by Stefania Mazzoni, pp. 29–45. Sezione di Egittologia e Scienze Storiche del Vicino Oriente; Università degli studi di Pisa. Giardini, Pisa.

Mazzoni, Stefania 1994 Aramaean and Luwian New Foundations. In *Nuove fondazioni nel Vicino Oriente antico: realta e ideologia*. Atti del colloquio 4–6 dicembre 1991; Dipartimento di Scienze Storiche del Mondo Antico, edited by Stefania Mazzoni, pp. 319–339. Sezione di Egittologia e Scienze Storiche del Vicino Oriente; Università degli studi di Pisa. Giardini, Pisa.

——— 1995a Aramaean Period in Syria: Continuity and Development. In *Proceedings of the Symposium on Syria and the Ancient Near East 3000–300 B.C.*, edited by F. Ismail, pp. 125–141, Aleppo.

——— 1995b Settlement Pattern and New Urbanization in Syria at the Time of the Assyrian Conquest. In *Neo-Assyrian Geography*, edited by Mario Liverani, pp. 181–192. Università di Roma "La Sapienza," Dipartimento di Scienze storiche, archeologiche e anthropologiche dell'Antichità, Quaderni di Geografia Storica 5: Sargon srl, Roma.

——— 1997 The Gate and the City: Change and Continuity in Syro-Hittite Urban Ideology. In Die orientalische Stadt: Kontinuität, Wandel, Bruch, edited by G. Wilhelm, pp. 307–338. Saarbrücker Druckerei und Verlag, Saarbrücken.

——— 2000 Crisis and Change: The Beginning of the Iron age in Syria. In *Proceedings of the First International Congress on the Archaeology of the Ancient Near East*, edited by Paolo Matthiae, Alessandra Enea, Luca Peyronel and Frances Pinnock, pp. 1045–1058. Università degli studi di Roma "La Sapienza," Dipartimento di Scienze Storiche, Archeologiche e Anthropologiche dell'Antichità, Roma.

———— 2002. "Temples in the City and the Countryside: New Trends in Iron age Syria," *Damaszener Mitteilungen* 13: 89–99.

Mazzoni, Stefania (ed.) 1994 *Nuove fondazioni nel Vicino Oriente antico: realta e ideologia*. Giardini, Pisa.

Modena, Letizia 2011 *Italo Calvino's Architecture of Lightness: The Utopian Imagination in An Age of Urban Crisis*. Routledge, London and New York.

Mouton, Alice 2018 Water and the Gods: Ponds and Fountains in the Hittite State Cult According to Hittite Textual Evidence. *Ash-sharq Bulletin of the Ancient Near East Archaeological, Historical and Societal Studies* 2(1): 112–120.

Müller Karpe, Andreas 2015 Planning Sacred Landscape. In *Sacred Landscapes of Hittites and Luwians. Proceedings of the International Conference in Honour of Franca Pecchioli Daddi Florence, February 6th-8th 2014*, edited by Anacleto D'Agostino, Valentina Orsi and Giulia Torri, pp. 83–92. Firenze University Press, Firenze.

Nail, Thomas 2017 What Is Assemblage. *SubStance* 46.1 (Issue 142): 21–37.

Neve, Peter 1993 *Hattusa—Stadt der Götter unde Tempel: Neue Ausgrabungen in der Hauptstadt der Hethiter*. Mainz Am Rhein.

Novák, Mirko 2005 From Ashur to Nineveh: The Assyrian Town-planning Programme. In *Nineveh: Papers of the XLIXe Rencontre Assyriologique Internationale London, 7–11 July 2003*, volume 1, edited by Dominique Collon and Andrew George, pp. 177–186. British School of Archaelogy in Iraq, London.

Ökse, Tuba 1999 Grabungen am Quellteich Šuppitaššu. *Mitteilungen der Deutschen Orientgesellschaft* 131: 86–93.

Postgate, Nicholas 1992 *Early Mesopotamia: Society and Economy at the Dawn of History*. Routledge, London.

Purdy, Jedediah 2015 *After Nature: A Politics for the Anthropocene*. Harvard University Press, Cambridge, MA.

Ruddiman, William F. 2003 The Anthropogenic Greenhouse Era Began Thousands of Years Ago. *Climate Change* 61: 262–293.

Schachner, Andreas 2017 The Historical Development of the Urban Geography of Hattuša, the Hittite Capital City, and Beyond. In *Places and Spaces in Hittite Anatolia I: Hatti and the East*, edited by Metin Alparslan, pp. 29–51. Turkish Institute of Archaeology, Istanbul.

Schachner, Andreas, and Hartmut Wittenberg 2012 Zu den Wasserspeichern in Boğazköy/Hattuša und der Frage ihrer Befüllung. In *Wasserwirtschaftliche Innovationen im archäologischen Kontext*, edited by F. Klimscha, R. Eichmann, C. Schuler and H. Fahlbusch, pp. 245–255. Verlag Marie Leidorf, Rahden.

Schoop, Ulf-Dietrich 2009 Indications of Structural Change in the Hittite pottery Inventory at Bogazkoy-Hattusa. In *Central-North Anatolia in the Hittite Period: New Perspectives in Light of Recent Research Acts of the International Conference Held at the University of Florence (7–9 February 2007)*, edited by Franca Pecchioli Daddi, pp. 145–167. Studia Asiana, no. SA 5. Herder, Rome.

Seeher, Jürgen 2002 Die Ausgrabungen in Bogazköy-Hattusa 2001. *Archaeologische Anzeiger* 2002: 59–78.

———— 2006 Die Untersuchungen im Bereich der Ostteiche in der Oberstadt 1996–1998. In *Boğazköy-Berichte* 8, edited by Jürgen Seeher, pp. 1–23. Verlag Philipp von Zabern, Mainz.

———— 2010 Zur Wasserversorgung und Wassernutzung in der Unterstadt von Hattuša. *Istanbuler Mitteilungen* 60:67–80.

Shaw, Brent D. 2001 Challenging Braudel: A New Vision of the Mediterranean. *Journal of Roman Archaeology* 14: 419–453.

Simonds, Timothy 2012 The Architecture of the Burrow: Reforming the "Anti-Architectural" Prejudice of the Threshold. Unpublished MA thesis, Brown University.

Sørensen, Tim Flohr, and Stephen Lumsden 2016 Hid in Death's Dateless Night: The Lure of an Uncanny Landscape in Bronze Age Anatolia. In *The Archaeology of Anxiety: The Materiality of Anxiousness, Worry, and Fear*, edited by Jeffrey Fleisher and Neil Norman, pp. 67–93. Springer, New York.

Stone, Elizabeth C., Paul Zimansky, Piotr Steinkeller, Vincent Pigott, Lisa Wells and Tony Wilkinson 2004 *The Anatomy of a Mesopotamian City: Survey and Soundings at Mashkan-shapir*. Eisenbrauns, Winona Lake, IN.

Tabak, Faruk 2008 *The Waning of the Mediterranean 1550–1870: A Geohistorical Approach*. Johns Hopkins University Press, Baltimore, MD.

Tinney, Steve 1996 *The Nippur Lament: Royal Rhetoric and Divine Legitimation in the Reign of Išme-Dagan of Isin (1953–1935 B.C.)*. Occasional Publications of the Samuel Noah Kramer Fund 15. University Museum, Philadelphia, PA.

Ur, Jason A. 2017 The Topography of Nineveh. In *Nineveh, the Great City: Symbol of Beauty and Power*, edited by Lucas P. Petit and Daniele Morandi Bonacossi, pp. 58–62. Sidestone, Leiden.

Van de Mieroop, Marc 1997 *The Ancient Mesopotamian City*. Oxford University Press, Oxford.

——— 1999 Literature and Political Discourse in Ancient Mesopotamia: Sargon II of Assyria and Sargon of Agade. In *Munuscula Mesopotamica: Festschrift für Johannes Renger*, edited by B. Böck, E. Cancik-Kirschbaum and T. Richter, pp. 327–339. Ugarit Verlag, Münster.

Vidler, Anthony 2011 *The Scenes of the Street and Other Essays*. The Monacelli Press, New York.

Westenholz, Joan Goodnick 1998 The Theological Foundation of the City, the Capital City and Babylon. In *Capital Cities: Urban Planning and Spiritual Dimensions*, edited by J. G. Westenholz, pp. 43–54. Bible Lands Museum, Jerusalem.

Wilkinson, Tony J. 1990 Late-Assyrian Settlement Geography in Upper Mesopotamia. In *Neo-Assyrian Geography*, edited by Mario Liverani, pp. 139–159. Università di Roma "La Sapienza," Dipartimento di Scienze storiche, archeologiche e anthropologiche dell'Antichità, Quaderni di Geografia Storica 5: Sargon srl, Roma.

——— 1997 Environmental Fluctuations, Agricultural Production and Collapse: A View from Bronze Age Upper Mesopotamia. In *Third Millennium B.C. Climate Change and Old World Collapse*, edited by H. N. Dalfes, G. Kukla and H. Weiss, pp. 67–106. Springer, New York.

——— 2000 Regional Approaches to Mesopotamian Archaeology: The Contribution of Archaeological Surveys. *Journal of Archaeological Research* 8: 219–267.

——— 2003 *Archaeological Landscapes of the Near East*. The University of Arizona Press, Tucson.

——— 2010 Empire and Environment in the Northern Fertile Crescent. In *Landscapes and Societies: Selected Cases*, edited by Peter Martini and Ward Chesworth, pp. 135–152. Springer, London and New York.

Yoffee, Norman 2005 *Myths of the Archaic State: Evolution of the Earliest Cities, States and Civilizations*. Cambridge University Press, Cambridge.

Wittenberg, Hartmut, and Andreas Schachner 2012 The Ponds of Hattuša—Early Groundwater Management in the Hittite Kingdom. *Water, Science and Technology: Water Supply* 13(3): 692–698.

10

COMMENTARY

The City and The City

Oliver J. T. Harris

Introduction

In China Miéville's (2009) magnificent novel, *The City and The City*, two different cities occupy the same space, but in different dimensions. These cities, named Ul Quoma and Besźel, are what the people in Miéville's novel call 'crosshatched'. That is their parallel existence overlaps, and the occupants of each city learn to 'unsee' the occasional moments where events in one city 'breach', as they call it, into the other. The novel has a huge amount to recommend it. In addition to being an excellent detective story, one featuring perhaps the world's most sympathetic murder victim,[1] it is a book that speaks to how we learn to move and live in cities; the ways our eyes are trained to glide over the homeless person asleep in the doorway, or to avoid eye contact with strangers on public transport. More than this, the book shows us how cities are always multiple. Cities exceed what we can know about them through their depth and complexity, via the things we see and do not see. They reveal themselves to us unexpectedly. Archaeologists working in urban spaces are like the detective in the novel, Inspector Borlú: They work precisely in the 'crosshatched' realm between dimensions, between past and present, between the city that was and the city that is.

The chapters in this volume bring us a new way of understanding past cities. Rather than focusing on them as bounded entities, they approach their ongoing emergence through the activities of humans and non-humans alike. Materials, memories, people and things come together to form and maintain these spaces, to territorialise them in the terms of Deleuze and Guattari (2004; see especially Van Dyke, Chapter 3). They also leave and deterritorialise themselves, allowing parts of cities to detach and move elsewhere, even as other elements endure. These are places of affect, where bodies press into one another, shaping each other and being shaped in turn. These are bodies far beyond the human. Where an older generation of archaeologists might have pointed to social evolution as a key mechanism that produced cities, here we find everything from coral reefs to mountains, from gods to toads, playing their part in the emergence of urbanity. From the karstic caves of the American Bottom to their counterparts in Anatolia, these chapters make room for all manner of beings to play critical roles in the histories they tell.

Bringing cities together, as Miéville shows us, changes how we understand them and, when taken as a whole, this is what the chapters in this volume do as well. Together they are an assemblage, each one adding to and contributing to the others. They come together to give us multiple snapshots of the ways in which architecture, people, materials, places, landscapes, movements, religions and more assemble – stratify – into what we call cities today. These chapters undoubtedly offer new accounts of the cities under discussion – indeed they do so with far more richness and complexity than I can do justice to here – in Timothy Morton's (2017) terms they 'subscend' my account. But they also do more than this: together they do more than they can alone. Specifically, I suggest, they offer us a clear demonstration of the ways in which 'New Materialism' can transform our narratives of the past. They show us how New Materialist approaches allow new kinds of history to emerge.

In my closing contribution to this volume I seek to do four things. First, I want to tease out how the chapters in the volume, together rather than individually, point to other areas of New Materialist thought that can help further develop our thinking. In particular I suggest we can draw on Deleuze's (2004) ideas of the virtual and the actual to add an additional dimension to how we conceptualise the emergence of these places. Here, I will also outline how thinking about the virtual as structured in particular ways can further aid our understanding of these processes. Second, I look at the manner in which these accounts demonstrate how seemingly generic substances, like water and stone, are as historically situated as any human being. Third, I will examine where our New Materialist accounts may need further development, especially in relation to other ontologies and to issues of power and politics. Finally, I return to the notion of the city itself to consider it as a form of articulation, in Deleuzian terms, and use that device to consider what these various cities have in common.

The (virtual) city and the (actual) city

The City and the City, the doubled title of Miéville's novel, points us towards other ways in which we can consider urban places, and how they are always more than the immediate physical materials that surround us. In Deleuzian terms, when we think about cities as assemblages (cf. Jervis 2017), as so many of the chapters in this volume ask us to do, then we have to think about their virtual as well as their actual elements (Deleuze 2004; Harris 2017; see especially Joyce, Chapter 4). For Deleuze (2004, 260), the virtual is not opposed to the real, but to the actual. The virtual is a means for thinking about the very real capacities that an assemblage has that are not yet made manifest in the world. The potential that a knife has to stab or cut is very real – especially if it is being waved at you – and the knife cannot be understood without them. Equally, the capacity a tree has to conduct a lightning bolt is entirely real all of the time, without usually being actualised. Deleuze (2004) distinguishes between the virtual and the actual as a means of thinking through the potential for change located in any assemblage. In a city we can think of the capacity to come together in times of disaster or triumph, to celebrate a sporting success or the reburial of a long-lost king.[2] These capacities are real, without always being actual, and are central to how a city works[3].

Many of the chapters reveal, both explicitly and implicitly, the relationship between the (virtual) city and the (actual) city, and this works at a number of scales. Landscapes around the world contained virtual capacities actualised in the building of urban assemblages. At Chaco Canyon, Fajada Butte created a landscape ripe with virtual potentials, already present before people began to construct the great houses of Pueblo Bonito and Chetro Ketl (Van Dyke, Chapter 3). As Van Dyke comments, the topographic properties of the canyon connected with the way in which people saw the world. Here a specific assemblage of material, landscapes, and people created a set of virtual capacities within an assemblage that could be actualised through the construction of the great houses and kivas of the Chacoan world.

In the Anatolian countryside, Hittite cities actualised the virtual capacities of sinkholes and caves in their karstic landscape through the way their building technologies mimicked these specific places (Harmanşah, Chapter 9). Alongside this, specific architectural elements explored the way in which landscapes acted to actualise their capacities differently. So constructed ponds drew on the ability of water to seep out of the ground during winter and spring months, but stored it over summer, actualising a new property that had previously only been virtual.

It is worth comparing this with the other karstic landscape discussed in this volume, that which lies close to Cahokia (Alt, Chapter 2). Karst sinkholes in this context offered many virtual capacities, including potential access to lithic resources, but also to underworld realms and flows of water. The St Louis mound centre, in particular, becomes an entirely different place once we think of the way in which its construction above 'karst and caves' (Alt, Chapter 2) drew out the virtual capacities of the landscape. This becomes a city that blurs above and below ground, one that reaches into other worlds, and the landscape of sinkholes becomes something entirely central to this place's very existence.

At a different, more intimate scale, virtual capacities also became actualised properties (sensu DeLanda 2006) in the specific encounters these different cities afforded. At Tiwanaku (Janusek, Chapter 5), for example, the stone monolith chachapumas that guarded the portals to temples drew out particular qualities in human beings, ensuring they were ready to encounter other stone persons within the city. We are used to thinking of how human beings draw out qualities from stone through knapping or sculpting, but here the reverse took place. Within the city of Tiwanaku and its assemblages of water, stone, monoliths and people, it was the monoliths that made virtual aspects of the human actual, and not necessarily the other way around.

The close virtual

We can push this further by considering how changes in the actual also recursively effect the virtual, changing its structure and the capacities therein. The virtual, after all is not a blank space. It is one characterised by singularities, by potentials, and by topological forces (Deleuze 2004; DeLanda 2016). We might, as the sociologist Bob Carter and I have recently argued (Carter and Harris 2018), distinguish a 'close virtual': those elements of the virtual that are more likely to become actualised than others. To give a simple example, whilst it might be a virtual capacity of any US citizen to become president, it is very much more likely to happen if you are a male orange-skinned tweeting billionaire, than say, a working-class African-American woman. The capacity is virtual for both, but in one case we might consider it part of the close virtual and in the other it is not. Similarly, whilst the virtual capacities of any city are almost endless, many are more likely to be actualised than others. It is more likely that San Francisco falls into the sea following an earthquake, or that New Orleans is swamped by a hurricane, than either of those two events is to befall my home city of Leicester. The potential for disaster is virtual for all three cities, but clearly that presence is much more potent − even if unrealised − for the two American examples.

The make-up of the close virtual of an assemblage is not fixed, however, but changes through time, in part because of events that happen in the actual, and we can see this clearly in this volume. When people began transforming the architecture and make-up of San José Mogote (Joyce, Chapter 4) they not only altered what might happen at this locale in the future (the close virtual of this assemblage), they also altered what might take place at the nearby mountain we know today as Monte Albán. In the former case, for example, acts of sacrifice and the deposition of offerings opened up the potential for human sacrifice at the site, making something that had always been possible, likely − moving it into the close virtual and then actualising it. In turn, the reworking of relations that Joyce describes at San José Mogote, as materials, people, gods, and objects gathered in new ways, raised the possibility that to the south a new city could come into being. It was always potentially possible to build a site at Monte Albán, but the construction of San José Mogote made it likely, transforming the close virtual of the former site through the ways in which new relations were actualised at the latter. In this sense we can only understand the emergence of Monte Albán both through the actual changes at San José Mogote and the way in which this began the process of territorialising new connections and relations at Monte Albán.

On the Deccan plateau of Southern India, the existing hill at Maski Durgada Gudda offered many virtual capacities (Bauer, Chapter 8). These were shaped, however, over millennia as Neolithic rock art motifs were carved on its slopes, which changed the capacities of the site for Iron Age people, who in turn transformed the site for the later medieval occupation. The actions of people in one period, working with the materials of the hill and its topography, shaped the close virtual of later periods from which differing settlement patterns could be actualised.

A third example of the transformation of the close virtual comes from Fleisher's chapter. In his analysis of the construction of mosques on the Swahili coast, Fleisher (chapter 7, this volume) reveals how the construction of *Porites* coral mosques drew on the materials of the nearshore and foreshore in new ways. *Porites* coral, beach sand and mangrove had always had the capacity to be used as building materials, of course, and indeed they still do today. This was, and is, in other words, a virtual element of the nearshore of the Swahili world. At around 1000 CE these new materials come to be incorporated into the building of mosques. In so doing, what was a virtual capacity becomes first a part of the close virtual, and then actualised in the mosques themselves. The assemblage of both the existing mosques and also the nearshore materials themselves is thus transformed. Such an alteration was only temporarily territorialised within the assemblage, however. From the thirteenth century coral rag became dominant, and the use of *Porites* coral and other near/foreshore materials faded. Within the assemblage of these materials it was still potentially possible to build with them, it was part of their virtual, but it was no longer likely, no longer part of their *close* virtual.

Adding a notion of the virtual and the actual here, and a consideration of the way in which the virtual is structured, thus helps us to add to the rich affective textures created in the assemblage of the chapters of this volume. It helps us to see how these urban assemblages emerge through the interplay of the virtual and the actual, the way changes in the latter rework the former, as individuated solutions emerge to the problems and challenges of urban living raised by both the human and the non-human elements of the assemblages we study.

The cities and New Materialism

Yet these chapters do more than just offer us detailed, theoretically informed accounts of different cities, ones that allow us to trace their territorialisation and stratification in new ways. They contribute to, indeed in my view significantly advance, the position of New Materialism within the discipline of archaeology. There is no need for me to reiterate here what New Materialism is or how it is working its way into our discipline (see Pauketat, Chapter 1, for a further review see Harris and Cipolla 2017, Chapter 8). The chapters in this volume embrace the active world of materials. The karstic sink holes are central attractors that gather the mound sites of Cahokia (Alt, Chapter 2). The tidal bore that sweeps up the Qiantang River plays a critical role in the history of Liangzhu (Pauketat, Chapter 6). In many examples, weather, celestial beings, sounds and objects play their roles, too (e.g., Alt, Van Dyke, and Joyce, Chapters 2–4). Yet the chapters – together – do more than just tell us about this historical role of materials: They tell us about the very historicity of materials themselves; they show us how these are not natural components of the world called into human projects, but just like people themselves, are historically emergent within specific assemblages (cf. Conneller 2011; Jones 2012). This is the central point where New Materialism makes its decisive break with older narratives. It would be one thing – and an important step at that – to argue that

250 Oliver J. T. Harris

a material plays a critical role in the emergence of a specific site or city, but quite another again to show how the material is itself historically different depending on the assemblage through which it emerges. Yet this is what these chapters so clearly demonstrate. Let me show how with reference to water and stone.

Water

Water in many of the examples in this volume emerges as a key element, and critical component, of urban centres. This is hardly surprising: Of course, gatherings of human beings will require supplies of water. However, what this volume achieves is to show us how water is not the same sort of thing at each of these centres (as Pauketat explicitly draws out in his contrast between Liangzhu and Paquimé in Chapter 6), even as at many of the sites water 'ordered people's lives' (Pauketat, Chapter 6). Each of the chapters identifies the different assemblages in which water is caught up. This means that water in each case has different virtual capacities and actual properties. Water here, in other words, is not a universal substance that humans employ in different ways (to drink, or to bathe in) but rather a historically emergent entity. Water here is as immanent (see Pauketat, Chapter 6), contingent, and as situated as the human beings it comes into contact with and becomes part of. This goes far beyond the idea that 'people have different beliefs about water' – this is not an epistemological claim. Instead it is ontological: Water can do different things, and so *is* something different in these various contexts.

Almost all the chapters in the volume draw out the historical contingency of water. At Emerald, water acted to help create plastered floors, was elicited from people in sweat lodges and helped to close buildings when people were finished with them (Alt, Chapter 2). Water would have oozed from the sides of the Emerald Ridge; this was a landscape from which water emerged, and disappeared, in specific and particular ways. At Cahokia, water enveloped the dead and flowed through the karst formations that surrounded the city. At Chaco Canyon (Van Dyke, Chapter 3) water was quite different. With rainfall such a rare occurrence in the canyon, water took on different qualities, emerging differently in the hot and dry assemblage of people, weather and materials at this place. This meant that when rain did fall the landscape was radically transformed in colour, sound, and environment, with the emergence of the call of the spadefoot toad and the sight of flying ants. People related to water very differently in a landscape where all the water available needed to be retained, and where the effects of rainfall on the land were so transformative. Water could do things at Chaco it cannot do in other urban assemblages.

As the volume moves southward from North to Central and to South America, we can see new relationships with water emerging. At Paquimé (Pauketat, Chapter 6) water was managed in complex ways, drawing on its capacities to flow and pool, and relations were created to the waters of the coast through the millions of discarded pieces and artefacts of marine shell. At San José Mogote materials including marine shells, river sand, and fish bones were incorporated into offerings, linking these to water through their ability to 'index' this substance, as Joyce puts it. At Monte Albán (Joyce, Chapter 4), rain, clouds, and the Rain Deity were all incorporated within the assemblage of the mountain. Here, up high, water acts differently; it has different capacities and properties than elsewhere. Monte Albán could be enveloped in clouds in the rainy season, water filling the air as much as it filled the bodies of the people who lived there.

The relationships with water were more mediated at Tiwanaku (Janusek, Chapter 5). Indeed the city itself emerged at a moment when the climate became wetter. Here a monumental 'hydrolithic' network was constructed linking water with stone directly. Tiwanaku involved different kinds of water, from the marshy waterlogged areas that surrounded the city, to the water-rich temples in its interior. The huge perimeter canal connected to the south on an aquifer and drew on the capacity of this element of the landscape to guide water to and around the city. As Janusek notes, these canals acted to enhance and control the occurrence of water, in effect modulating both the actual (how water operated) and the virtual (how water might operate). Here the capacities of humans, materials, landscape and water came together in historically specific ways.

Outside of the Americas, water operates differently once again. At Liangzhu, Pauketat (Chapter 6) shows us how the assemblage of river and moon produces a tidal bore to the southeast that must have been inescapably involved in the emergence of this city. Liangzhu, in turn, was a water city, where the flow was managed and controlled by people, in notable contrast to the way the moon controlled the flow of the bore. Water gates guided the movement of water and people together, and people travelled over water, took fish from water, planted their rice in water. Here, water is very different from the chemically identical compound at other cities that centred themselves on water like Tiwanaku or Paquimé.

Similarly to some of the connections emphasised in the shells at Paquimé or San José Mogote, water was made material in the Swahili mosques through other materials. Mangrove, beach sand and coral brought the sea into the mosques, 'the sea was built into the floors, the walls and the roof' as Fleisher (chapter 7, this volume) puts it. Water also brought other capacities to this assemblage, however. There were the water spirits on the one hand, and water's material effects on the coral on the other. *Porites* coral, Fleisher tells us, can only be worked when wet. So, water here is a construction material directly, you cannot build the *Porites* mosques without it. This capacity only emerges in the historical conjunction of people, coral, water and religion in the construction of the Swahili mosques.

Finally, on the Anatolian plain water has other properties (Harmanşah, Chapter 9). The urban infrastructure in this context drew on the way water seeped out of the ground at certain places. Water here was a landscape feature that went far beyond being a 'neutral natural substance' as Harmanşah rightly points out. This was a world where the 'hydro-geological' capacities of water were drawn out by people and the landscape together, where the karstic geology, political struggles and religious beliefs created new possibilities for being and becoming.

Stone

If water is a differentially emergent substance, with alternative capacities and properties depending on its assemblage within the urban spaces of the past, then the same can be said for stone. Here again we encounter a material that varies historically in its urban settings, not just in what people think or believe about stone, but in what it fundamentally *is*. As we will see, on occasion it was stone's connection with water that drew out these dimensions.

Janusek (chapter 5, this volume) discusses how, at Tiwanaku, stone flowed like water into and out of the site. Different kinds of stone, sandstone and volcanic andesite, were used at different times. Each of these stones had different capacities that could be brought out with different techniques of working, requiring different assemblages. In turn, each of these kinds of stone had differing origin points, and in tracing their movements we can detect links into and out of Tiwanaku, and the connections these stones formed (cf. Gillings and Pollard 2016). The constructions of Akapana and Pumapunku at the city linked stone to specific mountains and drew on materials that connected these locales to those places of origin. This was indeed an index, as Janusek states, a series of topological connections that moved mountains through the movement of stone. The monoliths at Tiwanaku represented another form of stone, one that was clearly alive in different ways. These were stones with homes constructed for them, stones that had capacities that humans did not – like having two left hands, placing them always above the humans they interacted with.

At Monte Albán, stone offered different possibilities. For example here, through carving both on orthostats and on incised slabs (Joyce, Chapter 4), it could be coded (sensu Deleuze and Guattari 2004, 59) with images, dates and identities. These helped to stratify social groups through the organisation of the images. Narratives became territorialised in stone through these carvings. This, of course, was a virtual capacity of stone at any of the urban centres under discussion, but it was at Monte Albán that this capacity became an actualised property in this specific assemblage. The construction of these narratives in stone helped to territorialise one kind of gathering, and their disassembly and destruction at the end of the Terminal Formative had the reverse effect. The destruction of the stone 'overcoded' (Deleuze and Guattari 2004, 222) the plaza, and so deterritorialised the previously dominant narrative.

If stone as mobile is a key theme at Tiwanaku and Monte Albán, a great stationary stone hill, an incelberg, is the critical territorialising factor at Maski in India (Bauer, Chapter 8), gathering occupation to it through its interactions with humans and non-humans over millennia. This is both at once an emergent hill formed on a geological timescale and a constantly changing assemblage. As Bauer emphasises, the processes and effects of sedimentation have affected the way in which people engaged with the locale over five thousand years. Not some timeless lump of rock, then, but rather a place with its own historical narrative of emergence, one that involves, but is not determined by, human beings. The interaction of people, climate, erosion and geology here brought out specific historical qualities in the materials, which shaped the construction of urban spaces. Although not built upon

Commentary: *The City and The City* **253**

in the same way, it is clear that the territorialising force of Fajada Butte and the stone walls of Chaco Canyon played a similar role (Van Dyke, Chapter 3). Indeed, we can reach back to water here once again, as the stone walls of the canyon were once muddy strata beneath the sea. Water is a building material here, too, forming stone, although without the involvement of human beings.

Whilst stationary stone and mobile stone contrast with one another, there is another capacity for stone settings that were actualised both around Cahokia and on the Anatolian plain. Here a shared karstic geological setting created capacities that could be actualised differently. In the greater Cahokia region, it created spaces that could be experienced and decorated from the inside (Alt, Chapter 2). Rock art inside caves was fixed in specific places, allowing links to be drawn with differing people, beliefs and genders in ways that could not be deterritorialised through dismantling, as happened with depictions at Monte Albán. Alt argues convincingly that it is these caves and sinkholes, which dominate the landscape around Cahokia, that led to the formation of this urban environment in this place. In the Hittite context in Anatolia, the caves opened up a 'Divine Road of the Earth' as a form of cultic place, which provided a mirror, a co-designer, in the construction of Hittite urban places (Harmanşah, Chapter 9). Whereas Cahokian mounds rose above the karstic caves around them, Hittite cities constructed chambers to territorialise, topologically, these places within their urban spaces. The affective power of caves was central in both cases, but affects too are historically contextual, and so the experience of them and their consequences was different in the Cahokian and the Hittite worlds in which they emerged.

We can finish with one final stone, the fallen star from Paquimé (Pauketat, Chapter 6), something that Deleuze and Guattari (1994, 86) might refer to as a 'celestial stranger'. Whether or not this sparked the construction at this city is hard to know, but its treatment and deposition mark it as an extraordinary moment of territorialisation, where stone from beyond even our planet becomes part and parcel of the assemblages of our urban spaces.

Looking at water and stone together in these different contexts shows us that embracing the vibrancy of matter, to follow Jane Bennett (2010), is only the first step. Yes, materials are alive, but the question is how? In what way? How does this emerge historically? This does not mean that stone at Tiwanaku has nothing in common with stone at Chaco, or that water gushing through a Hittite city does not have the same chemical make-up (on average) as water at Paquimé. It does mean that what stone and water can do, what their virtual capacities are, and what is in their close virtual, depends as much as human beings do on the assemblages in which they find themselves. Just as we can begin to trace what humans have in common *without* demanding a universal humanism (Dawney et al. 2017), so we can do the same with materials. The point is not merely to bring materials to life, but rather, as Deleuze and Guattari (2004, 454) challenge us, to understand 'a life proper to matter'. Such a life is importantly, and intensely, historical. To understand the cities of the past is to embrace the historical nature of materials as well as people, as these chapters clearly show.

Further assembly required?

As noted, it is clear that the great strengths of this volume are both what the chapters bring to our understanding of ancient cities and the manner in which they demonstrate what New Materialism can do for our accounts of the past. The chapters also identify, both implicitly and explicitly, other topics that may require us to think a little more. Specifically, I want to flag two areas here. Below I discuss the relationship between power and politics within New Materialist thought. First, though, it is worth examining the relationship between the New Materialist position that authors take in this volume, and the ontological claims of non-Western people, especially in the regions where descendent communities can be found.

Native ontologies

One of the strengths of the chapters in this volume is their ability to draw upon the insights of New Materialism, but also to leaven these with connections to insights from ethnographic or historical records derived from groups with a direct connection to those under examination. These insights clearly provide an enormous resource, from the Swahili belief in spirits that adds so much to Fleisher's account, to the textual evidence of Hittite perspectives on the world in Harmanşah's chapter. However, this leaves unresolved the ontological status of these beliefs vis-à-vis the ontological status of New Materialism. In archaeology there has been some tension between these different positions (Alberti 2016; Wilkinson 2017). Is New Materialism simply an attempt to adopt Indigenous thought without acknowledgement (Todd 2016)? Does it represent a meta-ontology that supresses difference (Alberti 2016)? Does the co-option of animism (for example) by New Materialists supress the variation in Indigenous thought and represent a new liberal consensus (Wilkinson 2017)? Does Indigenous thought getting raised to the status of ontology prevent critique, impose otherness, and deny historicity (Cipolla 2018; Harris and Crellin 2018)? What would happen if we applied these ideas to an Indigenous context where stones were understood as inert dead matter and human agency was celebrated as uniquely different to everything else?

The answer, it seems to me, is that we need to allow our accounts to be sensitive to these differences, and to draw out the relations between them, rather than demanding that one account be accorded ontological supremacy over another (cf. Harris and Robb 2012). Here, the multiplicity that Deleuze and Guattari (2004) always emphasise comes to the fore. Rather than demanding, we ask what something *is*; rather than privileging being, Deleuze (e.g., Deleuze and Parnet 2006, 42) suggests we always focus on the *and*, on how things link together. Here, the chapters demonstrate this by linking the attention to detail and to materials that New Materialism calls for, to an acknowledgement of the ontological power of indigenous knowledge claims. So, for example the eating of maize in Mesoamerica can be the consumption of vital forces in both the New Materialist sense, and in the religious sense of the people doing the consuming (Joyce, Chapter 4). Attending to the specific materialities of mosques around 1000 CE allows Fleisher to both reveal their connections with the sea and to trace back the relationships people have with spirits over a millennium. The naivety recommended by Fleisher allows us to trace assemblages that tack between past and present, materials and ideas, and to include, as Deleuze and Guattari urge us to, 'whole regimes of signs' (2004, 157). These regimes include the libations and songs accompanying the movement of stones around Tiwanaku, the connections to Chaco Canyon Native Americans have today, the oral history of the Sioux and the way religion affects the founding and structure of cities in medieval India. As archaeologists, the question is not whether New Materialism or Deleuzian philosophy are true, in an existential sense, but rather whether they allow us to ask interesting questions, and indeed to develop new concepts that link and connect with our material, historic and ethnographic records[4] (cf. Deleuze and Guattari 1994, 27). Such an emphasis on the *and* need not be seen as simply an appeal to multiple truths. It is, as Deleuze and Guattari (1994, 130) said, not about the relativity of truth, but rather about the truth of relations. What New Materialism allows is then both an authority to be granted to the onto-logical claims of people in the present and in the past, and for those ontological claims to be historicised alongside the testimony that materials present. This means that these chapters show us that we need not reduce the past to the ontologies of the present, but that we can allow these ontologies to articulate with and inform our understandings of the past.

Politics and power in New Materialist cities

A second and perhaps more contentious issue relates to the role of power, politics and indeed the question of the human in these accounts. Some critiques of New Materialism have argued that it ignores or downplays politics and power relations (e.g., Bauer and Kosiba 2016; Van Dyke 2015). The danger, these critics claim, is that the emphasis upon a flat ontology risks leaving us in a position where we cannot assign blame to human actors or institutions. Worse still, the reduction of the human to just one actor amongst many runs the risk of reducing people in the past to objects and undoing the good work post-processual archaeology did in for-cing us to attend to gender, identity and power in the past.

The chapters here suggest that this need not be the case, as Pauketat argues in the introduction. Van Dyke shows us how a concern with territorialisation and deterritorialisation leads us not only into the past, but into the present as well with the connections and contestations that revolve around Chaco Canyon today. In turn Harmanşah traces a politics of authority in the Hittite world that revolved around water as a critical element, drawing on the assemblage through which water emerged and flowed. In Joyce's account of Monte Albán there is no disguising the violence, human sacrifice and increasing social differentiation at the site, even as mountains, gods and clouds also play a role in its emergence. Bauer emphasises the political role of materials in the construction of spaces, noting the way in which the defensive architecture of medieval Indian cities like Vijayanagara were partially,

256 Oliver J. T. Harris

but still actively, produced by geology as well as by people. Bauer is concerned to ensure that the political decisions of human beings continue to attract our attention and is surely right to do so, and further stresses how politics is caught up in both the planned and the unplanned cities he discusses. Perhaps there is more to say in this context about whether the charismatic 'leaders' Bauer discuses who took political advantage of urban spaces might include non-humans as well as human beings. The monoliths of Tiwanaku (Janusek, Chapter 5) immediately spring to mind.

Beyond this volume, the explicit driving force of feminist analysis within New Materialism (e.g., Braidotti 2013) also suggests that concerns around the absence of power and politics are not fundamentally disabling to these theoretical ideas. Whilst it is clear that we need to be vigilant, we also need to ensure that such responses are not used to disable an approach that offers new ways of thinking about peoples' place in the world in the past, present and future (Dawney et al. 2017). Fundamentally the flat ontology of New Materialism does not demand an equality of responsibility or agency between people and things. Rather, it demands that the relative balance is not decided before the fact, but only through the process of investigation itself.

Conclusion: Difference, differentiation and the double bind

What these chapters lay to rest, then, is the worry that New Materialism might simply be an overriding meta-ontology that renders the world the same through space and time. New Materialism offers us instead the potential for thinking through difference. Difference, in this case, not merely as a negative (how different are women from men, how different are the 'others' to us?), but rather difference as a productive force, one that allows new potentials in the world to lead to new worlds themselves (Deleuze 2004; Deleuze and Guattari 1994). Indeed, we have only begun to scratch the surface of what these chapters, and the wider world of New Materialism, have to offer. There is much more to be said and thought about affect, immanence, temporality and emergence. There is more too to think about how our ideas of design are forever changed in this new world of materials (see Bauer, Chapter 8). I will finish, though, with one last point.

Deleuze (2004) writes about how the world comes into being through intensive differences; that is through the way in which difference itself creates first individuation, and then actualisation. This takes place through what Deleuze and Guattari (2004, 45) call the double articulation, or the double bind. This is not the imposition of form onto content, or content dictating form, but rather an articulation where both happen, like the pincers of a (god-like) lobster. It is through this articulation, Deleuze and Guattari argue, that stratification, territorialisation and coding take place, the processes through which the world continually becomes.

It is this process of double articulation that these chapters reveal to be so central to the emergence of urbanity across the ancient world. What we see with these chapters are the ways in which cities act as particular forms of articulation, bringing together materials, religious affects, ontologies, people, places and landscapes and binding them together. These emerge not as separate elements of content that are then given form, nor as forms needing content that can be filled in later. Instead, they become stratified through the processes that bring them into being, just as geological strata emerge through both formation and sorting simultaneously (Deleuze and Guattari 2004, 46). At Chaco Canyon, Van Dyke traces the gathering of people, materials, sounds and sites in an emergent landscape, and at Paquimé, Pauketat shows us how birds were territorialised into the site even as their feathers were deterritorialised from them. At Monte Albán, Joyce reveals the stratification of social class through the reworking of temples and the sacrifices of human bodies. At Tiwananku, different stones link to different places and flow through the site as water flows alongside them, the stones and canals binding together in the hydrolithic ecology that Janusek describes. Its boundaries, as Janusek rightly notes, can hardly be limited by the simple edges of the site. Cities here are the point of the pincer, the point where content and form emerge, folding and linking these different places, materials and people together.

What these chapters show is how the emergence of urban spaces works differently with different materials, people and landscapes; with different flows of intensity drawing in water and weather, belief and power, things and animals. Critical here, as I stressed earlier, is embracing both the vibrancy of materials, and the way in which they emerge as immanent and historically situated elements of the world. Yet they also reveal what links these processes. We need no longer search for the concrete features that a city will share, for the Platonic ideal that makes a city what it is (a certain size, a certain number of people, a certain form of infrastructure). This is because what cities share lies not in the actual, but in the virtual, and in the way in which the structure of the virtual leads to the articulations described above. This structure, the shape of the virtual both close and distant, is what Deleuze (2006, 30) calls a diagram. These chapters have revealed to us how this diagram can be actualised in ways that reveal the historical specificity of cities, people and religion, yet also share a process that links them historically across time and space. Archaeology was once a discipline that had to choose between small-scale specificity and large-scale generalisation. What New Materialism and its wonderfully folded approach to scale has given us, and what these chapters have shown us, is the paucity of that choice. Each of the chapters here opens up the multiplicity of cities, their complex, nuanced and specific histories. They are all virtual cities and actual cities. The city and the city indeed.

Acknowledgements

Taking part in the seminars at both the School of Advanced Research and the Amerind Institute was an enormous privilege; I owe a huge debt of gratitude to all the participants for their intellectual generosity across both occasions, and to Susan Alt and Tim Pauketat in particular for their invitation. My attendance at the seminars was supported by funding from the Templeton Foundation, the School for Advanced Research, the Amerind Foundation and the Leverhulme Trust, the latter through a Philip Leverhulme Prize (PLP-2016–109). Tim and an anonymous reviewer offered helpful comments that have improved this chapter immensely. Neither (or anyone else for that matter) should be held responsible for my errors, or as Deleuze (2004: 185) would say, my misadventures of thought.

Notes

1 A post-processual archaeologist more interested in 'Foucault and Baudrillard than in Gordon Childe' (Miéville 2009, 106) no less.
2 Both of which have happened in the city I live in within the last five years.
3 To be explicit here there is no sense in which the virtual pertains to the realm of ideas, and the actual to the realm of materials. A tree's capacity to conduct lightning is entirely dependent on material things, with no regard for the ideas people might have about it. Both the virtual and the actual are part of all assemblages, including those that have no relation to the human or, indeed, to organic life at all.
4 With thanks to Jeff Fleisher for reminding me of this.

References

Alberti, Benjamin 2016 Archaeologies of Ontology. *Annual Review of Anthropology* 45:163–179.
Bauer, Andrew M., and Steve Kosiba 2016 How Things Act: An Archaeology of Materials in Political Life. *Journal of Social Archaeology* 16:115–141.
Bennett, Jane 2010 *Vibrant Matter: A Political Ecology of Things.* Duke University Press, Durham, NC.
Braidotti, Rosi 2013 *The Posthuman.* Polity, London.
Carter, Bob, and Oliver J. T. Harris 2018 Rethinking the 'Crisis' in Contemporary UK Higher Education: The University as Assemblage. *Paper presented at the Post-human reading group, Leicester University, January 2018.*
Cipolla, Craig N. 2018 Earth Flows and Lively Stone: What Difference Does 'Vibrant Matter' Make? *Archaeological Dialogues* 25:49–70.
Conneller, Chantal 2011 *An Archaeology of Materials: Substantial Transformations in Early Prehistoric Europe.* Routledge, London.
Dawney, Leila, Oliver J. T. Harris and Tim Flohr Sørensen 2017 Future Worlds: Anticipatory Archaeology and the Late Human Legacy. *Journal of Contemporary Archaeology* 4:107–129.
DeLanda, Manuel 2006 *A New Philosophy of Society: Assemblage Theory and Social Complexity.* Continuum, London.
——— 2016 *Assemblage.* Edinburgh University Press, Edinburgh.
Deleuze, Gilles 2004 *Difference and Repetition.* Bloomsbury, London.
——— 2006 *Foucault.* Continuum, London.
Deleuze, Gilles, and Félix Guattari 1994 *What Is Philosophy?* Verso, London.
——— 2004 *A Thousand Plateaus: Capitalism and Schizophrenia.* Continuum, London.
Deleuze, Gilles, and Claire Parnet 2006 *Dialogues II.* Continuum, London.
Fowler, Chris, and Oliver J. T. Harris 2015 Enduring Relations: Exploring a Paradox of New Materialism. *Journal of Material Culture* 20:127–148.
Gillings, Mark, and Joshua Pollard 2016 Making Megaliths: Shifting and Unstable Stones in the Neolithic of the Avebury Landscape. *Cambridge Archaeological Journal* 26:537–559.

Harris, Oliver J. T. 2017 Assemblages and Scale in Archaeology. *Cambridge Archaeological Journal* 27:127–139.

Harris, Oliver J. T., and Craig N. Cipolla 2017 *Archaeological Theory in the New Millennium: Introducing Current Perspectives*. Routledge, London.

Harris, Oliver J. T., and Rachel J. Crellin 2018 Assembling New Ontologies from Old Materials: Towards Multiplicity. In *Rethinking Personhood: Animism and Materiality in Dialogue*, edited by M. Astor-Aguilera and G. Harvey, pp. 55–74. Routledge, London.

Harris, Oliver J. T., and John Robb 2012 Multiple Ontologies and the Problem of the Body in History. *American Anthropologist* 114:669–680.

Jervis, Ben 2017 Assessing Urban Fortunes in Six Late Medieval Ports: An Archaeological Application of Assemblage Theory. *Urban History* 44:2–26.

Jones, Andrew M. 2012 *Prehistoric Materialities: Becoming Material in Prehistoric Britain and Ireland*. Oxford University Press, Oxford.

Miéville, China 2009 *The City and The City*. Pan Books, London.

Morton, Timothy 2017 *Humankind: Solidarity with Nonhuman People*. Verso, London.

Todd, Zoe 2016 An Indigenous Feminist's Take on the Ontological Turn: 'Ontology' Is Just Another Word for Colonialism. *Journal of Historical Sociology* 29:4–22.

Van Dyke, Ruth M. 2015 Materiality in Practice: An Introduction. In *Practicing Materiality*, edited by R. M. Van Dyke, pp. 3–32. University of Arizona Press, Tucson.

Wilkinson, Darryl 2017 Uncertain Allies? The Place of Indigenous Metaphysics in Posthumanist Thought. *Paper Presented at The Theoretical Archaeology Group Conference*, Cardiff, December 2017.

INDEX

Aberdeen 9
actants 160, 172, 238; spiritual, 172
affectivity 8, 145, 207; of city, 225
affects 4, 7–9, 12, 14, 32, 35, 40, 66–67,
76–77, 86, 96, 130, 132–134, 142–143,
145, 147, 149, 150, 159, 194, 238,
253, 255–256; aura 8; enchanting 133;
maelstrom 35, 88, 131; watery 130, 138
agency 8, 97–98, 159, 227, 238–239, 256;
anthropocentric 220; of assemblage 228;
of ecologies and climate 224; human
72, 254; human and nonhuman 221, 224
agential cut 11, 67–68, 72, 74–75, 81–83,
86; stratifying 88
Alt, Susan 7, 10, 11, 253
alterity 12, 88, 186, 192, 202
Ames, Kenneth 5
Amin, Ash 147
ancestor veneration 82, 86
ancestors 21, 40–41, 45, 48, 52–55, 68, 70,
72–74, 78–80, 82–88, 105, 160, 221, 225,
228, 232–233
ancestral forces 98
animism 134, 254
Anthropocene 224, 226
anticipation 12, 133; and knowledge, 210
Antiquities Act 57
archaeoastronomical alignments and
observations 42, 52–53
Aristotle 132
assemblage 4–13, 21–22, 41–44, 48, 55–56,
66–70, 72, 75–78, 82–86, 88, 94, 95–96,
108, 111, 130–132, 146, 151, 158–160,

175, 180, 185, 238–239, 247, 249, 250,
252–253, 255; and agential cuts 74;
ala Deleuze and Guattari 21, 41; of
assemblages 67; and human beings 67;
beings and things 96; coalescence 86;
cosmic 147; defined 5, 44; emergent 249;
fish, faunal 171; fish-head 113;
intra-actions 67; material 160;
Mesoamerican reconfiguration 70;
mosques 159; nonhuman 21;
overlapping 84; political process 212;
pottery 22; processes 67; reconfiguration
73, 86; scaling up 82; sensorial 87;
of soil and water 209; spiritual 160;
stratified 151; thinking 219; of traces and
practices 219; in traditional sense 21; and
transfer of vitality 75; ungoverned 13;
urban 131; US-Mexico border 207; of
wood, water, and spirits 174
assemblage conversions *see* conversion
atmospheric phenomena 148
attachment, following Latour 7, 145;
immanent 138
axiality 94, 99, 184, 188, 190
axis mundi 44–45, 54, 65, 72, 74,
77, 82, 86
Aztec West 50, 56

balanced dualism 45, 54
Barad, Karen 3, 7, 11, 41, 67, 132
Bauer, Andrew 8, 12, 199, 252, 255–256
Bell, Catherine 108
Benjamin, Walter 3

Index **261**

Bennett, Jane 3, 22, 41, 97, 172, 228, 238, 253
Bergson, Henri 3
Black Elk 27, 33
Braudel, Fernand 224
building-in versus building-out 175
bundle 8, 10, 21, 41, 68, 71; of ideas, 51
bundling 72, 121, 130

cacao 40, 42, 51
Cahokia 4, 5, 7, 10–11, 14, 19, 21–28, 30–35, 247, 249–250, 253; greater 19, 22, 28, 35; St. Louis precinct 30–31, 33
Calvino, Italo 218
Caplan, Pat 173
Carter, Bob 248
causal relationships 2, 10, 97, 132, 133
caves 19, 30–31, 35, 70, 81, 173, 221, 225, 228, 232, 235, 238, 246–247, 253
Chaco 5, 9, 11, 14, 40–46, 48, 49, 50–57, 135, 247, 253, 255, 257; multiscalar and distributed, 44
Chaco Canyon 9, 40–45, 48–49, 52–56, 247, 250, 253, 255, 257; description 41; environment 48; recreated at Aztec 55; sensorial qualities 50
Chacoan outliers 42
Chacoan phenomenon 4, 11, 42, 49, 51, 247
Chavín de Huantar, Peru 118
Chesson, Meredith 4, 148
Chicago 96
Childe, V. Gordon 97
Chimney Rock, Colorado 53
cities as assemblages 130, 218, 221, 246; as architectonic reality 220; attraction 9; defined 9; Near Eastern 220
city foundation tropes 222
clouds 6, 40, 67, 69–70, 74, 77, 82, 87–88, 133, 144, 149, 251, 255
communitas 44, 51
communities 12, 42, 46, 48, 50–52, 55, 76, 83, 85–86, 88, 96, 103, 108, 119–124, 135, 162–163, 166, 168–169, 172, 174–175, 193, 210, 211, 223, 227, 254; climatic and environmental entanglements 223
constructivism 11, 224
conversion 4–5, 146, 149; assemblage 148; inter-assemblage 148; religious 134, 148–149, 175
coral, *Porites* 166, 168, 170, 174–175, 249, 251
cosmograms 184, 187, 210–212

Coulanges, Fustel de 4, 9, 151
Cowgill, George 192
Crown, Patty 51

Dawdy, Shannon 8, 194
de Certeau, Michel 193, 224
De León, Jason 207
Deccan plateau, India 184
DeLanda, Manuel 3, 43
Deleuze, Gilles 3, 6, 8, 13, 21, 41, 43, 67, 132, 220, 245–246, 254–256
deterritorialization 7, 41, 53, 67, 73, 77, 88, 159; places of 172; *see* territorialisation
Diaz-Granados, Carol 33
"disembedded" capitals 222

earth 4, 7, 9, 10–12, 22, 27, 32–33, 40, 44, 46, 48, 54, 65, 67–78, 82–84, 86–88, 103, 107, 113, 124, 132, 142, 145, 147–148, 151, 221, 228, 232; community relations 72; water-saturated 145
Eaton, Richard 196
ecoregime 11, 95, 96, 124; monumental 111
Eliade, Mircea 45, 149
Emerald Acropolis 4, 19, 24, 27, 30–31, 34, 250
entanglement as process 202
Escobar, Arturo 95

Fajada Butte 44–45, 247, 253
fields: affective 72, 82, 85
Flannery, Kent 73
Fleisher, Jeffrey 7, 12, 158, 249, 251, 254–255
flows 3, 4, 9, 10, 11, 12, 14, 69, 70, 72, 87, 95, 96, 97, 98, 99, 102, 111, 117, 121, 122, 124, 133, 134, 140, 151, 158, 219, 228, 232, 235, 237, 247, 257; of beings and things 202; political ecology of 237; symbolic and discursive 221; water 225, 228
Fowles, Severin 40
frogs 28, 48, 50, 83; *see also* toads

gathering 40, 42, 44, 46, 52–53, 55, 94, 106, 120–121, 158, 166–167, 174–175, 180, 252, 257; community 175; as spatial transformation 178
Gobekli Tepe 4
groundwater *see* water
Guattari, Felix 6, 8, 21, 41, 43, 67, 132, 220, 226, 245, 254–256
Gupta, Akhil 226, 239

262 Index

haecceity 4, 6, 8, 11, 67, 76, 88, 131
Hall, Robert 7, 132
Hamilakis, Yannis 7
Hansen, Thomas 193, 194, 206
Harman, Graham 3
Harmanşah, Ömür 8, 12, 218, 254–255
Harris, Oliver 13, 65
Hausmann, Baron 226
Hawkins, J. David 232
Heidegger, Martin 2
Heitman, Carrie 52
Heitzman, James 191
heterogeneity 67, 159, 238; temporal 220
Hewett, Edgar 57
hierophany 149
historicist perspective 223
Hodder, Ian 202
Horton, Mark 163, 165, 166, 168, 180
humanity 9
Hutson, Scott 69
hybridity 10
hydrololith 98
hylomorphism 132, 203, 209

imaginaries 190–191, 219
immanence 7–9, 11–12, 130, 132, 134,
    138–139, 146–149, 151, 250, 256–257;
    water, 133
individuation as quality of assemblage
    process 6
infrastructure 5, 12, 67, 75, 81, 86, 88,
    131–134, 139, 144, 146–147, 193,
    218, 221–222, 225, 227–228, 233,
    237–239, 251, 257; conceptualized 225;
    functionalist 226; immanent 149;
    technosphere 226; water 146, 221
Ingold, Tim 2, 8, 41, 158, 193, 203, 209, 224
inselberg 194–198, 202, 204, 211

jade 84–85, 87, 144, 146, 149
Janusek, John 8, 11, 251–252, 257
Johansen, Peter 199
Joyce, Arthur 8, 11, 255, 257
Judd, Neil 57

Kalhu 9, 223
karst 30–33, 221, 225, 227–228, 232, 235,
    237, 239, 247, 250
key operators 96
Khonkho Wankane, Bolivia 98–99, 103,
    120, 123

Lambek, Michael 172–173
landscape: problematic concept 97;
    relational 21; rural 192
Latour, Bruno 3, 8, 40

Lefebvre, Henri 224
Leick, Gwendolyn 220
Liangzhu 5, 12, 14, 130, 132, 134, 140–151,
    249, 250–251; period 142
liminality 70, 83, 86, 119, 196, 225
Liu, Bin 142

maize 11, 65, 68, 69, 70, 71, 72, 74, 75, 76,
    77, 82, 84, 85, 86, 87, 88, 135, 145, 146,
    147, 149, 254
Marcus, Joyce 73
marine shell 33, 71, 84, 85, 139, 250
Maski 5, 12, 14, 185–186, 194–195,
    197–199, 202, 204–207, 209–211,
    248, 252; production of landscape 202
materiality 4, 65, 98–99, 106, 108, 111,
    124, 184, 198–199, 219, 225; coral 175;
    fluvial 239; urban space 221
Mecca 165, 174–175, 184, 188, 190
mediators 3, 14, 75, 145, 151, 186, 209
memory 8, 9, 40, 49, 52–53, 56, 66, 73, 88,
    131, 219–220, 245
Mexico City 14
Michell, George 188
Middleton, John 173
Miéville, China 245
Mills, Barbara 51
Mitchell, W. J. T. 97
modernity 224, 226
Monaghan, John 67, 69
monoliths: human relations 123; nonhuman
    persons 117; see also Tiwanaku
Monte Albán 4, 5, 11, 14, 65, 70, 72, 75–80,
    82–83, 85–88, 248, 251–253, 255, 257
moon 33–34, 46, 53, 131, 140, 142–143,
    147–150, 251
Morrison, Kathleen 199
Morton, Timothy 246
mosques: as assemblages 159; and
    community identity 163; coral 170;
    materials 158; shift to coral
    construction 168; wattle-and-daub 170
mountains 8, 11, 12, 65, 68, 70, 75–76,
    81, 94–96, 98, 109–111, 120, 124, 133,
    140, 144, 146, 148–150, 207, 228, 246,
    252, 255; animate 121; surrounding
    Liangzhu 140
multiplicity 8, 10, 22, 34, 254, 257
Mumbai 9

New Materialism 1, 2, 3, 10, 21, 66,
    96–97, 221, 238, 246, 249, 254–257;
    approaches 13; criticisms 2; feminist
    analysis 256; perspective 34, 42,
    66, 67, 148, 221; plural usage 2;
    skepticism 41

Index **263**

offerings 27, 69, 71–72, 75, 78, 82–86, 98, 106, 108, 119–120, 123, 150, 180, 235, 248, 250; animating 74; sacrificial 69
ontogenesis 158
ontological: defined 1; entanglements 86; fields 97; underpinnings 4, 12, 158
ontology: dangers of equating to religion 187; Hittite 221; modern 68; non-western 41, 254; vibrant 227

Painted Cave, Missouri 33
Paquimé 12, 14, 130, 132, 134–139, 145–151, 250–251, 253, 257
Paris 14, 226
Pauketat, Timothy 97, 251, 255, 257
Peeples, Matthew 51
Pepper, George 57
phenomenology 2, 224
pilgrimage 4, 52, 111, 119–120, 123, 135, 139, 187, 191
pilgrims 40, 42, 51–52, 95, 99, 106, 112, 116, 120, 123
political ecology 96–97, 120, 124, 221, 228, 237; vital 95
politics: considered further 254–256
Polo, Marco 218
portals 34–35, 48, 99, 107, 112, 221, 232–233, 238, 247
positionality 144, 148
power: spiritual 8
Prince Rupert Harbour 5
procession *see* pilgrims, pilgrimage

Qiantang River 140, 143, 249

rain 6, 25, 27, 32, 48, 50, 65, 67–78, 80–88, 133, 137, 147, 149, 250–251; community relation 72; invocation 72
rainfall 65, 82, 86, 88, 250
realist philosophies 3
relational approaches 2
religion 1, 10, 12–13, 69, 94, 149, 186–187, 190, 209–210, 221, 232, 238, 251, 255, 257; Chacoan 42; compared to ontology 65; formalized 149; Formative 73; Hittite 228; as immanence 132; and politics 239; state 187
rhizome 4, 8, 44
rice 140, 142–149, 251
Richards, Colin 132
roads 41–42, 46, 49, 51, 53, 57, 104, 113, 138, 190
Robb, John 65

sacrifice 69–70, 82, 85, 123, 257; acts of 69, 72, 74; human 70, 73–75, 78–81, 83, 85, 88, 119, 248, 255; victims 82, 84–85
Sahlins, Marshall 98
San José Mogote 65, 70, 72–73, 76–78, 82, 84, 86, 248, 250–251
Santa Fe, New Mexico 9
Schachner, Andreas 232–233
Schoop, Ulf 233
Seeher, Jürgen 233
seeps *see* springs
sensory experience 9, 11, 41, 49, 52, 112, 172; taste 51
Shanga, Kenya 163, 166, 168
shrine 11, 19, 22, 24–27, 31, 33–34, 49, 52, 111, 118, 137–138, 173, 206
Silver Dragon 141, 145, 148–149
Singapore 14
sinkholes 19, 21, 28, 30–33, 35, 221, 225, 228, 232–233, 237–238, 247, 253
sky 10–11, 25–26, 33, 44–46, 48, 53–55, 65, 70–71, 74, 77, 82–83, 86–87, 96, 99, 111, 117, 124, 131, 133, 137, 140, 149, 151
smoking pipes 33
Sofaer, Anna 53
soil 10
springs 6, 25–26, 30, 32, 35, 48, 77, 88, 94, 98–99, 101, 117, 120–121, 147, 221, 225, 228, 232–233, 237
Stahl, Ann 159
Steadman, Sharon 186
Stein, John 50
Strang, Veronica 133–134
stratification 4, 7–8, 67, 75, 83, 132, 146, 246, 249, 256–257; agriculture 145; human-nonhuman relations 145; in sense of Deleuze and Guattari 9; social 87
Sundberg, Juanita 207
Swahili: conceptual frameworks 159; expansion 162; overview 160; spirits, land and sea 173; town development 166–168
sweat lodges 26
symmetrical archaeology 3

Tabak, Faruk 223
TallBear, Kim 160
temple 27, 33, 71–72, 74, 86, 96, 98–99, 101, 107–108, 111, 113, 115, 117, 118–119, 187–188, 191, 196, 198, 209, 211, 222, 235; Hindu 184, 198; personnel 191; rituals 191; water 124, 134
temporalities 73, 97, 122, 147, 149, 184, 198–199, 211, 219, 224–225, 239, 256; of cities 219

264 Index

territorialisation 4, 5, 9, 11, 22, 44, 46, 48–55, 67, 78, 132, 145, 149, 151, 159, 172, 175, 249, 253, 255–256; by assemblage 174; forces 53; ideological 54; pottery 145; through gathering 49; water 221
Thapar, B. K. 194
thinghood 6, 8; absence of 8
Thrift, Nigel 3, 131, 147
tidal bore 140, 143–144, 148, 249, 251
Tiwanaku 5, 11–12, 14, 94–124, 247, 251–253, 255–256; as monumental hydrologic complex 108
toads 50, 250
Turner, Victor 123

urbanism: American Indian, 19; as assemblage 247, 249; compared to religion 67; constructed sensibilities 193; cosmographic 209; defined 1, 3, 10; despotic hydraulic 226; dry 134; fast 5, 148; interassemblage haecceity 6; low-density 4; materiality 194; Muslim 160; Native American 65; nonhuman 101; older approaches 4; ontology 11; placemaking 192, 219; planned versus organic 206; and religion 10, 132, 184–185; slow 5; and water 147; wet 134; *see also* multiplicity
urbanity 5, 9, 14, 67, 86, 88, 131, 134, 148, 246, 256
Urcid, Javier 79, 83

Van de Mieroop, Marc 220
Van Dyke, Ruth 8, 11, 247, 255, 257
VanPool, Christine 139
VanPool, Todd 139
Venice 9
Verkaaik, Oskar 193–194, 206
vibrancy 8, 19, 68, 219, 221, 225, 253, 257; and landscapes 35; of matter 3, 19, 22, 227

Vijayanagara 184, 188, 190–191, 196–198, 206–212, 255
virtual versus actual 246
vital materialism 228, 238
vitality 66, 68–70, 72, 75, 77, 82, 84–86, 97, 117, 124, 160, 172, 238; flows 69; forces 65, 68–69, 73, 88, 254; tendencies 7–8; transferal 87
Vivian, Gwinn 48
Vranich, Alexei 116

Wagoner, Phillip 190, 196
water 3, 7–9, 11–12, 22, 25–28, 30, 32–34, 40, 44, 48–50, 55, 70–71, 81, 83, 85, 94–99, 101–103, 107–113, 117, 121–122, 124, 132–134, 137–139, 142–143, 145–149, 151, 171–172, 174, 209–210, 218, 221, 225, 227–228, 230, 232–233, 235, 237–239, 246, 247, 250–253, 255, 257; bird 137–138; and distanciation 147; Divine Road of the Earth 221; and life 48; ecologies of 225; erosion 44; foreshore and nearshore 171; gates 142; ground 6, 10, 25, 28, 102, 232, 233; hill 25; immanence 130; infrastructure 139; management 28; materiality 99; moat 101; monuments 221, 225, 227–228, 238–239; and the moon 148; offerings 27; presence and absence 147; qualities 109, 133, 251; and the realm of the dead 28; retention reservoirs 207; and sea spirits 174; spirits 33, 144–145; and stone 103; subterranean 102; table 24, 148; temple 124; transpiration cycle 147, 149; transport 146; types 26; vapor 133
Wetherill, Richard 57
Wills, Wirt 48
Wirth, Louis 94, 120
Wittenberg, Harmut 232–233
Wright, Henry 166
Wynne-Jones, Stephanie 163